Maureen Junker-Kenny
Religion and Public Reason

Praktische Theologie im Wissenschaftsdiskurs

Practical Theology in the Discourse of the Humanities

Herausgegeben von
Bernhard Dressler, Maureen Junker-Kenny,
Thomas Klie, Martina Kumlehn und Ralph Kunz

Band 16

Maureen Junker-Kenny

Religion and Public Reason

A Comparison of the Positions of John Rawls,
Jürgen Habermas and Paul Ricoeur

DE GRUYTER

ISBN 978-3-11-048796-1
e-ISBN 978-3-11-034732-6
ISSN 1865-1658

Library of Congress Cataloging-in-Publication Data
A CIP catalog record for this book has been applied for at the Library of Congress.

Bibliographic Information published by the Deutsche Nationalbibliothek
The Deutsche Nationalbibliothek lists this publication in the Deutsche Nationalbibliografie;
detailed bibliographic data are available in the Internet at http://dnb.dnb.de.

www.degruyter.com

To the memory of my mother,
Dr Mary Junker,
née Brennan,
1915 – 2012

Contents

Preface —— XIII

Introduction —— 1

1 **Public reason as a neutral mediator in pluralist democracies in John Rawls's political philosophy** —— 5
1.1 The normative framework and its two methods of justification —— 5
1.1.1 Justice as founded by contract and as found in reflected cultural standards —— 6
1.1.2 Assessments of the contract foundation: The circularity of the device of the "original position" —— 8
1.1.2.1 Onora O'Neill: A metaphorical contract between idealized parties —— 9
1.1.2.2 Otfried Höffe: A ruse of rational egotists —— 13
1.1.2.3 Paul Ricoeur: Oscillating between disinterest and mutuality —— 14
1.1.2.4 Between philosophical and empirical concepts —— 17
1.1.3 Beyond a constructed procedure: Convictions formed in religious and cultural history in "reflective equilibrium" with principles —— 19
1.1.4 The completion of a contextual foundation in *Political Liberalism* —— 22
1.2 "Idea of the good" and "sense of justice" as elements of moral personhood in *Theory of Justice* —— 23
1.2.1 Rationality as a good and its realization in a life plan —— 24
1.2.2 Comparison and critique of Rawls's concept of the good of self-respect —— 27
1.2.3 "The sense of justice" —— 31
1.2.4 The "sense of justice" compared with principled autonomy in Kant —— 33
1.2.5 Natural contingency and self-respect —— 36
1.3 Society as a cooperative venture for mutual advantage —— 38
1.3.1 From a system of benefits and burdens to a "social union of social unions" —— 39
1.3.2 Withdrawing from metaphysical assumptions: Classical republicanism versus civic humanism —— 41
1.3.3 Lack of "natural assets" as grounds for intervention? —— 44
1.3.4 Sources and significance of plurality in *Theory of Justice* and in *Political Liberalism* —— 46

1.3.4.1   Plurality in contract, associations, and primary goods — **46**
1.3.4.2   Setting the stage for the task of public reason: Philosophies as
           "comprehensive doctrines" in *Political Liberalism* — **48**
1.4   Democratic life and public reason — **50**
1.4.1   The search for a neutral ground between irreconcilable
           worldviews — **52**
1.4.1.1   Public reason converting comprehensive into political conceptions
           of justice — **53**
1.4.1.2   The paradox: Civility as abstention — **55**
1.4.1.3   The dual motivation of the overlapping consensus: comprehensive
           and civic — **57**
1.4.2   The spheres of democratic life — **64**
1.4.2.1   The composition of the background culture — **64**
1.4.2.2   Religious contributions to nonpublic reason? — **66**
1.5   "Public reason" and practical reason: Critiques from a Kantian
           perspective — **68**
1.5.1   Distinct starting points: "Public reason" between theory of law and
           morality — **68**
1.5.2   An alternative guiding principle for the constitutional order: Human
           dignity — **70**
1.5.3   *The Law of Peoples:* Transnational scope for human rights and
           justice? — **71**
1.5.3.1   Human rights, urgent and universal, versus constitutional and
           contextual — **72**
1.5.3.2   Justice – bounded or transnational? — **78**
1.5.4   The public and the private use of practical reason — **81**
1.6   Religion in the limits of Rawls's concept of public reason — **84**
1.6.1   A philosophical approach to God: Kant's "highest good" and the
           antinomy of practical reason — **85**
1.6.2   A proviso and translations in due course – how attractive for
           religions? — **89**
1.6.2.1   Addressing the hermeneutical deficit of procedural theories of ju-
           stice: Christian sources of identity formation (Elke Mack) — **89**
1.6.2.2   Self-restriction by religions on what basis? (Stefan Grotefeld) — **95**
1.6.3   The sources of public reason – free-standing, or indebted to a hi-
           story of formation? — **99**

Introduction to Parts Two and Three — **102**

2   **Practical reason in the public sphere: Jürgen Habermas's rehabilitation of religion as a resource within the project of modernity —— 103**

2.1   The normative framework: The foundations of discourse ethics —— 104

2.1.1   The basis of communicative rationality: Reason as embodied in language —— 105

2.1.2   The competence of philosophy —— 106

2.1.2.1   Constructivist and reconstructive elements in discourse ethics —— 107

2.1.2.2   Philosophy as "stand-in" and "interpreter" —— 109

2.1.3   Postmetaphysical thinking reconfirmed —— 113

2.2   An anthropology of the lifeworld —— 116

2.2.1   The interactive constitution of self-consciousness —— 118

2.2.2   Pragmatic reconstruction of normative implications, or moral recognition of the other? —— 121

2.2.3   Between a reservoir of shared meanings and postconventional morality: the role of the lifeworld —— 125

2.2.4   Religion after the abysses of reason —— 130

2.3   The public use of reason in the democratic public sphere —— 132

2.3.1   The moral core of public reason —— 133

2.3.2   Public reason as generated in the practical discourse of citizens —— 136

2.3.3   The basis of justification: Moral, ethical, or civic? —— 137

2.3.4   From religion to public reason: Habermas's comments on continuities in Rawls's thinking from its theological origins —— 142

2.3.4.1   Human individuality in response to God and as normative in the construction of just social structures —— 142

2.3.4.2   Anchoring the right in a personal view of truth —— 147

2.4   Religion as a resource for the project of modernity —— 150

2.4.1   The persistence of religion and the task of reconstructing the genealogy of human reflection in religions and philosophies —— 151

2.4.1.1   From the secularization thesis to the consciousness of a post-secular constellation —— 151

2.4.1.2   The shared origins of religions and philosophical reason in the axial period —— 153

2.4.1.3   The distinction between the two axial formations of reflection: Comparing Jaspers and his interpretation by Habermas —— 154

2.4.2   The heuristic and semantic potential of religions in the pathologies of rationalization —— 160

2.4.2.1 The ongoing intellectual potential of religious traditions for self-understandings formed in the lifeworld —— **160**

2.4.2.2 The origin of "the political" in the encounter between religious and secular self-understandings —— **164**

2.4.2.3 Postsecular society or postsecular state? —— **167**

2.4.3 Theological critiques: Religion in the limits of postmetaphysical reason —— **175**

2.4.3.1 The means of translation —— **176**

2.4.3.2 The specific difference of religion —— **177**

2.4.3.3 The limits of translatability —— **181**

3 **Religions as co-foundational of the public space in Paul Ricoeur's hermeneutical philosophy —— 184**

3.1 The normative framework: A phenomenology of desiring, capable and fallible human beings —— **186**

3.1.1 Theory of action based on "desire and effort to exist" —— **187**

3.1.2 Self-understanding as a result of appropriation —— **188**

3.1.3 Symbols and conflicts of interpretation —— **190**

3.1.4 Cultural uniqueness, utopia and ideology —— **192**

3.1.4.1 Particularity versus homogenization and historicist relativism —— **193**

3.1.4.2 Between foundational hopes and strategies of legitimation: Utopia and ideology —— **195**

3.1.4.3 Tradition and emancipation: Ricoeur's comments on Habermas's critique of Gadamer —— **197**

3.1.5 A hermeneutics of the self as *idem* and *ipse*, and as self and other —— **199**

3.1.6 Insights from Ricoeur's philosophical anthropology as a framework for ethics —— **200**

3.2 The self and its agency: Three types of ethical reflection —— **202**

3.2.1 A phenomenological reconstruction of the three dimensions of ethics —— **202**

3.2.1.1 The wish to "live well, with and for others, in just institutions" —— **204**

3.2.1.2 The deontological level as the "sieve of the norm" —— **206**

3.2.1.3 "Practical wisdom" as a "heartfelt conviction" —— **208**

3.2.1.4 The wish for a reconciled memory and the status of forgiveness in a theory of agency —— **210**

3.2.2 Differences to Rawls and Habermas in the outline of ethics —— **214**

3.2.2.1 Questions to Rawls —— **214**

3.2.2.2 Questions to Habermas — 218
3.2.3 Conclusions from perspectives on ethics — 221
3.3 Co-founding the public space: Types of authority, legitimation, and citizens' convictions — 222
3.3.1 Democracy between foundational myths and self-authorization — 223
3.3.1.1 The narrative model: Myths of foundation, *potestas* and *auctoritas* — 224
3.3.1.2 The model of self-authorization — 227
3.3.1.3 The model of recognizing heterogeneous traditions as co-foundational — 228
3.3.2 Domination and obedience, or initiatives in plural spheres of negotiation? — 231
3.3.2.1 Pluralizing the category of *Herrschaft* in Max Weber's theory of social action — 232
3.3.2.2 Explicit and implicit theory decisions in Weber's approach — 234
3.3.2.3 Enunciative and institutional authority — 240
3.4 Religion and agency: Fallibility, hope, and translation — 247
3.4.1 Fallibility and freedom in religious experience and in philosophical reflection — 249
3.4.2 A dialectic that gives a place to hope: Kant's concept of the "highest good" — 253
3.4.2.1 Reason as structurally oriented towards completion — 254
3.4.2.2 The endpoint of reason in Kant and Hegel: Demand of unconditional meaning versus absolute knowledge — 255
3.4.2.3 The epistemological status of hope — 259
3.4.2.4 Kant's treatment of evil in *Religion within the Limits of Reason Alone* — 262
3.4.2.5 Comparison of the three Kantian argumentations on the scope of reason — 264
3.4.3 Translations, particularity and plurality of religious traditions — 267
3.4.3.1 The possibility of intercultural understanding — 268
3.4.3.2 The goal of translation between a search for equivalents and engagement with particularity — 269
3.4.3.3 Epoch-making translations of biblical texts — 275
3.4.3.4 Plurality of interpretations in foundational scriptures and histories of effect — 278

4   **Conclusion of the comparison of the three positions** —— **280**
4.1   Reason in its three dimensions —— **280**
4.1.1   Theoretical reason —— **280**
4.1.2   Practical reason —— **282**
4.1.3   Judgement —— **286**
4.2   Religion and public reason —— **289**
4.2.1   Three views of religion in relation to reason —— **289**
4.2.2   Co-founders of the public sphere —— **294**

Bibliography —— **302**

Person Index —— **312**

Subject Index —— **315**

Preface

The themes treated in this book have accompanied me for some time. I am grateful to Trinity College Dublin for its Berkeley Research Fellowship award that allowed me to spend the academic year 2002–03 on issues treated in the public sphere: from ethics of memory, concepts and implications of human dignity in biomedical ethics and in education, to the differences and links between traditions of ethical thinking. A Visiting Fellowship to the Fondazione Bruno Kessler in Trento, Italy, in June/July 2011 offered an inspiring place to reimmerse myself into the writings of Paul Ricoeur and complete much of Part Three. To the colleagues who organized conferences in Vienna, Leuven, Mainz, Freiburg, Leeds, Padova and Trento, Frankfurt, Münster, Paris, Istanbul and Chicago, heartfelt thanks for providing productive encounters at memorable venues. My greatest debt of gratitude is owed to my family: to Peter in his resourcefulness and to Fiona and Kilian for understanding that book projects can become absorbing; to my sister Roseleen and brother-in-law Thomas for caring for our mother; to Betty, and to our friends who have shared and enhanced our lives, who will know what a difference they make. My thanks are also due to the editors at De Gruyter's and to my colleagues in the series for their professional care and patience.

I dedicate this book to the memory of my mother whose zest for life and trust in God must be part of the reason why I have been drawn to the questions treated in this study.

Dublin, October 26, 2013

Introduction

The diversity of cultures co-existing in one society and the pluralism of convictions have become every-day experiences for citizens. They encounter them in their workplace and in their circle of friends, in their neighbourhoods and in the media, as well as in the political sphere in which the future of their lifeworld and of future generations is being shaped. As members of democratic societies, they are not just passive recipients of decisions made elsewhere. They contribute to the life of society through their personal and professional pursuits, their social initiatives, informal debates and different ways of instructing their representatives of their views. Within the conflicting interests, outlooks and claims of many parties, the call for "public reason" as the lynchpin for assessing procedures and solutions is a positive move. It indicates that the democratic process has to answer to criteria beyond sectional interests, and offers a joint horizon for law-makers and members of civil society in their attempts to work out their vision of the republican project in concrete matters for decision. What sources there are for sustaining motivation and which new ways can be found to create cohesion have become relevant issues in the ongoing question of the legitimation of the state.

What conceptions have been developed to delineate the contours and the content of "public reason"? How does it relate to the deep convictions to which citizens are entitled as persons who are protected by two core liberal rights, freedom of conscience and freedom of religion? What is its scope, from the local to the cosmopolitan? Is it self-propelled, or does it need resources to feed and renew it? How does it engage with religion, a factor seen by some as a potential threat to the stability of society: is "public reason" its opposite since it insists on generalizable criteria over any merely particular and not generally available insights? Or is religion seen as a possible partner for public reason, indeed, as a presupposition?

How these questions are answered, will delineate the space in which religious traditions can operate. The variety of responses will be informed by the distinctive frameworks of interpretation that can be identified in philosophical ethics. The three authors chosen for comparison in this study represent three approaches from different linguistic and conceptual backgrounds. They range from the liberal platform John Rawls has elaborated (Part 1), to Jürgen Habermas's discourse ethical reformulation of Kant's universalism and its realization in the public sphere (Part 2), to the co-founding role for the public realm that Paul Ricoeur's combination of hermeneutical and normative ethics attributes to the specific traditions of thinking that have shaped a culture and the different convictions of its citizens (Part 3).

Each of these philosophers has produced works that have generated new departures in research enterprises in and across different disciplines, and a series of responses or refinements over decades; their theories constitute valid areas of specialization in themselves. Why choose to bring three such vast and intricate *oeuvres* together when many of the analyses and critiques that follow here may have already been made? Specialists on each of them may find that reference to long-standing debates on their core concepts and theory decisions is lacking. My reasons for undertaking a comparison that is not intended to be comprehensive are two: one goal is to make contributions to the debate of their works in Continental languages, especially German, more accessible to English-speaking philosophical and theological ethicists; these communities of researchers should be reconnected at least in discovering where their intellectual concerns and conclusions differ. The second reason is my perception that Theological Ethics impoverishes itself when it gives up on the internal requirement to be conducted as one of theology's philosophically mediated subdisciplines. The heritage from Irenaeus to Schleiermacher, to name just two anchorpoints in antiquity and modernity, to connect with the general consciousness of truth as reflected in the philosophical approaches of an era,[1] has been losing ground to programmatic justifications of internal self-explications of faith. The hope in these understandings of theology is to achieve a revitalization through a *ressourcement* from its own wells.[2] It seems to me that theological movements which take this direction are often based on an undialectical concept of identity, and that they give up too early on what can be gained from contemporary work in the light and discipline of reason. Like the colleagues from different linguistic and intellectual traditions and disciplines with whom I shall be conducting the debates that follow, I do not think that Theological Ethics can do without taking into constructive account the paradigmatic approaches of the three philosophers compared in this study. Its intention is to clarify the theoretical premises that shape the three distinct formats they provide for religious contributions to the public realm. By comparing their conceptual frameworks, alternatives become visible that might be useful for the civic initiatives, political proposals and interventions from religions and their justifications that public theology and Christian ethics especially in their social and applied dimensions reflect on.[3]

---

1 Th. Pröpper, "Freiheit als philosophisches Prinzip der Dogmatik", in *Evangelium und freie Vernunft. Konturen einer theologischen Hermeneutik* (Freiburg: Herder, 2001), 5–22. The task of connecting with "public truth" is also recognized in approaches to "public theology" that see "theology as a public activity, conducted in the midst of public life and committed to the pursuit of public truth". W. F. Storrar/A. R. Morton, "Introduction", in Storrar/Morton (eds.), *Public Theology for the 21st Century. Essays in Honour of Duncan B. Forrester* (London/New York: T & T Clark, 2004), 1–21, 8.

2 For an insightful comparison of the diverging concerns of theology in the United Kingdom and in Germany, see Johannes Hoff, "German theology in contemporary society", in *Modern Believing* (Special Issue, ed. by J. Hoff) 50/1 (2009) 2–12.

3 In his "Foreword" to the *Festschrift* for D. Forrester, Raymond Plant points out the danger that despite the value judgements implicit in the shaping of public policy the decisions are made by

The analysis of the three philosophical approaches to the foundations of public reason and its relationship to religion takes the following steps. After outlining the normative framework which determines the specific function of public reason, the (explicit and implicit) anthropology and theory of action that inform it are investigated. The dimensions of social life and its concretization in a democratic political framework are explored next. Finally, the understanding of religion that ensues from these factors is treated: the status of metaphysical and religious truth claims; the role of religion as a practice and conviction in a pluralist society; and the critical reflections of theologians from Continental and English-speaking contexts on the history and future of their faith traditions, and the role they might have in the diversity of world cultures for shaping a shared horizon of judgement and action.

A final word on the two key concepts juxtaposed in the title of this study, "public reason" and "religion". Their definitions emerge from histories of thinking that also form part of their current debate. The first now stands for the quest for a common foundation for opinion and will formation in pluralist democracies and includes the question of the legitimation of state action. What will turn out to be crucial is whether its origin is sought in a theory of law, or in morality.[4] As a term of Kantian origin, its precise meaning in its opposition to the "private use of reason" remains a decisive benchmark for judging its current use in political philosophy and ethics. This distinction is elaborated succinctly in Onora O'Neill's comparison of Kant's and Rawls's understandings of this term.[5] The emergence of an independent public sphere constituted a historical novelty and breakthrough that permitted the expression of a variety of worldviews and forms of life. For citizens and office-holders, being held accountable to public reason implies the recognition that while they will be shaped and motivated by different traditions, they share the human capability for morality that allows them to argue for positions that can be jointly agreed on. The scope of public reason and the methods of activating, ascertaining and concretizing this level of reflection differ among the three authors treat-

---

"those with instrumental expertise... But... there are no experts in respect of the nature and the ranking of the values which lie at the heart of public policy, and hence our predilection to leave these matters to experts is ultimately illusory...To engage in debate about the morality of what is done in our name is immensely difficult but it is a human responsibility that we cannot avoid." He argues that the way to "arrive at moral and civic insight" is to provide "a public forum in which such debates can take place between policy-makers, practitioners, theologians and philosophers", as the Centre for Theology and Public Issues at the University of Edinburgh's Divinity School has done. R. Plant, "Foreword", in Storrar/Morton (eds.), *Public Theology*, ix–xi, ix–x.

4 Cf. H. Nagl-Docekal, "Moral und Religion aus der Optik der heutigen rechtsphilosophischen Debatte", in *Deutsche Zeitschrift für Philosophie* 56 (2008) 843–855.

5 O. O'Neill, "Bounded and cosmopolitan justice", in *Review of International Studies* 26 (2000) 45–60.

ed; its Kantian origin, however, requires attention to be paid to its link to the unique moral self-reflection that humans are capable of.

Like "public reason", "religion" owes its origin as a concept that refers to a distinct and irreducible realm of human conscious life to the period of modernity. The classical theological author who inaugurated a new justification of religion in the context of the critical examination of reason in modernity is Friedrich Schleiermacher. The term "religion" denotes both this unique realm of human experience, and the particular historical traditions that exemplify its variety. In many cases, the general term, "religion", will encompass the second, "religions", for historical traditions in their particularity. The contexts of analysis where the two references need to be distinguished will become clear in the discussions that follow. The "semantic potential" that religious traditions are able to offer to secular reason in Jürgen Habermas's view can only be illustrated from particular traditions;[6] his examples, such as being made in the image of God, are taken from the Jewish and Christian monotheisms that have been co-creators of the roots of Western culture. Also Ricoeur uses classical texts from the Bible in the variety of its genres as well as from Greek and Roman philosophy and literature to indicate thresholds to new stages of reflection. Their "semantic" contents, marked by the specific translations of key terms in Hebrew, Greek and Latin that shaped their subsequent reception, need the conversation between philosophers, theologians and philologists in order to interpret religion not just at the generic level, but also within the historical development of the self-understanding of particular traditions. The hermeneutical task of charting the choices made in the inculturation of the biblical message of salvation within the intellectual currents of different eras needs a theology that is able and willing to be bilingual. A key term for the relationship between religion and public reason will turn out to be "translation". The attempt of this study to bring three philosophers into conversation will show that the exercize of translation already applies before religion comes into the analysis. The need for this effort does not only announce itself with contrasts such as reason and revelation, but appears in their different interpretations of the same key terms, for example, morality, autonomy, justice, principles, political, public, and reason. Before contemplating possible bridges over the gulf supposed to separate religion from reason, it will be helpful to practice measuring the distances between their uses of concepts derived from one background they share, the language of Kant.

---

6 Cf. Th. Schmidt, "Der Begriff der Postsäkularität", in J. Manemann/B. Wacker (eds.), *Politische Theologie – gegengelesen* (Münster: LIT-Verlag, 2008), 244–254, 252.

1 Public reason as a neutral mediator in pluralist democracies in John Rawls's political philosophy

The normative framework of John Rawls's classical Neo-Kantian proposal will be approached from the problems he identifies as paramount for his social theory, and from the moral philosophical terms in which he engages with them. Taking the task he poses himself as the entry point also allows one to trace the development that the parameters of his enterprise and the expectations for solutions undergo over several decades, reflecting critiques as well as new political constellations and cultural developments which his theory responds and adapts to. The first section will present the initial vision of a society governed by principles of justice and their two methods of justification (1). Section 2 analyses the concepts of moral personhood and agency in *Theory of Justice* (2). The social dimension including his vision of a well-ordered society is thematized next. Having analysed how individuality, sociability and structural justice are defined and related (3), it is then possible to examine his understanding of democratic life and his proposal for the role of public reason (4). Section 5 will submit the designation of this concept in *Political Liberalism* and the scope it allows for transnational justice to critiques from a universalist Kantian perspective (5). Having assembled the main elements of his approach, it will then be possible to treat the role that is allocated to religions when they are understood as "comprehensive doctrines". Part 1 concludes with the reception and critique of this framework by two German theological ethicists (6).

1.1 The normative framework and its two methods of justification

The theory design of the first book moves between contract and context. I shall present its outline (1) as well as its assessment by three other authors on justice (2), and end with the final foundation put forward in *Political Liberalism:* justice as a value institutionalized in Western democracies (3).

1.1.1 Justice as founded by contract and as found in reflected cultural standards

The initial task which Rawls sets himself in his *Theory of Justice* is to "formulate a reasonable conception of justice for the basic structure of society".[6] Rather than assess the performance of existing social systems and their agencies regarding the norm of justice, Rawls goes back to the level at which basic principles are devised: "Justice as fairness begins... with the choice of the first principles of a conception of justice which is to regulate all subsequent criticism and reform of institutions" (TJ, 13). Once defined, they will exert a powerful role of delineating what type of concrete social order conforms to the standard of justice, what kind of claims are permitted and what falls outside their conceptual borders and is a matter for private decision: "These principles are to regulate all further agreements; they specify the kinds of social cooperation that can be entered into and the forms of government that can be established." (TJ, 11) Rawls explains the qualifier "fairness" as pointing to an understanding of justice that is generated by the social contract theory of state legitimation, with "Locke, Rousseau, and Kant" (TJ, 11) named as ancestors of this tradition.

The fairness of the principles is established by removing from the protagonists of the original situation any knowledge of their personal condition. In order to guarantee impartiality, the foundational principles are to be chosen behind a "veil of ignorance" (TJ, 12). The principles agreed upon in this original position are two. The first principle is to ensure the greatest degree of liberty for each member, qualified by the requirement to be "compatible" with that of others: "Each person is to have an equal right to the most extensive total system of equal basic liberties compatible with a similar system of liberty for all." (TJ, 302) Besides making equality of opportunity mandatory, the second principle contains a normative orientation towards improving the position of the most disadvantaged members by only permitting inequalities if they work out to their benefit. In its final formulation this "difference principle" is stated as follows:

> Social and economic inequalities are to be arranged so that they are both: (a) to the greatest benefit of the least advantaged, consistent with the just savings principle, and (b) attached to offices and positions open to all under conditions of fair equality of opportunity. (TJ, 302)

The two principles and the two priority rules which put liberty first and subordinate efficiency and welfare considerations to justice, lead to the following conclusion:

---

6 J. Rawls, *A Theory of Justice* (Cambridge/Mass.: Belknap Press of Harvard University Press, 1971), 8 (=TJ). Further page numbers are included in the text.

"All social primary goods – liberty and opportunity, income and wealth, and the bases of self-respect – are to be distributed equally unless an unequal distribution of any or all of these goods is to the advantage of the least favoured." (TJ, 303)

What are the reflections which have led the founding members of this society to agree to these two far-reaching principles? It is here that with the "maximin" calculation of the participants a new element is brought into social philosophy, one derived from game or decision theory. It roots the motivation to adopt principles of justice in a comparison of possible outcomes imagined in a situation of uncertainty. Guided by caution, the goal is to achieve the "*maximum minimorum*" (TJ, 154), by adopting "the alternative the worst outcome of which is superior to the worst outcomes of the others". (TJ, 153) By not knowing whether they will be in the position of the least advantaged, the founders take the wise move to create structures as equitable as possible.

While the way in which both principles are fleshed out by the concept of "primary goods" will be examined in section 2 as part of Rawls's anthropological assumptions, what needs to be clarified first is the status of the proposal, starting with its basis in the contract tradition: since the authors cited for the origins of this heritage – Locke, Rousseau, Kant – differ considerably, how will they be combined? Whose concepts of personhood, of republicanism, of freedom will be dominant? By first situating his proposal within the contract theory of legitimating state power, Rawls has opted for a specific procedural justification. Justice is not to be defined by contents or individual value orientations, nor by discussing concrete issues of distribution. The state will have to conform to and put into action the principles of justice freely accepted as binding in the hypothetical original position. Yet the very way in which the decision is portrayed to have been reached is a matter for critique. How has the proceduralist part of his justification been judged (2)? A second line of justification already announces itself in the choice of the term "reasonable" within the initial definition of the task, to "formulate a reasonable conception of justice for the basic structure of society" (TJ, 8). "Reasonable" will turn out to mean that it is validated by "considered convictions" (e. g., TJ, 19). Thus, an alternative basis is constituted through the process of "reflective equilibrium" (TJ, 20): a coherentist one (3). This second method of drawing on an already existing currency of shared values implicit in Western political culture will then become the sole new foundation in *Political Liberalism* (4).[7]

In *Theory of Justice*, the two strategies of justification complement each other, as three commentators from different linguistic and cultural spheres

---

7 Rawls, *Political Liberalism* (New York: Columbia University Press, 1993) (=PL).

agree: the British Kantian scholar Onora O'Neill, the German social philosopher Otfried Höffe, and the French hermeneutical theorist Paul Ricoeur. While they all insist on the need for a deontological level of reasoning, their critiques of Rawls examine different features and offer distinct conclusions. I shall present their nuanced objections as immanent critiques, insofar as they all are sympathetic to using principles of reason in the project of establishing a framework for justice.

1.1.2 Assessments of the contract foundation: The circularity of the device of the "original position"

The two foundational principles of a just society are portrayed as the outcome of an agreement made under specific conditions. One is that they are to be chosen behind a "veil of ignorance" regarding the agents' own positions and features:

> The choice which rational men would make in this hypothetical situation of equal liberty... determines the principles of justice... Since all are similarly situated, and no one is able to design principles to favor his particular condition, the principles of justice are the result of a fair agreement or bargain. (TJ, 12)

The other is the understanding that the agents are "rational" in a specific, yet "widely accepted" sense:

> One feature of justice as fairness is to think of the parties in the initial situation as rational and mutually disinterested. This does not mean that the parties are egoists, that is, individuals with only certain kinds of interests, say in wealth, prestige, and domination. But they are conceived as not taking an interest in one another's interests. They are to presume that even their spiritual aims may be opposed, in the way that the aims of those of different religions may be opposed. Moreover, the concept of rationality must be interpreted as far as possible in the narrow sense, standard in economic theory, of taking the most effective means to given ends. I shall modify this concept to some extent... but one must try to avoid introducing into it any controversial ethical elements. The initial situation must be characterized by stipulations that are widely accepted. (TJ, 13–14)

O'Neill, Höffe and Ricoeur each argue that this argumentation is circular. Their observation is that the "original position" is stylized in such a way that all bias is removed in advance from the foundational members of the projected society. The shared thrust of their critiques can be explained as follows. The intent of Rawls's reformulation was to "generalize and carry to a higher level of abstraction the familiar theory of the social contract" (TJ, 11). The move that makes this contractual foundation, unlike its classical predecessors', circular, is that it guarantees the sought-for fair outcome of the procedure by introducing a "veil of ignorance" for the founding members as an impartial basis to generate principles for their future structural decisions.

On the one hand, this strips the protagonists of information on their qualities and condition, creating an artificial similarity of interests; on the other, as Onora O'Neill highlights most clearly, it actually enriches the hypothetical original position with unwarranted premises. Far from providing a more abstract level, it brings in new presuppositions: such as, that agency is self-interested, and that it is out to maximize its opportunities in competition with others. The circle between these two moves – stripping away and investing with specific features – results in the choice of the two principles of justice. While their verdict – that the argumentation is circular – is the same, their analyses and alternatives differ. Onora O'Neill points out deficiencies in the logic of proceeding from starting points to conclusions: first, she sees the goal of abstraction, a legitimate and unavoidable element in a course of argumentation, as not being reached but replaced with idealizations; secondly, she sees Rawls as offering competing answers. Her alternative proposal is to establish critically the guiding concepts at the level of practical reason rather than import unvindicated assumptions from empiricist theories (1). Höffe (2) and Ricoeur (3) equally evaluate the result of the constructed starting point as a saving move against the instrumental account of human agency that Rawls's reliance on rational choice theory leads to. While Höffe points out the effect of the second foundation on the understanding of human rights, Ricoeur considers the anchoring of the two principles in "considered convictions" as the necessary hermeneutically conscious counterpart to the contract foundation. After discussing the specific focus of each of their critiques, I shall conclude with a general point concerning the status of philosophy as a discipline; it is raised by the method taken in *Theory of Justice* of including an approach to empirical sciences, in this case the rational choice approach to economics, into the search for principles of justice (4).

1.1.2.1 Onora O'Neill: A metaphorical contract between idealized parties

Onora O'Neill takes on the circular character of the device of the original position by explaining the difference between regular "abstraction" and the "idealization" that occurs when unwarranted specifications are introduced. In this logical use, the term includes all features that are merely assumed, be they positive, negative or neutral. Thus, depicting the protagonists as self-interested is an "idealization" insofar as it introduces additional premises which may be misleading. "Appealing to true but abstract starting points appears uncontroversial... it does not introduce additional, possibly questionable or false, materials for reaching

conclusions",[8] such as interpretations of agents' motivations. By contrast, idealization, "rather than leaving it open... assumes that certain idealized predicates
apply, sometimes in the face of evidence that they do not" (MTJ, 33). The qualities claimed both for the contract parties and for their society in the establishment of the "original position" are such idealizations, as is the "veil of ignorance" itself: "Rawls assumes... that parties to the original position are
'mutually disinterested'", and "that 'a rational individual does not suffer from
envy'" (MTJ, 36), as well as that the polity to be founded is "'a closed system isolated from other societies'" (MTJ, 37). These initial assumptions are quite likely to
take on a life of their own at later stages of specifying just institutions. The circularity between the premises and the outcome of the foundational contract becomes evident with letting people choose behind a "veil of ignorance": "Rawls
assumes persons with quite specific patterns of ignorance... The defining ignorance... is not the *abstract* claim... but the *idealized* claim that they are without
certain sorts of information." (MTJ, 35–36) Thus, to speak of a "contract" is

> highly metaphorical. Everything that could differentiate one individual from another is hy-
> pothetically obliterated behind the veil of ignorance... The hypothetical "agreement" can-
> not be understood as the solution to any disagreement... since nothing differentiates
> those who are to "agree"... The supposed "contract" is simply the result of assuming
> away everything that could lead to disagreement. (MTJ, 32)

The effect of both areas of idealized premises is that the second cancels out the
negativity of the first: The "postulated ignorance undercuts the implications of
Rawls's assumption that agents are self-interested... The original position is designed to *prevent* self-interest from influencing the choice of principles of justice." (MTJ, 30)

  In face of a construction in which opposing assumptions are reconciled by
the circular nature of the proposal, the second foundation that constitutes an alternative to the renewed contract theory will have to carry all the weight, moving
his approach into a different tradition of argumentation. In her discussion of *Political Liberalism*, O'Neill shows that while this ethos of citizenship is contextual,
it differs from communitarianism in that a plurality of background cultures is acknowledged.[9] It does, however, still fall under "insiders' reasoning" by drawing

---

8 Onora O'Neill, "The method of *A Theory of Justice*", in O. Höffe (ed.), *John Rawls – Eine Theorie
der Gerechtigkeit* (Berlin: Akademie-Verlag, 1998), 27–43, 34. In this subsection, further page
numbers are included in the text under MTJ.
9 O. O'Neill, *Bounds of Justice* (Cambridge: CUP, 2000), 4 (=BJ): "Although he has not repudiated
universalist aspirations, and has not accepted the communitarian view that embedded social
norms form adequate starting points for ethical and political reasoning, Rawls has argued in his

an unvindicated line around the polity. From his first to his third and final book, Rawls argues for justice from the Rousseauian presupposition of a bounded society.[10]

In O'Neill's analysis, Rawls is the representative of contemporary Kantian approaches to justice who has taken the greatest care to elucidate his premises (cf. BJ, 72). In response to the reception of his thinking, he has revised his starting points in order to be able to uphold his conclusions, the two principles of justice. She traces the changes: from the "optimism" of being able to lay out a general theory in 1971, to his new foundation in a "Kantian concept of the person" in the early 1980s, and to the realization that only a "political" basis in the existing concept of citizenship would banish "metaphysical" borrowings, leading to the explicit reduction of the validity of his theory to Western liberal democracies.[11] While acknowledging the effort, O'Neill judges this trajectory as indicative of the enduring difficulties of trying to reach "Kantian" conclusions from empiricist conceptions of agency, reason and freedom. These are in effect shared by Utilitarians whose inability to include respect for persons into their framework is the typical objection from Kantians; in her analysis, it is this mismatch that is keeping current deontological work on justice from achieving the goal of establishing principles in a logically convincing, non-idealizing argumen-

---

later work that the agreements of fellow-citizens have fundamental status in an adequate conception of the reasonable, and thereby in political justification." Further page numbers are included in the text.

10 "In developing a conception of 'public reason' Rawls uses a term that is also central for Kant's conception of reason. However, his account of public reason is more Rousseauian than Kantian, in that he sees it as the public reason of a particular people who are fellow-citizens in a bounded and closed society. By contrast, for Kant public reason must be able to reach 'the world at large' and so cannot presuppose the shared assumptions of community or polity." (BJ, 72–73, n. 19, with reference to PL, 49–51). Drawing on the shared values of particular polities, the argument verges on "insiders' reasoning". As O'Neill states in *Towards Justice and Virtue. A Constructive Account of Practical Reasoning* (Cambridge: CUP, 1996), 53: "Particularist reasoning is intrinsically 'insiders' reasoning." Even if these insiders, unlike the communitarian approaches she critiques, are seen as having diverse worldviews, they do take for granted the borders of their polity and constrict the scope of their argumentation: "Those who see boundaries as the limits of justificatory reasoning will not take seriously... either the predicaments of those who are excluded or the alternatives for those who have been included." (BJ, 169)

11 "Across the years, one might say, Rawls has moved from optimism about the agenda of finding true, abstract starting points to the conclusion that the available starting points are socially determinate, and that they enable the construction of an account of justice based on and adapted to the reasoning that takes place among those who conceive of themselves as citizens of a bounded, liberal democratic society." (BJ, 73)

tation.[12] This includes the task of regaining a concept of human reason that goes beyond the instrumental capacity of choosing means; it lifts the argumentation from considering at a psychological level what agents *would* do, to one of ethical stringency, reflecting on what they *could*, or be justified to do:

> Many features of Rawls's work are clearly Kantian, above all his conception of ethical principles as determined by constraints on principles chosen by rational agents. However, Rawls's constructivism assumes a quite different account of rationality from Kant's. Rawls identifies the principles that *would* be chosen by instrumentally rational beings to whom he ascribes certain sparsely specified ends – not the principles that *could* consistently be chosen regardless of particular ends."[13]

In order to re-establish more adequate starting points, the elements which contemporary Neo-Kantians identify as in need of being superseded are to be re-examined: Kant's distinction between noumenal and phenomenal freedom, his critical assessment of the Rationalist metaphysics of reason, and his construction of the principles of ethics from the capabilities of finite and vulnerable humans in their plurality. Having first uncovered the idealizations at work in the parameters of the original position, O'Neill presents these properly abstract concepts as constituting the key to a successful vindication of practical reason and the specific proposals of justice it opens up. The alternative to an untenable combination of Kantian imperatives with empiricist interpretations of freedom, as, e. g., in identifying autonomy with independence and agency with preference, is to consistently follow Kant's non-metaphysical approach: not in all of its conclusions, but in its premises and in dividing the task into constructing principles, and devising virtue as an "intelligent, principled responsiveness to cases" (BJ, 78, n. 25), which are neglected by current Kantian proposals. I see her emphasis on the two levels of principles and of concrete judgement as a parallel to the second and third steps of Ricoeur's architecture of ethics which are equally separate tasks that are not reducible to each other. Her core objection to Rawls, using idealization instead of abstraction, not only gives rise to a counter-proposal based on minimal but justifiable assumptions that yield productive results by establishing clear constraints against "deceit, injury, and coercion"; it also avoids the

---

12 An "instrumental account of rationality and a preference-based conception of action... look ill chosen to develop a distinctively Kantian account of justice" (BJ, 73).
13 O. O'Neill, "Kantian Ethics", in P. Singer (ed.), *Companion to Ethics* (Oxford: Blackwell, 1991), 175–185, 184. She concludes her comment on other current accounts of ethics which are "even more loosely related" to Kant with the judgement, "nearly all rely on a preference-based theory of action and an instrumental account of rationality, all of which are incompatible with Kant's ethics."

vagueness and looming emptiness of concepts such as "equality" and "liberty",[14] and replaces them with ones that indicate the fragility of human life as the spring for devising principles of ethics.[15]

1.1.2.2 Otfried Höffe: A ruse of rational egotists

In Otfried Höffe's interpretation of the original position, the circle between the assumptions that steer the choice, and the desired outcome does not mark a failure, but an achievement. He goes as far as claiming that with "this artificial move (*Kunstgriff*) Rawls achieves a new reconstruction of the 'moral point of view'"[16]. As a device that manages to turn self-interested agents despite themselves into persons oriented towards the equal rights of others, the original position "with the knowledge it excludes achieves the target of rational egotists submitting themselves to a ruse (*Selbstüberlistung*)". Höffe notes how far the reformulation of contract in terms of rational choice is from the usual understanding of justice, but he is satisfied with the intention and the outcome:

> It could look as if justice were located only in the economic sphere of benefit calculation, maximizing yield and minimizing loss... It is true that the assumption of persons who seek to maximize their own advantage excludes an original interest in justice; yet the information deficit radically alters (*verfremdet*) this assumption... he screens off any individuality or particularity and achieves a general, i.e., moral or just, subject. (21–22)

In keeping with his assessment that Rawls succeeds in "(re)defining rational self-interest morally with the help of the information deficit" (23), Höffe goes on to interpret the first principle of greatest liberty as a reconstruction of human rights. Will this judgement continue to hold once the contract foundation is complemented by the normative background culture of values and convictions nur-

---

14 "We cannot offer reasons to all for adopting principles of deceit (one of Kant's favourite examples), of injury or of coercion... Of course, these are very indeterminate principles, but they are less indeterminate than many of the principles of liberty and equality that have recently been the preferred building blocks for theories of justice. One of the interesting respects in which they are more determinate is that they are evidently principles for finite, mutually vulnerable beings – for beings who might in principle suffer by being the victims of deceit, injury or coercion." (BJ 78–79)

15 "Much recent Kantian work has indeed been predicated on unvindicated idealizations, which undermine its applicability to human life. Kant's approach may be read in another sense, in which the finitude of human beings, of human rationality and the connectedness among human beings is stressed rather than denied." (BJ, 80)

16 O. Höffe, "Einführung in Rawls's Theorie der Gerechtigkeit", in Höffe (ed.), *John Rawls*, 3–26, 22. Further page numbers are included in the text. Translations from sources in German are my own.

tured in Western traditions? In a subsequent article, Höffe points to the reduced status and scope which a merely contextual foundation of principles on the existing, but contingent ethos of democracies leads to. He affirms against *Political Liberalism*'s restriction to Western political cultures a culture-transcendent validity of human rights and democracy as core elements of the constitutional state.[17] The move prepared by the second foundation in *Theory of Justice* and completed in *Political Liberalism* will be revisited in section 4 which examines his foundation of democratic life on an understanding of public reason in contextual terms. The change in Rawls's argumentative strategy will affect the validity of the two principles as expressing either human rights, or only a set of the liberal rights citizens enjoy in a democratic state. If they are meant to found universal claims due to each human being, prior to positive law in a state, by virtue of human descent, they will need a basis beyond actual citizenship.

1.1.2.3 Paul Ricoeur: Oscillating between disinterest and mutuality

Paul Ricoeur's sympathetic discussion of Rawls locates the circularity of the argumentation in the sense of justice presupposed, but at the same time allegedly generated by the contract foundation. He sees an ambivalence at work between the desired independence of the contract and the need to call on an already existing orientation towards justice. Yet in view of its function of standing against an alternative Utilitarian foundation, even the maximin rule borrowed from decision theory is evaluated as a "tacitly ethical" reason.[18] Like the first two commentators, he judges Rawls's first foundation of the principles of justice on contract alone as unconvincing. Ricoeur's "principal objection" is

> "that a moral sense of justice founded on the Golden Rule... is always presupposed by a purely procedural justification of the principle of justice... Rawls's extraordinary construction borrows its underlying dynamic from the very principle it claims to engender by its

---

17 O. Höffe, "Überlegungsgleichgewicht in Zeiten der Globalisierung? Eine Alternative zu Rawls", in Höffe (ed.), *John Rawls*, 271–293, 273.

18 Ricoeur, "Is a purely procedural theory of justice possible?", in *The Just*, trans. D. Pellauer (Chicago: University of Chicago Press, 2000), 36–56, 52–53: "At first glance, the argument has a purely rational appearance, giving an ethical conclusion to non-ethical premises. But if we look closer at the decisive argument directed against utilitarianism, namely, that it must be ready to sacrifice some unfavored individuals or groups if that is required by the good of the greatest number, I cannot help thinking that we have here an ethical argument disguised as a technical argument borrowed from decision theory in its most elementary form, game theory, where there are winners and losers divested of any ethical concern... It seems to me that the argument is a moral one." Further page numbers are included in the text.

purely contractual procedure. In other words, for me, the circularity of Rawls's argument constitutes an indirect plea in favour of the search for an ethical foundation for the concept of justice." (*The Just*, 37–38).

However, the attempt to establish principles through contract, rather than from the ethical self-reflection of humans, also undermines the second foundation on considered convictions. The "kind of circularity the search for reflective equilibrium seems to presume appears to be threatened by the centrifugal forces exercized by the contractualist hypothesis" (*The Just*, 56). As Ricoeur specifies in another text, there are two directions which the sense of justice as a "reasonable sentiment" can take. One is the "lower" atomistic level of a "contractualist conception" marked by "mutual disinterest", the other the "higher" level directed towards mutuality in the sense of a "desire for mutual dependence, mutual indebtedness".[19] In Ricoeur's evaluation, the argumentation of *Theory of Justice* fluctuates between the two.

Ricoeur's distinction of a lower from a higher level points to the difference between a contract and a moral foundation. Contracts are concluded for mutual advantage, whereas ethical striving and morality presuppose an internal orientation towards others and what is owed to them as well as to one's own moral self. In view of the tendency of contract theory to descend to the lower end of mutual disinterest with a Utilitarian *do ut des* mentality, to discount the original desire for a life with others in just institutions, and to replace it with centrifugal dispersion, Ricoeur uncovers the contract approach as a paradoxical attempt in itself: "It may be the burden of every contractualist theory to derive from a procedure agreed upon by everyone the very principles of justice that, in a paradoxical fashion, already motivate the search for an independent argument." (*The Just*, 56) It needs the counterweight of the sense of justice expressed in convictions which it tries to replace. Two competing methods of justification co-exist, one a-historical, in the shape of contract theory exemplified by the original position, the other culturally indebted, in the shape of the idea of the reflective equilibrium. Ricoeur concludes that Rawls wants to have it both ways, first constructivist, then grounded on convictions that are held by actual citizens:

> Rawls... seeks to have the best of both worlds – that is, to be able to construct a purely procedural conception of justice without losing the security offered by the reflective equilibrium between conviction and theory. (*The Just*, 56)

---

19 Ricoeur, "Theonomy and/or autonomy", in M. Volf, C. Krieg, Th. Kucharz (eds.), *The Future of Theology. Essays in Honor of Jürgen Moltmann* (Grand Rapids: Eerdmans, 1996), 284–298, 291.

For Ricoeur, the alternative lies in giving a philosophical account of the pre-understanding of the difference between good and evil through an analysis of human capabilities, and in tracing back their determination to specific cultural and religious histories of interpretation. He asks:

> In the final analysis, this ambiguity has to do with the role of rational arguments in ethics. Can they be substituted for prior convictions thanks to the invention of a hypothetical situation of deliberation (or a transcendental argumentation?) Or is their function instead to clarify in a critical way such prior convictions? (*The Just*, 56)

His answer makes it clear that only a reading in the context of the history of ethical thinking can rescue the purposive reason that dominates the original position including its "maximin" step from a merely economic understanding. This risk-minimizing decision in a situation of uncertainty to opt for maximizing the lowest basis which, in the worst case, the founding member might find himself at, can only be seen as more than calculation due to

> our pre-understanding of the unjust and the just that assures the deontological intention of the self-proclaimed autonomous argument, including maximin. Detached from the context of a Golden Rule (or a transcendental foundation of morality), the maximin rule would remain a purely prudential argument characteristic of every exchange relation. Separated from this cultural history, the maximin rule would lose its ethical character. Instead of being quasi-economic,... it would swerve toward a pseudo-economic argument, one deprived of its rootedness in our considered convictions. (*The Just*, 56)

Ricoeur appreciates the effort to demonstrate even to theories of justice that override individual rights for the sake of the majority's happiness that a contract approach is more promising also for the sake of self-interest; yet it lacks both a moral foundation and reflection on its specific histories of formation.[20]

The perspectives of the three fellow-authors on justice in its different aspects – the theories of action and reason informing it, its scope, its distinction into virtue and principle – will be drawn on again in subsequent sections. The goal is not to compare each of their theories of justice, but to shed the light of their reflections on the philosophical premises which will frame the position ascribed to religion. It is important to take account of the debate between fellow-philosophers in order to be able to detect where the bases of normative arguments ap-

---

20 Ricoeur's own approach to ethics that combines a phenomenological analysis of human capabilities with a hermeneutical approach that has the task of critically clarifying convictions formed in cultural and religious history, will be treated in Part Three.

pear to have been narrowed, and where conclusions are drawn that fall short of the scope required and that other approaches deem possible.

1.1.2.4 Between philosophical and empirical concepts

The critiques treated so far have been concerned both with the problem of devising two foundations, and with the material assumptions brought in through the rational choice background of decision theory; it seems to reduce ethics to self-interest, and regard for the other's equal claim to personal strategies of probable benefit, whatever about the underlying moral reasons for this construct. What is notable in addition to these points is the very fact that Rawls reaches for a discipline outside of philosophy for this attempt to attain the most general level possible. Despite his defense of this step,[21] it risks putting his own discipline in a subordinate position. By determining the term "rational" through rational choice theory – one among other approaches to the discipline of economics – he aims at a level that will provide greater generality. Instead of entrusting the generation of such principles to a philosophical account of human agency, receptivity and reason, one empirical discipline is enlisted to provide a plausible, widely acceptable foundation. This alignment of philosophy with individual sciences risks turning the relationship between critical reflection and empirical sciences on its head by crediting the latter with offering an additional or higher level of validity than philosophical analyses themselves. Rawls's reaching for rational choice theory to complement his reinterpretation of the contract tradition is an indication that the effort to distinguish sharply between philosophical and empirical concepts is not a concern of his.[22] The question of whether philosophy has a distinct method of its own, or whether it relies on empirical disciplines is a point that will reappear in Habermas's "postmetaphysical" understanding of

---

21 In TJ, 158, Rawls asserts that "there is no objection to resting the choice of first principles upon the general facts of economics and psychology. As we have seen, the parties in the original position are assumed to know the general facts about human society... What is essential, of course, is that these premises be true and sufficiently general."

22 In *Autonomy and Trust in Bioethics* (Cambridge: CUP, 2002), O. O'Neill has shown the consequences of this lack of distinction for medical ethics when a concept of autonomy is used which owes more to J. S. Mill than to Kant; autonomy then correlates with independence rather than the capacity for self-legislation as a matter of the good will, which downgrades social relationships and trust. In *Bounds of Justice,* she contrasts an empiricist understanding of autonomy reserved for those in control with positions that explain the "capacity for autonomy as an inherent feature of all human beings, even as the basis of human worth or dignity, and not as something which the more self-sufficient or successful or independent have developed to a greater degree than the rest of us, or that could be confined to one area of life." (BJ, 29)

philosophy, to be discussed in Part Two. Both authors are intent on leaving "metaphysics" behind, but take different routes to do so. Their specific understandings of the status and method of philosophy and of metaphysics that motivate this departure will need to be compared and assessed. As Onora O'Neill's alternative proposal shows, the question of what is unique to philosophical enquiry remains open.[23]

Another question worth asking is which other individual sciences could have been sought by an approach to social ethics to connect its enquiries to. One may wonder what shape *Theory of Justice* would have taken if Rawls had chosen the discipline of pedagogics to help him define rationality. Would there have been scope for considering action directed towards creating conditions for reason and autonomy under conditions of asymmetry?[24] Another more appropriate and defendable link from a philosophical anthropology that reflects on its core concepts, such as agency or rationality, would have been to history or to cultural studies. Instead, a specific and one-sided understanding of human agency, as espoused by one economic approach, is chosen. The inclusion of rational choice theory with its explicit and implicit assumptions about human individuality and sociability has been a key decision that is hard to reconcile with the content of the principles sought. In the quest for starting points that do not undermine the social ethical approach to be constructed, the subsequent foundation on values given in a democratic culture appears as an advantage to O'Neill; even if it narrows the sphere of validity, it leaves behind the guiding perspective of self-interest:

> This 'political' vindication of principles of justice was deepened in Rawls's 1993 *Political Liberalism*, in which a conception of the democratic citizen is used to introduce a distinctive

---

23 Also Paul Ricoeur requests that the avenues to these enquiries should be kept open: "There are no taboos in philosophy, and the terms 'mentalism', 'psychologism' have to stop denoting something forbidden." P. Ricoeur, *Discours et communication* (Paris: L'Herne, 2005), 15. This remark does not, in his view, constitute "a sufficient response" but indicates that the specific task of philosophy is to go behind what linguists and sociologists take as "social facts" (such as communication) (7–10); beyond their investigations, it is necessary to analyse the conditions of the possibility of communication. He states explicitly that the "order of intentions implied" in communicating can be "justified only by transcendental reflection" (15).

24 Cf. H. Peukert's approach in theory of education and theology, starting from theory of action, *Science, Action and Fundamental Theology. Toward a Theology of Communicative Action*, trans. J. Bohman (Cambridge/Mass.: MIT, 1986); *Wissenschaftstheorie, Handlungstheorie, Fundamentale Theologie*, 3rd German edition with a preface and postscript, Frankfurt: Suhrkamp, 2009), and the two *Festschriften*, S. Abeldt/W. Bauer et al. (eds.), *... was es bedeutet, verletzbarer Mensch zu sein* (Mainz: Grünewald, 2000) and O. John/M. Striet (eds.), *"... und nichts Menschliches ist mir fremd"*. *Theologische Grenzgänge* (Regensburg: Pustet, 2010).

account of public reason, thereby cutting loose from the instrumental account of rationality which had been one of the cornerstones of *A Theory of Justice*. (BJ, 72–73)

From different outlines of practical reason and agency, Rawls's contract foundation has been found to be circular: based on questionable idealizations, rather than on consistent conclusions drawn from abstract but justifiable basic predicates about humans (O'Neill); mitigating the self-interest of rational choice theory through the moralizing effect of the strategy of ignorance (Höffe); manifesting an oscillating lack of decision between self-oriented individualism and a morality based on the recognition of otherness (Ricoeur). In view of these objections, will the second foundation be able to offset the problems of the first?

1.1.3 Beyond a constructed procedure: Convictions formed in religious and cultural history in "reflective equilibrium" with principles

All three commentators agree that one can no longer speak of a contractual justification and that the ultimate foundation on which the "basic structure of society" in *Theory of Justice* rests is a contextual one. The decisive method is indicated in Rawls's move to "work from both ends... going back and forth" to reach a "reflective equilibrium" (TJ, 20) between judgements from the "considered convictions" a person arrives at by selecting from the values available in a society, and the principles established in the original position. Ricoeur's diagnosis that the safety net for Rawls's construction of a "purely procedural conception of justice" is the reflective equilibrium with already existing convictions is matched by Onora O'Neill's comment on his dual method:

> This second and more fundamental strategy of justification... justifies the hypothetically agreed principles... The appeal to reflective equilibrium entirely alters the character of Rawls's justificatory strategy. It reveals that he is not simply offering one more contractarian theory of justice which appeals to an idealized and perhaps questionable account of instrumentally rational choices by self-interested agents under supposedly canonical hypothetical conditions. His most fundamental justificatory strategy is an appeal to the fit between the implications of an appropriately tailored original position and 'our' considered judgements. It is these judgements which justify the construction of the original position, just as much as the original position justifies these judgements.[25]

Similar to Ricoeur and O'Neill, Otfried Höffe elucidates the resources that are being put to use as those of a historically shaped lifeworld:

---

25 O'Neill, "Method", in Höffe (ed.), *John Rawls*, 39–40.

> The methodical goal he wants to reach is of a coherence theoretical nature; it is called re-
> flective equilibrium... In order to reach it, Rawls begins with a normatively defined life-
> world, and thus relativizes the extent (*Tragweite*) of contract theory... in reflective equilibri-
> um history and the specific culture play a more than marginal role.[26]

The assessment that the contract approach is being contained or even superseded also means that rational choice theory is less decisive than it appears at
first.[27] The original position now seems to rely on a condensation of existing convictions and practices in the lifeworld. Despite the effect that the duality of methods reduces the scope and status of his theory, this conclusion is seen to give it a
much-needed everyday relevance. Yet, it also poses the question of where the
convictions at work in democracies come from, and how they cope with changes
in cultural supports. Onora O'Neill points out the need of a contract theory to
find traction in everyday practices, while Ricoeur is interested in the provenance
of the supportive convictions in which the sense of justice expresses itself, also
in view of the "fragility" of the reflective equilibrium. Höffe points out the uncertainty of this basis from a different angle, that of ideology critique, and from the
experience of cultural diversity. O'Neill reflects on the need of actual citizens to
have a reason to follow any such principles. If they do, it is because these concepts are already part of their repertoire:

> Why should we accept principles as fundamental to justice on the basis of the claim that
> they can be generated by curious hypothetical procedures?... unless Rawls provides further
> reasons for thinking that principles chosen in a hypothetical fair situation are appropriate
> in the far-from-fair situations in which we find ourselves, the justification is incomplete.
> What claim has Rawlsian justice on actual persons living in very different situations?
> Rawls anticipates this criticism. He argues that the fundamental justification... is not that
> they would be chosen in a situation which we regard as fair, but that these principles
> are in *reflective equilibrium* with our best considered judgements about justice: "these prin-
> ciples would lead us to make the same judgements about the basic structure of society that
> we now make intuitively and in which we have the greatest confidence".[28]

We have seen that Ricoeur welcomes the move to the new basis since it offsets
the dynamic of the instrumentalist rationality of the contract foundation. The

---

26 Höffe, "Einführung", in Höffe (ed.), *John Rawls*, 23.
27 O'Neill, "Method", in Höffe (ed.), *John Rawls*, 40, with reference to PL, 53n: "Since the
process of reflective equilibrium lends some (but never conclusive) weight to our considered but
pre-theoretical judgements about justice, Rawls's theory of justice cannot be regarded simply as
derived from considerations of rational choice (a claim that he makes in *A Theory of Justice*... but
repudiates in his later *Political Liberalism*)."
28 O'Neill, "Method", in Höffe (ed.), *John Rawls*, 38–39, quoting from TJ 19; cf. 579.

hermeneutical philosopher draws attention to the different sources from which this political culture developed. The deontological type of ethics itself did not arise in a vacuum; the normative order that generated it included the traditions of ethical monotheism as well as philosophical ethics: "The deontological intention, and even the historical dimension, are not simply intuitive; they result from a long *Bildung* stemming from the Jewish and Christian as well as from the Greek and Roman traditions." (*The Just*, 56)

On the one hand, the move to "considered convictions", feeding from the resources of the lifeworld, can be seen as progression: in the competition between the two methods of justification, the constructivist, a-historical contract theory exemplified by the "original position" is superseded by a culture-sensitive one which brings existing convictions into coherence with principles in a reflective equilibrium. This turn seems to suggest that the constructed level of a proceduralist approach may have to be supported by concrete values which people are already convinced of both individually and communally. On the other hand, is such recourse to culturally embedded ethical ideas trustworthy as a safety net? Can it deliver what is expected of it? Höffe wonders whether Rawls's "somewhat Hegelian" turn will be enough in times of crisis, or of cultural change and encounter with other traditions.[29] In her critique of commentators who diagnose Rawls as a communitarian, Onora O'Neill points out the republican, rather than community-specific nature of the civic virtues he appeals to.[30] Yet, the question remains what will happen if the hoped-for "mutual support of many considerations, of everything fitting together in one coherent view" (TJ, 21) does not materialize, if political culture and principles are hopelessly at odds. Rawls does provide for the possibility that situations for civil disobedience may arise but he restricts his treatment to the "context… of a state of near justice" (TJ, 351).[31]

---

29 Höffe, "Einführung", in Höffe (ed.), *John Rawls*, 25. "How does one behave when the presupposition, a substantial minimal consensus on justice, becomes fragile (*brüchig*) in eras of moral crisis or in the encounter of different cultures? When the substantive consensus dissolves, the possibility remains to draw a minimal criterion from the mere concept of justice. Since Rawls does not consider this method of a semantics of justice, he is left helpless in front of the dissolution of a substantial minimal consensus."

30 O'Neill, "Method", in Höffe (ed.), *John Rawls*, 41: "However, Rawls's appeal is not to the traditions of 'our' community… but specifically to the reasoning of citizens of liberal democratic polities, who may belong to multiple, diverse communities."

31 He defends civil disobedience despite the threat it poses to "civic concord" and stability: The "responsibility falls not upon those who protest but upon those whose abuse of authority and power justifies such opposition. For to employ the coercive apparatus of the state in order to maintain manifestly unjust institutions is itself a form of illegitimate force that men in due course have a right to resist." (TJ, 390 – 91)

At the same time, he subscribes to an analogy between systems of grammar and of ethos. Höffe points out that the fit between linguistic structures and native speakers' judgements of instances of spoken language, highlighted in Noam Chomsky's generative theory, cannot be applied, as Rawls tries to (TJ, 47), to everyday ethical notions.[32] Thus, rather than merely relying on "considered convictions" being in tune with principles, philosophical analysis has to submit them to a critique of their possible ideological content. This need is also seen by Ricoeur: "The task would be to discern what components or what aspects of our considered convictions require a continual eradication of ideologically biased prejudices."[33] For him as for Höffe, the second contextual justification harbours its own problems of reliance on a cultural basis that can neither be seen as immune against bias nor taken for granted. Which factors undermine the cultural support of a society oriented towards justice? Is it the loss of homogeneity through the arrival of foreign world cultures? Is it the subordination, or, in Habermas's term, the "colonization" of all spheres of life by the laws of the market? The threads of the safety net may be more prone to corrosion than the concept designating this balancing act, "equilibrium", insinuates. A lot will depend on the resources that fill the democratic ethos with life, and on how crisis-resistant they will turn out to be. It appears that the basis of citizens' convictions which the second method of justification invests its trust in may not be solid enough to take over the burden left by the questionable nature of the first. The final version of the contextualization in *Political Liberalism* will have to be examined for its points of anchorage.

1.1.4 The completion of a contextual foundation in *Political Liberalism*

The preceding analyses have shown that a contextually based justification already has an important function in the first book before *Political Liberalism* enacts the move to it as its single foundation. Published more than two decades

---

32 Höffe finds this analogy uncritical: "Rawls believes that an academic theory relates to everyday judgements on justice like linguistics do to everyday speaking… This analogy only carries that far… What native speakers agree on, does indeed constitute the German or English spoken language; yet what is judged to be just does not need to be just even if it is based on an overwhelming consensus. While it is meaningless to subject grammatical rules that are in practice to the suspicion of ideology and to draw up a 'normative' syntax that diverges strongly from the existing use, it can be meaningful to question with Plato's *Politeia* collectively validated convictions of justice. Existing convictions are indicators for principles of justice, but not an ultimately valid criterion." ("Einführung", in Höffe (ed.), *John Rawls*, 25–26)
33 Ricoeur, "Is a purely procedural theory", in *The Just*, 56.

after *Theory of Justice*, it fleshes out the programmatic clarification made in 1985, to offer "political, not metaphysical" foundations.[34] It draws on the institutions that democratic constitutional states have developed, and on the virtues they expect from citizens, and proposes the neutralising power of "public reason" as the level at which controversies are to be settled. The decisive new feature of society which political ethics has to do justice to is the "fact of pluralism" (PL, 4). While it is welcomed as an expression of the free use of reason, it also poses a problem for stability. Convictions reappear now in the shape of conflicting claims from plural origins, as a source of division rather than as an agreed existing basis in coherence with principles. The new task therefore is to secure the stability of a society oriented towards liberty and equality in the face of the multiplicity of "comprehensive doctrines" of philosophical and religious provenance. Will the second, inductive method be open to include the expressions of religious traditions of thought and practice in their contribution to an ethos of citizenship, or will it prefer to seek a platform that is equidistant to all traditions?

Before this question can be answered, it is necessary to turn to the anthropology (2) and theory of society (3) that flesh out the normative framework examined so far. Then the relationship between democratic institutions and public reason can be investigated (4), and compared with a Kantian understanding of practical reason and public reason (5). Having thus completed the parameters in which religions are to operate, Rawls's position on faith in God in relation to hope will be established from his discussion of Kant's postulate of God. Part One will conclude with a comparison of two responses from Continental theological ethicists to the role given to religions (6).

1.2 "Idea of the good" and "sense of justice" as elements of moral personhood in *Theory of Justice*

For the purposes of *A Theory of Justice*, the divergence in method, first constructivist, then contextual, does not pose a problem. Already in the explanation of the original position a Hegelian reliance on the ethical life existing in a polity has been added to the original contractualist "Kantian" foundation. It is necessary to identify the basic anthropological assumptions that allow this move between understandings of self, of moral experience and reason that are usually contrasted. While many colloquial observations of "facts" of human life and ex-

---

34 Rawls, "Justice as fairness: Political not metaphysical", in *Philosophy and Public Affairs* 14 (1985) 223–251.

amples of everyday pursuits are offered, two elements are specifically named as constitutive of the "moral person": Everyone has an "idea of their own good", and a "sense of justice". What does each of these concepts consist in (1 and 3), how do they relate, and how do they compare to their sources in Aristotle and Kant (2 and 4)? I shall conclude with a test case for Rawls's interpretation of these normative concepts: how is his demand for measures to compensate for a lack of natural assets to be evaluated (5)?

1.2.1 Rationality as a good and its realization in a life plan

Among the premises Rawls outlines, it is the idea of a person's good expressed in the ends pursued that serves to explain what motivates individuals to engage in society. The concept of the good contains a basic theory of action. In *Theory of Justice*, it is called the "Aristotelian Principle" and is specified into the concept of a "life plan" which needs for its realization "primary goods". It is here that the "sense of justice" will have to be called in, since it is assumed that these "primary goods" are scarce and finite. Once consumed, they are gone, so each person's use has to acknowledge a framework of agreed distribution, which is where the "sense of justice" takes over. In the definition of the original position, individuals were introduced as "moral persons", which was explained as "rational beings with their own ends and capable, I shall assume, of a sense of justice" (TJ, 12).

In order to find out how rationality, the good, and agency go together, it will be necessary to take a close look at the steps and formulations offered. Self-motivation is acknowledged as a premise deriving from Aristotle, but also compared to the modern or "idealistic" idea of self-realization.[35] The good is defined in a formal way, without committing anyone to a specific content; further, it is individualized into the concept of a "life plan": "The definition of the good is purely formal. It simply states that a person's good is determined by the rational plan of life that he would choose with deliberative rationality from the maximal class of plans." (TJ, 424)

---

35 TJ, 431 defends the reality of the Aristotelian Principle of realizing one's capacities from observation: "Like the idealist notion of self-realization, to which it bears a certain resemblance, it may have the ring of a philosopher's principle with nothing to support it. But it seems to be borne out by many facts of everyday life, and by the behavior of children and some of the higher animals. Moreover, it appears to be susceptible to evolutionary explanation. Natural selection must have favored creatures of whom this principle is true."

The good and the rational meet in the prioritization of goals achieved in this "plan". Standing for the coherence of a life, it is comparable to what other ethicists, such as Alasdair MacIntyre and Paul Ricoeur, have tried to capture as the "narrative unity of a life". For Rawls, the

> plan of life establishes the basic point of view from which all judgments of value relating to a particular person are to be made and finally rendered consistent (TJ, 409)... that plan which best organizes our activities and influences the formation of our subsequent wants so that our aims and interests can be fruitfully combined into one scheme of conduct... A plan, then, is made up of subplans suitably arranged in a hierarchy (TJ, 410 – 411).

At the same time, he warns against over-interpreting the extent to which it is possible to bind oneself in advance, and also defends the concept of a plan against the "misunderstanding" that it undervalues the importance of spontaneity: we are not to

> imagine that a rational plan is a detailed blueprint for action stretching over the whole course of life. It consists of a hierarchy of plans (TJ, 410)... It may be objected that this conception implies that one should be continually planning and calculating... It is not inconceivable that an individual, or even a whole society, should achieve happiness moved entirely by spontaneous inclination. With great luck and good fortune some men might by nature just hit upon the way of living that they would adopt with deliberative rationality. (TJ, 423 – 24)

The core of the satisfaction achieved by carrying out the plan is marked by the term "realized capacity". It comprises all the elements of diversity and creativity which the concept of "plan" seems to lack:

> human beings enjoy the exercize of their realized capacities (their innate or trained abilities), and this enjoyment increases the more the capacity is realized, or the greater its complexity... Human beings enjoy the greater variety of experience, they take pleasure in the novelty and surprises and the occasions for ingenuity and invention that such activities provide. The multiplicity of spontaneous activities is an expression of the delight that we take in imagination and creative fantasy. Thus the Aristotelian Principle characterizes human beings as importantly moved not only by the pressure of bodily needs, but also by the desire to do things enjoyed simply for their own sakes" (TJ, 426. 431).

The Aristotelian element of "realized capacity" stands for a "sense of mastery" (443), perhaps also in the face of unplanned turns, a confidence in one's own capabilities which a just society will foster. As a consequence, "in the design of social institutions a large place has to be made for it, otherwise human beings will find their culture and form of life dull and empty" (TJ, 429). The mark of a just society is that it allows its members to realize their capabilities. Rawls uses the terms self-confidence, self-esteem and self-respect interchangeably to denote the outcome of letting each member excel at their own level, in clear opposition to setting objectifying standards of perfection. He underlines how each sphere has its own measure of attainment, which outsiders have no business to judge. In

> a well-ordered society ... the members of (a variety of communities) have their own ideals appropriately matched to their aspirations and talents. Judged by the doctrine of perfectionism, activities of many groups may not display a high degree of excellence. But no matter. What counts is that the internal life of these associations is suitably adjusted to the abilities and wants of those belonging to them, and provides a secure basis for the sense of worth of their members. The absolute level of achievement, even if it could be defined, is irrelevant. (TJ, 441–42)

The "basic principle of motivation" contained in the "Aristotelian Principle" (TJ, 424–433) also includes the positive effects of such varied excellences on one's immediate others:

> Thus the familiar values of personal affection and friendship, meaningful work and social cooperation, the pursuit of knowledge,... beautiful objects... are not only... good for those who enjoy them but they are likely to enhance the good of others. In achieving these ends we generally contribute to the rational plans of our associates. In this sense, they are complementary goods (TJ, 425).

In view of the causal relationship between realized capacity and self-respect it is not surprising that the latter is developed two paragraphs later (TJ, 440–446) as the "most important primary good". I will first investigate the relationship between the good that occupies the highest position, and the enabling ones treated earlier, before concluding the analysis of Rawls's definition of the "good" by questioning the theory decisions that have become apparent so far.

Rawls is aware that the move to introduce the notion of "goods" into the contract approach needs to be explained. Above all, they have to be kept from being identified with the substantial goods of metaphysical accounts of personhood and *polis*. They need to be as formal or general as possible:

> The argument for the two principles of justice does not assume that the parties have particular ends, but only that they desire certain primary goods...The preference for primary goods is derived, then, from only the most general assumptions about rationality and the conditions of human life. (TJ, 253)

The "primary social goods" figuring in the "basis of expectations" in Part One as essential to carrying out one's life plan are identified as "rights and liberties, opportunities and powers, income and wealth", with the addition: "(A very important primary good is the sense of one's own worth)" (TJ, 92), to be followed up when dealing with "ends" in the third and final part of his book. If it is clear that each person has a basic interest in having "goods" at their disposal, and if the additional assumption is made that each desires more rather than less of them, society appears as marked by a tension:

> They assume that each has a conception of his good in the light of which he presses claims against the rest. So although they view society as a cooperative venture for mutual advantage, it is typically marked by a conflict as well as by an identity of interests. (TJ, 520)

It is this partly antagonistic situation which has to receive a framework that opens up the chance for each citizen to strive for his or her flourishing. It has to do justice to an impressive criterion: not to "wound his self-respect..., the main primary good" (TJ, 534). This demand is concretized by reference to the other primary goods which are material. A citizen should not be left in a "lesser position as measured by the index of objective primary goods" (TJ, 534). As the normative criterion of a programme of improving the basic conditions for each member's realization of their capacities, the orientation towards self-respect seems to offer an inspiring political vision, honouring the equal dignity of each: without self-respect

> nothing may seem worth doing... we sink into apathy and cynicism. Therefore the parties in the original position would wish to avoid at almost any cost the social conditions that undermine self-respect (TJ, 440)... the contract conception of justice supports the self-esteem of citizens generally more firmly... In the public forum each person is treated with the respect due to a sovereign equal; and everyone has the same basic rights (TJ, 536).

1.2.2 Comparison and critique of Rawls's concept of the good of self-respect

With this criterion for societies to qualify as just, to create conditions for self-respect, an impressive standard has been set. Yet how self-respect and self-realization are being defined needs to be assessed from the perspective of other philosophical anthropologies. The two defining aspects for Rawls are, first,

> a person's sense of his own value, his secure conviction that his conception of his good, his plan of life, is worth carrying out. Second, self-respect implies a confidence in one's own ability, so far as it is within one's power, to fulfill one's intentions... Associative ties strengthen the second aspect of self-esteem, since they tend to reduce the likelihood of failure and to provide support against the sense of self-doubt when mishaps occur (TJ, 440 – 41).

In comparison with other Kantian approaches, the "two aspects" Rawls distinguishes in "self-respect (or self-esteem)" leave out two dimensions: the internal one which is up to the moral agent, not to society, of the self-worth won through living up to the level of moral obligation; and the affirmation of other persons' equally original freedom. Combined with the unvindicated premise that all primary goods are to be maximized, the sense in which conditions for self-respect are to be secured is set in a problematic direction. By making the empirical capacities a person can realize the basis of self-respect, the self is not seen as a unique author, but defined in market terms as the owner of what are called "natural assets": "Yet... the application of the Aristotelian principle is always relative to the individual and therefore to his natural assets and particular situation" (TJ, 441).

Enough features have emerged for a first evaluation of the course of argumentation on the "good". It can be summarized as follows. The reception of Aristotle as a champion of self-realization is made possible by bracketing the substantive content of his ethics of virtues practiced in a *polis*. By becoming a "rational life plan", the idea of a flourishing life is turned into a formalized concept. However, the ends it strives for now appear as a complete matter of private choice which is outside the remit of public discourse. The observation that Rawls offers a selective and individualizing reception of the Aristotelian orientation towards the good life, however, does not mean that he deletes all social features in his account of the roots of human action. Social duties are portrayed as a fulfilling part of human self-realization;[36] education as a pursuit for its own sake, not subjected to efficiency calculations, is a core task of society;[37] individuals are oriented towards others for their own fulfillment.

Yet, despite the sustained effort of *Theory of Justice* to refute the view that contract approaches are deficient with regard to the communal dimension of human life, some of its assumptions remain questionable. They relate to the link between the rational and the good in Rawls's account of a life plan, to the content of self-respect as the main primary good, to basic motivation, and

---

[36] Explaining why the principle of "fair equality of opportunity" is paramount, Rawls argues that people excluded from the chance to cooperate would rightly feel they were being unjustly "debarred from experiencing the realization of self which comes from a skillful and devoted exercise of social duties. They would be deprived of one of the main forms of human good." (TJ 84)

[37] The "value of education should not be assessed solely in terms of economic efficiency and social welfare. Equally if not more important is the role of education in enabling a person to enjoy the culture of his society and to take part in its affairs, and in this way provide for each individual a secure sense of his own worth." (TJ, 101)

to society conceived as a system of distribution of quantifiable goods, rather than ones that need to be distinguished and prioritized by criteria of relevance. This general indication of lacunae in his argumentation can be specified from different angles.

(1) On the one hand, despite some effort to elaborate their equally spontaneous element, the individually conceived *life plans* which come to define happiness appear quite controlled. They are tied to a long-term discipline of gradual, step-by-step attainment. Yet, how does the process of working them out earn the attribute of being "rational" once they have been disconnected from the evaluated sequence of substantive goods offered in Aristotle's theory of striving? What takes the place of their prior connectedness in Aristotle? Could "rational" just amount to self-devised and disciplined, but otherwise arbitrary paths to personal meaning, instrumental to goals left undiscussed and unexposed to judgements of their rationality by shared criteria?

(2) Citizens become accountable to each other only when their use of primary goods exceeds the distributive framework. Are they also *accountable to themselves,* based on a concept of identity that differentiates the self in its spontaneity from the finite and conditioned expressions of its unconditional freedom? Is a "life plan" best described as a projection of fulfilling individual preferences on a time scale? Or does it need additional conceptions to capture other elements: for example, that a life plan is something hatched, tried, evaluated, abandoned, and recouped together with unchosen and chosen others, and that needs the narrativity of the self and of others to identify it retrospectively?

(3) Is it true of all *primary goods* that they diminish when they are drawn on, or can some contain a fruitfulness that creates more, rather than less, of them when they are realized together? Is the quantitative implication of "goods" not misleading when it comes to the hoped-for meaning of a life plan? The clearest candidate for such a socially augmented qualitative good would be the "most important primary good... self-respect" (TJ, 440). If it was based on a theory of recognition, it would generate more of, rather than absorb, the precious quantities deemed available in a framework of maximization. Instead of originating in a process of mutual recognition, its only basis in Rawls is a person's internal satisfaction with her achievements, which grows higher, the more intricate and complex the skills practiced are. It is here that the impression of the anti-intersubjective character of the theory of action underlying the first of the two features of the person finds the most ample evidence. It appears as *ab ovo* and irredeemably individualist, even "atomistic" since it overlooks both the reflexive and the intersubjective dimensions of self-respect. This concept would need to be analysed as a "good" which is attained not by proficiency in skills, but by a different capability that is key in other Kantian approaches. In Ricoeur's

terms, it is imputability, the moral experience of being a responsible agent, who does not simply express, but test, wishes for self-realization against the deontological "sieve of the norm".[38] This is where Aristotle meets Kant in Ricoeur's, but not in Rawls's combination of their approaches to ethics.

(4) The animating drive which the "Aristotelian Principle" tries to capture seems to be programmed in a rational choice direction of attaining ever-greater amounts of quantitative and exclusive maximal goods. How does this stand in relation to other elements Rawls takes from Aristotle, such as his account of the *self-motivated* character of *praxis?* Höffe observes that the premise of "more rather than less" (TJ, 93) primary goods leads *Theory of Justice* back to the Utilitarianism that it was meant to devise an alternative to.[39] Building a maximizing element into the primary goods that agents need seems more in tune with economic theories in which rational choice expresses itself in the imperative of increasing market shares. The admirable aim of bringing together the "rational" and the "good" would then descend into an instrumental rationality of exponentially increasing conditions for realizing goals that remain unassessed.

(5) Thus, Aristotle's striving for a flourishing life is in danger of being reconceived as assembling as many primary goods as possible, all on the same level, to have the wherewithall to carry out one's life plan, subject to a working system of distribution. One alternative would be to examine each of these goods for their distinctive contributions and connections in "realizing capacities". Then the question of a *teleology* which had disappeared in the contract situation where generalized, anonymous goods were subjected to principles for their allocation, could no longer be avoided. Once their concrete distribution had to be decided, it would become obvious that the different goods mentioned are neither at the same level, nor necessarily commensurable.[40] A subsequent step is required

---

38 Ricoeur, *Oneself as Another*, trans. K. Blamey (Chicago: University of Chicago Press, 1992), 170.

39 In his "Einführung", in Höffe (ed.), *John Rawls*, Höffe comments: "Does this thinking not lead to Utilitarianism under Rawls's own premises? Rawls understands the choice in the original position as a choice under uncertainty and opts for the risk-averse maximin rule...The criterion of rationality clearly is: maximize your expectations of benefit, which corresponds exactly to the average benefit of Utilitarianism." (22) He points out the internal problem of contradiction arising from Rawls's admission that for religious or other reasons one could renounce one's full share of primary goods, since it "contradicts either the concept of a primary good... as the unrenounceable basis of all life plans, or the maximizing task which is supposed to be an essential feature of rationality in accordance with game theory" (10 – 11).

40 The plurality of primary goods and of different cultural orders of priorities is the reason for Ricoeur to refer to the differentiation of justice into "spheres" as proposed in Michael Walzer's *Spheres of Justice. A Defense of Pluralism and Equality* (New York: Basic Books, 1983), or into

where goods are no longer treated at a formal level, and their ordering (for example, security over maximization of assets, or artistic expression over efficiency) has to be discussed.

After the individualizing account of human striving, how is the justice dimension anchored – as equally original, as a natural second step, as a conscious and voluntary transformation of self-interested agents into partners collaborating in the project of creating a just society, or even of fair conditions at a global level? In which way will this sense that Rawls takes up from the *sensus communis* tradition[41] to establish an orientation towards justice as a constitutive element of personhood be specified?

1.2.3 "The sense of justice"

If the "good" was drawn from Aristotelian philosophy, the criterion of what is "right" will be formulated in Kantian terms. Rawls refers to the faculty of extending equal regard to others as the human "sense of justice". While this sense has given rise to different ethical approaches, among them Utilitarianism, it is the foundation from which an alternative to its sacrificial principle is launched. The "least advantaged" fellow-citizen is the point from which justice is constructed. The term in which the view of individuals is expressed comes close to Kant's concept of human dignity: "Each person possesses an inviolability founded on justice that even the welfare of society as a whole cannot override." (TJ, 3)

To ensure such inviolability, far-reaching demands are established which include equal chances for future generations. Their foundation is a specific condition stated as part of the second principle of justice, subsequent to the first one of greatest equal liberty: the "difference principle". Its complex formulation includes the provision to ensure equal conditions of access to positions as well as measures to compensate for lower starting points. This requirement is to counteract the exclusion created by a "callous meritocratic society" (TJ, 110) which ig-

---

"cities" in Luc Boltanski and Laurent Thévenot, *De la justification: les economies de la grandeur* (Paris: Presses Universitaires de France, 1987).

41 J.-P. Wils, "Sensus communis – ein 'Vermögen'? Quasi-anthropologische und hermeneutische Aspekte in John Rawls' Sozialethik", in Wils, *Handlungen und Bedeutungen: Reflexionen über eine hermeneutische Ethik* (Freiburg i. Ue./Freiburg i. Br.: Freiburger Universitätsverlag, 2001), 126–163. For him, it does not constitute an anthropological assumption, but "a presupposition and product of a procedure of political constructivism. In it, the competences of judgement and of motivation are united at their origin." (153)

nores its own undeserved foundations. For Rawls, it is part of the "considered convictions" about justice within democratic societies that one's natural and social endowments are not due to one's own merit (cf. TJ, 102). It follows that the sense of justice demands that equally undeserved disadvantage be addressed. In view of such strong conclusions, it will be decisive how the normative dimension introduced by the term "justice" will be elaborated, beginning with how it is distinguished from "equality".

As the Protestant theological ethicist Wolfgang Huber explains, justice assumes the ability to carry out an operation that is more complex than a simple commitment to egalitarianism. In his elaboration of a Christian ethics of law he identifies Rawls's insight as follows: "Justice becomes a problem precisely because it cannot be understood as pure equality. Rather, it has to be asked which inequalities are compatible with justice or even required by justice."[42] Thus, while special contributions can be recognized and rewarded, the inequalities resulting from them have to meet a condition which the second principle specifies: All

> social and economic inequalities, for example inequalities of wealth and authority, are just only if they result in compensating benefits for everyone, and in particular for the least advantaged members of society. (TJ, 14–15)... Men share in primary goods on the principle that some can have more if they are acquired in ways which improve the situation of those who have less. (TJ, 94)

The overall goal is to offer people fair chances for developing their potential; differences can be justified if they contribute to this goal. Before examining what undeserved inequalities Rawls has in mind when he calls for compensation, one needs to take a closer look at the assumed "sense of justice" and the specific understanding of autonomy that shapes its crystallisation into the two principles:

> the members of a well-ordered society have the common aim of cooperating together to realize their own and another's nature in ways allowed by the principles of justice. This collective intention is the consequence of everyone's having an effective sense of justice. Each citizen wants everyone (including himself) to act from principles on which all would agree in an initial situation of equality. (TJ, 527)

---

42 W. Huber, *Gerechtigkeit und Recht. Grundlinien christlicher Rechtsethik* (Gütersloh: Gütersloher Verlag, 1996), 150. Rawls rejects a strict egalitarianism which he sees as the expression of an envy that rational agents should be free of: "As for particular envy, to a certain extent it is endemic to human life; being associated with rivalry, it may exist in any society... Strict egalitarianism, the doctrine which insists upon an equal distribution of all primary goods, conceivably derives from this propensity." (TJ, 537–8)

Here, an intention of genuine cooperation is the guiding perspective. A similar expression of an orientation towards the other can be found in one of Rawls's references to Kant's understanding of autonomy:

> Kant's main aim is to deepen and to justify Rousseau's idea that liberty is acting in accordance with a law that we give to ourselves. And this leads not to a morality of austere command but to an ethic of mutual respect and self-esteem. (TJ, 256)

Programmatic summaries such as this one explain the inspirational effect of Rawls's first book for policy-makers as much as its reception as a secular counterpart to Liberation theology's "preferential option of the poor" in some parts of theological ethics.[43] Yet, appeals to "mutual respect and self-esteem" stand side by side with other formulations which reveal a different understanding of Kant's project and the concept of autonomy on which it is based.

1.2.4 The "sense of justice" compared with principled autonomy in Kant

By interpreting "autonomy" in terms of "choosing principles" and "expressing" one's own free and equal rational nature, an understanding is adopted which risks reducing autonomy to empirical conditions of action and self-expression; it falls short of a moral self-legislation that recognizes all others as ends in themselves: "Kant held, I believe, that a person is acting autonomously when the principles of his action are chosen by him as the most adequate possible expression of his nature as a free and equal rational being." (TJ, 252) This explanation leaves out any constitutive orientation towards the other whose equally original freedom and status as an end in himself are to be protected, as especially the humanistic formulation of the Categorical Imperative shows. "Autonomy" in the Kantian sense of being subject to the moral law is now translated into the independence of "free and equal rational beings". In keeping with this empirical turn, the "noumenal" character of freedom, by which Kant distinguishes transcendental source and concrete, finite, empirical expressions, is operationalized as the quality that leads everyone to "consent to these principles". (TJ, 257) Freedom seems to be the opposite of natural and social givens. The result is that "het-

---

43 In "Fairness is not enough", in *Christian Justice and Public Policy* (Cambridge: CUP, 1997), 113–139, 130, D. Forrester asks: "Is the Difference Principle a secular transcription of what is now called the 'preferential option for the poor'?" His answer is that being motivated by Jesus's parables, such as that of Lazarus, would demand more of the Rich Man than acting in "his own reasonable self-interest".

eronomy" comes to be defined not by inclinations within the person herself which she can opt for or reject in her actions, but by natural and social chance:

> My suggestion is that we think of the original position as the point of view from which nou-menal selves see the world... The description of the original position interprets the point of view of noumenal selves, of what it means to be a free and equal rational being... Thus men exhibit their freedom, their independence from the contingencies of nature and society, by acting in ways they would acknowledge in the original position (TJ, 255–56)... The princi-ples he acts upon are not adopted because of his social position or natural endowments, or in view of the particular type of society in which he lives or the specific things that he hap-pens to want. To act on such principles is to act heteronomously. (TJ, 252)... We have acted as though we belonged to a lower order, as though we were a creature whose first principles are decided by natural contingencies. (TJ, 256)

But can natural or social contingencies rob a person of their autonomy, that is, their capability of being a moral agent? Kant's ethics is well aware of the empir-ical constraints within which agents work out their autonomy; but summarizing his understanding of freedom as "independence from the contingencies of na-ture and society" can easily be misunderstood as declaring a particular state of being as irreconcilable with the human ability to be a self-legislator. What is evident in Rawls's reinterpretation is an empirical understanding of autonomy as freedom of choice, rather than "principled autonomy"; it is a reductive under-standing which Onora O'Neill's critique of his normative framework has already shown to be an ambiguous foundation for ethics.[44]

Rawls also misinterprets Kant's reason for discounting "benevolence" as a moral principle. The author of the autonomy approach does so because he sees it as based on fleeting and shallow emotions, rather than on the moral ex-perience of obligation, not because he wants agents to ignore each other: the "motivational assumption of mutual disinterest accords with Kant's notion of au-tonomy... the concept of benevolence, being a second-order notion, would not work out well." (TJ, 253–4)

What emerges from these observations of Rawls's interpretation of concepts and quotes from Kant is that, despite some formulations expressing the "desire to treat one another not as means only but as ends in themselves" (TJ, 179), nei-ther moral self-reflection, nor the possibly one-sided recognition of others as ends in themselves play a role. Self-contained agents, rational, free, equal, and not indebted to one another, are the protagonists; the concept of person is empirical, not transcendental; no self or *ipse* as the condition of the possibility

---

44 See above, 1.1.2.4.

of reflection and outreach to the other is assumed.[45] The rational choice origin of the principles resurfaces when the aim is declared, "to replace moral judgments by those of rational prudence" (TJ, 94). Even if the construction of the original position makes it impossible for agents to out-manoeuvre each other,[46] the anthropological premises of moral agency in Rawls do not seem to allow for anything beyond a balance of mutual interests. Then even the compensation principle may appear to be conceived in the interest of safeguarding greater future stability, that is, as self-serving in the long term. For Rawls whose interpretation of Kant can move within a few pages from "mutual disinterest" (TJ, 253) to "an ethic of mutual respect" (TJ, 256), such dual interests may not constitute a contradiction. In *Political Liberalism* where the difference principle is downgraded and the "reasonable" becomes the basis of justification, it is stated clearly that justice is satisfied by strict reciprocity: "Persons are reasonable...when, among equals..., they are ready to propose principles and standards as fair terms of cooperation and to abide by them willingly, given the assurance that others will likewise do so." (PL, 49) In view of these formulations, it seems clear that Kant's paramount concern with the need to distinguish between self-interest and morality is not shared by Rawls.

For approaches to social and political ethics based on morality in its Kantian scope, as well as for theological ethics, this interpretation of justice in terms of strict reciprocity is a restriction. It remains conditional, only to be maintained if a response is forthcoming. As Herta Nagl-Docekal observes, the premise of a sense of justice can be interpreted in different ways: as an anthropological feature, or as a presupposition required in political theory. Its use as a condition for co-existing in a society is what the course of Rawls's thinking leads to. What needs to be remembered, however, is that it "is not coextensive with moral ought in its

---

45 This becomes clear in Rawls's explanation of the humanistic formulation of the Categorical Imperative: in an "original position of equality... men have equal representation as moral persons who regard themselves as ends and the principles they accept will be rationally designed to protect the claims of their person." (TJ, 180) Kant's prohibition of instrumentalizing the other is turned into a justification of self-protection, of one's own claim, not that of others as equal to mine and as a limit not to be transgressed in realizing one's own capacities.
46 In his "Einführung", in Höffe (ed.), *John Rawls*, 21, Höffe highlights the difference between "rational prudence" and "antique phronesis or medieval prudentia" in that the first denotes the "choice of a will that is oriented not to general but particular interests". Yet, he equally tries to show that since "the difference of general and individual will is deleted", it does not result in "cleverness in the modern sense... With the help of the information deficit he screens off any individuality or particularity and achieves a general, i.e., moral or just, subject... The subjects of the original situation cannot maximize a benefit of their own."

totality. It focuses our – morally founded – acting as citizens."[47] If the sense of justice, initially understood as one of the two capacities of moral personhood, slides into a property required for political institutions, morality is in danger of being usurped by legality. As the external framework for the interaction of free citizens, it cannot take the place of the measure of internal reflection on justification that morality offers. If a merely institutional understanding of the moral sense of justice is used to supply the basis of a normative concept of democracy, positions that demand more of its foundations may appear as excessive and possibly intolerant. The new view put forward in *Political Liberalism* of all philosophical approaches as "comprehensive doctrines" themselves will be explored in section 4.

What remains to be checked here are the effects of Rawls's empiricist reinterpretation of autonomy and heteronomy. If the new obstacles to autonomy, understood as pertaining to "free and equal rational beings with a liberty to choose" (TJ, 256), are natural chance and social contingencies, what light does this throw on the natural basis of individual personhood? Which tasks will it entail for the state in its role of compensation?

1.2.5 Natural contingency and self-respect

The "egalitarian demand" to compensate for undeserved inequalities is expressed early on in the aim to find a "conception of justice that nullifies the accidents of natural endowment and the contingencies of social circumstance" (TJ, 15). This strong formulation is softened later on by allowing distinctions to persist (TJ, 102), rather than be "nullified", but it insinuates that the natural features which go into personal identity have no value in themselves. They are put on the same level as socially constructed differences and are seen as something either to be remedied, or as undeserved "good fortune" which has to be paid back: the

> difference principle represents, in effect, an agreement to regard the distribution of natural talents as a common asset and to share in the benefits of this distribution...Those who have been favored by nature... may gain from their good fortune only on terms that improve the situation of those who have lost out. (TJ, 101)

In both cases, natural givens appear as undignified contingencies external to individual freedom and as bearers of a "bias": to

---

47 H. Nagl-Docekal, "Moral und Religion", 847.

provide genuine equality of opportunity, society must give more attention to those with fewer native assets and to those born into the less favorable social positions. The idea is to redress the bias of contingencies in the direction of equality (TJ, 100 – 01).

In addition to the negative view of natural chance, the sources of inequality are defined by assuming stark alternatives between persons: those who are naturally and/or socially endowed, and those who have lost out in either or both. No reference point or criterion is given in relation to which someone's gifts may be useful, lacking, or irrelevant. Before, in the chapters outlining the good of the life plan, equal regard was given to a person's favourite pursuits; now a different measure of evaluation seems to take over, some objective standard of what can count as a natural gift, and what as a deficiency. Having celebrated the multiplicity of interests and excellences as well as the associations arising from them, this sudden turn from appreciating variety to an objectifying stance carries undeclared intentions into the compensation principle. The turn to empirical evaluations can be seen as running counter to the vision stated above, of a society built to further the self-respect of its members.

Thus, upon examination, the two features of the moral person, a sense of the good, and a sense of justice, have shown themselves to be based on a combination of Aristotle and Kant that is marked by reductions of both approaches. They result in curtailing the role of intersubjectivity and in losing the origin of self-respect in the moral experience of obligation. The idea of an original sense of morality which would motivate initiatives also under asymmetric conditions, stalled by a lack of immediate response, indifference, or enmity, disappears. Is the anthropological basis of the two justice principles able to support the standpoint expected: "just institutions are collectively rational and to everyone's advantage from a suitably general perspective" (TJ, 567)? What would motivate people to take this view, rather than their own urge to acquire as many primary goods as possible to realize their capacities?

A second problem has emerged in the basic assumptions that inform the demand for compensation: it is narrowly oriented towards making up for lower starting conditions due to a person's poor natural or social endowments. Not pursued is the wider question, what role the functional frameworks of a society play and what allows it to judge one person's capacities as poor, and another's as undeserved, but ample. Kant clearly distinguishes measurable features like intelligence from moral capacity. To draw the line between those with greater and those with lesser natural "assets", even if it is in the interest of just compensation, can itself be seen as an expression of a particular system of values. When it was introduced, the difference principle appeared like the essence of justice: the demand that beyond safeguarding the conditions of realization of the primary goods, it was necessary to advance the most disadvantaged citizens the most. Yet when taken together with Rawls's view of natural assets, Höffe's judgement of it as "paternalistic" makes sense.[48] His remark could mean that there are evaluations and initiatives that are best left to citizens themselves. The assumptions emerging in Rawls's concretization of the difference principle as extending to compensation for natural features of human embodiment have given rise to an extensive debate in disability studies.[49] The implicit value decisions transported in these considerations need to be checked in the context of his theory of society.

1.3 Society as a cooperative venture for mutual advantage

The previous analyses have shown that Rawls's anthropology oscillates between the assumption of enlightened self-interest as the driving force, and a desire to share one's gifts with others in the creation of a just society. In discussing the "Aristotelian principle" it also became clear that even at the level of concrete, situated freedom, the starting point was the individual and intersubjectivity was thematized subsequently. It is for this reason that I am treating the social dimension, including his vision of a well-ordered society, as a separate section. By contrast, in Parts Two and Three, the anthropological starting points of his two fellow-theorists, Habermas and Ricoeur, will include the communal dimension of human action and morality.

The discussion of the two aspects of moral personhood has shown that expectations to citizens are high: they are seen as self-motivated; as oriented towards guaranteeing equality of respect in real terms through equal access to primary goods, achieved, if necessary, by compensating for natural or social disadvantage; and as non-judgemental and tolerant of other people's ways of realizing their ideas of the good. The list of attitudes desired in citizens raises the question of the cultural resources and values which can sustain the motivation required by the difference principle. The negative interpretation of contingency resulted in a call for specific measures to tackle disadvantage which included the proposal to improve society's genetic basis. Before returning to this point (3), however, first the guiding concept of society has to be reconstructed, from the admission made in the description of the original position that society is a

---

48 Cf. Höffe, "Einführung", in Höffe (ed.), *John Rawls*, 13.
49 Cf., e.g., several chapters in E. F. Kittay/L. Carlson (eds.), *Cognitive Disability and its Challenge to Moral Philosophy* (Oxford: Wiley-Blackwell, 2010).

place of conflict, to the contrasting ideal view of what a just society would accomplish (1). The self-correction voiced in *Political Liberalism* regarding some assumptions made in the first book will then be examined to establish what remains of the initial orientation towards a societal and public dimension of self-realization (2). The critique of "civic humanism" as a "metaphysical" stance to be avoided affects the scope and shape of what the second book develops as "public reason". I shall conclude by assessing the sources and significance of diversity in his theory of society (4).

1.3.1 From a system of benefits and burdens to a "social union of social unions"

It has already emerged that the "life plan", a formalized and individualized version of Aristotle's striving for a flourishing life, contains the seeds of societal conflict by needing primary goods which are in scarce supply. It is to everyone's ultimate advantage, be it for reasons of stability or to express the sense of justice that comes with one's rational nature, to create a system in which equal benefits and equal burdens for everyone are the guiding rule. The call for cooperation ensues not as a primary wish or because life plans are directed towards the hope of substantial exchanges with others, but as a realistic and sensible means of adjudicating conflicting claims to goods. Yet, beyond his individualistic starting point, Rawls offers descriptions which identify this cooperation and its outcome, a "well-ordered" society, not just as a by-product but as a goal in itself. A

> well-ordered society... is itself a form of social union. Indeed, it is a social union of social unions. Both characteristic features are present: the successful carrying out of just institutions is the shared final end of all the members of society, and these institutional forms are prized as good in themselves. (TJ, 527)

What are the elements of this vision, and how do the different levels relate to each other? We have heard of the "complementary" nature of the life plans of "our associates" to our own (TJ, 425), each "contributing" to the other and thus forming a "social union" at the lower level. Is society as the highest "social union" that unites them portrayed as the umbrella for such various groupings, or does it constitute a goal beyond their internal exchanges? Clearly, the individual has a social dimension and feels "publicly affirmed" (TJ, 441) when she finds associations which share her interests. Their value is primarily motivational. But is society the overarching structure in which such units co-exist, providing a framework and meeting point, comparable to a shopping mall? Or is it the space for multiple and direct interactions between such groups and individuals, a laboratory and enterprise in which its current and future shape are forged? A closer look into the vision expressed in Rawls's original approach is needed.

On the one hand, it is already clear that such associations provide an affirmation that is welcome and much-needed, but they have a secondary role to the individual's original interest or capacity.[50] The meeting point is in a "plan" or "scheme" where each is free to pursue their native excellence alongside each other: they

> call upon their educated endowments and arouse in each a sense of mastery, and they fit together into one scheme of activity that all can appreciate and enjoy. (TJ, 441)... There must be an agreed scheme of conduct in which the excellences and enjoyments of each are complementary to the good of all. Each can then take pleasure in the actions of the others as they jointly execute a plan acceptable to everyone. (TJ, 526)

These activities do not seem to need the spontaneity and free response from others to create something new. At the opposite end are key statements about "shared final ends" which use the language of Greek ontology to express the necessary and not just incidental orientation of humans towards each other:

> The social nature of mankind is best seen by contrast with the conception of private society. Thus human beings have in fact shared final ends and they value their common institutions and activities as good in themselves. We need one another as partners in ways of life that are engaged in for their own sake, and the successes and enjoyments of others are necessary for and complimentary [sic] to our own good. (TJ, 522–23)

Here, "common institutions" are not just ancillary to prior social unions. At the same time, they are not envisaged as overarching in the sense of proposing a defining content or a guiding ambition. Examples given for this rejected role are national or religious unity and the excellence of a culture. The aim compatible with citizens' plans, themselves enriched by "adjusting" to others, is more modest: to "realize the principles of justice". Yet for this to happen, is it up to citizens to engage with each other, or can they leave it to the "constitutional order" to realize these principles? The

> plan of each person is given a more ample and rich structure than it would otherwise have; it is adjusted to the plans of others by mutually acceptable principles. Everyone's more private life is so to speak a plan within a plan, this superordinate plan being realized in the public institutions of society. But this larger plan does not establish a dominant end, as that

---

50 It is only in rare circumstances that a chef-d'oeuvre is achieved by "a limited association of highly gifted individuals united in the pursuit of common artistic, scientific, or social ends" (TJ, 441).

of religious unity or the greatest excellence of culture, much less national power and prestige, to which the aims of all individuals and associations are subordinate. The regulative public intention is rather that the constitutional order should realize the principles of justice. (TJ, 528)

Even before the second book adjusts the more ambitious statements of the first to the level it sees as compatible with the social and political fact of pluralism, society does not seem to be conceived as a joint project in which the unpredictable input from different quarters of the citizen body and their traditions could play a role. It remains the "cooperative venture for mutual advantage" (TJ, 84) that justice as fairness strives for. This lack of a shared enterprise where concrete identities engage to realize the principles themselves by creating new structures and meanings may be due to one major drawback of Rawls's description: what appears are rational beings with life plans, but no selves whose actions originate from a self-understanding which includes the dimension of other, equally open selves from the start. It will take hermeneutical philosophers like Paul Ricoeur to excavate the depth dimensions of cultural self-understandings, the sources which imprint themselves in the imagination that shapes the concrete use of freedom: the encounters and translations, foundation histories, and processes of formation that lead to self-initiated projects. Rawls's "free and equal rational beings" are too impersonal and exchangeable for such concrete creations of meaning. Without such accounts of collaboration between rational beings in their situated freedom, however, the next decisive step also lacks contour: the road that leads from struggles of distribution to the goal of a "social union" uniting the parties through a constitutional bond.

1.3.2 Withdrawing from metaphysical assumptions: Classical republicanism versus civic humanism

Although *Theory of Justice* had already stressed the importance of avoiding strong metaphysical assumptions about the nature of persons, it saw no problem in borrowing freely from classical approaches in the history of philosophical ethics, such as Aristotle and Kant. *Political Liberalism* assumes a cautionary position towards some aspirations which *Theory of Justice* felt free to voice, and identifies these schools as "comprehensive doctrines" in themselves. Rawls now distances himself from the view that they can be used to inform a non-metaphysical theory of justice. What does this self-correction mean for the concept of society?

The second book completes the turn to a contextual foundation that was already under way in giving a role to "considered convictions" in the "reflective equilibrium" which citizens are to create with the principles established in the contract situation.

> a political conception of justice... presents itself as a reasonable conception for the basic structure alone;... it is not formulated in terms of any comprehensive doctrine but in terms of certain fundamental ideas viewed as latent in the public political culture of a democratic society. (PL, 174–5)

The task of extracting "fundamental ideas... latent in the public political culture" poses interesting hermeneutical questions about the origins and histories of interpretation contained in them which will animate exchanges on their current use. All that can be examined here, however, is the argument why previously admitted conceptions are now rejected or toned down in order to respect the limits drawn by the new "political" foundations. In relation to the conception of society, these limits become clear in the discussion of Charles Taylor's proposal of a "civic humanism". Viewed from Rawls's new attention to pluralism and from his wish not to alienate other approaches in advance, the problem is that this ideal indicates a normative self-understanding; it retains its Aristotelian roots, making it incompatible with the required "political, not metaphysical" view of justice. In the outline of his new approach several of the key statements discussed above are taken back: that common institutions are a good in themselves, that it is a "shared final end" to cooperate in them, that humans are social beings. These views are now attributed to the comprehensive doctrine of Aristotelianism:

> But with civic humanism... there is indeed fundamental opposition. For as a form of Aristotelianism, it is sometimes stated as the view that man is a social, even a political animal whose essential nature is most fully realized in a democratic society in which there is widespread and vigorous participation in political life. Participation is not encouraged as necessary for the protection of the basic liberties of democratic citizenship, and as in itself one form of good among others... Rather, taking part in democratic politics is seen as the privileged locus of the good life. (PL, 206)

Sketching "classical republicanism" which he accepts as compatible with liberalism, he reiterates some of the terms but plays down the previous claim of their central importance:

> justice as fairness does not of course deny that some will find their most important good in political life, and political life is central to their comprehensive good... in the same way that it is generally beneficial that people develop their different and complementary talents and

skills, and engage in mutually advantageous cooperation. This leads to a further idea of the good: namely, that of a well-ordered society as a social union of social unions. (PL, 206)

The question is what remains from the concept of society, which already in *Theory of Justice* was not conceived as a joint project, after taking the Aristotelian elements away? The joint horizon of realizing the institutions of justice now seems to be relegated to the same level as any other capacity or pursuit. A citizen who chooses not to participate in the different circles that make up the public sphere but remains within the horizon of the freedoms of private life is not missing out on anything essential. It is mainly society that is worse off if too many of its members withdraw into their private lives:

> Classical republicanism I take to be the view that if the citizens of a democratic society are to preserve their basic rights and liberties, including the civil liberties which secure the freedoms of private life, they must also have to a sufficient degree the "political virtues"... and be willing to take part in public life... without a widespread participation in democratic politics by a vigorous and informed citizen body, and certainly with a general retreat into private life, even the most well-designed political institutions will fall into the hands of those who seek to dominate and impose their will through the state apparatus either for the sake of power and military glory, or for reasons of class and economic interest, not to mention expansionist religious fervor and nationalist fanaticism. The safety of democratic liberties requires the active participation of citizens who possess the political virtues needed to maintain a constitutional regime. (PL, 205)

This comment on participation in public life principally in terms of a desirable safety precaution for keeping civil liberties out of the grasp of interest groups seems far removed from the earlier explanation of society as a "social union of social unions"; it identified as "the shared final end of all the members of society... the successful carrying out of just institutions" which were "prized as good in themselves." (TJ, 527)

A closer examination of what is rejected in "metaphysical" statements will be postponed until it can be compared to Habermas's "postmetaphysical" understanding of philosophy and his debate with a contemporary interpreter of German Idealism, Dieter Henrich, in Part Two. Yet, one problem can be identified at this stage: Metaphysical accounts are rejected because they violate the need to find a neutral basis that can be accepted by different positions on a theory of democracy. Yet, how neutral is Rawls's proposal itself? The reconstruction of his argumentation so far has shown that there are elements in his theory that, far from avoiding metaphysical assumptions, bring in borrowings from undiagnosed worldviews. Especially the rational choice conception of the person as a choosing economic agent, but also his reductive interpretations of Kant, can count as a liberal metaphysical premise, rather than as a neutral, or, in Onora

O'Neill's use of the term, truly "abstract" basis. In theological ethics, the danger of assuming one particular interpretation as a general basis is well-known from the moral theological debates on classical and revisionist understandings of Natural Law.[51] Will the "political conception of justice" and the political virtues expected from citizens qualify as such a general, unbiased framework? Or will they reveal themselves as quite particular expressions of a liberalism that is unaware of its tacit premises? Before seeking an answer in section 4 on how "public reason" is being conceived, I will return to a test case that exemplifies the task of institutions to safeguard justice; it leads into the practical politics of a society faced by new scientific and technological options. One of the two factors *Theory of Justice* identified as curtailing autonomy was natural chance. The complex of assumptions inherent in singling out a disparity in natural assets as a cause for prevenient action will be analysed as an indicative case of conflicting principles, before examining plurality as a final issue in his theory of society.

1.3.3 Lack of "natural assets" as grounds for intervention?

In his treatment of the benefits of social unions Rawls gave a convincing critique of perfectionism. Members are to decide themselves what levels they strive to attain in their capacities. However, since just institutions are also called to compensate for natural contingencies, the question of a standard for such capacities arose. Here, the power given to the two principles may become a problem: They "are to regulate all further agreements; they specify the kinds of social cooperation that can be entered into and the forms of government that can be established." (TJ, 11) If the "kinds of social cooperation" and "forms of government" that can be ruled out as not respecting either fundamental liberties or the distribution of primary social goods refer, for example, to apartheid or caste systems, there is no reason to disagree. Rawls compares how a caste system "tends to divide society into separate biological populations, while an open society encourages the widest genetic diversity. In addition, it is possible to adopt eugenic policies, more or less explicit" (TJ, 107). Despite the ominous last sentence, this may still be a position that affirms and protects both liberty and diversity.[52] But subsequently,

---

51 Cf. R. Gula, "Natural Law today", in Ch. Curran/R. McCormick (eds.), *Natural Law and Theology (Readings in Moral Theology No. 7)* (Mahwah: Paulist Press, 1991), 369–91. D. Mieth, "Autonomy of ethics – neutrality of the Gospel?" in *Concilium* 18 (Edinburgh: T & T Clark, 1982), 32–39.

52 Not wanting to debate the issue of eugenics in detail, he prefaces the evaluation to be taken behind the veil of ignorance by a remark which makes any increase in ability a social goal

the maximization element of the second principle takes over and leads to contestable conclusions. From the observation that it is one of the "fixed points of our considered judgments that no one deserves his place in the distribution of native endowments" (TJ, 104), he draws the consequence that the founding members in the original position would want "the best genetic endowment" for their children. And from this it follows that one generation owes it to the next to intervene to stop the "diffusion" of genetic disorders:

> But it is also in the interest of each to have greater natural assets. This enables him to pursue a preferred plan of life. In the original position, then, the parties want to insure for their descendants the best genetic endowment (assuming their own to be fixed). The pursuit of reasonable policies in this regard is something that earlier generations owe to later ones... Thus over time a society is to take steps at least to preserve the general level of natural abilities and to prevent the diffusion of serious defects... I mention this speculative and difficult matter to indicate once again the manner in which the difference principle is likely to transform problems of social justice. (TJ 107–08)

In these short notes on eugenics the extent of the powers opened up by the compensation principle becomes evident. Persons' physical specificity, their features as embodied selves, seem to be considered only in terms of market value, as an "asset" for realizing life plans. A new perspective is admitted that seems to have more in common with Utilitarianism than with protecting the "inviolability" of the individual, a central criterion of the counter-proposal which *Theory of Justice* wanted to develop. Now "society" is to "take steps... to prevent the diffusion of serious defects". Questions such as, which concept of self, which definition of illness, which weighting of genetic versus environmental and cultural components are presupposed, and which basic human rights are granted against societal interests, are all left open. Regarding enhancement, the assumption that parents would wish their children to have either anonymous best genes, or those inherited from them, but "only the best" of them (as the Science Fiction film Gattaca demonstrates) strikes one as ignoring basic rights and historical achievements in recognizing children's equal status. Appreciation of diversity, respect for fragility and for children's birthright to be accepted as themselves lose out against an imperative based on undisclosed criteria, to maximize conditions for life plans.[53] The debate on genetic selection and enhancement will be revis-

---

desirable by all: It "is not in general to the advantage of the less fortunate to propose policies which reduce the talents of others. Instead, by accepting the difference principle, they view the greater abilities as a social asset to be used for the common advantage." (TJ, 107)

53 The presuppositions implied in the idea of matching and optimizing genes and lifeplans are questioned by the philosopher Ludwig Siep in "Genomanalyse, menschliches Selbstverständnis

ited in Part Two when Habermas elucidates with Kant and Kierkegaard the concepts of moral authorship and of unique selfhood; he defends symmetric rather than paternalistic relations as a presupposition of moral and political autonomy. The counter-position in favour of allowing parents to decide to enhance their children's genes, laid out by Alan Buchanan, Daniel Brock, Norman Daniels and Dan Wikler, follows in the steps of Rawls's negative view of natural contingency as well as of the drive to maximize assets. Unsurprisingly, it commends the progression, as the title expresses, from "chance" to "choice",[54] specifically, parents' choice, rather than as a power given to the state, to move the fight against inequality forward to the genetic basis.

The final area in which I shall test the anthropological and societal presuppositions of Rawls's proposal is the realm of cultural diversity. It is true that the paradigm for social thought in the 1970s was the concept of society, and that the "cultural turn" took place only subsequently. Aware of the different contexts of both books, I shall look for possible sources of plurality in each of them.

1.3.4 Sources and significance of plurality in *Theory of Justice* and in *Political Liberalism*

The political and cultural insight which sparked the revision of key elements of *Theory of Justice* was the "fact of pluralism" (PL, 4). Before examining its premises in *Political Liberalism* (2), I shall treat the ways in which diversity, plurality or difference surface in the combination of contract and reflective equilibrium of principles and considered convictions in the first book (1).

1.3.4.1 Plurality in contract, associations, and primary goods

There are three occasions where difference as a constitutive factor of society is acknowledged as relevant for justice: it is the very reason for the contract; it explains the number of associations or social unions; and it affects the primary goods. How is the plural constitution of each of these occasions developed in the argumentation of *Theory of Justice*? In the first instance, "*contract*" stands both for "plurality" and for a "public" mode of agreement:

---

und Ethik", in L. Honnefelder (ed.), *Was wissen wir, wenn wir das menschliche Genom kennen?* (Köln: Dumont, 2001), 196–205. I have quoted some of his points in translation in "Genetic perfection, or fulfillment of creation in Christ?", in C. Deane-Drummond/P. M. Scott (eds.), *Future Perfect? God, Medicine and Human Identity* (London: T & T Clark, 2006), 155–167.
54 A. Buchanan/D. Brock/N. Daniels/D. Wikler, *From Chance to Choice* (Cambridge: CUP, 2001).

Principles of justice deal with conflicting claims upon the advantages won by social cooperation; they apply to the relations among several persons or groups. The word "contract"
suggests this plurality as well as the condition that the appropriate division of advantages
must be in accordance with principles acceptable to all parties. The condition of publicity
for principles of justice is also connoted by the contract phraseology. (TJ, 16)

The decisive differences between the founding partners, however, as already indicated in O'Neill's critique, are not played out since they are hidden by the veil.
In the second case, *capacities* and the *social unions* that confirm an individual's
sense of worth are diverse;[55] but since the different associations do not seem to
engage with each other, the potential for encounters, conflicts and syntheses is
lost. The descriptions are evocative: talents are diverse; the more practice they
take, the more they allow for "feats of ingenuity and invention. They also
evoke the pleasures of anticipation and surprise..., individual style and personal
expression" (TJ, 427). The most eloquent portrayals of diversity concern the "internal life of associations" which form an intermediate level between the individual and the system of institutions:

It follows that the collective activity of justice is the preeminent form of human flourishing... it is by maintaining these public arrangements that persons best express their nature
and achieve the widest regulative excellences of which each is capable. At the same time
just institutions allow for and encourage the diverse internal life of associations in which
individuals realize their more particular aims. Thus the public realization of justice is a
value of community... Only in a social union is the individual complete (TJ, 529. 524).

In these descriptions, individuality and sociability seem to have found the most
perfect mediation. Yet, neither as an opportunity nor as a challenge does plurality come into view. The possibility of surprise responses from free counterparts,
unexpected insights through shared interpretations or through unpredictable expressions of the freedom of others that cannot be calculated in advance do not
appear; the circles seem to be complete in themselves and are not depicted as
interacting with each other. Multiple memberships and cross-fertilisation are
not evident.

The third occasion for plurality are the *primary goods*. Introduced with a
view to the competition they unleash to secure sufficient, even maximal
amounts, the question is whether they display any signs of profoundly different
options. These could lead to radically different expectations, life forms and prac-

---

55 "Thus what is necessary is that there should be for each person at least one community of
shared interests to which he belongs and where he finds his endeavors confirmed by his associates." (TJ, 442)

tical solutions which a society might find hard to contain. In positions as different as those of Michael Walzer, Paul Ricoeur and Rainer Forst, they open up the insight into the historical constitution and changing orders of evaluating the material presuppositions of life plans. *A Theory of Justice*, however, treats them as if they were all on the same level, and true for every society, including the desire to increase them. What is ascribed to the social unions, an internally agreed standard of excellence, could be applied with much more reason to the spheres which each "good" denotes. By assuming a singular concept of distribution, the inherent diversity of the primary goods is lost from sight. An adequate theory of justice would have to take cognizance of the complexity of the different "spheres" with the difficult task of negotiating between them, each with their own internal logic. This includes the need to protect them from the encroachment of alien standards, as when education and family life find themselves colonized by the criteria of economics.

A further missed opportunity for discovering differences between cultures can be found in the serial ordering of the two justice principles. The priority of liberty over justice mirrors one typical development in Western modernity; it takes different concrete shapes in European and North American political cultures; it does not, as Höffe points out, constitute a normative standard in other cultures or eras.[56]

1.3.4.2 Setting the stage for the task of public reason: Philosophies as "comprehensive doctrines" in *Political Liberalism*

The discovery of pluralism is the one single phenomenon that makes it necessary for Rawls to work out a new proposal for the solution of conflicts in a well-ordered society. He gives this normative level an already established name: "public reason". Its mediating function will be analysed in the next section. What may constitute a continuity from the first to the second book is a feature "social unions" and "comprehensive doctrines" share: the assumption that they are defined solely by the interest around which they assemble. They keep to themselves, do not interact with the next group and are linked only through the overarching canopy of "society" as the highest social union which comprises all of them, but with no project transcending and uniting them.

What is new, by contrast, is the status ascribed to the discipline of philosophy. *Political Liberalism* presents philosophical theories not merely as distinct approaches but as completely different "comprehensive doctrines". They do

---

56 Höffe, "Einführung", in Höffe (ed.), *John Rawls*, 14.

not appear able to use their analytic and synthetic powers to think through and engage with other positions; nor does it seem possible to combine them, as Rawls did in his own initial proposal of a theory of justice based on contract, rational choice, Kantian and Aristotelian elements. They now have to be reconciled, in a realm removed from their proper and original activity, by the peace-making powers of "public reason". Not only religions are identified as competing systems of adherence, they are joined by philosophical traditions as well which are treated as entities similar to worldviews. I shall sketch the three reasons why their new understanding as "comprehensive doctrines" appears problematic to me: the dialectical history of philosophical thinking; their own self-understanding as open investigations directed towards a truth that is to be justified in argumentations; and the danger of self-immunization for the level that will take over from their attempts to seek clarification and reach agreement, namely public reason.

First, re-conceiving philosophical approaches as closed-off systems seems to undervalue that they are part of a dialectics of response. They contribute to the problems posed in the preceding history of thinking by offering correctives, new distinctions and directions, as well as rediscoveries of previous solutions.

Secondly, leaving their truth claims in abeyance is at odds with the self-understanding at least of universalist philosophies that there is a general consciousness of truth. The task of establishing knowledge that can be critically justified as true implies the distinction that a claim is either universally true, or not at all, in which case it has to be critically unmasked as mere opinion, error or ideology. Rawls treats such argumentations as local ones, interior to certain approaches, and seeks the basis for resolving differences elsewhere.

Thirdly, portraying them as "comprehensive" in themselves also means that engagement with their distinctive proposals can be avoided; each is seen to have its own relative claim which is left to its own school to discuss, but it does not constitute a competing foundation that has to be argued with. The new, single foundation for dealing with the open questions arising in everyday social life, politics and human history is established elsewhere, in the precincts of a "public reason" that can no longer be challenged by them. On its territory, each coherent system of thinking has to bracket its ideas. It seems that they cannot be treated as if they had anything to offer to the public realm. Yet once Kant, Mill, and all the other "reasonable" alternative approaches are no longer engaging each other in publicly relevant argument, the danger is that debate will only circle around an already agreed common ground that has been immunized against critiques from these traditions of thinking. Whatever the more specific definition of "public reason" will be, it is clear that it will carry a unique weight of expectation for problem-solving competence, since other avenues of insight and exchange have been blocked off for fear of privileging one above another.

In summary, from the anthropology that informs Rawls's concepts of moral personhood and of a well-ordered society two premises emerge that set parameters for his theory of democracy: (1) Persons come into view as authors of individual life plans and as finding completion with like-minded peers; (2) They interact with their peers seeking a common basis of just distribution as well as confirmation of themselves in their projects. From the perspective of other approaches in social ethics, especially those with an interest in the formation of ethical and moral identity, important dimensions are lacking: there is no emphasis on biographies in the making, inspired by values to be realized in one's self-conception, open towards initiatives and inviting others, and no reflection on discontinuity and conflict in the self; sources of deficiency are mainly external ones which impact on a person's self-confidence. It is to be expected that rationality in its public function will again presuppose players who enter the scene of contemporary society with worked-out plans. So far, there is also no indication of an analysis that reckons with the possibility of social pathologies afflicting an entire culture, or of resources of social cohesion being progressively eroded. With the main concern turning from structures of justice to those of stability as a precondition of maintaining both justice and equality, the brief for public reason has been set as conciliatory. How it is to carry out its role of achieving a balance between diverse worldviews, will be explored in the following section.

1.4 Democratic life and public reason

The ideal of society outlined in *Theory of Justice*, a "social union of social unions" governed by principles of justice, clashes with the experience of ongoing dissent. *Political Liberalism* explains its lasting character from the "burdens of judgement" which lead to different conclusions among reasonable citizens. Thus, against the hope that the principles found behind the "veil of ignorance" and the "considered convictions" of citizens would resonate and mutually confirm each other,[57] the scenario encountered is one of centrifugal forces. The focus has shifted: from the individual agents working out a reflective equilibrium be-

---

57 In "The Idea of Public Reason Revisited", published first in 1997, repr. in J. Rawls, *The Law of Peoples* (Cambridge/Mass.: Harvard University Press, 1999), 129–180 (= LP), he summarizes: "A *Theory of Justice* hopes to present the structural features of such a theory so as to make it the best approximation to our considered judgments of justice and hence to give the most appropriate moral basis for a democratic society." (LP, 179)

tween general principles and their personal convictions, to communities in their relation to society and to political decision-making. A new term has entered the analysis: "comprehensive doctrines", judged to be mutually irreconcilable. No self-limitation was asked of citizens before, since the theory of justice outlined was put forward as one to which everyone could agree, or had agreed, and personal convictions were deemed open to consideration and revision; these now seem to have hardened into complete and exclusive worldviews for which limits have to be set. From this diagnosis of pluralism, the way forward to curb the potential for conflict that threatens stability is to introduce a level to which all can consent, a neutral ground on which mediation is possible. This function is assigned to "public reason" which submits the variety of worldviews in the background culture to a framework and to criteria which distil reasonable "political conceptions" of justice out of them. By disconnecting "reason" from "truth" and redefining the epistemic status of public reason as "reasonable", it becomes possible to find an "overlapping consensus" on specific political issues between different worldviews. Accepted as internal bases for consent but not as rival truth claims in civic debate, their convictions can no longer be divisive. By abstaining from truth claims itself, "public reason" does not appear as a competitive player in the arena of convictions and can function as a protective roof over all communities of conviction (1). While demanding support from the virtues and the background culture of citizens, the operation of "public reason" itself does not take place in the public realm of civil society, but beyond the institutional threshold in the houses of parliament and of the courts. It is located closer to the official representation of citizens than to their own multiple forms of democratic agency. What this means for the input of citizens from their background cultures, for institutions in civil society which are deemed to engage in "non-public reason", and for the democratic project itself, will be evaluated subsequently (2).

Having mapped out the steps proposed in *Political Liberalism* to ensure the stability of a democracy committed to respecting liberty and equality, I shall profile the route it suggests against one of the roads not taken. The penultimate section of Part One will treat the alternative Kant offers for relating practical reason and public reason in their distinctive functions of judging the morality of actions and of deliberating on and legitimizing political decisions. Built on the foundational principle of human dignity, it also allows a different, namely a cosmopolitan understanding of the scope of justice and of human rights to be developed (1.5).

The final section of the first part will then deal with the question of how attractive Rawls's definition of "public reason" is for religions as comprehensive doctrines. As a correction to the impression that mainly religious positions were asked to agree to a self-limitation of the reasons they present in their political advocacy, the concept of public reason was extended: "The Idea of Public Reason Revisited" proposes a "wider view" in 1997 which admits a "proviso" for religious comprehensive doctrines. They will now be permitted to bring their categories and intuitions into political debate as long as these can be backed up by equivalent "properly public" concepts at some future point. Before discussing the concession of the "proviso" and the opposite assessments of two Continental Christian ethicists on the space it gives to religions, I will examine Rawls's position with regard to the "highest good", a concept which leads to the intersection of ethics with philosophy of religion in Kant. The issue of such limit questions between practical reason and religion will open the concluding assessment of public reason in relation to religion as the final point of Part One (1.6).

1.4.1 The search for a neutral ground between irreconcilable worldviews

Rawls's new retrospective insight from the experience of ongoing disagreement is that his *Theory of Justice* did not succeed in offering a platform true for all possible approaches; it had to be reclassified as a comprehensive doctrine itself, in this case, one specific proposal among others within Western liberalism.[58] In view of the two modes of justification, constructivist and contextual, and of some tacit assumptions uncovered so far, his readiness to relativize the status of the theory as only applying to the realm of Western culture seems appropriate. The conclusion he draws is that the basis of agreement has to be defined with less specific presuppositions. Named "public reason", it is presented as a process, a manner of arguing matched to "free and equal" citizens, on a subject, "the public good", circumscribed by shared "political values". I shall first present his threefold definition of reason in its "public" capacity, and then analyse the two counterparts, the required "political" as opposed to a "comprehensive" interpretation through which citizens with other worldviews may feel misrepresented, offended, or excluded. The failure to find some shared level would affect the legitimacy of the use of power in a democracy (1). However, because of the abstention demanded from citizens who are asked not to base their contributions

---

58 "(J)ustice as fairness is presented there as a comprehensive liberal doctrine (although the term 'comprehensive doctrine' is not used in the book) in which all the members of its well-ordered society affirm that same doctrine. This kind of well-ordered society contradicts the fact of reasonable pluralism and hence *Political Liberalism* regards that society as impossible." (LP, 179)

and electoral choices on their convictions of "the whole truth as they see it" (PL, 216), public reason faces a "paradox" (PL, 216–19) (2). The solution to this is the effort to reach an "overlapping consensus", which needs to be more than a "*modus vivendi*" (PL, 145–149). Public reason has to be able both to draw on reliable sources of motivation and to enjoy a validity independent of its vital roots in worldviews, by being "free-standing" (PL, 9–11) (3).

1.4.1.1 Public reason converting comprehensive into political conceptions of justice

The idea of public reason comprises three aspects. In Rawls's definition,

> reason is public in three ways: as the reason of free and equal citizens, it is the reason of the public; its subject is the public good concerning questions of fundamental political justice, which questions are of two kinds, constitutional essentials and matters of basic justice; and its nature and content are public, being expressed in public reasoning by a family of reasonable conceptions of political justice reasonably thought to satisfy the criterion of reciprocity. (LP, 133)[59]

The first element of the definition refers to the bearers of this reason, who are identified formally as "the public" in their quality as "free and equal" citizens; the second specifies its subject matter, the public good, as comprising both "constitutional essentials" and issues of "basic justice". The third element links public "nature and content" in that the first is elaborated by an array of approaches to justice which in their commitment to democracy and reasonableness are called a "family"; their willingness to anticipate the chance of reasonable acceptance or toleration of their positions by others ensures that the content meets the criterion of "reciprocity".

What are the implications of this description of the role of public reason? It assumes elements of different provenance, in need of directed mediation, guided by a specific understanding of legitimacy. The outcome is the emergence of "reasonable conceptions of political justice". How are the counterparts characterized? The core designation of the "other" of public reason is that it is "comprehensive". Here, Rawls takes care also to exclude the "secular" as a possible basis, since it constitutes a worldview in itself (LP, 143. 148); it equally has to anticipate what is acceptable to others. He illustrates the limits of what is permitted

---

59 In PL, 213, the "nature and content" was formulated as "public, being given by the ideals and principles expressed by society's conception of political justice, and conducted open to view on that basis."

to be used as an argument in public deliberation with the example of "autonomy" as a "comprehensive" and as a "political" concept. At the level of comprehensive doctrines – either Mill's individualist Utilitarian or Kant's deontological approach to ethics – it would be divisive; at the "political" level, autonomy is allowed as a shared value.

> It may take two forms: one is political autonomy, the legal independence and assured integrity of citizens and their sharing equally with others in the exercise of political power; the other is purely moral and characterizes a certain way of life and reflection, as in Mill's ideal of individuality... it fails to satisfy, given reasonable pluralism, the constraint of reciprocity, as many citizens, for example, those holding certain religious doctrines, may reject it. Thus moral autonomy is not a political value, whereas political autonomy is. (LP, 146)

Other examples to explore what is being opposed under the labels "metaphysical" or "comprehensive" versus "political" include the model of the Good Samaritan, and concepts of marriage. In each case, the fear is that a comprehensive and thus, it is held, divisive understanding will be imposed on fellow-citizens from other persuasions. This lack of restraint would counteract their equality and rob democratic practice of its legitimacy. Against this danger, the independent standing and coherent nature of the various reasonable political conceptions that result from the work of public reason are emphasized.

One is faced, therefore, with a distinction between the level of worldviews, called comprehensive doctrines, each rivalling the next, and each with their complete religious or metaphysical assumptions, on the one side, and that of public reason and "political conceptions" on the other. While they differ in that one side is marked by particularity, the other by general acceptability, the second also depends on the first in that each comprehensive movement supplies grounding reasons: "All those who affirm the political conception start from within their own comprehensive view and draw on the religious, philosophical, and moral grounds it provides." (PL, 147) Examples given of acceptable political conceptions that have purged themselves of their metaphysical or comprehensive elements are Habermas's discourse theoretical reconstruction of legitimacy, and the values which Catholic Social Teaching can contribute independently of its doctrinal connections: orientation towards the common good, and the virtue of solidarity (LP, 142). Yet despite these roots, the political conceptions derived from these foundations end up with "replacing" their truth claims: In

> public reason ideas of truth or right based on comprehensive doctrines are replaced by an idea of the politically reasonable addressed to citizens as citizens. This step is necessary to establish a basis of political reasoning that all can share as free and equal citizens. (LP, 171)

The problem this poses for the initial willingness especially of religiously bound fellow-citizens to submit to the requirements of public reason is explored and shown as a paradox that can be resolved.

1.4.1.2 The paradox: Civility as abstention

Rawls is aware that, depending on their comprehensive doctrines, citizens may see the condition for passing into the sphere of "reasonable" political conceptions, namely suspending their truth claims in political argumentation and practice, as an imposition. He admits

> a basic difficulty with the idea of public reason, one that makes it seem paradoxical...: why should citizens in discussing and voting on the most fundamental political questions honor the limits of public reason? How can it be either reasonable or rational, when basic matters are at stake, for citizens to appeal only to a public conception of justice and not to the whole truth as they see it? (PL, 216)

In his answer, he first refers to the "principle of liberal legitimacy", then to the possibility of an overlapping consensus between different worldviews on the basis of public reason. Only worldviews that qualify as reasonable by understanding the need for a "political conception" form part of this effort of finding a level of mutual agreement. The principle of democratic legitimacy is interpreted with reference, first, to one's fellow-citizens in a bounded society, and secondly, to democratic power as that of "free and equal citizens as a collective body" (PL, 216). Voting means "exercising their coercive political power over one another" (PL, 217); in order to be legitimate, it has to be justified to fellow-citizens. Being a citizen is given normative standing; from it, a moral duty is derived: the

> ideal of citizenship imposes a moral, not a legal, duty – the duty of civility – to be able to explain to one another on those fundamental questions how the principles and policies they advocate and vote for can be supported by the political values of public reason. This duty also involves a willingness to listen to others and a fairmindedness in deciding when accommodations to their views should reasonably be made. (PL, 217)

Thus, democratic legitimacy is spelt out as the need for citizens to be directly answerable to one another and to restrict themselves to political values in their political opinion and will formation and in their voting. Here the moral duty of civility exerts pressure to abstain from one's own complete worldview, and to be open to offer concessions.

The less of a gap there is, however, between the different communities' convictions and the position developed by public reason, the more the paradox dissolves. Rawls assumes that, inspired both by the ideal of citizenship and supported by their background tradition, they will promote the ideal of anticipating each others' acceptance as a value of their own:

> Thus, when the political conception is supported by an overlapping consensus of reasonable comprehensive doctrines, the paradox of public reason disappears. The union of the duty of civility with the great values of the political yields the ideal of citizens governing themselves in ways that each thinks the others might be reasonably expected to accept; and this ideal in turn is supported by the comprehensive doctrines reasonable persons affirm. Citizens affirm the ideal of public reason, not as a result of a political compromise, as in a *modus vivendi*, but from within their own reasonable doctrines. (PL, 218)

Since the political conceptions derive from these doctrines, there is no clash whatsoever, as Rawls asserts in "The Idea of Public Reason Revisited" in even stronger terms: "a true judgment in a reasonable comprehensive doctrine never conflicts with a reasonable judgment in its related political conception." (LP, 173)

By contrast, unreasonable doctrines are seen as "a threat to democratic institutions, since it is impossible for them to abide by a constitutional regime except as a *modus vivendi*." (LP, 178–79) Being reasonable in the sense of having "adapted to the conception of justice itself" (PL, 219) is the entry ticket to democratic life.

Positive points in this outline of the elements of public reason are that, first, the cost for religious and other traditions to abide by these expectations is admitted. Secondly, mutual interaction and knowledge of other traditions is encouraged. Thirdly, it is envisaged that one learns and adjusts one's own position in taking the perspective of others on board, at least as far as their probability to fit into the democratic mould is concerned. For each of them, fourthly, an internal motivation to follow the duty of civility is assumed. Finally, public reason would be unable to function without the virtues held and practiced by citizens.

On the other hand, as a programme of responding to pluralism it throws up several questions: First, it is already remarkable that comprehensive doctrines in their diversity are now being called a "family", the members of which are related to each other by being reasonable; even more astonishing and in need of explanation is the expectation that they might overlap in crucial points.

Secondly, the two poles opposed to each other need to be further examined. The adversarial status of the "whole truth" claims of the traditions against each other and to the level of public reason could be one more (negative) idealization, and the counterpart to the insistence of particular communities on their truths is much less clear. What is the content of the general, accessible and acceptable level that each of them has to conform to? In what does the unity between democratic citizens consist? The question of what it is that they have to sacrifice some of their convictions to will be of greater relevance to those comprehensive doctrines which are steeper than others, and harder to reconcile with the level of convergence reachable by less demanding background views. What if a world-view is judged unreasonable because it expects too much from a constitutional regime, and sees the need to adapt to what the least ambitious doctrine pre-scribes as confirming a status quo that cannot be justified and needs to be sur-passed? Could there also be a threat to democratic institutions from settling pre-maturely on targets that are undemanding? While the readiness to anticipate what other doctrines may find acceptable is an expression of fairness, the danger is that it becomes the benchmark itself, with no other criterion that the "ideal of public reason" has to meet than this contingent overlap.

Thirdly, also in light of the possible divergences described above in the con-tent and scope of policy proposals arising from the political conceptions of the different traditions of interpretation, the sources of motivation become an urgent question.

1.4.1.3 The dual motivation of the overlapping consensus: comprehensive and civic

The quotes above have made it clear that on the one hand, the close connection between comprehensive doctrines and their political conceptions is emphasized to the point that any disagreement between them is deemed impossible. On the other hand, the "freestanding" character of the political conceptions is para-mount for there to be any agreement located at a sufficient distance from the communities themselves, which continue to engage in rivalling truth claims. For Rawls, a steady, self-supporting desire to fulfill the ideal of democratic citi-zenship marks the difference from a pragmatic and changeable *modus vivendi.* While being assured that they are supporting their own versions of politically ad-justed conceptions, the different worldviews are equally expected to envisage a motivation independent of the roots they provide to support the mediating mis-sion of public reason. However, beyond its function for the stability of a demo-cratic society, the question of motivation is a sensitive one. It relates to self-iden-tity and thus to a limit of state power that especially the liberal tradition has defended as the right to privacy; motivation is a personal matter that cannot be made mandatory and that belongs to the right of persons over any system, be it a person's culture of origin, or the state.[60] It is thus a neuralgic point

---

60 Habermas points to this limit when he distinguishes between "motives" and "actual con-

and touchstone of whether persons are respected in their own self-understanding. I shall proceed by analyzing statements concerning the two different sources of motivation for political conceptions, their coherent character, and their relative value in the steps of justification; this is to clarify what scope the platform offered for civic agreement provides for the contents that comprehensive doctrines could offer. My conclusion regarding the capacities attributed to each side, comprehensive and political, will be that a move to a different level of analysis is required, distinct from reflecting on religions as social facts and on citizens' motivations as a psychological matter: what is needed is the step from an empirical to a systematic analysis of reason in its practical dimension, to be conducted in moral theory and philosophy of religion, with the aim of investigating the conditions of the possibility of such an overlap.

The capacity for generating motivation that communities of conviction display in their plurality is strongly acknowledged in the 1997 move to "revisit" the idea of public reason. The convertibility of this energy into support for democracy is a reason for granting them the "proviso" of being allowed to introduce comprehensive motifs into conversation as long as "properly public" reasons are added at a later stage: "When these doctrines accept the proviso and only then come into political debate, the commitment to constitutional democracy is publicly manifested." (LP, 153–54) The vitality they supply is valued:

> Citizens' mutual knowledge of one another's religious and non-religious doctrines expressed in the wide view of public political culture recognises that the roots of democratic citizens' allegiance to their political conception lie in their respective comprehensive doctrines, both religious and non-religious. In this way citizens' allegiance to the democratic ideal of public reason is strengthened for the right reasons. We may think of the reasonable comprehensive doctrines that support society's reasonable political conceptions as those conceptions' vital social basis, giving them enduring strength and vigor (LP, 153) ... a conception of public reason must recognize the significance of these social roots of constitutional democracy and note how they strengthen its vital institutions (LP, 154, n. 52).

On the other hand, Rawls stresses the complete and consistent character of political conceptions. They provide a framework and absorb the impulses from their related worldviews into a systematic and self-contained proposal that dis-

---

tributions" in Habermas, "'The political'. The rational meaning of a questionable inheritance of political theology", in J. Butler/J. Habermas/Ch. Taylor/C. West, *The Power of Religion in the Public Sphere* (New York: Columbia University Press, 2011), 15–33, 32–33, n. 22: "Apart from the fact that motives for actual voting behavior are not, in any case, subject to any form of regulation, only public utterances, hence actual contributions to the formation of opinion and consensus building, and not mind-sets, are relevant for the legitimizing power of democratic discourses."

connects itself from its comprehensive origin. While they offer their specific interpretations of substantive principles,[61] they are equally indebted to the "public political culture" from which they draw and which makes them "freestanding" (PL, 9–10). Part of their features is that they "can be presented independently from comprehensive doctrines" and "can be worked out from fundamental ideas seen as implicit in the public political culture,... such as the conceptions of citizens as free and equal persons, and of society as a fair system of cooperation". (LP, 143)

Their independence from their origins in specific worldviews is enhanced by a further requirement which is to ensure that political values "are not puppets manipulated from behind the scenes by comprehensive doctrines" (LP, 145):

> What we cannot do in public reason is to proceed directly from our comprehensive doctrines to one or several political principles and values, and the particular institutions they support. Instead, we are required first to work to the basic ideas of a complete political conception and from there to elaborate its principles and ideals, and to use the arguments they provide. Otherwise public reason allows arguments that are too immediate and fragmentary. (LP, 145–46)

What this insistence on the systematic and coherent nature of the political conceptions seems to exclude is the possibility of 1:1 conversions, for example, of key terms of monotheism, such as *imago Dei*, creation, or salvation, into concepts that can be used in political life. Instead, it is marked out as a "feature of public reasoning... that it proceeds entirely within a political conception of justice" (LP, 144). Also the revisited version of the idea of public reason, while trying to minimize the difference, anchors the back and forth movement between comprehensive origins and a general validity generated from its attunement to the existing public political culture in the latter. Any closer enquiry ends with an inability to decide which element is more basic:

> different political conceptions of justice will represent different interpretations of the constitutional essentials and matters of basic justice. There are also different interpretations of the same conception, since its conception and values may be taken in different ways. There is not, then, a sharp line between where a political conception ends and its interpretation begins (LP, 145, n. 35).

---

61 "Some may think the fact of reasonable pluralism means that the only forms of fair adjudication between comprehensive doctrines must only be procedural and not substantive... however, I assume the several forms of liberalism are each substantive conceptions." (LP, 141, n. 26)

The question remains unresolved whether political values dominate the themes provided by the comprehensive worldviews. In his reply to Jürgen Habermas on the status and method of his justification, Rawls distinguishes different types of justification and states his hope that they will agree: the "pro-tanto" level using only political values, the "complete" one, enacted by members of civil society, embedding it in their worldviews, and the ultimate embedding that is achieved with "public justification" in political society. Once more it is left open "how the claims of political justice are to be ordered, or weighted, against non-political values. The political conception gives no guidance in such questions, since it does not say how nonpolitical values are to be counted".[62]

The priority which the justification in political terms is given by the "pro-tanto" and the "public" steps receives a final support in the finding that it can rely on a motivation from its own roots: there is a "knowledge and desire on the part of the citizens… to follow public reason and to realize its ideal in their political conduct." (LP, 139) One of the "political and social roots of democracy" that is "vital to its enduring strength and vigor" expresses itself in the "disposition… to repudiate government officials and candidates for public office who violate public reason" (LP, 135 – 36).[63] The free-standing nature even of the motivation to argue in the limits of political conceptions is thus being emphasized; the public political culture on which it is based ultimately becomes the key provider of content and support.

Thus, two distinct motivations are assumed that may be difficult to disentangle in concrete political argumentations but that are rooted in a dual allegiance, one comprehensive, the other civic. The hope that they will mutually reinforce each other shows that Rawls accepts each in their ability to supply such support despite different origins. On the civic side, this appreciation of a genuine ethos of citizenship marks a major change from the "rational choice" motivation put forward in *Theory of Justice*. On the comprehensive doctrine side, he could equally have harboured the suspicion that faith communities have only adjusted externally to the societal framework in which they have to exist and still resent the loss of previous privileges to the state in its modern neutrality. His positive appreciation of internal sources in these traditions themselves to welcome the freedom of a personal choice of worldview, rather than automatic or enforced allegiances, has to be noted.

---

62 Rawls, "Reply to Habermas", in Rasmussen/Swindal (eds.), *Jürgen Habermas*, vols. I – IV (Sage Masters of Modern Thought) (London: Sage, 2002), vol. II, 99 – 139, 104.
63 Putting this requirement to holders and candidates for office reflects the move that takes place between *Political Liberalism* and "The Idea of Public Reason Revisited" from citizens as engaged in public reason, to their official representatives, which will be further discussed below.

The only element in the comprehensive doctrines that seems to be of interest, however, is their motivational potential for civic virtues, not the distinct content they could offer for interpreting political conceptions and their values. This lack of interest contrasts with Jürgen Habermas's high regard for the "unspent semantic potential" of religious traditions for discussion in the public sphere. With Rawls it seems that they are enlisted for the project of keeping democracy stable only because of their vitality. Yet it is possible that the remarkable energy democracy may gain from comprehensive truth communities goes beyond the scope of a bounded society to which Rawls restricts his analysis. The restrictions imposed by the limits of the overlapping consensus emerge clearly in his rejection of any hope beyond values that ensure internal political stability, a hope that would be typical especially of religious worldviews. His examples are "a more perfect union, justice, domestic tranquillity, common defense, general welfare, blessings of liberty for ourselves and for our posterity." (LP, 144) These goals do not go beyond the given society itself; efforts towards international peace, reconciliation after enmity, or environmental conservation are not mentioned. Greater hopes have to be "abandoned" as candidates for agreement across society. To suggest them is to cross the line to making a particular vision a coercive one. In the following response it becomes clear that for Rawls, the alternative to an overlapping consensus is the presumed unity advocated by communitarian proposals. Discussing a counterposition that calls for a more ambitious goal than his idea of political unity based on an overlapping consensus allows for, he states: to the objection that

> it abandons the hope of political community and settles instead for a public understanding that is at bottom a mere *modus vivendi*... we say that the hope of political community must indeed be abandoned, if by such a community we mean a political society united in affirming the same comprehensive doctrine. This possibility is excluded by the fact of reasonable pluralism together with the rejection of the oppressive use of state power to overcome it. (PL, 146)

In this analysis, the choice is between unitary visions and reasonable political conceptions, and the latter have to protect pluralism and the basic rights of citizens in their own society against the former:

> Liberalism rejects political society as a community because, among other things, it leads to the systematic denial of basic liberties and may allow the oppressive use of the government's monopoly of (legal) force. Of course, in the well-ordered society of justice as fairness citizens share a common aim... of insuring that political and social institutions are just, and of giving justice to persons generally, as what citizens need for themselves and want for one another. (PL 146, n. 13)

This dichotomous portrayal may reflect the experience of robust debates having degenerated into culture wars in a society already fragmented by other factors. From a comparative perspective on approaches to the public sphere, however, this division with its built-in rejection of proposals that go beyond the segment in which they all overlap seems to be the greater danger: it limits the scope of political goals a society is permitted to aim towards. More encompassing hopes have to be shelved at the minimal shared level. While it is portrayed as an expression of the "criterion of reciprocity" on which "political legitimacy" depends (LP, 137), it is clear that reciprocity is being restricted first to fellow-citizens, and then interpreted in terms of reasons which they "reasonably think that other citizens might also reasonably accept" (LP, 137). The willingness to follow this criterion is welcomed as "civic friendship" (LP, 137). But relationships in which the sharing of one's self-understanding is discouraged appear more like contracts than friendships.

In summary, which capacities are attributed to the two counterparts? The work of public reason is to make encounters possible by converting each comprehensive doctrine into substantive political conceptions; by formalizing and purging them of their worldview-indebted elements, they are made fit for an overlapping consensus. The extent and depth of this work depends on how "comprehensive", doctrinal, other, or self-enclosed a belief system is. Its capacities are to generate motivation and orientation from their original perspective on the world. Yet this sense of direction becomes associated with its "zeal" to think in categories of "friend or foe", and of a "relentless struggle to win the world for the whole truth... The zeal to embody the whole truth in politics is incompatible with an idea of public reason that belongs with democratic citizenship." (LP, 132–33) This is why each of them can only be allowed access after conforming to the exigencies of public reason by keeping their specific truth claims silent.

One capacity that comprehensive doctrines do not seem to have is conversing directly with one another in order to understand each other's perspectives: On their own, they "cannot reach agreement or even approach mutual understanding on the basis of their irreconcilable comprehensive doctrines." (LP, 132) Thus, by definition, there cannot be any overlap between them as such. Each is able to speak its own tongue or dialect, and attempt to learn the standard or high language of public reason to make themselves understood and encounter others like themselves through its service of translation. Even their stories are not seen as able to convince through their literary power and evidence across cultural divides as narratives of human action, moral choices and religious horizons; they have to be lifted to a generic level before they can find a hearing. The parable of the Good Samaritan gains entry to public reason through Kant's concept of imperfect duties (cf. LP, 146. 155, n. 55). This lack of capacity for communication between worldviews is the opening for public reason and its own platform of agreement: "I propose that in public reason comprehensive doctrines of truth or right be replaced by an idea of the politically reasonable addressed to citizens as citizens." (LP, 132)

What remains unanswered is how public reason can create an overlapping consensus if the partners are portrayed as so alien to each other. How is it possible that they can agree not just on a vague, but on a rather specific understanding of what "free and equal" means, that is also compatible with the next worldview's interpretation, and that resounds with citizens' moral experience of the recognition they offer each other? There are two unexplained premises in this coincidence which would otherwise remain unlikely: one is a capability for morality that underlies the new genuine regard between citizens that replaces the self-interest of the contract. The other underlies the astonishing ability of comprehensive doctrines to overlap after all. As Herta Nagl-Docekal points out, without the "thesis that all religions have their origin in the same need of reason (*Bedürfnis der Vernunft*)", it cannot be explained what Rawls assumes, namely that they are able to overlap in supporting freedom and equality.[64]

The investigation of these two premises, however, requires moving the level of analysis from the perspective in which both the comprehensive and the political side have been viewed so far: as external social facts, that is, as existing entities open to social scientific, for example, psychological, and political ethical analysis. The dominating external perspective also explains why the self-understandings of the different traditions were not explored themselves. It led to the view that "faith"- or "doctrine-based" traditions are unitary entities and that their members are just spokespersons for them; there seems to be no history of religions engaging with their own culture and with foreign ones. Their interpretive relationship to their foundational documents, the epoch-making translations they undertook, and the self-reflexive quality they share with the great philosophical systems since the axial age – themes relevant for the other two authors – do not figure. Before examining which premises lead to these interests for Habermas and Ricoeur, however, Rawls's outline of public reason and religion has to be completed, first by putting it into context with its counterpart, "non-public reason".

The restrictions of public reason only apply to one of the three spheres of democratic life, the admittedly "shallow" (PL, 242) ground of neutralized political conceptions. What other forms of democratic life are there besides the public political forum?

---

64 Nagl-Docekal, "Moral und Religion", 854.

1.4.2 The spheres of democratic life

Rawls has made it clear that the political and public sphere is only a section of a person's complete life which can flourish quite independently from it. It is only in the public political forum that all contributions have to be submitted to the discipline of public reason. Its counterpart is called the "background culture" in which many forms of "nonpublic reason" co-exist. In addition, the "wide view" of the public political culture allows religions and other distinct systems of conviction to express their views. If one wants to assess the place and role of religions in Rawls's framework, one has to include the other spheres of democracy in the analysis. While the "forum" was marked by the concern for stability in view of past and present conflicts, the wider range of activity in society might bring into focus other forces that are shaping its current and future life. Rawls's treatment of the background culture (1) will be followed by an examination of the function of religions within it (2).

1.4.2.1 The composition of the background culture

The counterpart to the public political forum and the wider view of political culture is not simply the private life of individuals. There are associations and institutions in civil society which offer possibilities of social encounter, expression and reasoning.[65] While it is not itself the space of democratic deliberation, in which candidates for election, campaign managers and officeholders (cf. LP, 133) engage with citizens, it offers space for reflection and debate on matters relating to its own circles. Only in comparison with the requirements of the overlapping consensus can it be called "nonpublic", in its own sphere it is social and visible:

> This way of reasoning is public with respect to their members but non-public with respect to political society and to citizens generally. Nonpublic reasons comprise the many reasons of civil society and belong to what I have called the "background culture," in contrast with the public political culture. These reasons are social, and certainly not private. (PL, 220)

---

[65] The "background culture... is the culture of civil society. In a democracy, this culture is not, of course, guided by any one central idea or principle, whether political or religious. Its many and diverse agencies and associations with their internal life reside within a framework of law that ensures the familiar liberties of thought and speech, and the right of free association." (LP, 134)

Which matters are allocated to the critical powers of the background culture? Rawls mentions issues of theological doctrine for the churches, of educational policy for the universities, and assessments of harm to the public from nuclear accidents in meetings of scientists (PL, 221). By including "the culture of churches and associations of all kinds, and institutions of learning at all levels" (LP, 134, Fn. 13), the background culture comprises the professional segment and operates through its discourses, too. Some of the problems it deals with clearly also belong to the brief of public reason, such as education and technology. In view of the range it encompasses from free associations to expert consultations, in what way are citizens involved?

Responding to critiques which question the division political liberalism makes between public and nonpublic reason, Rawls agrees to the "need for full and open discussion in the background culture" (LP, 134) and quotes approvingly an assessment by David Hollenbach:

> Conversation and argument about the common good will not occur initially in the legislature or in the political sphere (narrowly conceived as the domain in which interests and power are adjudicated). Rather it will develop freely in those components of civil society that are the primary bearers of cultural meaning and values – universities, religious communities, the world of arts and serious journalism. It can occur wherever thoughtful men and women bring their beliefs on the meaning of the good life into intelligent and critical encounter with understandings of this good held by other peoples with other traditions. In short, it occurs wherever education about and serious inquiry into the meaning of the good life takes place.[66]

A subsequent quote also highlights the need for exchange between traditions of conviction. It expresses the "hope that communities holding different visions of the good life can get somewhere if they are willing to risk conversation and argument about these visions."[67] Adduced by Rawls as pointers to the significance of the "social roots of constitutional democracy" which "strengthen its vital institutions" (LP, 154, n. 52), such forms of nonpublic reason are clearly accepted. Will exchange at this level give a different role to religions that may ultimately support the task of public reasoning?

---

66 LP, 134–35, n. 15, quoting from D. Hollenbach, "Civil Society: Beyond the Public-Private Dichotomy", in *The Responsive Community* 5 (Winter 1994–95) 15–23, 22.
67 LP, 154, n. 52, quoting from D. Hollenbach, "Contexts of the Political Role of Religion: Civil Society and Culture", in *San Diego Law Review* 30 (1993) 879–901, 891.

1.4.2.2 Religious contributions to nonpublic reason?

The concern of religions that under the "constitutional regime" of public reason, they may "not prosper…, and indeed may decline" has been taken seriously (LP, 149. 151). On the other hand, their enduring vitality is a factor that could be harnessed for motivating adherence to public reason. The positive acknowledgement of the reflective capacity provided by religious communities within the background culture could be expected to offer a bridge between the two spheres of reason, public and nonpublic. However, despite the mutual explorations and insights gained into each others' visions, public reason is still seen as operating by "conjecture". By using assumptions on what others may hold, the aim of its argument is to show that "despite what they may think" (LP, 155–56), it is reasonable for religions and in keeping with their own motivation to subject themselves to the political values specified. These formulations show that public reason does not make use of the knowledge that exists in the background culture through such exchanges. At the political level, the fear of a "hegemony" of worldviews (LP, 150) remains, if left unchecked by public reason. From its vantage point, the insistence of all "comprehensive convictions" on what they "see as the whole truth" makes them comparable to private interests. Although "offhand quite different" cases, they are as much in breach of the duty of civility and of the limits of public reason as citizens are who vote based on their own "preferences and interests, social and economic, not to mention their dislikes and hatreds" (PL, 219).

Also within the background culture, their function remains pale and unspecific; no unique contents or attitudes are named that only a religious orientation towards transcendence could provide. Apart from his quotations of David Hollenbach's illustration of the type of reflections on meaning that especially religious associations provide on the common good, the educational, heuristic and integrating potential of religious perspectives is not mentioned by Rawls.[68] In my view, two factors contribute to this lack of profile at the level of the lifeworld where communities of conviction should come into their own: firstly, citizens remain a collective and abstract concept, removed from the opportunities and threats their differences pose: "we don't view persons as socially situated or otherwise rooted" (LP, 171). Secondly, in the absence of an analysis of cultural pathologies, it seems as if the major threat to liberty and equality comes

---

68 It is interesting to compare Hollenbach's awareness of the educational contribution of religions with Rawls's discussion of funding for church schools which is left without a conclusion, as a matter of local circumstances. It served as an example for the difficulty of deciding whether opposite stances are the result of different interpretations of the same political conception, or two different political conceptions.

from communities of conviction, in particular from religions. One reason for this lack of analysis of all factors that can erode a democratic ethos is that the background culture as such is not examined for the resources and avenues it might provide for social cohesion. This is only a theme addressed at the level of public reason and its ethos of citizenship. As a consequence, even in the exchanges of the background culture, religions do not figure as multilingual mediators with a potential to reconcile deep differences; they could do this by providing a perspective which links the good and the right as well as a horizon in which singularity and universal justice can be reconciled.

The specifics of Rawls's separation between the spheres of nonpublic and of public reason, including his 1997 restriction to holders or candidates for political or juridical office, will be further examined in Part Two against Habermas's concept of discourse in the public sphere before and beyond the "institutional threshold". The discourse ethicist does not isolate the realm of public reason from the background culture. Its initiatives and venues of discourse are, as the American political philosopher Thomas McCarthy summarizes his approach, the basis of popular sovereignty. The "public use of reason" includes within the

> unofficial arenas of the political public sphere... (i)ndependent public forums, distinct from both the economic system and the state administration, having their locus rather in voluntary associations, social movements, and other networks and processes of communication in civil society – including the mass media".[69]

As will be seen below in 2.3.2, the public reason citizens generate according to Habermas in their practical discourses contributes a heuristic capacity different both from the levels of expert cultures, which Rawls subsumes into nonpublic reason, and of institutional politics.

The two final sections of Part One will treat the two counterparts separately: First, objections from more consistently Kantian positions on practical reason and public reason (1.5); then religion as a comprehensive, but not a self-enclosed doctrine with a truth claim that can be reconstructed within philosophy of religion in its relevance for reason, and in two specific interpretations (1.6).

---

69 Th. McCarthy, "Kantian constructivism and reconstructivism: Rawls and Habermas in dialogue", in *Ethics* 105 (1994) 44–63, 48–49.

1.5 "Public reason" and practical reason: Critiques from a Kantian perspective

Objections from fellow-Kantian positions will be treated in the following sequence: the reduction of expectations from the standard of morality to that of
civility (1) will be contrasted with the alternative of founding the constitutional
order on the principle of human dignity (2). This principle allows us to regain a
cosmopolitan scope for justice that the foundation on an overlapping consensus
cannot supply (3). This horizon is the one originally intended in the Kantian concept of public reason as distinct from the private use of practical reason which
Rawls's theory is shown to amount to (4).

1.5.1 Distinct starting points: "Public reason" between theory of law and morality

The high demands addressed to citizens, including that of casting their votes in a
publicly justifiable way, obscure the fact that this is the one and only level where
accountability is required. It has absorbed a different, prior level: that of morality as an experience of self-reflection and expectation to oneself and others.
Taken on their own, the descriptions of the person and of his duty to fellow-citizens seem exacting; yet they remain silent about its basis, thus conflating the
distinct logics of a theory of morality and of a theory of law. As we have seen
in Herta Nagl-Docekal's previous comments on Rawls's argumentation in comparison with Kant's, one crucial question is: what makes it possible for persons
to endorse the proposed values? In Rawls's ethics of citizenship they are asked to
anticipate the consent of others; by doing so, the direct access of individuals to
their conscience is replaced by an intermediate adjudication of what is right.
Nagl-Docekal points out that a sense of justice and the scope of civic virtues it
limits itself to differ in content from morality, indeed, can end up in tension
to it. If this is true, then a justification that eclipses a person's conscience has
to be rejected and its results resubmitted to its own more stringent test.

Nagl-Docekal shows that the origin of Rawls's concept of public reason is in
theory of law, seeking to establish the rational acceptability of constitutional
principles by all citizens. The problem arises when this approach of grounding
the legitimacy of law is applied to "all justification of norms *toto genere*", and
morality itself is reconstructed through contract theory.[70] Kant takes the opposite

---

70 Nagl-Docekal, "Moral und Religion", 843.

approach, aware of the "aporia" that a contractual agreement is unable to found moral conduct: Since it "cannot be part of a contract to have an inner conviction", which would "sign one's future conscience away", his

> proposal for the mediation of law and morality begins with morality. Here it is crucial that individuals are first seen as human beings and only in secondary instance as citizens. We are characterized as humans by being confronted with a categorical ought founded in our reason. It is decisive that the validity sphere of this ought is encompassing, since the categorical imperative relates to each of our actions.[71]

Thus, for her, the sense of justice is "derived" from our original human capability for morality. As pointed out before, in the context of explaining the two faculties attributed to moral personhood, the sense of justice "is not coextensive with moral ought in its totality. It focuses our – morally founded – acting as citizens."[72] By differentiating between its different areas of application and the genuine human experience of moral obligation, the irreducibility of the foundational capability for morality to its contexts and its distinctiveness from given or agreed social norms become evident. Nagl-Docekal draws the conclusions from Kant's distinction between external principles of law and the self-obligation of morality for the understanding both of "reciprocity" and of moral self-examination. In contrast to the

> principle of reciprocal benefit, the Categorical Imperative is not led by such symmetry. The point is to respect human dignity in the other and in myself (strict duty) and to make the ends of others my own as far as possible (wide duties), independently of the fact of whether others treat me in the same way. This is the point of the concept of moral autonomy, as opposed to heteronomy.[73]

This renunciation of symmetry highlights that morality is unconditional: "reciprocity is not a condition for specific services (*Leistungen*), but a consequence of unconditional moral action."[74] Her insistence that the sense of justice and morality constitute "two distinctive criteria of judgement" manifests itself in the observation that for the same person "the result of assessing the same action

---

71 Nagl-Docekal, "Moral und Religion", 846.
72 Nagl-Docekal, "Moral und Religion", 847.
73 Nagl-Docekal, "Moral und Religion", 847. As quoted and commented on before, Rawls's insistence on strict reciprocity rules out the risk of one-sided, asymmetric initiatives that might not be requited: "Persons are reasonable … when… they are ready to propose principles and standards as fair terms of cooperation treatment and to abide by them willingly, given the assurance that others will likewise do so" (PL, 49).
74 Nagl-Docekal, "Moral und Religion", 847, n. 29.

can be different... there are many ways of violating the Categorical Imperative without breaking a law. Something that is legally permitted is not *eo ipso* morally permitted."[75]

From this analysis, it becomes clear why the high expectations addressed to citizens still fall short of the moral point of view. On the one hand, they remain below it by not basing the moral obligation towards oneself and others on Kant's understanding of autonomy as self-legislation; on the other, they overtax it by asking citizens to supersede their own reflected moral perspective by unexamined "duties of civility", for example, in the area of voting. By skipping over the individual's own moral judgment, the validating reflection is passed on to an exterior authority. From here it is not surprising that it is not the moral agent, but philosophy that decides on reasonableness, and on what touches on constitutional essentials. Demanding too much unnecessarily of the citizen, and too little of the moral agent, also affects the aspirations permitted for democracies.

1.5.2 An alternative guiding principle for the constitutional order: Human dignity

Having successfully established the inviolability of the individual against Utilitarianism and libertarian liberalism in his *Theory of Justice*, taking human dignity as the supreme principle should appear as natural to Rawls as it is to Habermas. The orientation towards it seems to be implicit in the difference principle. It would offer the following advantages:

First, declaring human dignity as the standard and aim of political community would make it clear that the overlapping consensus strives for more than upholding a status quo of interlocking interests. It would offer a motivation and a basis of argumentation for accepting sacrifices,[76] for example, to long-established standards of distribution, and would point civic debate to a goal beyond accepted but unjustified conventions. It would secondly re-establish the possibility of a direct connection to one's own conscience that was exchanged for the exigency to anticipate other citizens' views, casting the democratic activity of voting

---

75 Nagl-Docekal, "Moral und Religion", 847–848.

76 Rawls also mentions the readiness for sacrifices, but interprets "fairness" overall as symmetry between what each one offers and receives. "Citizens are reasonable when... they are prepared to offer one another fair terms of cooperation,... and when they agree to act on those terms, even at the cost of their own interests in particular situations" (LP, 136).

in the light of coercion.[77] The "basic requirement... that a reasonable doctrine accepts a constitutional democratic regime and its companion idea of legitimate law" (LP, 132) could be fulfilled if the aim was specified as a commitment of that regime beyond itself to uphold and promote human dignity. Thirdly, human dignity as founded on the capability for morality in Kant, is also not in competition with religion. Committed to the inviolability of human dignity, there would be no need to curb particular worldviews *per se*. In addition, individuals and communities holding religious and other comprehensive views would be expected to fulfill exactly the same exertions and burdens, those posed to them by their moral nature. The real adversary to be faced, as will be discussed in the final section, is not the paradox of public reason, but a deeper one: the antinomy of practical reason.

The reason that human dignity is not chosen as the aim and benchmark of constitutional democracies in his later work, must be that since the move from metaphysical to political foundations it is viewed as falling under the comprehensive anthropologies that are in need of transformation into political conceptions. What platform does the contract approach offer for conceiving of human rights and international justice?

1.5.3 *The Law of Peoples:* Transnational scope for human rights and justice?

A final horizon to be explored in the total constellation of public reason and religion before coming to a theological evaluation is the question of the connections and limits drawn between a liberal society and the globe in which it is situated. The consequences of the increasingly contextual foundation for the scope of justice and human rights need to be examined. The frame for creating a just basic structure in *A Theory of Justice* admittedly was a bounded society. The task was to

> formulate a reasonable conception of justice for the basic structure of society conceived for the time being as a closed system isolated from other societies...The conditions for the law of nations may require different principles (TJ, 8).

---

77 Rawls's interpretation of voting as exercising "coercive political power over one another" which has to be justified to each other (PL, 217) presupposes that the sphere of individual rights is primary and antagonistic. It could equally have been expressed in terms of visions for a just society and international order and included an invitation for mutual exchange between citizens and election candidates on such shared aspirations.

After the programmatic move to a completely contextual foundation in *Political Liberalism* questions beyond the confines of domestic politics were mentioned together with national ones as examples of the need for civic education: "without a public informed about pressing problems, crucial political and social decisions simply cannot be made." (LP, 139) Deliberative democracy demands continuous, sustained efforts to access and examine information. The 1997 "Idea of Public Reason Revisited" analyses that if

> farsighted political leaders wish to make sound changes and reforms, they cannot convince a misinformed and cynical public to accept and follow them...(f)or example... about the importance of support for international institutions (such as the United Nations), foreign aid properly spent, and concern for human rights at home and abroad. (LP, 140)

The third major work, *The Law of Peoples*, takes on the task of developing a proposal of international law. Begun as an Oxford Amnesty Lecture in 1993, revised, and completed just after "The Idea of Public Reason Revisited", it offers principles of international relations based on social contract. Explicitly taking his "lead" from Kant's *Perpetual Peace* (LP, 10), Rawls agrees that "a constitutional regime must establish an effective Law of Peoples in order to realize fully the freedom of its citizens". For Kant, too, the starting point is the citizen at the local level; according to the 1795 treatise, as Rawls mentions, that person is capable of a "cosmopolitan point of view". (LP, 10, n. 14)

It will be instructive also for the framework in which religion is located in relation to reason, to investigate the following points: what rights do human beings have, on the basis of which concept of personhood (1), and which global structures are they obliged to promote (2)? Theologically, these requirements can be reconstructed as what creatures owe to each other and to their creator who gave them stewardship over the earth in its fecundity. A philosophical approach that stops short of equality in human rights and justice in the use of global resources will be less compatible with positions of faith in a creator, and, for the Christian faith, the redeemer, of all humanity, than universalistic ones. The objections of two Kantian critics, the Frankfurt philosopher Rainer Forst, and Onora O'Neill, will show up the theory decisions where Rawls opts for a liberal and contextual rather than a deontological and universalistic framework.

1.5.3.1 Human rights, urgent and universal, versus constitutional and contextual

The basic division *Political Liberalism* has made between the level of comprehensive doctrines, including all philosophical approaches, and the neutral level of public reason which constitutional democracies conduct their debates on, poses the following questions once the borders of citizenship are crossed: how is it possible to conceive of human rather than citizens' rights? On what basis can democratic electorates and leaders accord rights beyond a society's original contract? Like Kant, Rawls assumes an interest beyond the confines of the state, but what interest? Unlike the element of correction present in the turn from *Theory of Justice* to *Political Liberalism*, the third book sees itself in continuity with the foundations laid in the second. Its inclusion of the global political reality beyond Western democracies happens by way of "extension of a liberal conception of justice for a domestic regime to a Society of Peoples" (LP, 9). The *Law of Peoples* fleshes out the core concepts of the second work in a new area of application: the international relations of liberal states. Keeping to the limits of public reason, it reconstructs human rights "as a necessary, though not sufficient standard for the decency of domestic political and social institutions". (LP, 80) It avoids founding them on any comprehensive concept:

> Comprehensive doctrines, religious or nonreligious, might base the idea of human rights on a theological, philosophical or moral conception of the nature of the human person. That path the Law of Peoples does not follow. (LP, 81)

Accordingly, the first article of the Universal Declaration of Human Rights is understood as one that can be disconnected from the list of rights that follows. It is reinterpreted as expressing not a comprehensive, but an aspirational concept that liberalism can identify with:

> Of the other declarations, some seem more aptly described as stating liberal aspirations, such as Article 1 of the Universal Declaration of Human Rights of 1948: "All human beings are born free and equal in dignity and rights. They are endowed with reason and conscience and should act towards one another in a spirit of brotherhood." (LP, 80, n. 23)

Assuming this liberal basis to be universal, is seen as committing the fault of ethnocentrism. Both the foundation and the list of rights have to be examined in order not to overextend their cultural limits. The list of rights is reduced to "proper" ones with unlimited validity, and those which presuppose a Western framework both of values and of institutions able to deliver on them.[78] What then

---

78 "(S)ome think of human rights as roughly the same rights that citizens have in a reasonable constitutional democratic regime; this view simply expands the class of human rights to include all the rights that liberal governments guarantee. Human rights in the Law of Peoples, by contrast, express a special class of urgent rights, such as freedom from slavery and serfdom, liberty (but not equal liberty) of conscience, and security of ethnic groups from mass murder

makes certain rights universal? It is neither that they are followed everywhere, nor that they can be founded metaphysically on a concept of human nature. The universality of the class of human rights "proper" derives from their contractual foundation, on the one hand: they are "intrinsic to the Law of Peoples" (LP, 80). On the other hand, the geographic spread of their appeal, their political force across state boundaries is also part of their universality: "That is, their political (moral) force extends to all societies, and they are binding on all peoples and societies, including outlaw states." They do not need local support everywhere to have "political (moral) effect" (LP, 80 – 81). It is on the basis of "decency", then, which unites liberal states with those built on a hierarchical political culture, that rights to life, liberty and security of person apply everywhere, and that "outlaw states" are to be excluded from the "Society of Peoples" because they violate these "urgent" human rights. Articles 3 and 5 and the rights implied by them belong to them:

> First, there are Human Rights proper, illustrated by Article 3: Everybody has a right to life, liberty and security of person, and by Article 5: No one shall be subjected to torture or to cruel, degrading treatment or punishment. Articles 3 – 18 may all be put under this heading of human rights proper, pending certain questions of interpretation. Second, there are human rights that are obvious implications of the first class of rights. The second class of rights covers the extreme cases described by the special conventions on genocide (1948) and on apartheid (1973). These two classes comprise the human rights connected with the common good (LP, 80, n. 23).

Others can only be supported by a liberal political conception of justice, and thus need the values present in them, endorsed by their citizens. They "appear to presuppose specific kinds of institutions, such as the right to social security as in Article 22, and the right to equal pay for equal work, in Article 23" (LP, 80, n. 23), institutions typical for liberal societies.

As far as the contextual basis of this argumentation is concerned, which begins from the political values, virtues and institutions of Western culture, the argumentation is stringent. Every element, including the diversity of cultures, is developed from the experience of liberalism.[79] From the first "original position" expounded for a bounded society in *Theory of Justice*, a second original position

---

and genocide. The violation of this class of rights is equally condemned by both reasonable liberal peoples and decent hierarchical peoples." (LP, 78 – 79)

79 "What can be the basis for a Society of Peoples given the reasonable and expected differences of peoples from one another, with their distinctive institutions and languages, religions and cultures, as well as their different histories... (These differences parallel the fact of reasonable pluralism in a domestic regime.)" (LP, 54 – 55)

between liberal societies, and a third one of the representatives of decent peoples are constructed by way of extension. Although the title chosen, *"Law of Peoples"*, is to reflect the crucial fact that international law refers to peoples rather than states (LP, 23), the "moral character" (LP, 25) uniting humanity in its different parts is again played down. It is only on the basis of an extension that these rights apply elsewhere; they remain foreign and are characterized as part of the external relations of liberal states (cf. LP, 10), not as the original and unconditionally valid property of all individuals and peoples.

Both this method of justification and its conclusions have attracted philosophical critiques which are important for theological ethics. The three central "deficits" which Rainer Forst detects concern morality, democracy, and equality.[80] The "moral deficit" in the method of extension is judged as arising, first, from the failure to see the need for a genuinely universalist foundation in the concept of moral personhood which (again, as it already did in the difference principle of *Theory of Justice*) remains implicit:

> His "fair ethnocentrism" (so to speak), that is, the attempt to move within a "liberal," non-universalizable framework is doomed to failure for two reasons. First, when the minimal conditions of justice are specified for nonliberal "decent" societies, the perspective of a liberal "foreign policy" is essentially transformed into a universalist moral position, and Rawls implicitly operates with a concept of unconditional respect for moral persons, who have certain rights as human beings and as citizens, rights that apply, moreover, without restriction in outlaw states and can even justify intervention. Here we encounter moral content that is not sufficiently acknowledged, which calls his liberal modesty into question.[81]

As a consequence, Forst rejects the division into urgent and merely constitutional human rights as being without foundation:

> Second, an opposing moral deficit arises when... the list of human rights is so reduced that central rights contained in the 1948 Universal Declaration of Human Rights drop out, such as equal treatment of the sexes, full freedom of conscience, freedom of speech and association, and the right to democratic participation. It is questionable whether such rights, in comparison with others that Rawls holds to be universally valid... should be regarded as particularly "liberal"... In my view, all these rights are equally more and equally less "liberal": demands for them arise out of various experiences of injustice and oppression, whatever the society, and they can be brought to bear and institutionalized in a variety of ways.[82]

---

80 R. Forst, "Constructions of transnational justice. Comparing John Rawls's *The Law of Peoples* and Otfried Höffe's *Democracy in an Age of Globalisation*", in *The Right to Justification. Elements of a Constructivist Theory of Justice*, trans. J. Flynn (New York: Columbia University Press, 2011), 229–240, 231.
81 Forst, *Right to Justification*, 232.
82 Forst, *Right to Justification*, 232.

Thirdly, taking up critiques from Charles Beitz and Thomas Pogge, the drift of a normative philosophical into a pragmatic political argumentation is deplored and its result identified as a paternalism which the attempt to steer clear of ethnocentrism was meant to avoid:

> When it comes to the normative construction of a universalist conception of human rights which covers an array of absolutely nonrejectable normative claims by persons, there is thus no reason to qualify the status of moral persons with an eye toward being able to get "decent" regimes to agree, from the perspective of "foreign policy," so to speak. This would not only improperly mix normative and political-pragmatic questions, it would also be – contrary to Rawls's own intentions – a paternalistic gesture coming from the "outside": who is to say which rights people are entitled to other than those affected *themselves* in discourses of reciprocal justification?[83]

The second major deficit, concerning the role of self-determination granted in a decent polity, confirms and extends Forst's diagnosis of paternalism. Exploring it is relevant for a Christian Ethics interested in contemporary questions of inculturation and the concretization of human rights. By recognizing countries which honour the first set of human rights if not as fellow-liberal, but as "decent" societies, Rawls makes a distinction between types of government and basic moral orientations which gives a place to cultural difference.[84] It seems to offer a tolerant and culturally sensitive attitude which renounces a spirit of crusading on behalf of a particular understanding of liberty. "Decent" countries have not made the distinction between a comprehensive doctrine and political conceptions and are examples of the type of communitarian unity rejected before in favour of one achieved by overlapping consensus which leaves it to individual liberty from what basis to agree. The evidence of this democratic life form does not have to be accepted elsewhere. So what is Forst's specific point of critique? The Frankfurt philosopher agrees with Rawls's position of conceiving the nature of the sovereign, the "people", not in "substantialist" terms but – apart from other factors such as history and common sympathies – by "agreement on a collective political project of justice",[85] even if this is "nonliberal" (LP, 70). It is this

---

83 Forst, *Right to Justification*, 232. In LP, 58, Rawls takes care to refrain from speaking for others: "The reason for going on to consider the point of view of decent hierarchical peoples is not to prescribe principles of justice for *them*, but to assure ourselves that liberal principles of foreign policy are also reasonable from a decent nonliberal point of view. The desire to achieve this assurance is intrinsic to the liberal conception."

84 "Leaving aside the deep question of whether some forms of culture and ways of life are good in themselves, as I believe they are, it is surely a good for individuals and associations to be attached to their particular culture and to take part in its common public and civic life." (LP, 111)

85 Forst, *Right to Justification*, 233.

consensus that creates its legitimacy. Conversely, Forst argues, once this consensus is questioned, the basis for judging a country as adhering to the standard of "decency" becomes questionable. The argument itself shows that Rawls should have left the right to democratic participation in the list of human rights proper, rather than reserve it as a constitutional right for liberal states.[86]

Rather than accept decent nonliberal societies as static well-governed entities, space has to be made for an internal forum of debate beyond the life of their various internal associations. Forst uses Rawls's own theory of legitimacy to argue for structures of participation in political opinion formation and decision making as a matter of right. As we have seen, one of the deficits he identified as relevant to morality was an only partial admission of freedom of conscience. While the critique itself of only granting them to a certain degree can be fully backed, it raises the question of the relationship between freedom of conscience and freedom of religion: are they on the same level, or is the latter subordinated to the first, and what is the content of each? Here, both Rawls's subordination of freedom of religion to freedom of conscience with his explanatory footnote, and Forst's comment are instructive: Included under the right to "liberty" are "freedom from slavery, serfdom, and forced occupation, and to a sufficient measure of liberty of conscience to ensure freedom of religion and thought" (LP, 65). Footnote 2 explains:

> this liberty of conscience may not be as extensive nor as equal for all members of society: for example, one religion may legally predominate the state government, while other religions, though tolerated, may be denied the right to hold certain positions. I refer to this kind of situation as permitting "liberty of conscience, though not an equal liberty." (LP, 65, n. 2)[87]

---

86 Forst, *Right to Justification*, 233, with references to LP: "The basic argument for why 'decent' peoples and their regimes are tolerable lies, accordingly, in their being the expression of the self-determination of their members (61). Thus, internal order is upheld by those members on the basis of, for example, a 'comprehensive doctrine.' We are met here with 'a people sincerely affirming a nonliberal idea of justice' (70), thus not a fully democratic society but one that is nonetheless completely supported by all of its members without coercion. Thus, it is not without reason that Rawls stresses the internal duty of justification within a decent regime (77–78). But then there seems to be no legitimate possibility of not granting a human right to democratic participation since it is the basis – in a rough form – for the legitimacy of the regime itself... as soon as the existing order is challenged and democratic rights are more strongly demanded, the reasons for denying such rights by referring to the integrity of the society no longer apply... it would be hard to see how we could talk of a 'well-ordered society' anymore."

87 This toleration of a state religion is not without limits: "Although the established religion may have various privileges, it is essential to the society's being decent that no religion be

Thus, both Rawls and Forst classify the right not to have to submit to a comprehensive religious doctrine governing the self-understanding of a state as freedom of conscience. However, it would have been equally valid and more to the point to invoke the freedom of religion which includes the freedom to leave a religion. There are properly religious reasons to insist on the freedom of the human person in relation to the call of their God. As a free commitment, it includes as a necessary external condition the freedom to disconnect oneself from a religion, including a state-backed one.

Equality, the third complex where Forst diagnoses a deficit, relates to the role of justice on the international stage. His and Onora O'Neill's responses to the analysis offered in *The Law of Peoples* complement each other. They also agree on the need to identify causes of poverty and domination in what Rawls calls "burdened" societies with a more self-critical awareness of first world collusion with their oppressive elites.[88]

1.5.3.2 Justice – bounded or transnational?

Already in *Political Liberalism*, the difference principle was reduced in its importance even for its own liberal context. Although it named questions of basic justice as one of the two areas of public reason, it was considered "more urgent to settle the essentials dealing with the basic freedoms", the realisation of which was also "far easier" to ascertain. The conclusion was that "freedom of movement and free choice of occupation and a social minimum covering citizens' basic needs count as constitutional essentials while the principle of fair opportunity and the difference principle do not." (PL, 230) Since they "fall under questions of basic justice", they "are to be decided by the political values of public reason" (PL, 229, n. 10) which will be interpreted by different political conceptions linked to the worldviews present in a specific liberal culture. As both commentators observe, the application to international relations leaves out the principles of distributive justice. Forst wonders with regard to the construction of the third original position why only representatives of decent peoples and not all the individuals of the globe are considered as negotiating partners. But even

> if one accepts Rawls approach, it is still questionable why at the level of the international original position, in which the representatives know neither the size of their country nor its population, nor the extent of their natural resources, nor their degree of economic develop-

---

persecuted, or denied civic and social conditions permitting its practice in peace and without fear." (LP, 74)

88 Cf. Forst, *Right to Justification*, 234–35.

ment ..., only the stated principles of international law are considered as candidates and not more comprehensive principles of distributive justice.[89]

Examining the reason given, equal respect as independent peoples (cf. LP, 41), rather than the baseline of equality in primary goods, as in *Theory of Justice*, he judges: "This independence would certainly not have to be abandoned if they were to consider and accept stronger distributive or redistributive principles than the terms of fair trade and the duty of assistance that Rawls provides."[90]

He adds that this duty of assistance which for Rawls includes "material support" as well as "advice on institutional reform" (LP, 110) has to begin with the "political and economic hindrance" that the "global 'order' is to achieving this autonomy", marked more by "force and domination" than by "voluntary 'cooperation',... reciprocally stabilizing relations of injustice vis-a-vis the powerless strata of the population which are dominated in multiple ways."[91] Instead of a contract approach with its first and secondary stages, beginning with a specific society, he proposes a "discursive, moral-political construction of *co-original* principles of local and global justice."[92]

The approach taken by Onora O'Neill to develop principles of justice from a basic theory of practical reasoning offers one way of fulfilling this programme. Part I of O'Neill's 2000 book *Bounds of Justice* treats "philosophical", Part II "political" limits. The first part thus alerts to theory decisions that might result in justifying exclusion. It argues for a theory of action in which duties and rights correspond to each other, and puts forward an alternative to empirical and contextual models of practical reasoning.

---

89 Forst, *Right to Justification*, 233. The disappearance of the distributive part of the two justice principles demanded in the first book is equally pointed out in O'Neill's comments on *The Law of Peoples* in BJ, 133: "The first echoes the libertarian view that all should have equal and maximal liberties; the second, the so-called difference principle, qualifies this with the requirement that inequalities be permitted only where they would be to the advantage of the representative worst-off person. Since the construction assumes the framework of a closed society, the 'representative worst-off person' is not thought of as representing the worst off of the whole world. When Rawls finally relaxes the assumption that justice is internal to states, he argues only for selected principles of transnational justice. He repeats the thought experiment of the original position... but claims to establish only those principles of international justice which are the analogues of his first principle of justice: non-intervention, self-determination, *pacta sunt servanda*, principles of self-defence and of just war. There is no international analogue of the difference principle, and hence no account of transnational economic justice."
90 Forst, *Right to Justification*, 234.
91 Forst, *Right to Justification*, 234.
92 Forst, *Right to Justification*, 240.

The Cambridge philosopher starts her analysis with the need not to accept but to critically question borders. The concept of public reason proposed by her former doctoral adviser is viewed from the effect it has of separating fellow-citizens and "outsiders":

> Rawls has argued in his later work that the agreements of fellow-citizens have a fundamental status in an adequate conception of the reasonable, and thereby in political justification. The thought may seem convincing if we take for granted that an account of justice may presuppose that we are fellow-citizens of some state, or (as Rawls puts it) of a "bounded society"... but the approach is strangely silent about the predicaments of outsiders, and about the justice of a world that is segmented into states, a world in which for each of us most others are emphatically not fellow-citizens... on the contrary, an adequate account of justice has to take seriously the often harsh realities of exclusion... Why should the boundaries of states be viewed as presuppositions of justice rather than as institutions whose justice has to be assessed?[93]

The basis of what is ultimately judged to be reasonable has to be found at a more original and at the same time universal level than a consensus between citizens. Public reason is rendered provincial if the mere feature of being fellow-citizens is allowed to restrict reasonable argumentation to the horizon they happen to share: In "our world reasoning must reach beyond the like-minded... based on principles widely accessible."[94] The capacity that allows individuals to subject apparent givens to scrutiny and to judge the validity of presuppositions is that of critical reasoning. A theory of action that insists on the link between duties and rights also avoids the danger of empty claims of rights with no specific addressee for the corresponding duties which pervade an "abstract" cosmopolitanism.[95] O'Neill shows the connections between Kant's account of rationality with its priority of practical reason and his theory of agency which oblige human beings to "devise institutions and practices that secure and sustain basic capacities for agency and autonomy for all", including as their "source or precondition...

---

93 O'Neill, *Bounds of Justice*, 4.

94 O'Neill, *Bounds of Justice*, 24.

95 "Abstract cosmopolitanism of this popular sort dilutes rather than promotes understanding of universal human rights: if we are to take rights seriously, we cannot begin by taking them so lightly" (BJ, 189). Her critique of the Universal Declaration of Human Rights is based on premises opposite to those of Rawls whose distinction of liberal from urgent rights gives priority to the boundaries between societies. For O'Neill, whose starting point is the respect owed to the individual members of humanity, these very boundaries have to be justified to them. The assumption of the 1948 Declaration that states are sovereign, that "they can make and enforce law, and so they can make and enforce just laws" leads her to the conclusion, the "Universal Declaration does not endorse very much institutional cosmopolitanism" (BJ, 179–80).

morally valuable... forms of dependence and interdependence". She concludes that "(e)thics and politics are not spectator sports".[96]

In Part II of her book the political bounds of justice are investigated from a theory of action that is empowering by not beginning with claims, but with the capacity of agency to recognize what it owes to others. Analyses such as those of the practical contradictions women face as "impoverished providers in marginalized and developing economies"[97] call for a moral response. While, as Forst shows, some of Rawls's conclusions can be critiqued from his own premises, a different framework is needed overall to establish transnational justice as a demand of political philosophy. It has to be based on taking the shared status of being human as more foundational than that of being a citizen.

1.5.4 The public and the private use of practical reason

In the context of her critical discussion of Rawls's restriction of justice to bounded societies compared to Kant's scope of humanity as sharing a finite globe, O'Neill also analyses the main differences between their concepts of public reason. Their points of reference are quite distinct: for Rawls, it is the possible empirical overlap between traditions in their contingency with the political values of liberty and equality; for Kant, it is the normative judgement that a proposed course of action or maxim is followable, having submitted it to the standard of practical reason. Kant's understanding of reason and of public reason as "nonderivative"[98] makes Rawls's definition a case of the "private use of reason" since it presupposes social arrangements and authorities without which agents would not be engaging in it:

> It follows that the sorts of reasoning exhibited in democratic political debate and in communitarian thought, as well as in the civic reasoning Rawls commends, are all in Kant's

---

96 O'Neill, *Bounds of Justice*, 49.
97 O'Neill, *Bounds of Justice*, 144: "These women may depend on others but lack the supposed securities of dependence... They are powerless, yet others who are yet more vulnerable depend on them for protection. Their vulnerability reflects heavy demands as much as slender resources... this domestic sphere is embedded in an economy that is subordinate to distant and richer economies... A serious account of justice cannot gloss over the predicaments of impoverished providers in marginalized and developing economies."
98 O. O'Neill, "Bounded and Cosmopolitan Justice", in *Review of International Studies*, vol. 26 (entitled: *How Might We Live? Global Ethics in a New Century*) (2000) 45–60, 52.

view private, because each presupposes the authority of civilly and socially constituted roles, institutions and practices. [99]

One could say that this is even more the case after 1997 when "Public Reason Revisited" entrusts its exercise to office-holders and candidates who are clearly acting in political roles, rather than in virtue of the Kantian capability for morality. With citizens, it could have been either in the derived role of a citizen, or as a moral thinker that the individual could have used practical reason to test the justifiability of proposals.

Public reason for Kant is exemplified by a scholar using reason in relation to the world at large, not a bounded framework. This does not mean, however, that it is an individualist exercize, since the thinker has to fulfill the criterion that its use is "communicable" to and "followable"[100] by others. Its criteria are the underived, disciplined and law-like nature of reason. In its practical realm, it also requires political institutions to be answerable to the principled autonomy spelt out in the Categorical Imperative. This is the horizon deemed necessary, beyond the overlapping consensus against which its adequacy can be judged.

In conclusion, the line of argumentation I have offered and the critiques I have explored do not reject the distinction Rawls makes between particular doctrines and a general standard of reason. From a communitarian or a postliberal perspective, this may be voiced as the main objection. From a platform shared with Rawls, which affirms modernity's turn to the subject and his or her obligations and rights, his recasting of public reason as a mode of thinking that turns internal worldviews towards the shared enterprise of democracy is not problematic. It was a prior theory decision of *Political Liberalism* that has caused a principal deficit. It consisted in relegating all philosophical approaches to the segment of worldviews, and making their truth claims internal, incommunicable and incontestable. For ethics, this means that all candidates supporting a shared basis of a universally binding morality could be removed from the general sphere of public reason. They may even risk being rendered "unreasonable" in Rawls's definition if they insist on offering their own original argumentations for this position, rather than convert them into political conceptions. Thus, such contenders for a shareable standard of reason are reclassified as rival parties in need of prior reconciliation even before argumentation can begin. Ironically, this move which tends to promote a self-immunisation of political liberalism especially against universalist critiques happens in the name of the self-application of tol-

---

99 O'Neill, "Bounded and cosmopolitan justice", 53.
100 O'Neill, "Bounded and cosmopolitan justice", 55.

erance by philosophy. Not only could this use of "tolerance" facilitate its opposite, also other key terms such as "respect", "reciprocity", and "legitimacy" lose their critical moral edge. In the end, the distinction between certifying "validity" through a critical examination by reason, and accepting mere existing opinion is levelled. The scrutiny of institutions is in danger of being replaced with an elucidation of current common sense in a bounded society.[101]

When practical reason becomes reduced to public reason, its own orientation towards the "highest good" with its internal connection to limit questions between reason and religion is disrupted. Placed in the realm opposite to public reason to which no internal link is assumed, the danger for religious comprehensive doctrines is that they could be turned into fideist instances of witnessing. Thus, theology has every interest in the radical reflection on the powers and limits of reason which Kant provides.

---

101 In "Public Reason", in S. Freeman (ed.), *The Cambridge Companion to Rawls* (Cambridge: CUP, 2003), 368–393, 377–78, Charles Larmore sees this objection as a misunderstanding: "If the nature of justice is to be defined by reference to what a society's members happen to agree upon, how can there be any room to argue that current opinion is wrong?... these worries are ill-conceived." Public reason will not just settle for an "appeal to the common denominator of existing opinion" because the conception of justice has its own independent basis established prior to its confirmation. Quoting from PL 64 and 140ff, he points out that Rawls distinguishes two "stages", the first of which is to establish "fair terms of cooperation among citizens"; the question of how to stabilize them in an overlapping consensus "only comes into play at this subsequent stage". Thus, each "person should have both sound and identical reasons to embrace them... Consensus so understood is therefore hardly identical to the extent of agreement about justice that actually obtains in a society." Thus, it is not a question of establishing this basis, but of how it "coheres with the comprehensive conceptions to which they are attached. Only if the consensus shaping their public reasoning about justice also forms an overlapping consensus, a common element in their otherwise different points of view, is the structure of their political life likely to endure... The notion of overlapping consensus serves therefore to connect a conception of justice already arrived at, and already marked by a more fundamental kind of consensus, to the question of its stability."

In my view, there are two reasons why even this priority of the principles cannot avert the danger of settling for the lowest common denominator: The "sound and identical reasons to embrace them" are not anchored in the human capability for morality, but only in a reciprocity that will be cancelled when the other is seen as breaching it. Secondly, in questions of application, as policy proposals are, it will be up to the "divergent visions of the human good" to concretize what liberty and equality mean, for example, in questions of disability. So while it is true that the "validating grounds" are not in the comprehensive doctrines, and the "conception of justice is freestanding", it is to discount citizens' own possible contributions, unique insights and their sustaining and renewing power if they are asked to "abstract" from them. The point whether it is possible to isolate "constitutional essentials" and "questions of basic justice" from the concrete questions of their everyday application, raised by Habermas, will be treated further in Part Two.

1.6 Religion in the limits of Rawls's concept of public reason

The opposition established between "comprehensive" and "public" made it difficult to see what links the two. Yet at the same time, Rawls thinks it possible that the two decisive criteria, liberty and equality, can be adopted by competing worldviews for internal reasons. At least here they can overlap, although they can neither understand each other, nor is there any general consciousness of truth to which they can relate. Herta Nagl-Docekal has pointed out the contradiction between the two assumptions of not being able to communicate, but still being able to overlap from internal sources.[102] Regarding communities of faith she suggests exploring the shared platform which philosophy of religion can establish.[103] In agreement with her analysis, I shall take as my starting point au-

---

102 It is worth quoting this objection in full from Nagl-Docekal, "'Many forms of nonpublic reason'? Religious diversity in liberal democracies", in H. Lenk (ed.), *Comparative and Intercultural Philosophy* (Berlin/Münster: LIT, 2009), 79–92, 90–91: Rawls asks, is "it possible... 'for citizens of faith to be wholehearted members of a democratic society' without having to struggle with an inner conflict? Rawls approaches this question in the following manner: While insisting that arguments concerning questions of fundamental political justice must be formulated in terms of 'public reason,' he states that this demand is not (necessarily) at odds with claims of faith. Religious people may, as their political statements appeal to the principles of 'liberty' and 'equality,' regard these principles, at the same time, as God-given commandments. While Rawls describes this possible congruence primarily with reference to Jewish-Christian conceptions, he does, in fact, include other religions as well... He suggests that, generally speaking, the manifold religious doctrines do agree on these two principles of justice. As is well known, he expresses the hope that there exists an 'overlapping consensus' among teachings that otherwise may be opposed to one another. Significantly, Rawls stresses that this consensus must not be understood as a compromise (for which all parties involved have abandoned some elements of their conviction), but rather as being based upon shared conviction.

Unfortunately, we do not find in Rawls a consistent theoretical basis for these views. To begin with, we are confronted with a contradiction. As mentioned before, Rawls at first characterizes religion as being shaped by a specific mode of reason, suggesting that, consequently, different religious convictions are bound to be incapable of mutual understanding. This point of view is, I think, hardly compatible with the assumption of an 'overlapping consensus'. But let us set aside this contradiction for a moment. We still face an open question: How could the assumed overlapping be accounted for? It seems unlikely that the consensus may be attributed to sheer chance – specifically, since Rawls maintains that the diverse religions do not vary in their overlapping with others, but do all agree on one and the same conception of 'liberty' and 'equality'. Obviously, Rawls draws upon an understanding of religion which implies that different doctrines share basic convictions. He fails, however, to explicitly define this conception."
103 Nagl-Docekal, "Many forms", 92, referring to the role given to churches in Kant's *Religion within the Boundaries of Reason Alone*: "I think that the way in which Kant constructs the encounter between the 'ethical commonwealth' and the given state would deserve to be examined with great care today. (In this context, it would also be important to critically discuss

tonomy in the moral sense and follow its connection to religion before analyzing how Rawls interprets Kant's dialectics of freedom as they appear in the concept of the highest good (1). Moving to receptions and critiques of Rawls's work within Christian Ethics, I shall compare two opposite views on the burdens public reason imposes on believers (2). Finally, the absence of enquiries into the interplay of reason and religion is traced back to a crucial dimension missing in his works: the history of formation of core intuitions of Western ethics, such as justice and mercy, responsibility and forgiveness in the encounters of Greek and Roman thought with biblical monotheism (3).

1.6.1 A philosophical approach to God: Kant's "highest good" and the antinomy of practical reason

Kant's division between duties of law and duties of virtue that led to the liberal distinction between the right and the good devises the priority of the right in a sense different from Rawls. While the right is established as foundational in terms of a morality of unconditional recognition of human beings as ends in themselves, the good is indeed seen as needing to align with the right, rather than detract from it, but not as divisive. There is no need to distance oneself from worldviews or communities of conviction in order to follow the moral law. The point is to establish autonomous freedom as the ground of moral obligation, instead of natural inclination, divine command, or traditional authorities;[104] yet, this insistence on the question of justification does not banish traditions of origin into a camp opposite to practical reason. Indeed, communities of virtue are welcomed as supportive for renewing motivations and not as replaceable by links at the level of legality.[105]

Kant's view that religion and reason can co-exist accords with one of the two conflicting positions held by Rawls. A "reasonable constitutional democracy" marked by liberty and equality can be accepted by religious groups in terms

---

Rawls's reading of Kant's conception of the 'highest good,' as he tends to interpret this conception predominantly in terms of a political perspective on the future.)"

104 Cf. O. O'Neill, "Kantian Ethics", in P. Singer (ed.), *Companion to Ethics*, 175: "His writings on ethics are marked by an unswerving commitment to human freedom, to the dignity of man, and to the view that moral obligation derives neither from God, nor from human authorities and communities, nor from the preferences or desires of human agents, but from reason."

105 Cf. Nagl-Docekal, "Eine rettende Übersetzung? Jürgen Habermas interpretiert Kants Religionsphilosophie", in: R. Langthaler/H. Nagl-Docekal (eds.), *Glauben und Wissen*, (Wien: Oldenbourg/Berlin: Akademie-Verlag, 2007), 93–119, 110–119.

of "the limits God sets to our liberty" (LP, 151). It may be doubtful both to qualify equal freedom as a limit, rather than as an implication of every member of humanity being created as *imago Dei* by God, and to rely on a divine command model for religious ethics, instead of one which reconstructs equality and justice, love and forgiveness as the creature's response to God's prevenient love. Yet, the correct point Rawls is driving at is that the overlapping consensus does not have to import foreign notions. Still, what remains missing, is to account for this possibility philosophically, and to establish at the same time that the question of meaning is one that connects all religions amongst each other and with philosophical anthropology. Nagl-Docekal refers to this as Kant's thesis that "all religions have their origin in the same need of reason".[106] However, to understand this "need" will involve a reflection on reason as the capacity for principles which does not stop short of limit questions. While Rawls keeps his theory of justice within the bounds of reciprocity, Nagl-Docekal's critique was that the Categorical Imperative expresses a different type of moral orientation which also holds in situations of asymmetry. Yet the readiness to offer unilateral recognition, for example, in histories of enmity, without calculating on a return, has a price: it ends in the antinomy of practical reason. For Kant, the highest good leads to the limit questions of moral agency which only the postulate of God's existence can contain. Before presenting Rawls's reading of it, the aporia practical reason runs into needs to be explained.

Kant reflects on the problem posed for the human quest for meaning or "happiness" when moral intentions encounter only hostility and fail. It is not the limit of human capacity experienced at the lower end, competing with self-interest, but at the highest level of morality, when its fulfillment is not something that more effort could attain, but something beyond human powers. It is here that the two meanings diverge which he distinguishes in the "highest good" (*summum bonum*) as the ultimate goal of willing. Doing everything in one's power constitutes the virtue of the *bonum supremum*. This is the part that is in human reach, and it makes them worthy of happiness (*glückswürdig*). Kant is ready to admit, however, that the deontological goal is not the end but points beyond itself to the hope of fulfillment: the "*bonum consummatum*" (*glückselig*) which is not at our disposal.[107] The gap experienced between moral effort and its failure risks turning morality into a vacuous and absurd idea.[108] As he repeats in *Religion within the Limits of Reason Alone:* "Yet an

---

106 Nagl-Docekal, "Moral und Religion", 854.
107 Cf. A. Anzenbacher's comparison of Kant's with Aristotle's concept of happiness and meaning in *Einführung in die Ethik* (Düsseldorf: Patmos, 1992), 151–55.
108 Kant, *Critique of Practical Reason*, trans. L. W. Beck (New York: Liberal Arts Press, 1956), 114.

end (*Zweck*) does arise out of morality; for how the question, *What is to result from this right conduct of ours?* is to be answered,... these cannot possibly be matters of indifference to reason."[109]

It is here that the postulate for the existence of God comes in. Hope in fulfillment is possible through a God who is the creator of a world which is open to moral effort; in contrast, a world in which one does the good in vain is the definition of absurdity.[110] Yet setting the *bonum supremum* of constant effort as the condition for fulfilled happiness could be misunderstood as a reward strategy: the *bonum consummatum* as the compensation for sacrifices undergone while struggling for the *bonum supremum*.

An interpretation of the antinomy in such empirical terms would miss the question posed by moral freedom of a "trans-moral" dimension of meaning.[111] It would also ignore that the postulate of the immortality of the soul can hardly be seen as a reward, constituting a never-ending quest to comply with the moral law. Kant's postulate of the immortality of the soul can be seen as a secularizing moralization of hope in a future that is opened up by God for each individual beyond their life span, confirming their irreplaceability. Against the functionalization of religion for morality in this postulate, it is all the more important that Kant's third question, "What may I hope for?" insists on the need of practical reason to see its best intentions redeemed. The theological ethicist Dietmar Mieth summarises the distinction of autonomous ethics between human freedom as the ground of obligation, and God as the ultimate ground of meaning as follows:

> The main feature of moral autonomy is simply a methodological separation of Kant's two questions, "What should I do?" and "What may I hope for?" The proof of moral obligation is methodologically independent of religious premises. On the other hand, it is clear that the ultimate interpretation of moral obligation leads into the question of faith... for Kant.[112]

How does Rawls deal with the problem of meaning in view of failure? Already in regard to his general concept of action, Onora O'Neill has observed that "reluctance to credit human agents with noumenal freedom lies behind Rawls's reluc-

---

109 Kant, *Religion Within the Limits of Reason Alone*, trans. Th. M. Greene and H. H. Hudson (New York: Harper & Brothers, 1960), 4.

110 This consciousness of a moral struggle that is necessary but will ultimately fail is what Albert Camus expresses in his later writings, especially in *The Plague*.

111 R. Langthaler, "Zur Interpretation und Kritik der Kantischen Religionsphilosophie bei Jürgen Habermas", in Langthaler/Nagl-Docekal (eds.), *Glauben und Wissen*, 46.

112 D. Mieth, "Autonomy of ethics", in *Concilium* 18 (1982), 35.

tance to go the whole way with Kant (TJ, 256 – 7)".[113] His consistent reduction to "the canons of reasonable empiricism"[114] is also evident in his treatment of this argument of Kant's. The limits and contradictions encountered by the moral subject, as Kant analyses them in the antinomy of practical reason, remain out of sight. Persons come into view as members of a polity; an analysis at the level of philosophical anthropology is seen as the domain of comprehensive doctrines, and their truth claims are left in suspension. The consequence of this approach in which "duties" or conditions for the public use of reason refer to the citizen, but not to the moral agent, is that public reason limits human reason as the capability for principles and as oriented towards the unconditional. It does not reach the radicality of Kant's questioning of the foundations of ethics. Rawls attempts to fill in the gap between sustained moral initiatives and the experience of their being thwarted with an unspecific hope in progress. In his lectures on moral philosophy he compares how the problem of the "highest good" is treated in the *Critique of Practical Reason* against the *Groundwork of the Metaphysics of Morals*. Interpreting them as alternative positions, he opts for the latter's orientation towards the "realm of ends" as the object of the moral law, and states his belief in a gradual ascent of history:

> When the object of the moral law is the secular ideal of a possible realm of ends, the basis for the postulates of God and immortality is far weaker."[115] In this case, it is sufficient to have "certain beliefs about our nature and the social world... a realm of ends is possible in the world only if the order of nature and social necessities are not unfriendly to that ideal. For this to be so, it must contain forces and tendencies that in the longer run tend to bring out, or at least to support, such a realm and to educate mankind as to further this end. We must believe, for example, that the course of human history is progressively improving, and not becoming steadily worse or that it does not fluctuate in perpetuity from bad to good and from good to bad (LM, 319 – 20)... The content of practical faith has now greatly changed. It fixes on nature's being (as we reasonably believe) not unfriendly to a realm of ends but instead conducive to it. (LM, 321)

This less ambitious goal, called in a departure from his classification of "secular" as a comprehensive doctrine, "the secular ideal of a possible realm of ends", is, as Rawls concludes correctly, not in need of a postulate of God. He admits the link between hope and faith in Kant:

---

113 O'Neill, *Bounds of Justice*, 45.
114 Rawls, "The basic structure as subject", in *American Philosophical Quarterly* 14 (1977), 159 – 65, 165, quoted by O. O'Neill, *Bounds of Justice*, 2.
115 Rawls, *Lectures on the History of Moral Philosophy*, ed. by B. Herman (Cambridge/Mass.: Univ. of Harvard Press, 2000), 318. (= LM, further page numbers in the text).

Without those religious beliefs, we might lose all hope that those who are just and good won't be pushed to the wall and come to think that the wicked and evil will dominate the world in the end. We lapse into cynicism and despair, and abandon the values of peace and democracy, since it is a need of reason, it might be said, to believe that there will be a certain matching, if not exact proportionality, between moral worth and happiness. (LM, 322)

His own solution is not to push the desire for happiness too far and to retreat from Kant's reasonable faith in order to "uphold our moral integrity" (LM, 322) with less demanding conditions.

Already in *Theory of Justice*, agency did not include the experience of its internal limits, nor was the transformative potential of unilateral, innovative action explored. When Rawls is willing to concede to adherents of religious comprehensive doctrines the "proviso" of initially using religious expressions which are then to be translated into equivalent political ones, it is not because religions have a unique contribution to make to the practice of public reason. This is where the two theological ethicists to be treated next disagree with him; they explicate the self-understanding of the Christian faith as a comprehensive doctrine in relation to its contemporary setting as a concretization and challenge that a pluralist democracy needs.

1.6.2 A proviso and translations in due course – how attractive for religions?

The two contrasting responses from theological ethics to his proposal to be discussed now present the Christian faith tradition as an indispensable source for public reason (1), and a necessary correction of it (2).

1.6.2.1 Addressing the hermeneutical deficit of procedural theories of justice: Christian sources of identity formation (Elke Mack)

The Catholic moral theologian Elke Mack begins her 2002 investigation entitled *Justice and the Good Life* by tracing the distinction between the right and the good from Kant to contemporary political ethics. She analyses the distinctive requirements of justification of each in terms of their scope: under modern conditions, the good life refers to the individual's sphere of action, the just relates to structural questions which belong to the sphere of law.[116] In complex mass soci-

---

116 Cf. E. Mack, *Gerechtigkeit und gutes Leben. Christliche Ethik im politischen Diskurs* (Paderborn: Schöningh, 2002), 60. Further page numbers will be included in the text. She later

eties, individual virtue is not enough.[117] To set them into a complete dichotomy, however, ignores how significant the institutional level regulated by norms of justice is for the formation of personal identity. The interplay between the two manifests itself when questions of personal responsibility and structural issues intersect (36–37), and when deficient conditions result in the inability to achieve a good life, as problems like homelessness show (105).

In view of the modern pluralism of basic orientations, the norms of justice can only be established by means of procedure, rather than of a substantive consensus. The task therefore is to find agreement on the basic principles that govern society, as Rawls's *Theory of Justice* attempts to do. The normative theory for creating the basic conditions for everyone's life plan is restricted to the structural level. What remains outstanding is to make it possible for individuals to develop their identities. Here, the irreplaceable function of worldviews comes in. Rawls's acknowledgement of the role of comprehensive doctrines is the reason why Elke Mack sees his proposal as more accommodating to religions than, for example, discourse ethics, which in her view pays too little attention to concepts of the good and to the bridge between the two types of moral theory.[118] In her analysis, it is Rawls who allows worldviews a full role for the task complementary to creating just structures, namely supporting the formation of identities. Her question is whether these consistent background views, among them religions, can also speak at the moral, universalizable level of the right, rather than only the good: "Does Christian Ethics have to restrict itself to being an ethical theory of justice in the political context?" (14) Drawing in many perceptive contributions from contemporary moral theological debate, the book asks about the capability of the Christian faith to participate in democratic society and contribute to generalizable norms of justice without "giving up the core of its own message of faith" (10). Before looking at her answers regarding the present significance of the Christian heritage and practice, I shall examine how her reconstruction of political liberalism compares to the assessments treated so far.

---

specifies her understanding of how individual theories of the good relate to a consistent comprehensive one. Cf. 281–85.

117 Mack, *Gerechtigkeit*, 80–81: "In a large anonymous society justice can no longer be secured sufficiently through individual virtue... the structural turn of modern ethics sees morality (*Moral*) in a society primarily secured through institutions and law."

118 Mack, *Gerechtigkeit*, 119–20 and 145: "In contrast to discourse ethics, the level of comprehensive theories of the good as provided by worldviews, is not left out in political liberalism." Her book was published only just after Habermas received the Peace Prize of the German Book Trade in Frankfurt a few weeks after September 11, 2001. The most recent stage of his thinking on religion, as put forward in his speech on Faith and Knowledge (*Glauben und Wissen*) has thus not been included.

Elke Mack carefully counters the incorrect conclusions that could be drawn from the experience of pluralism. The fact that moral positions feed from a "pluralism of humanisms" does not mean that morality itself is relative (12–13, n. 18). Distinguishing the critically tested validity (*Gültigkeit*) of norms from their factual acceptance (*Geltung*), she agrees that the confirmation they receive through consensus renders them effective, but does not itself validate moral principles (cf. 13). The method of agreement is not simply by majority decision or political compromise but expresses "the normative claim that in developed democratic constitutional states all societal groupings and all affected citizens can agree on the principles of essential political strategies for solutions" (10). What is the moral basis of this agreement?

Here, Elke Mack decides to follow the approach of "ethical constructivism which has taken a political turn in modern theory of justice" (28). She traces the process of reception of Kant's universalization principle for defining duties of law to the "consensus paradigm" (76). Its advantage over Kant is that it is exercized "not only in theoretical reflection, but at a practical-constitutive level through the agreement of all potentially affected people" (76). The "moral standpoint" consists in the question, "what can be justified reciprocally and universally, so to speak, in a hypothetical consensus" (76). Thus a "converging will to agree on just norms" (133) is manifested. Kant's original proposal has been modified by "two restrictions: by limiting moral theory to questions of justice, and of justice to political justice, that is, the framework conditions" (142). The new paradigm offers a "more modest and more cautious version of justification" and "pays the price of a more encompassing validity (*Gültigkeit*) with its limitation to political justice" (142). While the "formal" character of Kant's "claims, especially with regard to the constitution of duties of law" and the "internal connection between law and morality" (50) have been maintained, they have been "enlarged" into an "intersubjective social theory" (58). It stipulates society's duty of law towards its individual citizens (cf. 58).

For Mack, the new shape makes the theory of justice fit for purpose as an "institutionally converted ethics of large modern democratically constituted societies" (142). She correctly observes that political liberalism "restricts itself by withdrawing from a comprehensive metaphysical but also from a comprehensive philosophical foundational theory of the good, and limits itself to the framework conditions. It does not offer a contrasting programme, but a complement" to the good (135). While her sympathetic discussion of Rawls is conducted at a highly differentiated, learned and careful level as a constructive engagement of Christian social ethics with his political ethics, it is evident that it does not share the assumptions of the Kantian critics quoted so far. The modifications of the Kantian framework are seen as its necessary adaptation to complex democracies, not as reductions of depth and scope. My objections to her affirmative reception of Rawls are similar to those directed at his own approach: how a restricted use of the terms "moral", "universal", and "law" affects the overall understanding of constitutional democracy and its highest principle, human dignity.

Compared to the previous discussion of Herta Nagl-Docekal's and Onora O'Neill's critiques, one striking feature of this account is that it understands obligation only with regard to law. It does not explain its prior foundation on the morality found in and expected from everyone as a fellow-human being, not only as a fellow-citizen. The question, however, remains, whether a justification can be called "universal" (e. g., 50. 297) if it originates in a contract between avowedly self-interested "rational" agents, concluded in a bounded society marked by excluding the non-native other, and thus stopping short of the original cosmopolitan scale of Kant's roadmap for peace between republics? While she notes the restriction of Kant's moral theory to framework conditions of political justice, its effect, the reduction in the scale and quality of moral obligation as the original experience of encountering an "ought" towards oneself and others, is not mentioned. Mack refers to the "unconditional moral claim raised by Kant for duties of law" but affirms that his concept of duty and the contemporary use of the concepts of "rights and justice" are "similar in their determination of content and in the degree of their binding character (*Verbindlichkeit*) (58). Kant's distinction between the "moral law", the true basis of universality, and mere external laws, called "legality", is not investigated. Neither is the ambivalence of the term "political" reflected: that it concretizes the demands of universal morality on the one hand, but on the other reduces it to the horizon of generalized citizens who may be moved by nothing but self-interest in their own polity. If the justification of norms, especially of those which establish "just restrictions" (142), is built on procedure, their legitimacy is affected if the process itself is marked by tacit diminutions and exclusions. A method constrained to arguing from a contextual foundation in liberal democracies and conceiving of human rights as gradational does not really qualify as "universal". There is a danger that the term "democracy" is being charged with a justificatory task that it could only deliver if it was filled with the goal of protecting human dignity. Is it enough to state that "the societal order can only avail of (*verfügt... über*) the formal constitutional principle: protection of human dignity" (107)? Mack mentions "historical experiences of suffering and violations of human dignity" (107) and draws attention to the definition and status of personhood as one problem to be addressed also by the resources of the comprehensive doctrines (110. 331). Yet by allowing contemporary debate on justice to split Kant's theory of law from its foundation in morality, she loses the possibility of recognizing this principle as more than formal, namely as already filled by an understanding of humans as moral and vulnerable beings. The one candidate of convergence to a shared, rather than just an overlapping consensus, human dignity, is replaced with the principle of a democracy based on contract terms. How it affects religions if this is all they are expected and allowed to contribute to, will have to be asked at the end.

The fact that these two possible foundations, human dignity or contract, are not equivalent, becomes clear when the motivation attributed to citizens is examined. Mack greets the achievement of political thought since the Enlightenment to identify as central the task of securing elementary freedom and social rights (108). She sees the success of contract theory in establishing "how individuals of the same rank can come to an agreement" (108). That the basis of this is a reciprocity so strict that the agreement breaks down when one partner defaults, is not marked as a problem, although the section is subtitled as "The problem of the conditions of preserving liberal constitutional states" (108). Citizens are entitled to judge between what can be expected of them (*zumutbar*), and what can be rejected as an imposition. We shall see in the following chapter how Jürgen Habermas identifies as a core problem the degeneration that takes place when citizens use universal rights as "individual liberties... exclusively against one another like weapons".[119] Mack defends the liberal agreement on reciprocal-symmetrical terms with the argument that requirements to which one submits others need stronger reasons than those to which one submits oneself: "An ethics which wants to set just rules has to be intersubjectively binding (*verbindlich*), but also able to be generally imposed as acceptable (*zumutbar*)." (60) Symmetry becomes a condition: "individual rights to claims (*Anspruchsrechte*) have to be guaranteed, otherwise the people affected would not agree to certain norms of justice." (77)

Herta Nagl-Docekal has pointed out that a moral motivation is distinct from one that restricts itself to upholding legality, and that the first is foundational for the second. Thus expectations to moral beings should be exactly the same; the Categorical Imperative not to instrumentalize each other holds both for agents with regard to themselves and to others, and in personal as well as in public life. The point that moral and legal obligation cannot be reduced to each

---

119 J. Habermas, "Prepolitical foundations of the constitutional state?", in *Between Naturalism and Religion*, trans. C. Cronin (Cambridge: Polity Press, 2008), 101–113, 107: The "uncontrolled modernization of society could certainly corrode democratic bonds and undermine the form of solidarity on which the democratic state depends even though it cannot enforce it. Then the very constellation that Böckenförde has in mind would transpire, namely, the transformation of the citizens of prosperous and peaceful liberal societies into isolated, self-interested monads who use their individual liberties exclusively against one another like weapons".

other is manifested in the motivation to do what is right also when it is not reciprocated and the symmetry condition is broken.

As a consequence of this Kantian critique of Mack's position, a further claim has to be refuted, namely the presupposition of "political constructivism that the principles of justice on which reasonable persons agree in a fair procedure fulfill all the requirements of practical reason" (28). If this claim was granted, it would mean an enormous reduction. The replacement of a theory of morality by a theory of legality, as observed as problematic by Herta Nagl-Docekal, would be complete, and the near-identification of practical reason with law ratified. To elevate the principles of justice to the level where the highest good is situated in Kant, is problematic both for moral philosophical and for theological reasons. If "all requirements" can be met, does that include the two components of perfect virtue and corresponding happiness? Is the antinomy of practical reason still admitted, or is the question of fulfillment toned down to chances of pragmatic steps of progress? If theological ethics, as distinct from philosophy of religion, ceases to recognize the radical nature of Kant's questioning, who else is there to defend the need to keep open the unanswered limit questions of practical reason?

Finally, her assessment that because the overlapping consensus contains insights from religious and metaphysical worldviews, it "reaches further than the universalizable normative level" (145–46) equally has to be challenged. In my view, it remains below the level of morality, conforming to the anticipation of what generalized citizens might accept if their expectations of a symmetrical give and take have been met. It diminishes religions if their resources are only to serve a society which limits justice to its own boundaries, indeed, its own fortress.

I shall now turn to Mack's description of the concrete contribution of Christian ethics to contemporary discourses on just policies. It has already become clear that religions can have a bearing on public debate via the overlapping consensus, but also that their scope has been constricted. It will be necessary to ask whether a contract basis can produce what Mack assumes, namely a participative democracy. Rawls's critique of Taylor's "civic humanism" shows the need to check whether such an interest in participation in civil society and in the empowerment this may require can be assumed, or whether it is an optimizing reading that may be disappointed. All these open questions are factors in the decision of how acceptable and attractive political liberalism is for comprehensive doctrines. If the core of the message of faith is not to be renounced, how can it bring its potential to bear on the process of finding an overlapping consensus?

For Mack, the main lacuna of political liberalism is the "hermeneutical deficit" typical of procedural theories of justice. A "comprehensive Christian theory of the good" can address this gap for its own constituents and can thus supply the liberal state with a motivation for cooperation and solidarity. It is sustained by a hermeneutics of meaning which is based on its "reference to transcendence" (305–07). It "recontextualizes morality" (cf. 307–10) and offers a "rational approach to the themes of an ethically good life" (313–15), thus "stabilising legal persons and the foundations of law" (328–32). It promotes citizens' responsibility for shaping the polity (*Förderung staatsbürgerlicher Gestaltungsverantwortung*), yet also provides a "heuristics for a universal ethics" (288), for "political justice" (336–338) and "constructive criticism through a counterfactual perspective" (334–36). Mack conceives of the Christian and the Catholic institutional presence in society mainly as an intellectually respectable and resourceful complement that fills the structures of justice agreed on contractually with motivation and specificity. In directing justice towards love (cf. 339–41), it expresses its original calling by God. Especially since the Second Vatican Council it has been "open to a post-conventional discourse of ethics" (298–99). Defending the "modern difference between comprehensive worldviews and formal universalizable ethics of law," she judges with reference to *Gaudium et Spes*: "Even Christian Ethics will be interested in this difference since its research goals include the universal implications of just norms for all human beings in order to enable peaceful coexistence" (299–300). It is clear that her reading of Rawls is marked by trust in the "productivity of a universalizable morality of justice" (299) towards which Christian hermeneutics has a "debt of delivery" (*Bringschuld*, 301). In view of the more critical receptions by other philosophical and theological conversation partners, it is difficult to share her assessment that this is what Rawls's work achieves. I shall now turn to a theological ethical treatment which comes to opposite conclusions, and assess these in view of Mack's position and of the critiques from Kantian philosophers.

1.6.2.2 Self-restriction by religions on what basis? (Stefan Grotefeld)

Elke Mack's assessment that Rawls's idea of an overlapping consensus is successful in forging the much-needed connection between the right and the good was based on a division of labour: agreeing on principles for a just framework, on the one hand, and supplying the cultural background which nourishes the formation of personal identities, on the other: "Since… pluralism as such is affirmed, the proper (*eigentlich*) task to create complete identities is left to other forces, namely reasonable worldviews and institutions." (145) Religious comprehensive doctrines can also reach the public sphere through the political conceptions they develop. In her reading, this does not happen in isolation; she sees exchange and debate between worldviews as welcome elements of his theory. Quoting Rawls's positive reference to concepts of Catholic Social Teaching in

The Idea of Public Reason Revisited,[120] and his answers to David Hollenbach (270), her conclusion seems to be that the only condition imposed on religions is one they should be happy to meet, being one voice in the pluralism of constitutional democracies.

A counterposition to her view that his conception provides a "successful attempt of an answer to the problem of pluralism" (145) by not sidelining religions is taken by the Protestant theological ethicist Stefan Grotefeld. His detailed analysis of the English-speaking legal, philosophical and theological debate on the role which religious convictions are allowed to play in the public sphere and of its reception and critique in Protestant social ethics is conducted under the term "self-restriction" (*Selbstbeschränkung*). Unlike Elke Mack who sets out from an overview of the general relationship between the right and the good in Kant and in recent political philosophy, he begins his enquiry with the question: "Are we morally obliged to exclude or bracket (*aus- oder einzuklammern*) our religious convictions when we make political decisions?"[121] How does he make his case that from the perspective of comprehensive doctrines it is not an attractive but an unacceptable offer to be asked to distance oneself from the core of one's faith message in order to be able to gain access to the level of public reason?

Grotefeld begins his enquiry into *Religious Convictions in the Liberal State. Protestant Ethics and the Requirements of Public Reason* by diagnosing two camps. For the first, represented by Richard Rorty, "recourse to particular convictions... endangers social stability since their arguments are not accessible" to citizens of no faith or of other faiths. The contrasting view, for which Stephen Carter is quoted, is that they provide "important moral resources" and that their exclusion from the political public sphere would ask religious persons to act in a "schizophrenic" way (11). Grotefeld identifies as the core point of the argument of legitimacy that "every person deserves the same consideration and respect", and that "unjustified constraints" have to be excluded (15). His target is a specifically liberal understanding of the moral legitimacy of the political exercise of power. He judges perceptively that framing the issue in terms of an al-

---

120 "It is remarkable and significant for the reception of Rawls's theory of justice within Christian social ethics that he sees a special connection between Catholic Social Teaching which is based on a specific concept of the common good and the principle of solidarity, and his own approach" (194), quoting him (194, n. 154): "Political Liberalism (...) admits Catholic views of the common good and solidarity when they are expressed in terms of political values." (LP, 142)
121 S. Grotefeld, *Religiöse Überzeugungen im liberalen Staat. Protestantische Ethik und die Anforderungen öffentlicher Vernunft* (Stuttgart: Kohlhammer, 2006), 11. Further page numbers are included in the text.

ternative between the positive function of religious resources and the imposition (*Zumutung*) they mean in a pluralist society underdetermines the problem (cf. 27). The crucial point is the "essential feature of liberalism... that legitimating reasons have to be able to be accepted by everyone" (27). The conclusion liberalism draws is that religious – and possibly other comprehensive – worldviews have to restrict themselves, since "under pluralist conditions they are not shared by all" and are thus "not fit to justify political regulations... any exercise of political power invoking them is said to be illegitimate" (34).

In a nuanced presentation of the course of the English-speaking debate, Grotefeld investigates the premises that lead to the position of limiting the access of worldviews either to civic opinion formation, or political decision making, or both. His principal avenue towards discounting the argument for restriction is to question the alleged difference between "public" and "comprehensive". Thus, his objection goes in a different direction than the previous Kantian critiques of Rawls's empirical and overlapping understanding of "public" which did not reach the level of the universalizing reflection of morality. Grotefeld, by contrast, argues for the equal right of all worldviews to unrestricted access also to matters of political decision-making. For him, there is no difference between the universal level of moral arguments that everyone can share, and the particular insights of communities of conviction. The "epistemological premise of the liberal thesis of neutrality" that there is a "fundamental asymmetry between questions of the right and... the good" (178) is challenged. Commenting on Rawls's own procedure in *Theory of Justice*, he emphasizes the role of "considered convictions" in the "reflective equilibrium" against the first foundation sought for the principles of justice in the contract concluded in the original position (cf. 192, n. 20).

He agrees to the significance of worldviews for identity formation, which was the crucial argument in Mack's complementarity thesis, but denies their difference from the level of "reason". The insightful comments he quotes open up a debate that was becoming predictable to new arrays of questions. They put on the agenda the task of specifying the criteria for what "respect" under the conditions of pluralism can mean. Nicholas Wolterstorff's contributions are summarized as pointing out that "the respect that citizens owe to each other does not require a self-restriction concerning their religious convictions which levels their particular identities" (25). A similar point is made regarding the criterion of "reciprocity" which does not have to be interpreted as keeping to already accepted and "plain truths", rather than "whole truths". Lawrence Solum is quoted as revealing a different understanding of discourse in his 1993 comment:

"Such respect does not mean only giving other citizens reasons which they already accept as true. Treating others as free and equal does not mean catering to existing beliefs and desires; indeed, one could argue that catering only (*sic*) existing beliefs and desires is disrespectful because it treats others as unreasonable." (36, n. 5).

These insights are much to be welcomed. The categorization of truth as being either "plain" and accessible, or "whole" and inaccessible simplifies the democratic process of finding solutions to an undifferentiated choice between "common sense" and encompassing "doctrines". This disjunction does not foresee any intermediate position between already accepted values and insights from different worldviews; it does not allow for a quest for truth or even competition in an open forum of ideas. The moral demand for reciprocal respect does not include the self-understandings of the conversation partners.

Grotefeld's main argument against liberal public reason assuming the role of gatekeeper is that all we have are convictions, so the playing field should be a level one. This view is close to Rawls's own, that all we have are comprehensive doctrines, and there is no general consciousness of truth that they can relate to. He only objects to Rawls's insistence on the need to find a different, neutral, basis for legislation and political decision-making that affect all members of a pluralist society. While Mack accepts the reduction of morality to theory of law, and then adds the notions of the good that religions provide as crucial elements of concrete policy decisions, Grotefeld levels the difference between generally accessible and comprehensive or religious reasons.

An example of his view that "universalist" positions need to be superseded is his comment on Wolfgang Huber's interpretation of the distinction between the Golden Rule and the Christian idea of love. Having discussed different positions in Protestant social ethics on the Golden Rule and on human rights as a level of convergence, he refers to love of enemy as extending beyond (*Überbietung*) the principle of reciprocity. In Huber's treatment, when the Golden Rule is understood from the perspective of the Sermon on the Mount, it becomes

> much more than simple common sense. It shows how love makes use of reason without being exhausted in general reasonableness. It opens the way to making the radicality of love of enemy practical in steps of 'intelligent love of enemy'. It thus also discloses the way towards showing how love can use the reciprocity of the law without forgetting, however, that the unilateralism (*Einseitigkeit*) of love is never exhausted in this reciprocity.[122]

Grotefeld concludes from these theological ethical analyses that when the Golden Rule is thus "interpreted, it loses its universal character" (102). Rather than

---

122 Huber, *Gerechtigkeit und Recht*, 212, quoted by Grotefeld, 102.

losing it, one could equally see it as being interpreted in a superlative and, as Paul Ricoeur points out, hyperbolic way. It remains valid and continues to be a necessary counterpart to the "hyperethical" demand of love, as Ricoeur's analysis of this dialectical relationship shows.

Grotefeld's critique of the need for a level of general justification for intended policy proposals leads to the question of the "institutional threshold" that demarcates the spheres of a postsecular society and the neutral state in Habermas's position. His theological analysis highlights some of the distinctive traits and insights that are lost for public reason when the plural sources of identity formation and their different visions for society in its global relations are left out of such debates. If these traditions were explored and compared in their historical encounters and their existing exchanges, rather than being classified and kept apart under the formal label "comprehensive doctrine", the reservoir of their creative re-interpretations would become available, and "public reason" would be enlivened. Yet, by only allowing for communities of conviction, Grotefeld takes a position that is as culturalist as Rawls's. A different avenue would be to support the distinction between society and state, assume (with Karl Jaspers's thesis of the axial age) a shared genealogy of world religions and systems of reason, and acknowledge the interplay between universalism and particularity in the development of Western values and principles; this is the new direction Habermas has taken since 2000. While observations on the genealogy of concepts do not replace the question of their validity, these origins offer an instructive avenue to understanding their contents; tracing the formation of modern ethics to the history of encounter between antique intellectual traditions and monotheism provides insights into historical turning points.

1.6.3 The sources of public reason – free-standing, or indebted to a history of formation?

Rawls appreciates the normative heritage latent within democratic political culture. Already in *Theory of Justice*, it supplied the contextual part of the foundation of the two principles. The second book as well drew on input from citizens' worldviews to their public reasoning. It made it possible, as Onora O'Neill summarizes, to establish certain principles as legitimate and stable ways of organising the basic structure of a given society by showing that they will be endorsed by its citizens' public reasoning and expressed in its public political culture.[123]

Its function as a stock of cultural resources is suggested: We look "to our public political culture... as the shared fund of implicitly recognised basic ideas and principles" (PL, 228). Yet, when it comes to identifying which traditions have interacted to create this culture, Rawls is reticent in his answers. His interest in the overlap as an outcome rather than in the processes of cross-determination of key terms tends to exclude hermeneutical and comparative perspectives. The very diversity of the traditions in which they originate could have been valued in their productive tension. The lack of attention to religious factors that drove historical developments results in a simplified picture; the religious background especially of a universalizing understanding of social justice is rarely mentioned, in contrast to other philosophers, such as Ludwig Siep, who attributes its role in Western ethics to a "concrete history of values" in Jewish and Christian monotheism.[124] It is instructive in this context how the abolitionists' use of their religious convictions, above all the view of every human being as *imago Dei*, in the 19th century North American struggle against slavery is examined and judged as defensible by Rawls within a situation when "a society is not well ordered and there is a profound division about constitutional essentials".[125] By "basing their arguments on religious grounds" (PL, 249) when making the case against slavery already in the 1830s,

> the comprehensive doctrines they appealed to were required to give sufficient strength to the political conception to be subsequently realized... given the comprehensive doctrines they held and the doctrines current in their day, it was necessary to invoke the comprehensive grounds on which those values were widely seen to rest. (PL, 251)

In view of this admission of the significance of religious arguments "for a well-ordered society to come about in which public discussion consists mainly in the

---

123 O'Neill, "Method", in Höffe (ed.), *John Rawls*, 41.

124 L. Siep, "Moral und Gattungsethik", in *Deutsche Zeitschrift für Philosophie* 50 (2002) 111–120, 113, n. 5.

125 Rawls, *Political Liberalism*, 248–252, 249. In n. 38, he quotes W. E. Channing's argument for the abolition of slavery, in *Slavery*, 3rd ed. 1836: "He cannot be property in the sight of God and justice, because he is a Rational, Moral, Immortal Being, because created in God's image, and therefore in the highest sense his child, because created to unfold god-like faculties, and to govern himself by a Divine Law written on his heart, and republished in God's word. From his very nature it follows that so to seize him is to offer an insult to his Maker, and to inflict aggravated social wrong."

appeal to political values" (PL, 251, n. 41), is it possible to maintain that the difference principle is the product of a fictitious original position? Or could the idea of including compensation for unequal starting points into the task of justice also be owed to universalistic monotheistic values such as justice and compassion that originated in the Jewish prophetic tradition and in the emphasis on active mercy in Christianity?[126]

In conclusion, the task to examine the roots of the different traditions and life forms that are partners in the overlapping consensus remains undeveloped in Rawls. The historical encounters, processes of communication and the great translations out of which Western culture originated will surface in Part Three on Ricoeur. He assesses the hidden debt and the lines of continuity between Rawls's proposal and the normative orders and institutions that were generated in Mediterranean and European cultural history in the interaction with biblical monotheism. His analysis can serve as a transition to the enquiries of Parts Two and Three into Habermas's and Ricoeur's understandings of practical reason and religion in the public sphere: Rawls's

> "overlapping consensus" intersects with several cultural traditions: in addition to the project of the Enlightenment which Habermas rightly judges to be "incomplete", it encounters the reinterpreted forms of Jewish, Greek, and Christian traditions that have successfully undergone the critical test of *Aufklärung*. There is nothing better to offer, in reply to the legitimation crisis,... than the memory and the intersection in the public space of the appearance of the traditions that make room for tolerance and pluralism, not out of concessions to external pressures, but out of inner conviction, even if this is late in coming. It is by calling to mind all the beginnings and all the rebeginnings, and all the traditions that have been sedimented upon them, that "good counsel" can take up the challenge of the legitimation crisis.[127]

While Rawls is content with drawing on the normative understandings implicit in the public political culture of Western democracies, Ricoeur engages in a hermeneutical enquiry into the sources of these norms. He agrees with Habermas that the project of modernity is unfinished, and that it continues to be a learning process; indeed, that the present owes a debt to the past and that sources of renewal can be discerned from previous cultural encounters and conflicts. How each of them conceives of agency and language, reason and religion, discourse and traditions of interpretation in the public sphere, will be investigated in the following two parts.

---

126 Cf. F. Schüssler Fiorenza, "The works of mercy: theological perspectives", in *The Works of Mercy: New Perspectives on Ministry*, ed. F. A. Eigo (Philadelphia: Villanova Press, 1992), 31–71.
127 Ricoeur, *Oneself as Another*, 261.

Introduction to Parts Two and Three

What unites the two philosophers to be treated in Parts Two and Three is an awareness that religious traditions as part of the worldviews of citizens have to be able to articulate their insights, rather than only offer tacit support within a society oriented towards justice. Habermas and Ricoeur also both identify "mutual recognition" as the normative core of ethics in modernity which implies a critique of instrumental or calculating reason. They each devise a social anthropology which emphasizes role-taking and the significance of the other for the self, and an understanding of the importance of the heritage of shared meanings in the lifeworld, including the historical dimension of the encounter between "Athens" and "Jerusalem" in the translations that created European culture. Moving from anthropology to political ethics, they agree that democracy as a joint project aims at more than mere stability; it is motivated by a surplus or a utopian element in its histories of foundation and is oriented towards an idea of citizenship that links the local and the cosmopolitan. Their positions contrast with Rawls's limiting of justice to a bounded society. Philosophy draws on existing meanings, self-understandings, and practical initiatives, and it represents the faculty of critical self-reflection. Habermas explicitly highlights philosophy's role as mediator to the lifeworld, and the capacity for self-reflection which it brings to the collaboration with the social sciences and the humanities. For both, religion has the potential to be a resource rather than an obstacle to achieving a justifiable political consensus. They emphasize the dimension of hope which invigorates a reason that is becoming "defeatist", and the sensitivity of religion for pathologies and failure. Ricoeur also explores its unique promise of forgiveness.

Differences between their approaches will become clear in their theories of agency: Habermas keeps the "moral" and the "ethical" uses of reason separate. For Ricoeur, the entry point for ethics is individual striving for a flourishing life in Aristotelian terms which finds a counterpart in Kant's idea of the "good will"; the French philosopher explores the unsubstitutible role of narrative identity for morality, and the necessary "detour" of hermeneutical reason through cultural traditions which are much more than conventional life forms. It is necessary to take the long road through myths and stories to articulate the great questions of origin and destiny, of evil and of meaning, of self and other. Cultures supply resources on which future renewals depend. How the use of reason in the public realm is envisaged, is affected by the strands they select from their shared philosophical heritage.

2 Practical reason in the public sphere: Jürgen Habermas's rehabilitation of religion as a resource within the project of modernity

Jürgen Habermas's discourse theory, the second approach to be examined for the relation it envisages between religion and public reason, has equally been developed as a reconceptualization of Kant's deontological ethics. Several of the differences of his project to Rawls's liberal enterprise are relevant to his rediscovery of religion as a source of regeneration for the normative projects of modernity and of resistance against a growing imbalance between system and lifeworld. Before discussing his new view of religion with its call for mutual cooperation between religious and secularized fellow-citizens in translating intuitions from religions in section 4, I shall begin by outlining the normative framework. Habermas's theory of communicative reason understands agency as communicative action and as discourse in the public realm, developed in the "postmetaphysical" categories that the changed role of philosophy demands (1). Next to be examined are the anthropology and the theory of action implied in communicative reason. In his interactive concept of rationality he differs from Rawls; in his reliance on the shared meanings and socializing contributions of the lifeworld he assumes cultural foundations similar to the basis Rawls employs besides the contract, namely considered convictions. The fact of pluralism is traced back to structural factors in society rather than to burdens of judgement, and their effects on the lifeworld are analysed. One of the new roles for philosophy is to counteract the impoverishment caused by this segmentation (2). The key difference of his understanding of the use of reason in the public sphere comes out in his debate with Rawls on the crucial link of public reason to a participative concept of democracy. Distinguishing between principled justifiability and empirical acceptance, his alternative to a merely overlapping consensus is justification through discursive deliberation on the universalizability of proposed norms (3). From a normative understanding of modernity marked by the principles of self-determination and mutual recognition, the semantic and action-guiding potential of religion is seen as a resource. The danger of a "derailing" modernity needs to be countered with mentalities of "solidarity".[128] Religion offers a language and vision of an un-failed life against the pathologies of late modern societies, among them the logics of objectification and commercialization.

---

128 Cf. Habermas, "Prepolitical foundations of the constitutional state?", in *Between Naturalism and Religion*, 101–113, 107. 111.

Habermas insists that religion is not a priori irrational, and that believers have a right to contribute to the public sphere from their particular identities. Religious objections to new technological developments are seen as indications that a more profound debate of their effects on normative achievements, such as children's rights, is needed, and are accorded the "delaying veto"[129] of an early warning system. Thus, religions are sought as conversation partners not for their functional value but for contents that only they can provide. At the same time, by describing them as "opaque" and as "dogmatically encapsulated", they are given a place opposite to reason in its general accessibility. Their status of "discursive exterritoriality"[130] is part of the argument against Rawls's proviso. Theological assessments of this new understanding of religion in relation to reason (4) will conclude Part Two.[131]

2.1 The normative framework: The foundations of discourse ethics

The new starting point of the critical theory of the Frankfurt School that Habermas has elaborated since the 1960s is his rediscovery of the communicative capacity of reason; it marks the third phase of critical theory and reconnects with the interdisciplinary framework set out at the beginning by Max Horkheimer and Theodor W. Adorno. Their subsequent diagnosis of the total eclipse of a reason which had become purely instrumental, put forward in the *Dialectic of Enlightenment* written at the time of the Holocaust, is traced by Habermas also to the dualistic categories of the philosophy of consciousness. Seeking an alternative foundation, he reconceives the faculty of reason as embodied in linguistically

---

129 The ET of "*aufschiebendes Veto*" from "Faith and Knowledge", in *The Future of Human Nature,* trans. W. Rehg/M. Pensky/H. Beister (Cambridge: Polity Press, 2003), 109, uses a weaker expression, "dilatory plea".

130 Cf. Habermas, "Religion in the public sphere: Cognitive presuppositions for the 'public use of reason' by religious and secular citizens", in *Between Naturalism and Religion*, 114–147, 130.

131 I have treated the discussion of the different stages of his discourse theory and its reception and critique by German-speaking philosophers and theologians in greater detail in *Habermas and Theology* (London/New York: T & T Clark International, 2011). Some points of comparison with Rawls are outlined in "Witnessing or mutual translation? Religion and the requirements of reason", in L. Hogan/S. Lefebvre/N. Hintersteiner/F. Wilfred (eds.), *From World Mission to Interreligious Witness, Concilium* 2011/1 (London: SCM, 2011), 105–114. I shall extend my previous analyses with more specific comparisons to Rawls and Ricoeur, and by adding further responses from theologians as well as points he makes in the most recent explanation of his position in *Nachmetaphysisches Denken II* (Frankfurt: Suhrkamp, 2012), published so far only in German.

structured communication (1). The "paradigm change" to language from the "introspective" categories that marked the transcendental and idealistic approaches of German Idealism raises the question of the capacity of philosophy to offer such analyses. Many of its functions have been taken over by the natural and the social sciences. After clarifying the specific roles that remain in the competence of philosophy (2), his concept of "postmetaphysical" thinking, reconfirmed recently against the critiques of the last 25 years, will be treated in its relevance for the understanding of morality and of religion (3).

2.1.1 The basis of communicative rationality: Reason as embodied in language

The basis from which the interactive capacity of reason arises is a universal, distinctive feature of human beings: language. It is the potential for rationality embodied in language with its ability to forge mutual understanding that Habermas brings to bear against the result of Horkheimer's and Adorno's critique of instrumental reason that "denounce(s) the whole as the untrue".[132] He attributes its analysis of the complete transformation of reason into an instrument of domination also to the "exhaustion of the paradigm of the philosophy of consciousness".[133] The dualisms it construes between subject and object, reason and nature can be overcome by turning to a prior level from which these distinctions emerge, the shared structure of language:

> The human interest in autonomy and responsibility *(Mündigkeit)* is not mere fancy, for it can be apprehended a priori. What raises us out of nature is the only thing whose nature we can know: *language*. Through its structures autonomy and responsibility are posited for us. With the first sentence the intention of a universal and unconstrained consensus is unmistakeably expressed.[134]

From this new foundation for critical theory, offered in his inaugural lecture at the University of Frankfurt in 1965, Habermas develops his discourse ethics. Together with his account of the genesis of the public sphere, published in 1961, and his discourse theoretical reconstruction of law in 1992, it leads to a distinc-

---

132 Habermas, *Theory of Communicative Action*, vol. I, *Reason and the Rationalization of Society*, trans. Th. McCarthy (Boston: Beacon Press, 1984) 378.
133 Habermas, *Theory of Communicative Action*, vol. I, 386.
134 Habermas, "Appendix. Knowledge and human interests: A general perspective", in *Knowledge and Human Interests*, trans. J. J. Shapiro (Boston: Beacon Press, 1971), 301–317, 314.

tive theory of democracy.[135] The way in which Habermas develops this basic in-tuition of a consensus founded only on the force of the better argument, that is, on insight, not on constraint, is indebted to the linguistic and the pragmatic turns of philosophy to meanings generated in social interaction. Understanding human agency as communicative action, he focuses on discourse in the public realm as the meta-level at which theoretical and practical validity claims are to be justified. From the intersubjective praxis of argumentation he identifies the normative presuppositions that are at work in every act of communication in which partners mutually recognize their orientation towards objective truth, moral rightness and personal sincerity. Thus, the moral point of view is already embodied in linguistically structured communication. While Rawls's *Theory of Justice* had a dual foundation, a contract part which included the assumption of self-interested and in this sense "rationally" choosing agents, and culturally given values, there is only one starting point for Habermas's theory of communi-cative reason: the potential for agreement inherent in language which is un-equivocal in its orientation towards recognition. The new role philosophy is as-suming is one of collaboration with the sciences. Its argumentation is conducted with the means of postmetaphysical thinking which are the only ones available since the identity thinking, the idealism and the strong concept of theory that marked metaphysics are judged to be incompatible with modernity.

2.1.2 The competence of philosophy

How does Habermas seek to give a contemporary foundation to Kant's ethics, one that is based on distinguishing communicative action from self-serving or strategic purposes? In what way are constructivist and reconstructive elements combined in comparison with Rawls (1)? Secondly, how does he conceive of phi-losophy as a discipline which still retains its proper competence to establish a critically justifiable general truth claim over against the realm of worldviews

---

135 Habermas, *The Structural Transformation of the Public Sphere*, trans. Th. Burger (Cambridge, Mass.: MIT Press, 1989); *Between Facts and Norms. Contributions to a Discourse Theory of Law and Democracy*, trans. W. Rehg (Cambridge: Polity Press, 1996).

It is remarkable that John Rawls had developed a similar connection between public debate and a consensual elaboration of rules in his doctoral dissertation of 1950. In their "Introduction" to *A Brief Enquiry into the Meaning of Sin and Faith. With "On my Religion"* (Boston: Harvard University Press, 2006), 1–23, 10, Joshua Cohen and Thomas Nagel quote: a "democratic con-ception of government… views the law as the outcome of public discussions as to what rules can be voluntarily consented to as binding upon the government and the citizens."

but that renounces to its previous, now unsustainable position of superiority to the sciences (2)?

2.1.2.1 Constructivist and reconstructive elements in discourse ethics

Two core elements of Kant's ethics are transposed to an intersubjective level: the Categorical Imperative, and the concept of transcendental freedom on which it is based. For Habermas, in order to find impartial resolutions to contested claims, it is necessary to agree on moral norms as such, and on the norms relevant for the practical discourse in question. This cannot be done in a monological way; other participants' perspectives on what all those affected would be able to consent to have to be expressed and cannot be anticipated or assumed by conjecture. While the test of universalizability is retained and concretized as being realized by distinct participants, Kant's categories are detranscendentalized in a "universal pragmatics" which uncovers in the presuppositions of argumentation a basic recognition of the other. With an ironic description, Habermas explains the "performative contradiction" that would obtain if the rules posed by the "inescapable presuppositions" of argumentation were not honoured: "Having excluded persons $A, B, C,...$ from the discussion by silencing them or by foisting our interpretation on them, we were able to convince ourselves that N is justified." Another example of the "semantic paradox" incurred is the statement: "'Using lies, I finally convinced $\underline{H}$ that $\underline{p}$'."[136] Rainer Forst summarizes the reasoning which this long article on the foundations of discourse ethics developed in 1983: its

> most important feature is the replacement of the reflexive testing of moral maxims, as in the precedent (*Vorgabe*) of the Categorical Imperative, through an argumentative vindication of the validity claims of moral norms in a practical discourse. Methodically, the transcendental self-reflection of practical reason in Kant's sense becomes a pragmatic reconstruction of the normative implications of communicative rationality.[137]

The reconstructive part lies in seeking in language as a given feature of humanity an effective, enabling capacity of recognizing the role of the other and of reaching understanding. The constructivist part lies in jointly establishing norms

---

136 Habermas, "Discourse ethics", in *Moral Consciousness and Communicative Action*, trans. C. Lenhardt and S. Weber Nicholsen (Cambridge/Mass.: MIT Press, 1990), 43–115, 91. 89–90.
137 Forst, "'Diskursethik der Moral. 'Diskursethik – Notizen zu einem Begründungsprogramm' (1983)", in H. Brunkhorst/R. Kreide/C. Lafont (eds.), *Habermas-Handbuch. Leben – Werk – Wirkung* (Stuttgart: J.B. Metzler'sche Verlagsbuchhandlung/C.E. Poeschel Verlag und Darmstadt: Wissenschaftliche Buchgesellschaft, 2009), 234–240, 234.

which are not already given but need to be identified in a procedure that is inclusive and respectful. In his comparison of the use of reconstructive and constructivist moves in Rawls and Habermas, Forst comes to the following assessment:

> Habermas's argument for the need for a postmetaphysical conception of practical – or rather, communicative – reason does not arise primarily as it does for Rawls from the reflection on conditions of justification for a general conception of justice capable of securing agreement within a pluralist society... in human language, in its ability to produce reciprocal understanding, there lies a rationality potential on which philosophy can still build even when more substantive conceptions of the true or the reasonable have lost their universal validity... The idea of a "discourse ethics" or a "discourse theory of morality" is sustained by the notion that moral claims to validity can only be grounded in a particular form of practical discourse in which equal participants... agree on whether the general observance of a norm is equally acceptable for each affected person. Thus, discourse ethics is also based on a combination of reconstruction and construction, but in a different way than Rawls's theory. On the basis of a formal pragmatic reconstruction of the implications of raising and justifying validity claims, a discourse principle is formulated, which provides the procedures for an intersubjective construction of norms.[138]

Thus, the two elements take opposite places in the two approaches: Since the existing basis for morality is the human species' endowment with language, Habermas does not need the device of the original position to construct principles of justice. Here, he can use reconstruction in relation to excavating the moral dimension inherent in language, more precisely in the presuppositions of argumentation. The plurality of agents, however, makes it necessary to conduct a dialogue or discourse between real interlocutors on what course of action would pass the test of being universalizable. Here, Habermas constructs a procedure for an intersubjective construction of norms: the principles of discourse and of universalization. Rawls had turned to reconstructing both what is implied in the self-understanding of citizens and the specific values shared in a democracy, namely, liberty and equality. Both speak of rationality, but in Rawls's "rational choice" use, it stands for the prudential in the sense of calculating the best personal outcome; thus, it is not at the moral but at the ethical level of personal intentions, wishes and interests.[139] For Habermas, "rational" stands for the cognitive claim of moral reflection over against the merely "reasonable"; yet, the term "rationality" indicates an already reduced status of reason which takes a

---

138 Forst, *Right to Justification*, 86 – 87.
139 In *Right to Justification*, 83, Forst explains the "priority of the 'reasonable' over the 'rational'" as "(i.e., justice over the individual good)".

more collegial attitude in interacting with the research of the individual sciences rather than judging them from a superior position. Thomas Schmidt highlights the background for the contemporary use of the term "rationality" rather than "reason" as expressing the

> fundamentally changed situation of philosophy in the late 20th and the early 21st centuries. Rationality is not just another name for reason. The access to and the method of treatment of reason have changed... reason fulfills a specific function in human contexts of action... Philosophy no longer encompasses the totality of the world in its reach... it does not provide a unified worldview but becomes a meta-theory, a place of reflection of presuppositions of rationality in everyday life and in the sciences... "Rational" are utterances and actions of persons insofar as they are "justifiable" and "criticizable".[140]

Construction and reconstruction thus take place from an understanding of rationality as "a disposition of speaking and acting subjects" (*Disposition sprach- und handlungsfähiger Subjekte*).[141] The social sciences need philosophy to inject a guiding idea into identifying and devising research programmes. The lifeworld needs its capacity for translation.

2.1.2.2 Philosophy as "stand-in" and "interpreter"

Habermas's address at the Hegel-Congress in Stuttgart in 1981 in which he redesigned the role of philosophy has been singled out as "one, if not *the* key to his whole work".[142] In comparison with *Political Liberalism*'s relegation of philosophy to the level of particular worldviews, it retains much more of its original competence for Habermas despite the circumscribed functions it is given: It is to carry out the roles of "stand-in" or "placeholder" (*Platzhalter*) for universalistic questions in the sciences, and of "interpreter" between the expert cultures and the lifeworld, rather than of "usher" (*Platzanweiser*) and "judge" (*Richter*)

---

140 Th. Schmidt, "Objektivität und Gewißheit. Vernunftmodelle und Rationalitätstypen in der Religionsphilosophie der Gegenwart", in F.-J. Bormann/B. Irlenborn (eds.), *Religiöse Überzeugungen und öffentliche Vernunft. Zur Rolle des Christentums in der pluralistischen Gesellschaft* (Freiburg: Herder, 2008), 199–217, 200. He also draws a conclusion for what this understanding of reason means for philosophy of religion: "approaches to contemporary philosophy of religion... understand rationality as a property that is attributed to and justifies propositions and convictions". For this "functional or situated concept of reason... the reason [*Vernunft*] of faith is to be analysed as the rationality of religious convictions... not as a question of truth." (201)
141 Schmidt, "Objektivität", with reference to Habermas's definition in his *Theory of Communicative Action,* vol. I, 22, German original vol. I, 44.
142 Brunkhorst, "Platzhalter und Interpret", in Brunkhorst et al. (eds.), *Habermas-Handbuch*, 214–220, 215.

which is portrayed as Kant's view.[143] Yet philosophy as the power of reflection of a situated reason is undiminished in its ability to establish truth; this capacity for normative reflection is unquestioned, and its cognitive status defended. Against postmodern and conventionalist positions Habermas maintains the "unity of reason" and even the "moment of unconditionality" inherent in it.[144] Rawls's uncoupling of the concept of justification from that of truth is his primary target of critique in the in-depth exchange carried out between them in 1995; it will be treated in section 3.

The first function draws philosophy into a reconstructive operation within the sciences where its "strong universalistic claims" supply a focus from which new directions for research take off. Here, its previous "transcendental and dialectical modes of justification" are turned into the reduced or more modest (*ermäßigt*) remit of offering reconstructive hypotheses for empirically observable competences.[145] Examples of such fruitful cooperation between universalistic and empirical enquiries include the links "between cognitivist ethics and a psychology of moral development, between philosophical theories of action and the ontogenetic study of action competences".[146] The innovative capacity of this generative core is exemplified by "fertile minds" such as

> Freud..., ... Durkheim, Mead, Max Weber, Piaget, and Chomsky. Each inserted a genuinely philosophical idea like a detonator into a particular context of research. Symptom formation through repression, the creation of solidarity through the sacred, the identity-forming function of role-taking, modernization as rationalization of society, decentration as an out-

---

143 Habermas, "Philosophy as stand-in and interpreter", in *Moral Consciousness*, 1–20.

144 Habermas, "Stand-in and interpreter", in *Moral Consciousness*, 19–20: "The validity claims that we raise in conversation – that is, when we say something with conviction – transcend this specific conversational context, pointing to something beyond the spatiotemporal ambit of the occasion. Every agreement... is based on (controvertible) grounds or reasons. Grounds have a special property: they force us into yes or no positions. Thus, built into the structure of action oriented towards reaching understanding is an element of unconditionality. And this is the unconditional element that makes the validity (*Gültigkeit*) that we claim for our views different from the mere de facto acceptance (*Geltung*) of habitual practices. From the perspective of first persons, what we consider justified is not a function of custom (*Lebensgewohnheiten*) but a question of justification or grounding (*Begründbarkeit*)."

145 Habermas, "Stand-in and interpreter", in *Moral Consciousness*, 16. The English translation inserts an addition to the German text that is uncalled for, namely "venerable". By translating "reduced" ("ermäßigt") as "marked down in price", it gives an ironic tone to an originally appreciative statement: "Marked down in price, the venerable transcendental and dialectical modes of justification may still come in handy," for "Dabei können die ermäßigten transzendentalen und dialektischen Begründungsweisen durchaus hilfreich sein" ("Platzhalter und Interpret", in *Moralbewusstsein und kommunikatives Handeln*, 23.)

146 Habermas, "Stand-in and interpreter", in *Moral Consciousness*, 16.

growth of reflective abstraction from action, language acquisition as an activity of hypothesis testing – these key phrases stand for so many paradigms in which a philosophical idea is present in embryo while at the same time empirical, yet universal, questions (*empirisch bearbeitbare, aber universalistische Fragestellung*) are being posed.[147]

The new role means that philosophy itself shares in the revisable and fallible status of the knowledge explored in the individual sciences.[148] This alignment has been countered by severe critiques from Continental philosophers and theologians. His fellow-discourse ethicist, Karl-Otto Apel, questions the ability of philosophy to retain a critical role once it is assimilated to the level of empirical enquiries. The

> Habermasian strategy of avoiding a methodological distinction between philosophy and empirically testable reconstructive science seems to me openly inconsistent: I suspect Habermas will have to make up his mind one day whether he wants to persist in the inconsistency or give back to philosophy its genuine *justificatory function*, together with its a priori universal and self-referential validity claims.[149]

In *Nachmetaphysisches Denken II*, the independent and critical role of philosophy is again underlined,[150] without, however, responding to Apel's demand to identify what its own methodology consists in, namely a transcendental reflection. The alternative between conceiving it as facilitating the production of types of knowledge that are empirically testable and at one's disposition, and a genuine reflective and justificatory competence is not admitted.

The second role philosophy is to take over is an interpretive and mediating one. The "integrating" and "enlightening role of philosophy... directed toward the whole of life practices"[151] is applied to two tasks: the mediation of the expert

---

147 Habermas, "Stand-in and interpreter", in *Moral Consciousness*, 15.

148 "Fallibilistic in orientation", it rejects "the dubious faith in philosophy's ability to do things single-handedly (*im Alleingang*), hoping instead that... success... might come from an auspicious matching of different theoretical fragments." Habermas, "Stand-in and interpreter", in *Moral Consciousness*, 16.

149 K.-O. Apel, "Normatively grounding 'critical theory' by recourse to the lifeworld? A transcendental-pragmatic attempt to think with Habermas against Habermas", in Rasmussen/ Swindal (eds.), *Jürgen Habermas*, Vol. III, 344–378, 362.

150 In *Nachmetaphysisches Denken II. Aufsätze und Repliken* (Frankfurt: Suhrkamp, 2012), Habermas contextualizes the first collection of essays published under that title in a politically conservative period of a "return to metaphysics" (8). Almost 25 years later, it is now necessary to "distinguish philosophy – as a discursive form of understanding of world and of self conducted in an academic (*wissenschaftlich*) spirit – from the objectifying sciences" (10).

151 Habermas, "Metaphysics after Kant", in *Postmetaphysical Thinking. Philosophical Essays*, trans W. M. Hohengarten (Cambridge/Mass.: MIT Press, 1992), 17. 14.

cultures amongst each other, and with the communicative practices of the life-world. On both levels, it is a formidable programme: to "overcome the isolation of science, morals, and art and their respective expert cultures" seems to call for systems and industries propelled by their own dynamics to be answerable to each other by submitting themselves to the light of reason. These spheres, distinguished in Kant's three *Critiques*, and reinterpreted as separate value spheres of culture by Max Weber, are to be reconnected and joined "to the impoverished traditions of the lifeworld", establishing "a new balance between the separated moments of reason... in communicative everyday life."[152] Habermas uses a metaphor for a capability he still sees reason as able to perform: It is to "help set in motion the interplay between the cognitive-instrumental, moral-practical, and aesthetic-expressive dimensions that has come to a standstill today like a tangled mobile";[153] yet, lest reason get too confident, it is reminded that in this role of translator, philosophy is acting by invitation only. It "has lost its autonomy in relation to the sciences, with which it must cooperate", and also as interpreter, it "no longer directs its own pieces", having to "operate under conditions of rationality that it has not chosen": "Today, the illumination of common sense by philosophy can only be carried out according to criteria of validity that are no longer at the disposition of philosophy itself."[154]

Unlike Rawls, who does not claim any mediating competence for philosophy since it is made up of comprehensive doctrines itself, Habermas defends functions that are difficult to carry out if its status is reduced to one of such dependency. Thus, his statements are criticized by fellow-defenders of Kantian concepts as irreconcilable, radically pruning previously held competences, and still expecting philosophy to fulfill specific tasks.

In summary, as to the aspirations, not to the means recognized as being at philosophy's disposal, he still holds that its changed position in a scientific culture does not mean that it has to give up its claim to being the one authority able to conduct a critical analysis of reason that is open to all. It is expected to make research in the individual sciences answerable to the norms that guide democracy. No matter how modest the roles that remain for philosophy after the linguistic turn and the scientific diversification of reason, its core function of giving and critically examining reasons cannot be given up.[155] Rather than be co-opted

---

152 Habermas, "Stand-in and interpreter", in *Moral Consciousness*, 19.
153 Habermas, "Stand-in and interpreter", in *Moral Consciousness*, 19.
154 Habermas, "Stand-in and interpreter", in *Moral Consciousness*, 16.18.
155 Cf. Habermas, "Reconciliation through the public use of reason", in *The Inclusion of the Other. Studies in Political Theory*, ed. by C. Cronin and P. De Greiff (Cambridge: Polity Press, 1999), 49–74.

to the side of comprehensive doctrines itself, it remains a counterpart for religions and worldviews in their particularity. Its ability to provide differentiated analyses, for example, of the relationship between theory and praxis, and to mediate between the expert cultures of a complex society and the lifeworld of citizens, presuppose this independence. It is exactly by not being a comprehensive doctrine itself that philosophy can initiate structured dialogues between, for instance, the life sciences and historically achieved self-understandings. Rather than equating different philosophical approaches to worldviews, making them all particular and incommunicable, they are accepted as different proposals in a shared quest for truth. This is why discourse is needed as the one and only mode for arriving at a reasoned consensus on norms. Due to the difference of levels between the analytical and critical nature of philosophy, on the one hand, and individually held comprehensive doctrines, on the other, it is in the name of reason that participants in civil society can work out and own the outcome of practical discourses on the norms and policies that are to be adopted. Rather than leaving this task to the democratic institutions alone, it is by virtue of everyone's capability of insight into the demands of practical reason that citizens themselves conduct the crucial processes of opinion- and will formation that are the basis of legitimate decisions by parliament. Thus, it is crucial especially in pluralist societies which understanding of philosophy is put forward. Habermas objects to Rawls's reduction of the universal truth claim of reason to the level of the "reasonable" since it aims for less than a mutually shared identification and endorsement of justified policies on the basis of a practical reason available to all. Philosophy's task and competence is to establish the moral point of view in its validity independent of historical traditions or particular persuasions and their contingent overlaps.

2.1.3 Postmetaphysical thinking reconfirmed

Both Rawls and Habermas deem metaphysics a form of thought that needs to be superseded; for Rawls, the alternative to concepts of practical reason that are split into plural interpretations by various traditions of thinking is their "political" foundation on what can be explicated as implied in shared civic self-understandings. What Habermas rejects in "metaphysics" – identity thinking, idealism, and a strong concept of theory – is not the problem of controversial, opposing interpretations, but its lack of reflection on being situated, mediated by language and thoroughly historical. The abiding reconstructive and critical competences he attributes to philosophy, however, would seem "metaphysical" to Rawls, as Forst highlights:

> For Habermas, metaphysics... starts out from an absolute and "ultimate" reality that is ac-
> cessible to the human mind... and comprehended in a general theory that guides both
> thought and action. In the course of modernity... metaphysics has been gradually re-
> placed... But philosophy continues to believe it is capable of carrying out a reconstructive
> analysis of human communicative practice and of the rationality potential found within it,
> even while relinquishing "ultimate foundations"... Rawls's understanding of metaphysics,
> by contrast, is conceived so widely that it identifies even these forms of thought as meta-
> physical[156].

The problem with this use which is "too broad and undifferentiated" is that no
line can be drawn between "metaphysical" and general concepts and statements, including "scientific theories".[157] It can be seen as confirming Forst's critique that Rawls has also declared the secular as a worldview or comprehensive
doctrine in itself, leaving no space for a general or non-comprehensive consciousness of truth. The differences between his and Habermas's understandings
show that it depends on one's concept of metaphysics what exactly has to be superseded and what is still needed for a conscious and critical orientation in the
world. On the question of what definition of metaphysics is being proposed, in-
depth exchanges have taken place, first with Dieter Henrich in 1987 on the supposed alternative between metaphysics and modernity which disappears when it
is linked to the "self-relation of conscious life". The task Habermas had put to
philosophy in its interpretive, integrating role is explained by Henrich as one encountered by the human subject. The disparities and conflicts in its experiences
of the world and of itself need integration. For Henrich, the "internal lack of homogeneity in, and the conflict between, the primary world conceptions and self-
descriptions" are a matter for reflection and resolution. They "can then be translated into synthesizing second-stage conceptions".[158] These "figures of thought"
and tasks are unavoidable; "Habermas is wrong to think that his own theoretical
enterprise can do without" them.[159] For Henrich, to seek what he calls "a metaphysics of 'resolving closure' (Abschluss)" which gives up the claims of "absolute
knowledge"[160] corresponds to a "latent interest of every human being" since neither "reason, nor a life oriented towards reason... can simply remain in this state

---

156 Forst, *Right to Justification*, 91.
157 Forst, *Right to Justification*, 91.
158 D. Henrich, "What is metaphysics – what modernity?", in P. Dews (ed.), *Habermas: A Critical Reader* (Oxford: Blackwell, 1999), 291–319, 306 (German original 1987).
159 Henrich, "What is metaphysics", 292.
160 Henrich, "What is metaphysics", 306.

of incompletion and in such contradictions... It is a concern of reason, and as such a concern of humanity."[161]

Also for Herbert Schnädelbach, metaphysics cannot be simply viewed as a unitary block but only in the history of its transformations, and could only be superseded at a cost: Distinct from scientific knowledge, metaphysics is defined as "the effort to reach a cognitive comprehensive orientation with interpretive means"[162]. Unlike a knowledge claim regarding the world, as in the sciences, "interpretive" signifies that what is at issue is a question of the "meaning of it all (*Sinn des Ganzen*)".[163] While some responses have meanwhile become dated, the questions have not aged: "I still regard metaphysical questions as irrefutable (*unabweisbar*) since they are 'given to us by reason itself' (Kant); even if certain types of answers are no longer acceptable, it cannot mean that these questions can no longer be asked".[164] If they were no longer admitted, Schnädelbach is skeptical of what the attempt to overcome metaphysics would lead to:

> Could it not be that a thinking that has purged itself from anything that reminds one of metaphysics no longer deserves the label "thinking"? Does not the "postmetaphysical age" only begin when we – flooded by media and other tranquillizers – simply stop asking certain questions?[165]

Twenty years after the debate with Dieter Henrich, Daniel Henrich draws attention to the "naturalization" that is the consequence of shunning the type of self-reflection which is metaphysics in its modern form.[166] In *Nachmetaphysisches Denken II*, Habermas relates his earlier attempt at a new departure to the political context of a conservative renewal in the late 1980s.[167] He now emphasizes the reflective and critical power of reason in its response to the current cultural setting.[168] The normative framework and its ambivalent statements of method set

161 Henrich, 'What is metaphysics", 294.
162 Schnädelbach, "Metaphysik und Religion heute", in *Zur Rehabilitierung*, 144.
163 Schnädelbach, "Metaphysik und Religion heute", in *Zur Rehabilitierung*, 140.
164 Schnädelbach, "Metaphysik und Religion heute", in *Zur Rehabilitierung*, 137.
165 Schnädelbach, "Metaphysik und Religion heute", in *Zur Rehabilitierung*, 138.
166 D. C. Henrich, *Zwischen Bewusstseinsphilosophie und Naturalismus. Zu den metaphysischen Implikationen der Diskursethik von Jürgen Habermas* (Bielefeld: Transcript Verlag, 2007), 83–84.
167 Habermas, "Versprachlichung des Sakralen. Anstelle eines Vorwortes", in *Nachmetaphysisches Denken II*, 7–18.
168 Habermas, "Religion und nachmetaphysisches Denken. Eine Replik", in *Nachmetaphysisches Denken II*, 120–182, 122: "Even today, philosophy is distinguished from the objectifying sciences by the reflexive question about the understanding of self and world of 'the' human person or of individuals 'as such' (or of 'modernity')."

the parameters for what can be said in sections 2, 3, and 4 on his anthropology, theory of society and religion.

2.2 An anthropology of the lifeworld

The framework outlined in the previous section has given indications of the direction Habermas's theory decisions are taking, and of the objections they have encountered. First, the restrictions in the themes and method of philosophy through the "paradigm change" from the philosophy of consciousness to language makes reflection on the self a theme that is secondary and derived from the presuppositions of linguistic exchanges in the lifeworld. Factors that impoverish and threaten the lifeworld are external ones. The critical, diagnostic stance of the Frankfurt School is still maintained but carried out mainly in collaboration with the social sciences; the illuminating powers of analysis of the arts and humanities for past and present self-understandings are rarely drawn on. Thus, the capacities, aspirations and fault-lines of subjective agency are not core questions.

Secondly, by keeping to empirically researchable issues, language comes into view as a social fact. The public, visible features of grammar, such as the first, second and third person perspectives, are the starting points. Unlike the original position where the veil of ignorance hid all the differences between the participants, it provides a basis for reconstructing an undeniable plurality; but it leaves open the reasons for recognizing the other, both as a specific you, and as an anonymous other.

Thirdly, by focusing on discourse (carried out by multiple participants, in replacement of a monological test of universalizability), the theory of communicative action is located at the deontological level. Where does the question of motivation come in? The interactive foundation avoids the need for a device like the original position that builds on self-interest; yet it does not of itself answer the question of how to sustain the resolve to keep to the norms agreed, especially when they come at a cost. The problem of connecting the right and the good is exacerbated when the highest level of moral argumentation is identified as "postconventional", creating a barrier between itself and the lifeworld with its otherwise valued resources.

Finally, the empirical route was taken also to escape from the "abysses of the classical philosophy of reason"[169] which no longer seemed productive to dwell on. If they are removed from the agenda of legitimate themes, what happens to the questions previously put by reason, but judged to be unanswerable, such as the antinomy between freedom and determinism or the limit questions that led from ethics to philosophy of religion for Kant? Is the experience of well-intended actions failing or of one-sided, supererogatory deeds part of his critical theory, as questions of suffering and justice in and beyond history were for members of the first generation of the Frankfurt School, such as Horkheimer, Adorno and Benjamin? Will religion, along with language, only come into view as a social fact, or also as a dimension whose rationality can be uncovered in analyses of subjectivity and of the antinomies of agency?

The roots of Habermas's moral theory can be found in an anthropology for which the communicative character of rationality is foundational. The debate with Dieter Henrich that ensues from its guiding assumption of the priority of human interaction is centered on the relationship between intersubjectivity and reflexivity (1). The theory of communicative action is focused on uncovering the moral demands implicit in "discourse", that is, a meta-level of shared normative reflection on assumptions that have become problematic. Transposing the moral respect for others as ends in themselves into the level of premises of discourse provokes the question what the content of this recognition is (2). The ethical issue of motivation finds one answer in the resources of the lifeworld. Occupying a level similar to Rawls's "considered convictions" in *Theory of Justice* and linked to "comprehensive doctrines" in *Political Liberalism*, they are diagnosed as endangered by the purposive rationalities of the economic and political systems. Is Habermas's use of Kohlberg's stage theory of the development of moral competence in danger of invalidating them at the same time by calling the highest stage "postconventional"[170] (3)? And regarding the space to be allocated to religion in his subsequent revisions of an originally secularizing view: does the restriction of reason to the functions of placeholder and interpreter give up a direction of thinking that goes beyond the totality of the lifeworld? In his *Critique of Pure Reason*, Kant distinguished between *Denken* and *Erkennen*, the thinking carried out by reason (*Vernunft*) and the knowing established by understanding (*Verstand*) in collaboration with the senses (*Sinnlichkeit*). Reason's orientation towards the unconditional would be crucial for vindicating religion as

---

169 Habermas, *Moralbewusstsein und kommunikatives Handeln* (Frankfurt: Suhrkamp, 1983), 26. These abysses will be further discussed in 2.2.4.
170 Habermas, "Moral Consciousness and Communicative Action", in *Moral Consciousness*, 116–194, 122–125.

responding to a demand of reason, rather than a merely existing social fact the truth of which has to be left undecided by reason due to its fallibility (4).

2.2.1 The interactive constitution of self-consciousness

By taking his starting point with language as the defining anthropological feature, as expressed in his 1965 inaugural lecture, and building an interdisciplinary research programme on it, the evidence of human sociability distinguishes it from approaches that begin with isolated individuals; this is what he interprets the philosophy of consciousness as doing. In order to investigate the genesis of individual agency from intersubjectively constituted lifeworlds and relate its competences to the normative foundations of democratic self-organization, he brings in a range of individual disciplines. They include linguistics, sociology, history, theory of law, political theory, ethnomethodology and theory of civilizations, as well as developmental psychology and psychoanalysis. Based on the assumption of a shared faculty of human reason, they work out approaches and research steps for reconstructing different aspects that remain open to correction. By privileging the prior linguistic mediatedness of the subjects whose competences are being explored, however, he is choosing a premise for these enquiries that other philosophers regard as one-sided. His answer to the question, "Why be moral?" is revealing of the extent to which the new foundation replaces problems that other traditions of thinking explored: "this question does not arise meaningfully for communicatively socialized individuals".[171] By relativizing the importance of the distinction between self and other from the perspective of language, the opposite poles that should structure the enquiry are collapsed; instructive, insightful questions are withdrawn by declaring them to be no longer meaningful.

Dieter Henrich, the most prominent German fellow-philosopher outside the Frankfurt School to have entered into debate with Habermas, reactualizes the heritage of the thinkers of German Idealism when he explains that the individual capacity for self-reflection is equally primordial with intersubjectivity. It is the necessary counterpart to social connectedness that is not diminished by it, but must be reconstructed as one of two poles that remain in tension. As one of the colleagues who share the commitment to modernity that Habermas defends

---

171 Habermas, "Transcendence from within, transcendence in this world", in D. Browning/F. Schüssler Fiorenza (eds.), *Habermas, Modernity, and Public Theology* (New York: Crossroad, 1992), 226–250, 238.

against postmodern and metaphysical approaches, Henrich analyses the connection between self and other with the means of the philosophy of consciousness. Habermas had used George Herbert Mead's symbolic interactionism to replace Kant's transcendental method, making the ability for mutual role-taking a cornerstone of his theory. It provided the link between the levels of semantics and pragmatics, moving from speech act theory to agency. By performing the roles of speaker and listener, the self takes over the perspective of the other with the help of the grammatical pronouns "I" and "you." What speaks for the attempt to explain the constitution of the self with the help of a pragmatic theory of language is that an "introspective access to facts of consciousness" can be replaced by a reconstructive analysis of "(g)rammatical expressions" that are "publicly accessible".[172]

The methodological advantage claimed by Habermas leaves a crucial question open for Henrich: What is it in the subject's constitution that makes this possible? The very ability to change perspectives in mutual role-taking is what needs explanation. How can each perspective be internalized without confusing self and other? This question can only be answered by shifting to a different methodology than that of reconstructing linguistic and pragmatic facts as if they did not need further enquiry: a transcendental analysis into the conditions of the possibility of such initiatives and returned invitations. As the internal condition of the possibility of role-taking in both speaker and listener, a prior familiarity with oneself has to be presupposed. Thus, self-reflection cannot be derived from intersubjectivity, it remains its counterpart. The "introspective" step of distinguishing two levels cannot be superseded: concrete and publicly visible actions, on the one hand, and the condition of their possibility that remains invisible and accessible only by reflecting on the enabling capability as their source, on the other.

This is the position from which Henrich questions the thesis on which Habermas has "made his whole work dependent…, the primacy of the community of interaction".[173] Instead of proposing an equally one-sided solution, where the self would be constituted entirely by reflexivity, Henrich assumes an "equal primordiality" of both factors. For Habermas, "original self-consciousness is not a phenomenon inherent in the subject but one that is communicatively generated".[174] This position takes for granted what is in need of critical analysis: the communication assumed is itself unthinkable without a prior self-relation. The

---

172 Habermas, "Themes in postmetaphysical thinking", in *Postmetaphysical Thinking*, 45.
173 Henrich, D., 'What is metaphysics," in Dews (ed.), *Habermas – A Critical Reader*, 310 – 11.
174 Habermas, "Individuation through socialization: On George Herbert Mead's theory of subjectivity", in *Postmetaphysical Thinking*, 149 – 204, 177. The English translation leaves out an elucidating phrase after "*innewohnendes*" (inherent): "*ihm zur Disposition stehendes… Phä-*

functioning of linguistic communication presupposes a self-relation on the part of the 'speaker' – as one of its constitutive pre-conditions, one which is no less fundamental than the subject-predicate form of the proposition... Habermas finds... that the linguistically organized lifeworld, which for its part is self-sufficient, can generate self-relations – and hence the identity of speakers – out of itself... Such a view... would be incapable of describing or understanding language and communication... rather,.. the capacity of language can only develop *along (in einem) with* the spontaneous emergence of a self-relation. This emergence in turn requires explanation. And this would require us to speak of an implicit self-relation, which already appears or functions at the most elementary level of language acquisition.[175]

The attempt to overcome the distinctions of the philosophy of consciousness that were deemed dualistic with categories such as "language" and "lifeworld" has generated new perspectives and research insights; yet, it has not been able to reach the level of differentiation required to elucidate the shared premise of modern approaches to philosophy, namely, human freedom. The series of mutual responses begun by Henrich's *Laudatio* for Habermas in 1974, and continued in articles as well as in Habermas's contribution to the *Festschrift* for Henrich ended in 1987. A late result of Henrich's attention to what is implied in conscious life can be seen in Habermas's turn to an eminent philosopher of subjectivity around the year 2000: in his dispute with positions that defended the emerging possibility of genetic enhancement, Kierkegaard's category of the "ability to be a self" is used as a decisive argument against submitting a child to the genetic preferences of its parents. Here, the heritage of the philosophy of consciousness is taken up as a resource; even with its original setting within a religious framework, it is deemed to be compatible with postmetaphysical thinking.[176] Faced with technological developments that instrumentalize by imposing parental interests in designing the bodily specificity of their child, the concept of self as singularity is rediscovered and its contingency defended against a choice that is revealed as domination. The exchange with Henrich can be seen as an example of the fruitfulness of Habermas's insistence that it has to be left to discourse what will finally count as good reasons, even if he does not take them on board. The

---

nomen". The complete version is thus, "not a phenomenon inherent in and at the disposition of the subject".

175 Henrich, "What is metaphysics", in Dews (ed.), *Habermas – A Critical Reader*, 311. Habermas responds to his critique in "Metaphysics after Kant", in *Postmetaphysical Thinking*, 10 – 27, his contribution to the 1987 *Festschrift* for Dieter Henrich.

176 Habermas, *The Future of Human Nature*, 5.

question whether it is possible to deliver the results he claims on the basis of his premises remains unresolved.[177]

2.2.2 Pragmatic reconstruction of normative implications, or moral recognition of the other?

The key premise of the discourse theory of ethics is that inherent in the presuppositions of argumentation is a normative orientation towards the other participants. They are respected in advance as partners who strive to contribute their best judgement, who seek coordination with others as equals and who are sincere. These normative attitudes that are implied in communication are reconstructed by universal pragmatics as the universal conditions of possible agreement.[178] From these presuppositions already operative in linguistic interaction, the discourse rules of inclusion and symmetry are derived.[179] To restate Forst's summary of the method employed, "the transcendental self-reflection of practical reason in Kant's sense becomes a pragmatic reconstruction of the normative implications of communicative rationality".[180] What constitutes the discovery and realization of the foundational human capacity of the good will for Kant, is here sought in the conditions for reaching an agreement. It needs to be shown how the priority of communicative action oriented towards understanding over uncooperative, strategic action can be established.

---

177 He does not give up his thesis that the self-referential relations of the subject are made possible by social relationships, despite Henrich's argumentation for the equally primordial status of reflexivity and intersubjectivity. Cf. Habermas, "Freedom and determinism", in *Between Naturalism and Religion*, 175. 178.

178 Habermas, 'What is universal pragmatics?', in *Communication and the Evolution of Society*, trans. Th. McCarthy (Boston: Beacon Press, 1979), 1–68. Cf. the reconstruction of A. Anzenbacher, *Einführung in die Philosophie* (Freiburg: Herder, 2002, 8th ed), 197–9.

179 In order to carry out a communication that is committed to a "cooperative search for truth" and in which any "coercion other than the force of the better argument" is excluded, the following formal requirements are identified and stated as rules of discourse, as formulated by the legal theorist Robert Alexy:

(3.1) Every subject with the competence to speak and act is allowed to take part in a discourse.

(3.2) a. Everyone is allowed to question any assertion whatever.

b. Everyone is allowed to introduce any assertion whatever into the discourse.

c. Everyone is allowed to express his attitudes, desires, and needs.

(3.3) No speaker may be prevented, by internal or external coercion, from exercising his rights as laid down in (3.1.) and (3.2). Habermas, "Discourse ethics", in *Moral Consciousness*, 89.

180 Forst, "Diskursethik der Moral", in Brunkhorst *et al.* (eds.), *Habermas-Handbuch*, 234.

> I call interactions *communicative* when the participants coordinate their plans of action consensually, with the agreement reached at any point being evaluated in terms of the intersubjective recognition of validity claims... the actors make three different claims to validity in their speech acts as they come to an agreement with one another about something. Those claims are claims to truth, claims to rightness, and claims to truthfulness... I distinguish between communicative and strategic action. Whereas in strategic action one actor tries to *influence* the behaviour of another by means of the threat of sanctions or the prospect of gratification in order to cause the interaction to continue as the first actor desires, in communicative action one actor seeks *rationally to motivate* another by relying on the illocutionary binding/bonding effect (*Bindungseffekt)* of the offer contained in his speech act.[181]

The key reason for the priority of communicative over strategic action given to refute skeptics, cynics and relativists is that a "performative contradiction" is committed when inescapable presuppositions are put to a use that denies them at the same time. The role of moral theory is seen as twofold: to justify the "moral point of view", and to outline the procedure needed to set up and structure the practical discourses which only real participants, as distinct from moral philosophy, can carry out:

> It is incumbent on moral theory to explain and ground the moral point of view. What moral *theory* can do and should be trusted to do is to clarify the universal core of our moral intuitions and thereby to refute value skepticism. What it cannot do is to make any substantive contribution. By singling out a procedure of decision making, it seeks to make room for those involved, who must then find answers on their own to the moral-practical issues that come at them, or are imposed upon them, with objective historical force. Moral philosophy does not have privileged access to particular moral truths... philosophy cannot absolve anyone of moral responsibility.[182]

From the rules of discourse which explicate the presuppositions that are operative in all acts of communication, Habermas derives the "discourse principle (D)" and then sets out to justify the "principle of universalization (U)". The renewed attempt to construct this principle from premises that do not incur a *petitio principii* results in the final formulation,

> a contested norm cannot meet with the consent of the participants in a practical discourse unless (U) holds, that is, Unless all affected can *freely* accept the consequences and the side

---

181 Habermas, "Discourse ethics", in *Moral Consciousness*, 43–115, 58.
182 Habermas, "Morality and ethical life: Does Hegel's critique of Kant apply to discourse ethics?", in *Moral Consciousness*, 195–215, 210–11.

effects that the *general* observance of a controversial norm can be expected to have for the satisfaction of the interests of *each individual.*[183]

The universalization test that could be carried out in self-reflection for Kant is made into a dialogical and public procedure; in it, diverse participants come to a freely endorsed agreement that is geared to protecting the interests of all affected, including the effects of norms on them. How does this presupposition for the correctness of norms compare with Kant's Categorical Imperative as the guiding principle of moral action? One difference is that discourse ethical justification relates to validity claims of moral norms; they are the material of the practical discourses, not self-reflection on the moral permissibility of an intended act. A second difference arises from the first, since there is no direct relation to agency: what happens when the discourse has been concluded? Do the norms still hold, are they valid in real life? Put differently, what is the content of the recognition that the symmetrical conditions of access safeguard: is it of discourse partners as participants in argumentation, or is it the recognition of every human being who is therefore not to be instrumentalized? If so, can a pragmatics of argumentation make this case, or can it only show certain presuppositions to be factually inescapable? What does the argumentative vindication of validity claims achieve, and where is its limit?

In order to answer these questions, Habermas's various responses to theorists who are sympathetic to, or part of, the enterprise of discourse ethics, such as Albrecht Wellmer, Rainer Wimmer and Karl-Otto Apel, need to be examined. In them, he gives answers that restrict the scope of recognition to the situation of discourse itself. A sharp distinction is drawn between it and everyday behaviour, and a separate justification called for:

> It is by no means self-evident that rules that are unavoidable *within* discourses can also claim to be valid for regulating action *outside* of discourses. Even if participants in an argumentation are forced to make substantive normative presuppositions (e. g., to respect one another as competent subjects, to treat one another as equal partners, to assume one another's truthfulness, and to cooperate with one another), they can still shake off this transcendental-pragmatic compulsion when they leave the field of argumentation. The necessity of making such presuppositions is not transferred directly from discourse to action. In any case, a separate justification is required to explain why the normative content discovered in the pragmatic presuppositions of *argumentation* should have the power to *regulate action*. One cannot demonstrate a transfer of this kind as Apel and Peters try to do, namely by deriving basic ethical norms *directly* from the presuppositions of argumentation.[184]

---

183 Habermas, "Discourse ethics", in *Moral Consciousness*, 92–93.
184 Habermas, "Discourse ethics", in *Moral Consciousness*, 85–86.

Wellmer's request for clarification regarding the sense of "obligation", distinguishing between a "rational" and a "moral" intention, highlights two alternative directions in which the recognition extended in discourse, marked by presuppositions of symmetry, can be understood:

> the unavoidable presuppositions of argument do not in themselves constitute *moral* obligations... Obligations to rationality refer to the acknowledgment (*Anerkennung*) of arguments, moral obligations to the acknowledgment of persons. It is a requirement of rationality to acknowledge even the arguments of my enemy if they are good ones; it is a requirement of morality to permit even those people to speak who are not yet capable of arguing well. Overstating the point a little, we might say that obligations to rationality are concerned with arguments regardless of who voices them, whereas moral obligations are concerned with people regardless of their arguments (*Personen ohne Ansehen ihrer Argumente*).[185]

Habermas's response interprets the alternative posed between recognizing persons in their quality as contributors of rational arguments and "regardless of their arguments", that is, independently of the quality of their contributions to discourse, in a different direction. The alternative is no longer between purveyors of validity claims and persons in their human dignity; "regardless of their arguments" is taken as referring to "egocentric convictions":

> The obligatory character of justified norms involves the notion that they regulate problems of communal life in the common interest and thus are "equally good" for all affected. For this reason, moral obligations relate, on the one hand, to "persons regardless of their arguments", if by this one understands "without taking into account egocentric convictions that may be bound up with generally valid arguments from the perspective of individual persons". On the other hand, the moral principle owes its rigorously universalistic character precisely to the assumption that arguments deserve equal consideration regardless of their origin and, hence, also "regardless of who voices them."[186]

Thus, the universalization principle is restricted to a weak sense. The distinction between arguments and persons is not pursued; obligation relates to ensuring the unlimited nature of discourse on validity claims to which participants contribute in order to satisfy the criterion of an unrestricted quest for truth.

A perceptive comment is given in Rainer Wimmer's analysis of the part that Habermas's universal pragmatics takes over in the justification of discourse ethics. Having reconstructed systems of competencies as the conditions of commu-

---

185 A. Wellmer, *Ethik und Dialog* (Frankfurt: Suhrkamp, 1986), of which three chapters, without the appendix, have been translated as the fourth and final part of *The Persistence of Modernity*, trans. D. Midgley (Cambridge: Polity Press, 1991), 113–231, 184–85.
186 Habermas, "Remarks on discourse ethics", in *Justification and Application*, 33.

nicative action, he no longer seems to see the need to reflect on their *validity*, which was Apel's part in the division of labour between the two; on its own, however, his reconstruction commits a "naturalistic fallacy":

> At times, Habermas gives the impression that the problem of justification did not exist or became irrelevant once the question for the conditions of the possibility of discourses had been answered by way of a theoretical-hermeneutical reconstruction. Yet the mere reconstruction of "basic norms of rational speech" which contents itself with the universalization principle as the "ultimate (*allerletzten*) 'fact of reason'"... incurs the suspicion of committing a naturalistic fallacy or of moving in a circle. What has to be added is the proof of the normative inescapability of the universalization principle.[187]

In view of the limitations drawn repeatedly in debates with colleagues whose goals of justification (such as Apel's "ultimate justification") or recognition beyond the discourse setting he considers as too demanding, Paul Ricoeur's summary of his approach as an "ethics of argumentation"[188] seems accurate.

2.2.3 Between a reservoir of shared meanings and postconventional morality: the role of the lifeworld

From the hermeneutical factor in his philosophical heritage, Habermas chooses the term "lifeworld" in which values and symbolically structured practices, unthematized background assumptions and aspirations provide the material for socialization and everyday communication.[189] It offers forms of life that are receptive also for the principle of morality. The objection of "naturalization", however, in the first instance referred to taking the studies conducted to elucidate the generative capacities, stages of competencies and normative direction implied in the presuppositions of argumentation to be self-sufficient. Having identified these endowments and placed them in a structural framework, they were no longer judged to be in need of a different type of justification. Yet, it is also clear that these structural competencies depend on how different cultures and eras

---

187 R. Wimmer, *Universalisierung in der Ethik. Analyse, Kritik und Rekonstruktion ethischer Rationalitätsansprüche* (Frankfurt: Suhrkamp, 1980), 48–49.
188 Ricoeur, *Oneself as Another*, 286. He also speaks of an "ethics of discussion" (283), and "morality of communication" (281).
189 See C. Lafont, "Hermeneutik und *linguistic turn*", in Brunkhorst et al. (eds), *Habermas-Handbuch*, 29–34. The significance of this heritage was not obvious due to the stance taken in his debate with Hans-Georg Gadamer for critical self-reflection over against belonging to a history of effects.

shape them; the symbolic worlds and their ordering of cultural spheres and practices constitute backgrounds that can be seen as enabling or pathologizing, depending on a theory's designation of goals for a society to meet. In this second, material respect, "naturalization" can also refer to the role played by cultural conditions for the formation of morality. In Apel's view, Habermas reaches too directly for the potential of the lifeworld, as distinct from human structural competencies, as a basis for the moral orientation towards communication. What should be a philosophical justification of a principled ethics, is "supposed to be replaced by a recourse to the factually functioning ethical life of communicative action in the lifeworld".[190] Apel objects that instead of only leaving the constitution of "meaning" to its resources, Habermas

> in the final analysis,... also reduces the justification of validity, such as the grounding of moral validity, to such lifeworld resources, apparently for fear of otherwise losing contact with lifeworld praxis as the material basis of philosophy. One might call this a 'reconstructivistic naturalism' with respect to the justification of validity.[191]

Some of Habermas's statements confirm this view:

> It is true that a philosophy that thinks postmetaphysically cannot answer the question ...: why be moral at all? At the same time, however, this philosophy can show why this question does not arise meaningfully for communicatively socialized individuals. We acquire our moral intuitions in our parents' home, not in school. And moral insights tell us that we do not have any good reasons for behaving otherwise: for this, no self-surpassing of morality is necessary.[192]

The questions both of justification and of motivation seem to have always already been answered by assuming continuity between supportive life forms and a communication that strives for agreement. The lifeworld thus seems to play a similar role of safety net as Rawls's concept of considered convictions. The only problem then would be factors that erode the lifeworld in its contribution to forming rational identities in complex societies, a task identified by the Christian ethicist Arnold Anzenbacher as the core problem Habermas sets for

---

190 Cf. Apel, "Normatively grounding 'critical theory'", in Rasmussen/ Swindal (eds.), *Jürgen Habermas*, Vol. III, 350–51.

191 Apel, "Normatively grounding 'critical theory'", in Rasmussen/ Swindal (eds.), *Jürgen Habermas*, Vol. III, 364.

192 Habermas, "Transcendence from within", in D. Browning/Schüssler Fiorenza (eds.), *Habermas, Modernity, and Public Theology*, 239.

critical theory to pursue.[193] The lifeworld is seen as a trustworthy foundation for moral reflection, which, as has become clear above, is conceived more in terms of rational argument than of good will. Action regulation is not what the morality involved in discourse is about:

> No *direct* action-regulating force outside the context of argumentation may (or need) be ascribed to the "normative" content of presuppositions of argumentation that cannot be denied without falling into a performative contradiction or to the moral principle based upon them. The moral principle performs the role of a rule of argumentation only for justifying moral judgments and as such can neither obligate one to engage in moral argumentation nor motivate one to act on moral insights.[194]

These restrictive statements have come as a disappointment not only to fellow-Kantians, but also to the theological reception which interpreted his defense of the concept of universalization in the strong sense of recognizing every human being in their dignity. Faced with the question of how his moral theory can incorporate historical experiences such as failure, suffering and irredeemable loss that undermine the motivations supplied by the lifeworld, his answer moves these challenges outside the realm of philosophy. Distinguishing a moral interaction that can be generally expected from what is heroic or supererogatory, makes Kant's concept of practical reason that insists on the unconditional character of obligation appear as rigid. By attaching the term "unconditional" only to rarely demanding situations, all actions that go beyond strict reciprocity require a stronger motivation, such as the one supplied by religions:

> Since Schiller, the rigidity of the Kantian ethics of duty has been repeatedly and rightly criticized. But autonomy can be reasonably expected (*zumutbar*) only in social contexts that are already themselves rational in the sense that they ensure that action motivated by good reasons will not of necessity conflict with one's own interests. The validity of moral commands is subject to the condition that they are *universally* adhered to as the basis for a general practice. Only when this condition is satisfied do they express what all could will. Only then are moral commands in the common interest and – precisely because they are good for all – do not impose supererogatory demands. To this extent rational morality puts its seal on the abolition of the victim. At the same time, someone who obeys the Christian

---

193 Anzenbacher, *Einführung in die Philosophie*, 197: "Habermas's basic concern revolves around the question: 'Can complex societies form rational/reasonable (*vernünftig*) identities?' In previous societies, myths, religions, and metaphysical systems granted identity. Today these foundations of identity are no longer possible. But also the sciences cannot found them... Thus the question of the possibility of rational/reasonable identity points to the praxis of humans living together, to the contexts of the lifeworld from which convictions and interests arise and thus to linguistic interaction and its pragmatics."
194 Habermas, "Remarks on discourse ethics", in *Justification and Application*, 33.

commandment to love one's neighbour, for example, and makes sacrifices that could not reasonably be morally required of him, is deserving of our rational admiration. Supererogatory acts can be understood as attempts to counteract the effects of unjust suffering in cases of tragic complication or under barbarous living conditions that inspire our moral indignation.[195]

Thus, the shared meanings and motivations offered by the lifeworld are not seen as invalidated by such serious historical experiences of rupture. At the same time, the structural framework adopted from theorists of moral development posits the highest stages as being "postconventional". The gap between ethical life and morality that had been narrowed before is now again extended. Agents are expected to draw a sharp separation between the norms of their traditions of upbringing, and their independent moral judgements:

> Moral practical discourses... require a break with all of the unquestioned truths of an established, concrete ethical life, in addition to distancing oneself from the contexts of life with which one's identity is inextricably interwoven.[196]

Yet, even if lifeworld values and universalizable moral norms occupy different levels, the barrier between them is not completely hermetic. The possibility is admitted that values from particular life forms may become generalizable norms:

> While cultural values may imply a claim to intersubjective acceptance (*Geltung*), they are so inextricably intertwined with the totality of a particular form of life that they cannot be said to claim normative validity in the strict sense. By their very nature, cultural values are at best *candidates* for embodiment in norms that are designed to express a general interest.[197]

Despite noting the possible connection between values and norms, the chance of taking cultural and religious traditions in their particularity seriously as contributors to a universalistic ethics is not followed up, nor is a link sought between ethical and moral self-understanding. Such an internal connection could have been found in the validity claim of sincerity, as the systematic theologian David Tracy has observed.[198] Thus, even more at the individual level, the two

---

195 Habermas, 'Remarks on discourse ethics', in *Justification and Application*, 34–35.
196 Habermas, 'On the pragmatic, the ethical and the moral employments of practical reason', in *Justification and Application*, 1–18, 12.
197 Habermas, "Discourse ethics", in *Moral Consciousness*, 104.
198 Tracy perceptively points out the unused potential of the three validity claims: There "is further need to see how ethical discussions of the 'good' (the good life and happiness) might be related to (because already implied by) Habermas's formal analysis of the validity claims en-

realms of the ethical and the moral are left without a link. No integrated account of agency is attempted, indeed, a principled separation is introduced:

> If we define practical issues as issues of the good life, which invariably deal with the totality of a particular form of life or the totality of an individual life story, then ethical formalism is incisive in the literal sense: the universalization principle acts like a knife that makes razor-sharp cuts (*einen Schnitt legt*) between evaluative statements and strictly normative ones, between the good and the just... a deontological ethics... deals not with value preferences but with the normative validity of norms of action. [199]

Is this the rigour typically required within universalistic theories in order to distinguish a moral motivation from a self-serving one? Here, the perceptive comparisons with Kant by the Christian ethicist Hille Haker and by Paul Ricoeur offer a different perspective. Why should it be necessary to disconnect oneself from one's cultural world in order to make unconditional moral judgements?

> The Kantian principle of universalization does not presuppose this; it only demands to transcend in a fictive way the perspective of self-interest and of being bound to a specific situation of action, in order to clarify one's motives... Since (in Habermas's conception)... moral theory is to escape from the grips (*Fängen*) of a normative tradition, individual life histories, respectively life forms, are easily reduced to the aspect of hypothetical obligations and declared morally irrelevant. In a second step, however, they again have to be re-integrated since the moral perspective remains dependent on the "support" (*Entgegenkommen*) of life forms, and since without the perspective from a life history the problem of motivation appears unsolvable.[200]

In Haker's critique, a specific understanding of universalization which is not shared by Kant in his foundation of moral obligation results in distinctions that leave the right, the good and the authentic separate and closed to further elucidation. Transitions that could have been a matter for philosophical and for personal reflection are not considered. In Haker's understanding of the task of a moral theory that is interested in critical social analysis, this leaves out an area of enquiry which is crucial for the effectiveness of norms: It constitutes a problem if between ethical and moral self-understanding, there is a complete "discontinuity of evaluation, at first only in relation to one's own life his-

---

tailed by a morality of 'right'." Tracy, "Theology, critical social theory, and the public realm", in Browning/Schüssler Fiorenza (eds.), *Habermas, Modernity and Public Theology*, 19–42, 34.
199 Habermas, "Discourse ethics", in *Moral Consciousness*, 104.
200 H. Haker, *Moralische Identität* (Tübingen: Francke, 1999), 67. Apart from the transition from "good" to "right", discourse ethics also has a problem with the step from "justification" to "application". Cf. Haker, "Kommunitaristische Kritik an der Diskursethik" in *Ethik und Unterricht* 5 (1994) 12–18, 18.

tory. It radically endangers the formation or maintenance also of moral evaluative attitudes, so that *nolens volens* ethics has to pay attention to these developments."[201]

If it is not Kant's principle of universalization that leads to the downgrading of the ethical motivations nurtured by lifeworld traditions, what other theory decisions are involved? For Ricoeur, the heritage to be discerned here is that the concept of "convention" takes the place of "inclination" in Kant and is thus envisaged as an element in need of purification: "In this regard, the recourse to L. Kohlberg's model of developmental psychosociology reinforces the antinomy between argumentation and convention, to the extent that the scale of development is marked by preconventional, conventional and postconventional stages."[202] A further assumption is that of a complete discontinuity between modernity and tradition:

> I attribute the rigorousness of the argumentation to an interpretation of modernity almost exclusively in terms of breaking with a past thought to be frozen in traditions subservient to the principle of authority and so, by principle, out of the reach of public discussion. This explains why, in an ethics of argumentation, convention comes to occupy the place held by inclination in Kant. In this manner, the ethics of argumentation contributes to the impasse of a sterile opposition between a universalism at least as procedural as that of Rawls and Dworkin and a "cultural" relativism that places itself outside the field of discussion.[203]

As a hermeneutical philosopher, Ricoeur would doubt whether it is even possible to distance oneself to the extent demanded by Habermas from the categories, symbols and patterns of action in one's cultural world. To conclude the examination of his anthropology before turning to his theory of democracy, the effects for the role of religion of the routes taken so far shall be outlined.

2.2.4 Religion after the abysses of reason

Two consequences can be drawn from the positions Habermas takes in his anthropology and theory of action for the perspective in which religion will be able to appear. First, due to the limits that the interpretation of reason in terms of specific, universalizing rationalities sets, the only statement possible is negative: The truth of religion has to be left undecided due to the fallibility

---

201 Haker, *Moralische Identität*, 27.
202 Ricoeur, *Oneself as Another*, 286, n. 78.
203 Ricoeur, *Oneself as Another*, 286.

that reason shares with the revisable processes and results of the individual sciences. This gives only a negative answer which is not incorrect but incomplete. It would have been possible to locate the rationality of religion at the intersection that reason's limit questions create: its reflection on facticity, morality and meaning. The route of exploring the limit questions of practical reason is not taken since the unconditional character of morality cannot be sufficiently represented in the categories of presuppositions of argumentation to which it has been transposed. Thus, the insight that religious faith is a practical option, not one that can be objectified or only accessed as a social fact, escapes the conceptual possibilities held by the framework. Religious faith could be shown as a response to the antinomy opening up due to the two conflicting components of the highest good if analyses such as those of Kant were admitted. Habermas had decided to forego enquiries into the "grounds and abysses... of reason" (*Gründe und Abgründe der Vernunft*), and to search for the reunifying power of philosophy in its function as interpreter in the lifeworld: "Everyday life, however, is a more promising medium for regaining the lost unity of reason than are today's expert cultures or yesteryear's classical philosophy of reason."[204]

Its restriction to an interpretive function within the lifeworld poses another limitation. One of the abysses of reason, the question of facticity explored by F. W. J. Schelling and Kierkegaard, can no longer arise if philosophy is "to refurbish its link with the totality by taking on the role of interpreter on behalf of the lifeworld".[205] The totality of everything that can be experienced has been replaced with the totality of the lifeworld; one of the unavoidable questions of humanity, in Henrich's terms, the insight into the contingency of existence as such which modernity at its inception posed in its significance for human self-consciousness, is thus being deflected. The rational character of a religious response to these radical questions of reason cannot be shown if the abysses into which they lead are no longer deemed genuine tasks for reflection.

A second consequence for the angle from which religion will be viewed arises from the ambivalent treatment of the resources of the lifeworld. It affects religious traditions as part of the constitutive sources of self-understandings that have shaped the stocks of imaginative, conceptual, moral and affective understandings that make up a culture. On the one hand, the symbolic resources of the lifeworld are deemed irreplaceable; on the other, its particular traditions

---

204 Habermas, "Stand-in and interpreter", in *Moral Consciousness*, 18. The English translation chosen for "*in den Gründen und Abgründen der klassischen Vernunftphilosophie*" is less than accurate: "yesteryear's classical philosophy of reason". Habermas, *Moralbewusstsein und kommunikatives Handeln* (Frankfurt: Suhrkamp, 1983), 26.
205 Habermas, "Stand-in and interpreter", in *Moral Consciousness*, 18 – 19.

with their concepts of the good, practices and institutions are not availed of. Only recently has the role that religious communities can play in the emerging and uncharted moral challenges of technological societies been recognized; two decades after the 1988 conference at the University of Chicago's Divinity School, Habermas refers to the systematic theologian Francis Fiorenza's proposal of religious communities of interpretation as institutional venues to discuss questions at the intersection of the good and the right.[206] As long as traditions that explore these transitions are placed at the merely "conventional" stage, their insights remain at the existential level and are left without any potential for public debate. The opportunity is lost to gather instructive material for reflection from the sequence of mutually correcting proposals that such traditions consist of, and from the ongoing controversies they conduct within themselves and with their cultures on the core elements of their self-understanding. The most recent stage of Habermas's engagement with the ongoing reality of religion also in late modern society shows a growing awareness that input from all traditions is needed. In counterposition to Rawls's *proviso* the expectation is stated that the burden of translating their contributions cannot fall on the religious side alone. Between acknowledging their potential for resisting pathological social developments, and considering them as conventions in need of being surpassed towards a postconventional level, the issue of the place of religious resources in the lifeworld and in discourse remains open. Before their current position can be discussed in the concluding section of Part Two, the distinct understanding of public reason that is profiled in his debate with Rawls will be outlined.

2.3 The public use of reason in the democratic public sphere

Key themes in the exchange between Habermas and Rawls on the diverging paths they have taken in translating their Kantian heritage into the contemporary conditions of a pluralist democracy are the understanding of public reason (1), and its life in the civic discourse that marks participative democratic structures (2). Next to be examined will be its basis of justification: is it moral-deontological, or ethical-evaluative, or is it situated at a third level, the self-understanding of citizens? Here, the nature of the overlapping consensus advocated

---

206 Habermas, "Religion in der Öffentlichkeit der 'postsäkularen Gesellschaft'", repr. in *Nachmetaphysisches Denken II*, 308–326, 312–14, with reference to F. Schüssler Fiorenza, "The church as a community of interpretation: Political theology between discourse ethics and hermeneutical reconstruction", in Browning/Schüssler Fiorenza (eds.), *Habermas, Modernity, and Public Theology*), 66–91.

by Rawls as the only available, yet also sufficient level of agreement between citizens is at stake (3). The final point to be treated as illuminating Habermas's distinct understanding of democratic public reason in its difference from religions and worldviews is his comment on how the role of religion has changed between Rawls's posthumously published Bachelor's dissertation of 1942 and the position on public reason that he developed in the 1990s (4).

2.3.1 The moral core of public reason

While both Habermas and Rawls agree that an "autonomous" and "non-metaphysical" foundation is required, they diverge on the meaning of these crucial terms. The critical theorist sees the moral meaning of autonomy missed, and the levels of empirical, factual acceptance and of normative justifiability collapsed. Rawls responds that Habermas's approach itself is metaphysical[207] and that only a "political" understanding of autonomy will avoid the import of divisive metaphysical background theories. True reciprocity consists in not alienating other reasonable worldviews, and in providing a neutral level for them to contribute to.[208] To mark the difference to an existing contingent consensus, however, Rawls distinguishes three stages of justification which nevertheless only confirms Habermas's view that neither the "autonomous" nor the "public" character of civic discourse on norms have been accounted for sufficiently.

Having stated his agreement with Rawls's project,[209] Habermas sets out his critique that begins with the design of the original position in *Theory of Justice* in which agents are motivated by rational egoism. This bars the way to any insight of their own into obligations posed by justice. It underrates their capacity for mu-

---

207 As one of the main differences, Rawls notes that "his is comprehensive while mine is an account of the political and is limited to that" (Rawls, "Reply to Habermas", in *Studienausgabe* II, 97–139, 97).

208 The "political conception of justice is worked out first as a freestanding view that can be justified *pro tanto* without looking to, or trying to fit, or even knowing what they are, the existing comprehensive doctrines... It tries to put no obstacles in the path of all reasonable doctrines... by eliminating from this conception any idea which goes beyond the political... to do that violates the idea of mutuality." Rawls, "Reply to Habermas", in *Studienausgabe* II, 105–06.

209 In "Reconciliation through the public use of reason", in *Inclusion of the Other* 50, he states: "Because I admire his project, share its intentions, and regard its essential results as correct, the dissent I express here will remain within the bounds of a family quarrel. My doubts are limited to whether Rawls always brings to bear against his critics his important normative intuitions in their most compelling form."

tual perspective taking. The withdrawal from any truth claim and replacement of the "rational" by the "reasonable" in *Political Liberalism* then diminishes the "cognitive", that is, the discursively debatable, status of conceptions of justice.[210] Only in such public discussion can they be justified, rather than merely found as culturally available options. Therefore, conflicting validity claims cannot be ignored but have to be argued out.[211] The "moral core" of public reason which Habermas emphasizes in his answer is relevant in two dimensions: in the individual capacity for moral insight, and in the engagement of citizens in the networks of their lifeworld as a resource for democratic opinion- and will formation.[212]

Rawls in turn diagnoses Habermas's assumption of a human capacity for morality as being the expression of a comprehensive doctrine, and not as a level that can be generally shared. Worse, it is in danger of actively excluding other metaphysical positions. The objection is formulated in terms of virtues, namely tolerance and modesty. A view that is more modest in making less assumptions is a better candidate for public reason in that it shows the most respect. Rawls interprets the typical distinction drawn by autonomous ethics between a moral universalistic justification and all other types of motivating reasons as a disdain for religion on the part of the critical theorist.[213] By the

---

210 In "Reconciliation", in *Inclusion of the Other*, 53, Habermas asks, "but can the meaning of considerations of justice remain unaffected by the perspective of rational egoists? At any rate, the parties are incapable of achieving, within the bounds set by their rational egoism, the reciprocal perspective taking that the citizens they represent must undertake when they orient themselves in a just manner to what is equally good for all... if... the parties are to understand the meaning of the deontological principles they are seeking and to take sufficient account of their clients' interests in justice, they must be equipped with cognitive competences that extend further than the capacities sufficient for rationally choosing actors who are blind to issues of justice."

211 Habermas, "Reconciliation", in *Inclusion of the Other*, 50: "Further, I think that Rawls should make a sharper distinction between questions of justification and questions of acceptance; he seems to want to purchase the neutrality of this conception of justice at the cost of forsaking its cognitive validity claim".

212 For Habermas, *Political Liberalism* "represents a shift to an entirely new framework within which reason loses its central position. Practical reason is robbed of its moral core and is deflated to a reasonableness that becomes dependent on moral truths justified otherwise. The moral validity of conceptions of justice is now no longer grounded in a universally binding practical reason but in the lucky convergence of reasonable worldviews whose moral components overlap to a sufficient degree." "'Reasonable' versus 'true,' or the morality of worldviews," in *Inclusion of the Other*, 75–101, 82–83.

213 In his "Reply to Habermas", in *Studienausgabe* II, 99, Rawls states that Habermas "rejects naturalism and emotivism in moral argument... Moreover, he often criticizes religious and me-time of the exchange, 1995, Habermas's position on religion had developed into a recognition of its "ongoing coexistence" with postmetaphysical thinking and an appreciation of its "semantic potential";[214] Rawls, however, appears to understand his uncovering of the "presuppositions of argumentation" not as the weak transcendental foundation they are meant to be, but as existing values which, being autonomous or secular, end up in competition with religious motives.

Habermas's question about justification leads Rawls to specify three different stages in the testing and "embedding" of a conception of justice. Displaying its freestanding character at the "*pro tanto*" stage, it becomes assimilated to the individual background doctrines in a second step, and is "publicly" acknowledged at the third, again individually implemented stage. What is "public" about it is not the exchange of reasons but the mutual registration among citizens that each of them is equally performing the same act of vindication on their own.[215]

For Habermas, this still amounts to drawing the decisive reason for supporting a political conception of justice from the level of personal worldviews, and shortchanging practical reason: "The concept of practical reason cannot be drained of moral substance and morality cannot be relegated to the black box of comprehensive doctrines."[216] Thus, before the different levels of justification defended by each of them as the most general and inclusive one can be examined, it has to be explained how Habermas's assumption of an immediately accessible moral consciousness works itself out in political theory: in the idea of a public use of practical reason in democratic deliberation.

---

taphysical views. Habermas does not take much time to argue against them in detail; rather, he lays them aside, or occasionally dismisses them, as unusable and without credible independent merit in view of his philosophical analysis of the presuppositions of rational discourse and communicative action."

214 The following passage that concludes his essay on "Themes in postmetaphysical thinking", in *Postmetaphysical Thinking*, 28–51, 51, is requoted by him in his response at the Chicago conference in 1988, in "Transcendence from within": "Philosophy, even in its postmetaphysical form, will be able neither to replace nor to repress religion as long as religious language is the bearer of a semantic content that is inspiring and even indispensable, for this content eludes (for the time being?) the explanatory force of the religious language and continues to resist translation into reasoning discourses."

215 Rawls, "Reply to Habermas", in *Studienausgabe* II, 104–05: "3. Public justification happens when all the reasonable members of political society carry out a justification of the shared political conception by embedding it in their several reasonable comprehensive doctrines."

216 Habermas, "'Reasonable' versus 'true'", in *Inclusion of the Other*, 99.

2.3.2 Public reason as generated in the practical discourse of citizens

For Habermas, the feature in Rawls's argumentation that cuts short the moral competence of citizens is the device of the veil of ignorance. While their own access to the moral point of view is not elucidated, the conditions for choosing the principles of justice take over the role of reconciling divergent perspectives. Thus, rather than the moral subjects themselves, the conditions stand for the morality of the future political framework.[217] The critical theorist reconstructs political autonomy more radically from its basis in the ability for perspective taking implied in linguistic interaction. Citizens fill the democratic structures which are entrusted to their moral competence with their own deliberations; no material principles such as those agreed in the original position can be set, just the formal test of universalization:

> Under the pragmatic presuppositions of an inclusive and noncoercive rational discourse between free and equal participants, everyone is required to take the perspective of everyone else and thus to project herself into the understandings of self and world of all others; from this interlocking of perspectives there emerges an ideally extended "we-perspective" from which all can test in common whether they wish to make a controversial norm the basis of their shared practice; and this should include mutual criticism of the appropriateness of the languages in terms of which situations and needs are interpreted.[218]

The "political" thus denotes a process between citizens endowed with the capability of mutual perspective taking in which matters that are morally relevant are detected, and a consensus on norms for directing policies is reached.[219] In their

---

217 "Rawls imposes a common perspective on the parties in the original position through informational constraints and thereby neutralizes the multiplicity of particular interpretive perspectives from the outset. Discourse Ethics, by contrast, views the moral point of view as embodied in an intersubjective praxis of argumentation which enjoins those involved to an idealizing enlargement of their interpretive perspectives. Discourse Ethics rests on the intuition that the application of the principle of universalization, properly understood, calls for a joint process of 'ideal role taking.'... the veil of ignorance constrains the field of vision of parties in the original position *from the beginning* to the basic principles on which presumptively free and equal citizens would agree, nonwithstanding their divergent interpretations of self and world." Habermas, "Reconciliation", in *Inclusion of the Other*, 57–8.
218 Habermas, "Reconciliation", in *Inclusion of the Other*, 58.
219 In his comparison of both approaches, Thomas McCarthy summarizes Habermas's position as follows: "In this model of a deliberative decentering of political power, the multiple and multiform arenas for detecting, defining, and discussing society's problems, and the culturally and politically mobilized publics who use them, serve as the basis for democratic self-government and thus for political autonomy." "Kantian constructivism and reconstructivism", 49.

civic capacity, moral agents are exercising their dual property of being "authors" as well as "addressees of laws". This double designation exemplifies that "popular sovereignty and human rights are nourished by the same root".[220] In contrast, by according priority to individual liberal rights, Rawls's argumentation loses the element of popular sovereignty and restricts the field of the political; it then no longer includes a participative, co-creative understanding of democracy in which political conceptions are still to be designed, rather than merely confirmed and "embedded" in existing, unchanging worldviews. Thus, Habermas emphasizes the moral content as well as the procedural and the productive nature of public reason. It is the practical reason every agent has access to, and its public exercise works through conflicting positions to generate a new level of shared insight into obligations and rights, both negative and participative: "democratic self-legislation assumes the position occupied by the negative liberties in Political Liberalism."[221]

What remains open and unspecified, however, are the various resources agents draw from when they submit political questions to the discursive test of practical reason. The existing plurality of starting points, each of them open to a postconventional moral perspective, is recognized; it is also assumed that background perspectives are not fixed once and for all but open to further articulation, learning and development in mutual exchange. Yet no attention is given to the contents that such cultural formations could contribute to a public process of argumentation on concrete issues. By calling them "comprehensive doctrines", Rawls captures the historically rooted, coherent nature of these approaches and traditions,[222] but restricts their expression to the background culture. Habermas wants citizens and social movements to engage in public discourse but undervalues the particular insights of these worldviews because the ethical level is seen as disconnected from postconventional morality as a matter of principle.

2.3.3 The basis of justification: Moral, ethical, or civic?

What remains to be clarified are the understanding and the level at which there is a need for "justification". Habermas interprets Rawls's move in *Political Liber-*

---

220 Habermas, "Reconciliation", in *Inclusion of the Other*, 71.
221 Habermas, "'Reasonable' versus 'true'", in *Inclusion of the Other*, 78.
222 Their persistence from their origins in ancient history is one of the reasons why they are able to supply a "deep and enduring basis" for the "social unity... of a democratic regime". Rawls, "Reply to Habermas", in *Studienausgabe* II, 106.

alism, confirmed in his reply in the second step of embedding principles in comprehensive doctrines, as making the whole theory "ethical"; it thus reduces its standard of justification which should be universal to the level of particular cultural traditions. Rawls, however, sees the self-understanding of citizens at work, not individual metaphysical doctrines. For Habermas, validity claims in social anthropology and in political theory cannot be isolated from each other and are part of what needs to be discussed and justified. How much their paths diverge, becomes clear from their opposite interpretations of the concept of "legitimacy". To be assessed in conclusion is which analysis of Rawls's argumentation is more convincing: Habermas's interpretation of his solution as handing over too much to ethical worldviews, or Rainer Forst's diagnosis of an ambivalence that is ultimately resolved in favour of the initial political conception that is civic.

From a Kantian perspective, Habermas rejects the replacement of a moral judgement that is available to all with an array of individually convincing assessments that may, or may not, overlap. As a result of the retreat he observes in Rawls from searching for and arguing towards a moral consensus, judgement is split into two components: the "believer's" perspective as a participant in a worldview, and that of the "observer" who states as a secondary finding that there is an area of overlap. There is a

> division of labor between the political and the metaphysical that leads to a distinction between *what* all citizens can agree upon and *the reasons for* their individually accepting it as true… each citizen combines the perspective of a participant with that of an observer. Observers can describe… that an overlapping consensus has occurred… But in the objectifying attitude of observers, citizens cannot penetrate each others' worldviews and judge their truth content from the internal perspective peculiar to each. [223]

It is a matter of chance whether these individual background assumptions have anything in common:

> Only the lucky convergence of the differently motivated nonpublic reasons can generate the public validity or "reasonableness" of the content of this "overlapping consensus"… Agreement in conclusions *results* from premises rooted in different outlooks… the participants can only register this convergence as a social fact… Before an overlapping consensus is established, there is no public, intersubjectively shared perspective from which the citizens could make inherently impartial judgments.[224]

---

223 Habermas, "'Reasonable' versus 'true'", in *Inclusion of the Other*, 83.
224 Habermas, "'Reasonable' versus 'true'", in *Inclusion of the Other*, 84.

Habermas's main objection is that a reflection which is perfectly available to each agent is avoided, and is replaced by an agreement that has already been concluded:

> The citizens are denied the "moral point of view" from which they could develop and justify a political conception *in joint public deliberation*. What Rawls calls the "public use of reason" presupposes the shared platform of an already achieved political consensus on fundamentals.[225]

For Habermas, in contrast to Forst, this argumentation locates the individual reasons for support in the worldviews, making them incommunicable, indeed, unintelligible:

> Though struck from the public agenda, the metaphysical nevertheless remains the ultimate ground of the validity of what is morally right and ethically good. The political sphere, by contrast, is deprived of any source of validity of its own... The overlapping consensus rests on the converging moral segments of the diverging totalities of what each citizen holds to be true.
>
> Although the acceptance of a freestanding conception of justice is parasitic on complementary metaphysical truths, the political conception is nevertheless supposed to exhibit a reasonableness that *adds* the aspect of public recognition to those idiosyncratic and mutually nontransparent truths.[226]

Against this purely "comprehensive" reading by Habermas, Rawls affirms that while his justification gives greater significance to background beliefs, the crucial level is not provided by these, but by citizens' self-understanding. The real basis is found in its implications, and this is what makes the political conception "freestanding", not indebted to metaphysical doctrines, and independent of philosophical controversies. He assumes that by providing the theory of this given, "substantial" self-understanding, political liberalism supplies all the justification that is needed. His failure to grasp the Kantian concept of "legitimacy" as distinct from mere "legality" illustrates their different understandings of justification: For him, legitimacy

> says something about... pedigree: how they came to their office. It refers to whether they were the legitimate heir to the throne... under a democratic regime... (l)aws passed by solid majorities are counted legitimate, even though many protest and correctly judge them unjust or otherwise wrong. Thus, legitimacy is a weaker idea than justice and imposes weaker constraints on what can be done... democratic decisions and laws are legitimate,

---

225 Habermas, "'Reasonable' versus 'true'", in *Inclusion of the Other*, 84.
226 Habermas, "'Reasonable' versus 'true'", in *Inclusion of the Other*, 85.

not because they are just but because they are legitimately enacted... it may not be just and still be legitimate, provided it is just enough in view of the circumstances and social conditions... Legitimacy allows for an indeterminate range of injustice that justice does not.[227]

His subsequent questions of clarification equally show that he misunderstands how legitimacy in the Kantian sense is constituted by examining individual interests for their universalizability, and thus for their justice in relation to every human being's right to an equal share: "Are we to think that each person's interest are to be given equal consideration in ideal discourse? What are the relevant interests? Or are all interests to be counted...? This might yield a utilitarian principle to satisfy the greatest balance of interests."[228]

He does not see that for Habermas, it is precisely the "democratic principle of legitimation" that supplies the alternative to a utilitarian neglect of the need to account for basic rights. At the same time, this principle goes beyond a priority for "liberal basic rights"; they are not just givens but themselves in need both of deontological justification and of concretizations to be decided in discourse with others.[229] The quest for legitimation which should be at the core of the construction of the constitutional state is replaced with giving "primacy" to the class of undiscussed "liberal basic rights"[230] as such. Since Rawls's approach falls short of the level Habermas expects for a critical grounding of the state, he classifies it as giving precedence to comprehensive doctrines.

In Rainer Forst's analysis, however, it is not the particular background traditions that come out on top, but the political conception. Rawls's argumentation oscillates between the two but ultimately gives precedence to the *pro tanto* form of justification:

> This account raises the central question of how the moral force that the freestanding *pro tanto* justification of the conception of justice initially confers entirely independent of eth-

---

227 Rawls, "Reply to Habermas", in *Studienausgabe* II, 127.

228 Rawls, "Reply to Habermas", in *Studienausgabe* II, 128. In Fn. 77, he notes the difference of Habermas's understanding of legitimacy to Max Weber's, "who understood legitimacy as acceptance by a people of its political and social institutions. Acceptance alone without justification Habermas rightly holds is not enough" (139, n. 77). His addition to which he thinks Habermas could agree that "these institutions need not be perfectly just, and may, depending on the situation, be unjust and still be legitimate" misunderstands that legitimacy cannot be accorded without the test of universalizability and that it has to be reconfirmed in citizens' discourse on justice.

229 The level decisive for the legitimacy of the state is the "standpoint of impartial judgment of deontological principles of justice". Habermas doubts that the original position offers a successful argument for impartiality (Habermas, "Reconciliation", in *Inclusion of the Other*, 50 – 51).

230 Habermas, "Reconciliation", in *Inclusion of the Other*, 50 – 51.

ical beliefs can, on the one hand, be absorbed wholly by the ethical "truth" of comprehensive doctrines, while, on the other hand, it prevails justice in the political-public use of reason in its restriction to moral-political values of justice. Rawls is unable clearly to explain the moral justification of the political conception: he fluctuates between a form of justification based on an ethical-comprehensive doctrine and a freestanding moral justification. But ultimately he must opt for the latter, since otherwise the first type of justification would fail... The level of justification that is reached at the first step in a public, reciprocal and general justification must govern the other steps, for otherwise there could be no insight at all into the *priority* of justice over "non-political" values.[231]

Apart from being distinct from comprehensive doctrines, the level of the political conception is more than a hermeneutics of existing democratic culture for Forst, namely one that includes reflection on principles.[232] What is decisive, in my view, for the role accorded or denied to religion, however, is that there is no interest in the content of metaphysical and religious convictions; nor is there any change envisioned in the political conception in the course of embedding a comprehensive doctrine in them. There seems to be no use for them as resources apart from confirming and filling in the political conception that was developed without them; at the "political" level, in contrast to the background culture, they are also asked to keep silent about their differences. The "module" (PL, 12–13. 144–5) of the political conception can be plugged into them, but Rawls's hope is that it will shape them towards its own standard, rather than receiving impulses and insights from these worldviews. Integration is achieved by silencing their own original contents. Thus, with regard to the question whether historical communities of interpretation can draw on their intellectual heritage in current mat-

---

231 Forst, *Right to Justification*, 96. The following statement from Rawls shows a much greater appreciation for the consistency and historical depth dimension of the worldviews held by associations that "play a basic social role in making public justification possible", than Habermas's references to the ethical level: Pointing out the "deep and enduring basis" for the "social unity... of a democratic regime" that also religious associations provide, Rawls states: "these doctrines have their own life and history apart from their current members and endure from one generation to the next." "Reply to Habermas", in *Studienausgabe* II, 106.

232 In *Right to Justification*, 85–86, Forst argues against Otfried Höffe's objection that Rawls's argument remains at the level of a hermeneutics of already existing democracy that it does not "simply pick out what is contingently shared in a culture; rather, it confines itself to the ideas and principles of practical reason that are unavoidable (*unhintergehbar*) in a process of reflective equilibrium if one poses the question of justice for a pluralist society. The fundamental ideas are in no way contingent, but are those that can 'qualify' as reciprocal and general in public justification properly understood." In my view, this analysis implies two levels: the ideas are given as implications of the civic ethos, *and* they are critically appropriated which presupposes a move from cognitive rationality to will.

ters of political opinion formation, Forst's assessment of the priority of political conceptions over worldviews seems correct to me. Even if Rawls's own assessment is that he gives greater prominence to worldviews than Habermas does, the three levels of justification distinguished in Rawls's response ultimately subordinate comprehensive doctrines to the "political conceptions" which make up his concept of "public reason".

How does Habermas assess the development of Rawls's thinking from its theological origins in the 1940s to the role of religious background positions in the 1990s? His evaluation will also provide a transition to his own most recent evaluation of religion, to be analysed in section 4.

2.3.4 From religion to public reason: Habermas's comments on continuities in Rawls's thinking from its theological origins

In his comments that conclude the German edition of Rawls's posthumously published theological dissertation of 1942, Habermas identifies two lines of continuity that are unaffected by the negative answer to religion which Rawls gave in a personal document in 1997.[233] One is the originally theologically based insight into the inviolability of the human person that motivates his lifelong opposition to Utilitarianism (1). The second is the ongoing significance given to worldviews and to one's own conception of the good. Justification has to extend to this level (2).

2.3.4.1 Human individuality in response to God and as normative in the construction of just social structures

The first point is shared by Habermas who has himself emphasized the religious genealogy of key terms of Western ethics.[234] He sees Rawls's later work as providing a "philosophical translation of religious motives",[235] similar to the transformation into autonomous ethics offered by Kant. Specific intuitions of his social

---

233 Rawls, "On my religion", in *A Brief Inquiry into the Meaning of Sin and Faith*, ed. T. Nagel (Cambridge/Mass.: Harvard University Press, 2006), 259–269.
234 In a footnote, he refers to Rawls's "implicit polemic against Greek thinking in which he contrasts the Christian concept of the 'person' individuated in her life history who has shed the anonymity of the Roman *persona* to the ... (originally Greek) concept of the individual applied to all objects individuated in space and time." Habermas, "Nachwort", J. Rawls, *Über Sünde, Glaube und Religion* (Frankfurt: Suhrkamp, 2010), 315–336, 325, n. 12.
235 Habermas, "Nachwort", 315.

theory are founded in attitudes and insights that arise from an understanding of humanity and world structured by the relationship to God:

> The objections against Utilitarianism which Rawls presents in *Theory of Justice* are rooted (*angelegt*) in his religious ethics. The decisive features of individuality arise from the structure of a community of persons who relate in a performative attitude to an *irreplaceable* (*nichtaustauschbaren*) other by ascribing to each other reciprocally irreplaceability (*Unvertretbarkeit*) and unmistakeability (*Unverwechselbarkeit*)[236].

This "performative" rather than objectifying attitude originates in each believer's orientation towards God which is shared with one's fellow-humans. Its consequence is a universalism that Rawls embraces at this stage. Habermas interprets him as follows:

> The Christian belief in the existence of the one God before whom all humans are equal implies besides the egalitarian conception of the equal dignity of each one at the same time a delimitation (*Entgrenzung*) towards a confederation oriented towards complete inclusion. The young Rawls defends this universalism against contemporary forms of ethnocentric exclusion (*Abschließung*) of what is one's own from what is other, in a critical diagnosis of the time.[237]

Habermas does not comment on the fact that this cosmopolitan horizon is no longer kept open in *Theory of Justice* and abandoned in the *Law of Peoples*. Yet it is worth noting that once the religious motivation fades in Rawls, so does his early universalism. By giving up the universalist scope, a problem is removed that Habermas only hints at but which continues to provoke divergent answers in theological thinking: the question of whether all human beings, including perpetrators of evil, are going to be saved in an *apokatastasis panton*. It engages with the theological problem of how God's justice relates to God's mercy:

> The deontological and individual sense is complemented by two further aspects: demands of radically equal treatment and complete inclusion. An egalitarian universalism also appears condensed (*verdichtet*) in the image of the Last Judgement: the time when God will solve the paradoxical task of pronouncing on the deeds and omissions of each one in regard of each individual life story, an (ultimately salvific) judgement which is differentiated, and at once just and merciful [*zugleich gerechtes und gnädiges (letztlich erlösendes) Urteil*].[238]

---

236 Habermas, "Nachwort", 324–25.
237 Habermas, "Nachwort", 326–27.
238 Habermas, "Nachwort", 325. As examples of two opposite views, cf. J. Moltmann's defense of Origen's idea of a totally inclusive reconciliation and H. U. v. Balthasar who insists on the need

Habermas does not pursue the "paradoxical task" any further and just notes the contrast which the idea of complete inclusion forms to the political movements of the 1930s and 1940s on which Rawls comments in his thesis. His graduation was followed the same year by his enlistment into the United States' military forces. Habermas summarizes his analysis that ascribes to "'pride and vanity'... an egotism generalized in a collectivist way in the ethnocentric exclusion or oppression of incriminated races and classes, alien confessions, peoples, and cultures",[239] and quotes his judgement, "'closed groups are now tearing that civilization to pieces.'"[240]

The egalitarianism that Rawls upholds also after his retreat from a universalistic scope of inclusion is critical of meritocratic appropriations of success to one's own efforts, rather than propitious circumstances not of one's own making. According to Habermas, his opposition to libertarian liberalism is rooted here:

> No matter whether a creator God or nature's lottery decide on how these resources are distributed, those favoured cannot claim the availability of such potential as their own merit. Precisely this distinction has been obscured (*verwischt*) by a triumphant market liberalism. The fact that some persons can, and others cannot, be counted among a functionally conceived elite does not justify any difference in the respect and in the treatment that is equally due to each person based on their human dignity.[241]

The equal respect due to every human being, worked out for the basic structure of democratic societies, is mediated in a model analogous to the religious structuring of the relations between self, others and God; in Habermas's account, it was first transferred to a secular level by Kant. Besides this triadic structure with a mediating third between self and other, Habermas names as the second element crucial for the transformation from a religious to a moral basis Rawls's critique of ontological categories in favour of personalist ones. Both features together inform a theory of justice which is not "ontologically" given, neither by God nor in natural traits, but constructed by human reason; as in Kant, there is a move from God as the uniting "third" position to the moral law, or to the

---

to take the human freedom of the perpetrators in their choice of evil seriously. For an in depth treatment of the competing emphases on God's justice and on God's mercy in the history of theological thinking from the Bible to modernity, cf. D. Ansorge, *Gerechtigkeit und Barmherzigkeit Gottes* (Freiburg: Herder, 2009).

239 Rawls, *A Brief Inquiry into the Meaning of Sin and Faith,* 103–258, 196.
240 Habermas, "Nachwort", 327. Quote by Rawls, *Brief Inquiry,* 197.
241 Habermas, "Nachwort", 326.

conception of justice which takes the place of the "transcendent".[242] Habermas reconstructs the lineage as follows: The "deliberation on the right conception of justice" is achieved by the "transformation of the point of view of God into a structurally generated perspective of argumentation which urges participants in a self- interested way to use their practical reason morally". He identifies as the "linkage point in the thinking of the young Rawls" a "performative view":

> in the same manner as God was introduced in the performative view of a second person who is encountered in the community of communication, he now discloses what is morally demanded in the performative attitude of a person who experiences in communication what she owes to others or for what she is indebted to them.[243]

Habermas's observation on the underlying triadic structuring of both the monotheistic and the Kantian accounts is perceptive, although its implications would need to be drawn out: the affirmation of a responsibility for each other as a consequence of God's individualizing call, or of acceptance of the moral law, as a matter of appropriation by a person's will, rather than as an implication of linguistically mediated intersubjectivity. Yet his use of the term "performative" for both requires a comment. In the *Postscript*, Habermas's interest is to draw the lines of continuity from the early Rawls to the author of *A Theory of Justice*. Yet it is remarkable how the discourse ethicist, despite his previous critique of the device of the veil of ignorance, now sees two radically alternative conceptions as similar with regard to their supposedly equal "performative" character: namely the "performative" realization of what one owes to others, and the "structurally generated perspective of argumentation" of initially "self-interested" rational choice agents. How can the second one be reconciled with his objection that exactly that element which could be called "performative", namely the "insight" of agents in their moral capacity, was dropped, and the framework,

---

242 Habermas traces the "philosophical reshaping (*Umformung*) of religious thoughts that Kant was the first to carry out" as follows: "The basic traits of a religious community ethics can be sublated (*aufgehoben*) on the secular basis of practical reason into an individualistically conceived, egalitarian-universalist ethics of obligation, since the triadic pattern of relations of the monotheistic community of faith is also retained in the realm of ends (*Reich der Zwecke*) – that is, the universal community of intelligences that binds itself to given laws from its own insight. Here also, persons are not in an *immediate* relationship to other persons. Rather, all interpersonal relationships are mediated by the relation of each one affected to the authority of an impartial third element – to the authority of the moral law founded on reason. The place of the relationship of the individual to the one God who creates connection (*Zusammenhang*) is now taken by the moral point of view that unites all, under which all autonomously acting subjects examine conscientiously how they are to act in a case of conflict." Habermas, "Nachwort", 327.
243 Habermas, "Nachwort", 329.

namely the veil of ignorance, enriched instead with attributes of morality? His subsumtion of both approaches, one based on moral self-reflection, the other "structurally generated", under the term "performative" is puzzling; it invalidates the evidence of meaning this category had in its relation to the self-understanding of agents.

In his desire to uncover continuities between the origins and the later development of his thinking, the second feature, Rawls's opposition to natural theology, is also understood from this ongoing trait. "Ontological" is seen as the opposite to "performative"; the first stands for an approach that objectifies instead of reconstructing "implicit knowledge that is present from the participant's perspective". Categorizing the critique of ontology as a "postmetaphysical abstention (*Enthaltsamkeit*) from ontological statements", he quotes as proof the "polemical" remark of the preface: "An ounce of the Bible is worth a pound (possibly a ton) of Aristotle."[244] This early judgement of Rawls's is seen as the result of two theological traditions intersecting: a "dialectical theology marked by the influence of Kierkegaard, and Buber's philosophy of dialogue which was mediated by Brunner. Both traditions develop religious statements from the existential-religious context of experience of the communicative encounter with the other."[245] Could Habermas's view as commentator on Rawls's early religious beginnings, and his emphasis on the personalist rather than ontological categories he opts for to spell out biblical contents, be motivated by his own critique of metaphysics? Habermas does not follow up on the truth claim of personalist, encounter-oriented understandings and only marks the difference to ontological thinking. Does Rawls's view change on this issue, and if so, how does Habermas comment on it?

Quite in contrast to Rawls's early regard for persons individuated by their life stories and connected by their personal relationship to God, is his negative assessment of Christianity in 1997. Its "deleterious effects on one's character" are linked to the personal quest for salvation in a framework of double predestination. Now, Christianity is viewed as a "solitary religion: each one is saved or damned individually". Rawls goes on to state: "our own individual soul and its salvation are hardly important for the larger picture of civilised life".[246] Habermas sees this position as an expression of his "strict moral attitude (*Gesinnung*)" that demands "reasons for moral action to be sufficiently distinguished

---

244 Habermas, "Nachwort", 329–330, n. 17, quoting from Rawls's Preface with the preceding sentence: 'I do not believe that the Greek tradition mixes very well with Christianity, and the sooner we stop kow-towing to Plato and Aristotle, the better.' Rawls, *Brief Inquiry*, 107.
245 Habermas, "Nachwort", 329, n. 17.
246 Habermas, "Nachwort", 308.

from the self-oriented motives of the quest for personal salvation". He thus tunes into Rawls's new assessment of the non-objectifiable and not ontologically re-solvable question of personal response and relation to God as morally dubious. He could equally have questioned its suspicion of the longing for salvation and its alignment with a deleterious self-occupation. Even Kant recognized the legiti-macy of striving for happiness, although morality itself had to be distinguished from it. By declaring the lack of importance of the individual soul, Rawls is in danger of dismissing singularity as such. No comment other than the one quoted is available here from Habermas who otherwise clearly states his disagreement on other points, such as the following one, on truth.

What remains paramount throughout the course of Rawls's thinking is the emphasis on the individual. It also forms the bridge to the view of practical rea-son developed in *Political Liberalism* which compensates for its renunciation to a cognitively justifiable claim by being anchored in individually grasped personal truths.

2.3.4.2 Anchoring the right in a personal view of truth

Section 2.3.3 above dealt with Forst's disagreement with Habermas's judgement that comprehensive doctrines, as distinct from morality and from the self-under-standing shared by citizens, acquire the dominant role in Rawls's process of jus-tification. It is in keeping with this analysis that Habermas highlights the need expressed in Rawls's view for moral claims to gain "flesh and blood" by being anchored in encompassing worldviews. He also points out the awareness of a "vacuum" left by a previously religious endorsement of morality that is waiting to be filled.[247] On the one hand, Habermas shares Rawls's point about the signi-ficance of worldviews; he has emphasized in his most recent writings that the "secularization of state power is not to be confused with the secularization of civil society".[248] On the other hand, he disagrees with the weakening of the de-ontological level of justification by giving the monopoly of truth to worldviews.

---

[247] "As a consequence of the religious experiences of his youth Rawls allowed himself to be concerned (*beunruhigen*) by the vacuum that a marginalized (*verdrängte*) religion left behind in the Enlightenment thought of the law of reason. In the two decades since the publication of *Theory of Justice* Rawls was dealing with the question whether a practical reason shared by us all which is sufficient to construe a concept of political justice has enough substance to reach the level (*das Wasser zu reichen*) of a morality that is related (*verschwistert*) to religion. Finally, he reaches the view that a liberal conception of justice only acquires flesh and blood in a communal sphere (*Gemeinwesen*) when it finds support (*Halt*) in the contexts of religions and worldviews." Habermas, "Nachwort", 331–2.

[248] Habermas, "Nachwort", 316.

Here, he sees a lingering influence of Rawls's early religious conviction that the comprehensive doctrines which shape people's biographies cannot be separated from normative validity claims.

> Ultimately all personal relations are so connected for the reason that we all exist before God, and by being related to Him we are all related to each other although we may never have met one another. That personal relations form such a nexus leads us to the conclusion that religion and ethics cannot be separated.[249]

On this second point, Habermas retains his critical position against assigning the predicate "true" to comprehensive doctrines, while political conceptions of justice, the truth claims of which should be argued out in a discursive process, only earn the predicate "reasonable". He sees in this reduction of the cognitive status of practical reason a late effect of Rawls's "religious socialization": truth is private and foundational for a person's outlook. Yet even if pluralism in matters of the good is irreducible, the consequence drawn by Rawls, a strategy of avoidance, is not the only one possible. The fact that there are plural sources to the life and regeneration of civil society, even if they will offer conflicting solutions, allows for a more differentiated articulation of justice and for a more encompassing future stability.

What Habermas fails to explore, however, is whether the critical view of natural theology and ontology that Rawls held, both as a young theologian and subsequently as a social philosopher, does not promote a dissociation from truth claims by understanding faith exclusively in terms of personal encounter. Instead of investigating what the approach of natural theology intended, the connection of revelation as a nondeducible historical event to the subject's capability to recognize the fulfillment of its quest for meaning, Habermas dismisses it as only "objectifying". This robs religious faith of an opportunity to explain to a general consciousness of truth the rationality of its claim: not merely to personal evidence, as it appears in heightened form in an individual experience of conversion, but also to a possibly true interpretation of the world as created and saved by a transcendent God. Taking the side of the early Rawls and linking it to his own struggle against metaphysical thinking, he leaves religion in a realm separated from discursive justifiability.

Contemporary theologians have noted the duality between keeping religion as a compartment that is different and alien in comparison with every other communicable human insight, and deeming it open to "translation". Their objections to what they see as a contradiction will be followed up in the concluding part of

---

249 Rawls, *Brief Inquiry,* 116.

the fourth and final section on Habermas's position regarding religion and public reason. A second point for theological and ethical enquiry will be his critique of Kant's doctrine of postulates which unites him with Rawls. How each of them assess the antinomy of practical reason will have consequences for their views on the link between morality religion. When the scope of ethics is reduced to probable achievability, both morality in its reflection on the motivation for unconditional unilateral action, and religion are left short of the horizon Kant claimed as part of practical reason.

In summary, based on his early investigation of a normative concept of the public sphere and on his concretization of Kant's universalization criterion into an intersubjective forum of deliberation on justifiable policy directions, the critical theorist judges Rawls's concept of public reason as deficient. Its withdrawal from argumentation on truth claims is interpreted as advocating worldviews as the level that confers validity at least in the empirical sense; this falls short of claims for principled, context-independent validity which are the only ones that can confer legitimacy to political decisions. Habermas does not explore the possibility of a third level between the moral and the ethical, namely a self-understanding as citizens that is both principled and marked by particularity. In his review of Rawls's first academic work, his unpublished bachelor thesis, he attributes the attention *Political Liberalism* pays to people's personal backgrounds and convictions to his religious socialization but fails to note two changes: Rawls's reduction of the universal scope of justice that occurs after leaving the originally Christian motivation of his thinking behind, and his skeptical view of the significance of the individual that appears in his dismissal of the personal quest for salvation. In what Habermas calls the "paradoxical task" of reconciling justice and mercy, Rawls's moralistic formulations of 1997 disavow the self in its precarious position of responsibility and need for grace; by dismissing the hope for salvation as if the wish to reconcile morality and flourishing life was not a legitimate concern, the individual seems to be regarded as a *quantité négligeable* in view of the grand task of constructing and maintaining just structures. While the individual is still defended against the utilitarian calculus of average benefit, the prior existential-personalist regard in which it was held is no longer its basis.

Habermas's new position on religion, his invitation to secularized and believing fellow-citizens to engage in mutual translations, reflects his long-held position that a diversity of input into the public sphere is a valuable resource. Stability does not arise from avoiding exchange and conflict, but from creating cohesion in openness, curiosity and mutual respect within the framework of discourse. In my final section on Habermas's reconfiguration of the roles of public reason and religion, I will trace his new regard for the potential that religious traditions bring to public debate; it includes their institutional support as communities of interpretation of fora where options of the good and demands of morality can be voiced and related to each other. The threshold between civic deliberation and parliamentary law-making that he insists on for religious contributions will turn out not to be shared across the board by philosophical positions; theological responses to the latest phase of his thinking on religion will conclude Part Two.

2.4 Religion as a resource for the project of modernity

Both Neo-Kantian thinkers agree that democracy in its orientation towards justice, equality and recognition needs to find support in accommodating life forms which arise from value traditions, among them religions.[250] Habermas's new diagnosis of a "postsecular" society stands as much in contrast to his previous endorsement of the secularization thesis as Rawls's discovery of pluralism does with the framework in which *Theory of Justice* was conceived which featured neither religions nor other communal bases for society's pluralist constitution. For the discourse ethicist, a different perspective that explains the persistence of religion is opened up by Karl Jaspers's genealogical thesis of the joint origin of philosophy and world religions in the axial age (1). A counterforce to pathological aspects of modern developments is found in the reflective capacity of religions. Their heuristic and semantic potential leads to their new appreciation as communities of interpretation in which the existing and emerging challenges of complex societies can be approached from multiple angles. While Habermas defends the integral nature of religious believers' outlook against Rawls's "proviso" and values their encounter with non-religious citizens as the originating moment of the "political", the enrichment their contributions bring to the public sphere ends at the threshold of state institutions. Society is postsecular, the state remains neutral (2). A review of problems identified by theologians will conclude the second part. They can be traced back to the limits posed by Habermas's concept of postmetaphysical reason which conceives the translation

---

250 Their analyses based on contemporary differentiated societies are preceded by the parallel Kant draws between morality and the "ethical commonwealth" supported by religious resources; its significance in Kant remains disputed between Herta Nagl-Docekal's reconstruction in "Eine rettende Übersetzung? Jürgen Habermas interpretiert Kant's Religionsphilosophie", and Habermas's response, "Replik auf Einwände, Reaktion auf Anregungen", in Langthaler/Nagl-Docekal (eds.), *Glauben und Wissen*, 93–119. 366–414.

of religious motifs in terms that neglect the parts played by philosophy of religion, philosophical ethics, and the history of theological thinking (3).

2.4.1 The persistence of religion and the task of reconstructing the genealogy of human reflection in religions and philosophies

The main correction of the view of religion put forward twenty years earlier in *Theory of Communicative Action* lies in disconnecting the theory of modernity from a secularization thesis that predicted the end of religion. Now, the modern course of rationalization is seen as an open-ended process in which the currently observable "revitalisation" of world religions may, or may not, continue (1). The fact that religions have survived, despite the loss of functions that accrued to them in their histories, poses a challenge to secular self-understanding. Merely banishing religion from the public, as laicistic state forms do, is not an adequate way of dealing with the persistence of religious self-understandings. They need to be reconstructed in their relationship to the origins of reason (2). How Jaspers and Habermas distinguish the two axial formations of reflection, will be compared and submitted to a theological critique (3).

2.4.1.1 From the secularization thesis to the consciousness of a postsecular constellation

The changed relationship between religion and society in modernity captured as "secularization" has been subject to various sociological interpretations. Drawing on José Casanova's studies, Habermas now agrees that individualization and the loss of previous functions have not led to the disappearance of religion in the political public, in culture, nor in the personal lives of citizens with a religious allegiance. This is why now the term "postsecular" seems to offer a more adequate description of a society in which "religious communities continue to exist in a context of ongoing secularisation".[251] The new assessment, put forward in his speech on receiving the Peace Prize of the German Booktrade, held a few weeks after the attacks of September 11, 2001, of a "postsecular" stage of modern society, is subsequently qualified as describing a change of "consciousness" rather than an abrupt break between a secular and a postsecular period. This new awareness is ascribed to three factors. The first is the perception of global conflicts which the media often present as having religious roots. Habermas's

---

[251] Habermas, "Faith and Knowledge", in *The Future of Human Nature*, 104.

comment is that "frequently conflicts which have a different, profane origin are sparked into glowing conflicts by being coded in religious terms".[252] Secondly, the effect on European citizens of a new consciousness of the significance of religious traditions in other continents is that "all triumphalism is driven out of their secular understanding of the world"; its *certainty* that the ongoing cultural and societal modernization will happen *at the expense of* the public and personal relevance of religion is lost."[253] The third factor, immigration, presents religious and secular fellow-citizens with the vitality of other religions in their own neighbourhoods. It is necessary, however, to distinguish a "sociological" from a "genealogical" perspective:

> the expression "postsecular" is not a genealogical but a sociological predicate. I use this expression to describe modern societies that have to reckon with the continuing existence of religious groups and the continuing relevance of the different religious traditions, even if the societies themselves are largely secularized. Insofar as I describe as "postsecular", not society itself, but a corresponding change of consciousness in it, the predicate can also be used to refer to an altered self-understanding of the largely secularized societies of Western Europe, Canada, or Australia... In this case, "postsecular" refers, like "postmetaphysical", to a caesura in the history of mentality. But the difference is that we use the sociological predicate as a description from the observer's perspective, whereas we use the genealogical predicate from the perspective of one who shares in the goal of self-understanding.[254]

The task arising for social theory, political philosophy and ethics from such changes, both in the reality of contemporary culture and in the consciousness of it, is to add to the empirical level of enquiry a quest that is internal to reason. It is to re-examine the roots of the process in which philosophies and religions emerged together:

> This modern reason will learn to understand itself only when it clarifies its relation to a contemporary religious consciousness which has become reflexive by grasping the shared

---

252 Habermas, "Die Revitalisierung der Weltreligionen – Herausforderung für ein säkulares Selbstverständnis der Moderne?", in J. Habermas, *Kritik der Vernunft, Studienausgabe, Philosophische Texte*, vol. 5 (Frankfurt: Suhrkamp, 2009), 387–407, 390.

253 Habermas, "Revitalisierung der Weltreligionen", in *Studienausgabe*, vol. 5, 392.

254 Habermas, "Ein neues Interesse der Philosophie an Religion. Ein Interview von Eduardo Mendieta", in *Nachmetaphysisches Denken II*, 96–119, 101. I am using the English translation that appeared under the title, "A Postsecular World Society? On the Philosophical Significance of Postsecular Consciousness and the Multicultural World Society. Jürgen Habermas Interviewed by Eduardo Mendieta", trans. M. Fritsch, in the journal *The Immanent Frame* (February 3, 2010).

origin of the two complementary intellectual formations in the cognitive advance of the Axial Age.[255]

2.4.1.2 The shared origins of religions and philosophical reason in the axial period

This new perspective, that philosophical reason is encountering a related intellectual phenomenon in the world religions, makes them appear in a different light. A genealogical understanding renders a total separation questionable, given that religions were partners in the great cognitive and moral advance of the axial age. The enquiry into the shared origin of philosophy and the world religions in their turn from myth to reflection is for reason's own sake; this is why a securalist position cuts itself off from insight into the constitution of reason. Not surprisingly, it tends to identify reason with its objectifying mode and misses its self-reflective and critical element.

> For philosophy, there are *empirical* indications that religion has remained a *contemporary* configuration of spirit [*Gestalt des Geistes*]. In addition, philosophy also finds *internal* reasons for this, reasons in its own history. The long process of translating essential, religious contents into the language of philosophy began in late antiquity... a reflection on the position of postmetaphysical thinking *between* the sciences and religion... turns against a secularist self-understanding of philosophy that aspires to merge with science, or to emerge into one. Every assimilation to the sciences withdraws the reflective dimension that distinguishes philosophy's labor of self-understanding from research.[256]

The axial period brought forth a new self-consciousnesss that was marked by the tension of reflection, replacing the "tranquillity" of the preceding stage of myth of the great antique civilizations.[257] A "reflective push" or advance (*Reflexionsschub*) divides the old from the new and thus forms the axis for a subsequent, normative human self-understanding which continues into modernity. It encompasses several strands: the birth of a historical consciousness, transcendence and universalism, and the dawning of individual responsibility.

> A reflective push in three dimensions may be read in the worldview development of the Axial Age: a historical consciousness emerges with the dogmatization of a doctrine that is traced back to founding figures; from a transcendent viewpoint internal or external to

255 Habermas, *An Awareness of What is Missing*, trans. C. Cronin (Cambridge: Polity Press, 2010), 17–18.
256 Habermas, "Neues Interesse der Philosophie?" in *Nachmetaphysisches Denken II*, 96–119, 102.
257 K. Jaspers, *The Origin and Goal of History*, trans. M. Bullock (London: Routledge, 1953), 2.

inner-worldly events, one can get into view the entirety of interpersonal relations and judge them according to universal commands; and because individual fates separate themselves from the fate of the collective, the consciousness of personal responsibility for one's own life emerges. We can also describe this as a differentiation of lifeworlds in the course of increasing social complexity: a reflexive relation to traditions and to social integration emerges, an integration that now reaches beyond kinship groups and even beyond political borders; in the relation of individuals to themselves, reflexivity emerges as well. In European modernity, we observe a further cognitive push in the *same* dimensions. We observe a sharpening of the consciousness of contingency and an extension of futural anticipation; egalitarian universalism becomes more pointed in law and morality; and there is a progressive individualization. In any case, we still draw our normative self-understanding from this (disregarding short-winded, fashionable denials).[258]

Habermas quotes Jaspers's thesis as an innovative philosophical idea that elucidates historical sequences; it fits into his own emphasis on contemporary encounters between religion and secular reason as processes of learning.[259] However, his conclusion on the role of religion will differ, since his interpretation of Jaspers accentuates elements that result in a contrast between reason and religious certainty.

2.4.1.3 The distinction between the two axial formations of reflection: Comparing Jaspers and his interpretation by Habermas

For Jaspers, these unconnected simultaneous beginnings in the period of just a few centuries, 800 to 200 BCE, can be termed a "miracle"; they are interpreted as opening up different, equally valid avenues towards the deity.[260] While Jaspers's

---

258 Habermas, "Neues Interesse der Philosophie?" in *Nachmetaphysisches Denken II*, 108–9.
259 In "The Conflict of Beliefs: *Karl Jaspers on the Clash of Cultures*", in *The Liberating Power of Symbols*, trans. P. Dews (Cambridge: Polity Press, 2001), 30–45, 31, Habermas points out how Jaspers sought to overcome "the aporias of an unrestrained historicism" by attempting to "foster mutual understanding between alien traditions and forms of life" at the level of "(e)xistential communication." The problem of a historicist approach to cultures will also be taken on by Ricoeur.
260 Jaspers, *Origin and Goal of History*, 18–20: "The fact of the threefold manifestation of the Axial Period is in the nature of a miracle, insofar as no really adequate explanation is possible within the limits of our present knowledge." (20) Jaspers interprets "the historical fact of the threefold origin" as a call to "boundless communication" which is "the best remedy against the erroneous claim to exclusive possession of truth by any one creed" (19). In his view, "that tool of fanaticism, of human arrogance and self-deception, through the will to power, that disaster for the West – most intensely so in its secularised forms, such as the dogmatic philosophies and the so-called scientific ideologies – can be vanquished by the very fact that God has manifested

philosophy of existence is interested in the reflective element shared by the two new formations, the high religions and philosophy, Habermas focuses on them as two different "modes of taking-to-be-true". The emphasis is on the cognitive capacity for truth rather than on the aspect of subjective reflection. Since Habermas stresses the reflective character of thinking in the context of his dismissal of a philosophy that turns into scientism, it appears as if reflection was reserved for non-religious manifestations of reason. This affects his understandings of religion which then becomes the "other" of reason, with consequences for how the work and the goal of translation are conceived. The quote above on the two directions of reflection continues:

> On the other hand, we should not blur the difference that exists between faith and knowledge in the mode of taking-to-be-true. Even if thinking about the postsecular situation should result in an altered attitude toward religion, this revisionism may not change the fact that postmetaphysical thinking is a secular thinking that insists on distinguishing faith and knowledge as two essentially different modes of taking-to-be-true. I repeat: at most, we may call "postsecular" the situation in which secular reason and a religious consciousness that has become reflexive engage in a relationship, of which, for instance, the dialogue between Jaspers and Bultmann is exemplary.

If both faith and knowledge are modes of "taking-to-be-true" at the same level of objective claims, then the understanding of faith as a practical option is missed; instead, it becomes an epistemological competitor. The failure to identify the specific truth claim of religion as interpretive, rather than as objective, is followed by locating their difference in its "certainty", while postmetaphysical thinking is marked by fallibility. The next step is to attribute "discursive exterritoriality" to religion, by basing it on a unique experience of revelation which seems to confer certainty once and for all. The reflectiveness and interpretive self-understanding of religion which Jaspers points out in his "axial age" thesis are played down. Both the internal link of religion to reason is underestimated, and its real specificity does not come into view. For Christian theology, the difference between the human capacity of reason and the foundational testimony of a religion is that God's self-revelation had to be initiated by God; in the Christian faith, human reason can subsequently reconstruct the truth of the incarnation but could not have made it happen. The central difference between religion and philosophy thus cannot be captured as certitude versus fallibility. Religious faith and its reflection in theology can well be marked by doubts; in any case

---

himself historically in several fashions and has opened up many ways toward Himself. It is as though the deity were issuing a warning, through the language of universal history, against the claim to exclusiveness in the possession of truth." (19–20)

faith is a practical option, and not on a par or in competition with the work of theoretical reason. By isolating the aspect of existential commitment in the over-emphasized terms of an unshakable conviction, Habermas makes religion more fideist and less open to a reflection on limits, which is the point that Jaspers was interested in. By stressing its different "mode of taking-to-be-true", Habermas undervalues the capacity of reason in which religious believers share as human beings; it also puts into question the central plank of his discourse ethics, G. H. Mead's concept of the ability to take the other's perspective. Despite the wish for a "dialogical relationship",[261] this allocation of roles is then in danger of making translation one-sided; its goal is an appropriation that only expands secular reason by alerting it to a forgotten heritage, but that does not question its self-sufficiency. The role of translation is to "set free" religious contents from the grasp of their original encoding: "Who is to say that they do not contain encoded semantic potentialities that could provide inspiration if only their message were translated into rational discourse and their profane truth contents were set free?"[262] The praise for the abiding evocativeness of religion is ambiguous; it makes it appear like an enclosed tower to which reason comes externally as a liberator:

> Philosophy has repeatedly learned through its encounter with religious traditions... that it receives innovative impulses when it succeeds in freeing cognitive contents from their dogmatic encapsulation in the crucible of rational discourse. Kant and Hegel are the most influential examples of this... Religious traditions appear to have remained present in an even more vital sense than metaphysics, even if they at times present themselves as the opaque other of reason. It would be unreasonable to reject out of hand the idea that the major world religions – as the only surviving element of the now alien cultures of the Ancient Empires – can claim a place within the differentiated architecture of modernity because their cognitive substance has not yet been exhausted ... we cannot exclude that they involve semantic potential capable of exercising an inspirational force on society *as a whole* as soon as they divulge their profane truth contents. [263]

---

261 Habermas, "Neues Interesse der Philosophie?" in *Nachmetaphysisches Denken II*, 102: "We cannot know whether this process of appropriating semantic potentials from a discourse that in its core remains inaccessible has *exhausted* itself, or if it can be continued. The conceptual labor of religious writers and authors such as the young Bloch, Benjamin, Levinas, or Derrida speaks in favor of the continuing productivity of such a philosophical effort. And this suggests a change of attitude in favor of a dialogical relationship, open to learning, with *all* religious traditions, and a reflection on the position of postmetaphysical thinking *between* the sciences and religion".

262 Habermas, *Between Naturalism and Religion*, 6.

263 Habermas, *Between Naturalism and Religion*, 142.

To conclude the discussion on Habermas's use of the concept of the axial age, some comments from the reception of Jaspers in theology will highlight the different perspectives. They begin with theological assent to his own previous critique of Jaspers and end with questioning what Habermas assesses as a "model dialogue" between Jaspers and Rudolf Bultmann: between a philosopher open to religious faiths as shapes of the transcendence that human existence is oriented towards, and an exegete whose programme is to demythologize biblical faith.

In Habermas's treatment of Jaspers in one of his philosophical-political portraits, the heritage of critical theory becomes evident in his objection to a method that reconstructs the history of philosophy as that of great individuals who set in motion a new stage of thinking.[264] This emphasis plays down the particular cultural and intellectual conditions of their time and focuses on the resonance their original insight has in reflective modern individuals. For Habermas, this angle is an abstraction which misses the particular and leaves the question of criteria of greatness unanswered. "Greatness" is too indeterminate and open to questionable definitions which might in the end only confirm a current common sense or status quo.

This is a critique that is especially convincing for theology with its interest in the particularity of God's self-revelation. In his discussion of Jaspers in *The Jesus of the Philosophers and the Jesus of Faith*, the German systematic theologian Thomas Pröpper quotes the suspicion arising from the lack of criteria in its memorable formulation by Habermas: "Wherever it remains confined to the forms of appearance proper to greatness, does it not lead toward the apologetic equation of what is ponderous (*wuchtig*) with what is important (*wichtig*) and of what is important with what is right (*richtig*)?"[265]

---

264 Habermas, "Karl Jaspers: The Figures of Truth" (1958), in *Philosophical-Political Profiles*, trans. F. G. Lawrence (Cambridge/Mass.: MIT Press, 1983), 45–52, 47–48: 'Jaspers treats the history of philosophy as the history of great philosophers... The existence of great persons is like a guarantee against nothingness. Any present that is not reflected in meditation on its past 'greats' stays caught in a void without history. Great individuals make themselves evident wherever something novel enters history by a leap; they are not conceivable as a possibility before they become a reality... The import and scope of their existence overflow the proportions of their historical context. In time, they are beyond time... And if a thinker can be adequately grasped by historical analysis alone, he does not belong among the 'greats'. The latter come before us in their purity when they are released from their ties to their historical moment and are gathered into the eternal realm of the spirits."

265 Habermas, "Karl Jaspers: The Figures of Truth", in *Philosophical-Political Profiles*, 52, for "apologetische Gleichsetzung des Wuchtigen mit dem Wichtigen und des Wichtigen mit dem Richtigen," in "Die Gestalten der Wahrheit" (1958), in *Philosophisch-Politische Profile* (Frankfurt:

Here, a theological perspective can agree with Habermas's interest in naming criteria for judging an individual's historical influence and esteem. On a second point, however, his perception of the "philosophical faith" Jaspers subscribes to differs from its view in a theological critique. For Habermas, this concept breaches the boundary between philosophy and faith.[266] For a theological analysis, however, Jaspers's statements that "'God'" remains a "'cipher'" (*Chiffre*) and that revelation cannot be conceived show the difference to religious understandings of God in the specific terms of their particular historical tradition. Although distinct from human transcendence, the concept of "God" remains indeterminable and indecisive.[267]

A third point of significance is discussed in Pröpper's theological assessment of Jaspers: he counts Jesus among the four "paradigmatic figures" (*maßgeblicher Mensch*) for humanity, together with Confucius, Socrates, and Buddha. Jaspers offers a careful portrayal of Jesus through a method that combines essential idea and historical details. Not only the element stressed by Nietzsche, his voluntary defenselessness and renunciation to power, are highlighted in his readiness to suffer, but also his fighting spirit and determination.[268] Yet, this appreciation is set on the background of attributing a markedly negative understanding of the world to Jesus.[269] The cross becomes a symbol for the necessity of failure in a world that does not support the unconditional.[270] The specific contents of

---

Suhrkamp, erw. Ausgabe 1987), 87–96, 95, quoted in Th. Pröpper, "Jesus – Maßgeblicher Mensch (Jaspers)", in *Der Jesus der Philosophen und der Jesus des Glaubens* (Mainz: Grünewald, 1976), 19–28, 27.

266 Habermas, "The boundary between faith and knowledge: On the reception and contemporary importance of Kant's philosophy of religion", in *Between Naturalism and Religion*, 209–247, 238: "Karl Jaspers attempts to go further by rationally reconstructing the radical tension between transcendence and worldly existence from the secular standpoint of the 'illumination of existence.' He succeeds, however, only at the cost of assimilating the validity claim of philosophical assertions to the status of truths of faith."

267 Cf. Pröpper, *Jesus der Philosophen*, 26.

268 Cf. Pröpper, *Jesus der Philosophen*, 22–23.

269 This is the point where Pröpper comes to opposite conclusions, based on the Christian faith in a God who has become incarnate. This points theology towards history in order to determine its "tasks and its promise... The world and history have been accepted by God and identified as the location in which humans find and represent their destination. Even if the meaning of existence cannot be fully realized in the world, it is more than the scene of failures that repeat themselves like a destiny. It has been given the destination to become the reality of a human freedom recognized by God." (*Jesus der Philosophen*, 28).

270 Cf. Pröpper, *Jesus der Philosophen*, 23. Jaspers's interpretation is not unlike the early Romantic reading of the cross given by Friedrich Schleiermacher in his fifth speech on religion: F.

Jesus's proclamation and ministry remain pale. Could this reticence of Jaspers despite the new debate on the "historical Jesus" begun in 1953 by Ernst Käsemann also be due to theological reference positions like Albert Schweitzer who had pointed out the dependence on changing contemporary horizons,[271] and dialogue partners such as Rudolf Bultmann in his skepticism about what could be established historically about the person of Jesus? Is Bultmann in his advocacy for "the that not the what" of Jesus's life and testimony not a congenial theological interlocutor for the wrong reasons, for whom the *kerygma* is all that is needed, and the historical detail remains unattainable?[272] Should a model dialogue between a philosopher and a theologian not rather lead to unexpected discipline-specific insights, rather than meet in the confirmation of abstract truths?

Despite the lack of more particular insights and directions that could have been gained from research into the life of Jesus, Jaspers's insistence on the unconditional and irreplaceably personal character of response, the generous welcoming of distinctly different forms of humanity[273] and his moral seriousness un-

---

Schleiermacher, *On Religion. Speeches to its Cultured Despisers*, trans. J. Oman, with an introduction by R. Otto (New York: Harper & Row, 1968), 210 – 265, 247 – 48.

271 A. Schweitzer concludes his review of the reconstructions of the "life of Jesus" in the 18th and 19th centuries with the judgement that each subsequent epoch in theology found its own ideas in Jesus. For the "Rationalists", he was a "moral preacher", for the "Idealists" an "inclusive concept of the human person", for the "Aesthetes" a "genius of rhetoric", for the "Socialists" a "friend of the poor" and "social reformer": "He is a figure designed by rationalism, endowed with life by liberalism, and clothed by modern theology in an historical garb." Jesus himself was not a modern man but someone alien and mysterious, resisting all attempts at modernisation: "The historical Jesus will be to our time a stranger and an enigma. The study of the Life of Jesus has had a curious history. It set out in quest of the historical Jesus, believing that when it had found Him it could bring Him straight into our time as a Teacher and Saviour. It loosed the bands by which He had been riveted for centuries to the stony rocks of ecclesiastical doctrine, and rejoiced to see life and movement coming into the figure once more, and the historical Jesus advancing, as it seemed, to meet it. But He does not stay; He passes by our time and returns to His own." A. Schweitzer, *The Quest of the Historical Jesus. A Critical Study of its Progress from Reimarus to Wrede*, with a preface by F. C. Burkitt, trans. W. Montgomery (London: A. & C. Black, 1910), 398 – 399.

272 Recent studies treat, for instance, the interpretation of his own Jewish faith tradition that becomes evident from his selection of specific prophets regarding concrete details of their view of Zion and the Nations, or of prayer and sacrifice in the Temple, and from the link he made between the gift of creation and justice for the poor in Galilee. See, for example, S. Freyne, *Jesus, a Jewish Galilean* (London/New York: T & T Clark International, 2004).

273 In comparison with the different cognitive stances philosophy has taken towards the Christian religion, Habermas recognizes this generosity as rare: "In the face of other religions Western philosophy was very rarely sympathetic or even generous. In this respect Jaspers represents an interesting exception. Certainly, he stresses the gulf between modernity and tradi-

derline a point that is relevant for communities and individuals: the irreplaceable role of historical self-understandings. Habermas now values religious traditions as "communities of interpretation" that keep the heritage of intuitions alive which secular reason needs to be reminded of for their diagnostic and heuristic value.

2.4.2 The heuristic and semantic potential of religions in the pathologies of rationalization

What content does Habermas see as unique to religions (1), how do they contribute to the collective self-understanding of a polity in the informal public sphere (2), and why does he uphold the neutrality of the state against proposals that argue for allowing it to become postsecular (3)?

2.4.2.1 The ongoing intellectual potential of religious traditions for self-understandings formed in the lifeworld

In numerous comments dating also from the second phase of his thinking that saw religions no longer as destined to disappear but as worldviews philosophy would "co-exist" with,[274] Habermas has acknowledged the genealogy of core concepts of modern self-understandings in the encounter of antique philosophy with biblical monotheism:

> Without this subversion of Greek metaphysics by notions of authentically Jewish and Christian origin, we could not have developed that network of specifically modern notions which come together in the thought of a reason that is both communicative and historically situated. I am referring to the concept of subjective freedom and the demand for equal respect for all – and specifically for the stranger in her distinctiveness and otherness. I am referring to the concept of autonomy, of a self-binding of the will based on moral insight, which depends on relations of mutual recognition. I am referring to the concept of socialized subjects, who are individuated by their life histories, and are simultaneously irreplaceable individuals and members of a community; such subjects can only lead a life that is genuinely their own through sharing in a common life with others. I am referring to the concept of liberation – both as an emancipation from degrading conditions and as the utopian project of a harmonious form of life. Finally, the irruption of historical thought into philosophy has fostered insight into the limited span of human life... This awareness includes a sense of the

---

tion. But he sets Greek metaphysics alongside the great world religions and assigns it a place within a more comprehensive process of the overcoming of myth, one which is driven forward on both wings." Habermas, "The conflict of beliefs", in *Liberating Power of Symbols*, 36.
274 Habermas, "Themes", in *Postmetaphysical Thinking*, 51.

fallibility of the human mind, and of the contingent conditions under which even our unconditional claims are raised.[275]

It is thus possible also for non-religious citizens to relate to ideas which are part of the cultural heritage of Western modernity and even to recognize forgotten intentions that secular reason has lost sight of. For Habermas, it belongs to the lifeworld to produce encompassing questions that such rediscoveries can draw on:

> As matter-of-course and as something about which we must be reassured, this totality of the lifeworld is near and far at the same time; it is also something alien from which insistent questions emerge – for example, "What is a human being?" Thus, the lifeworld is the almost naturelike wellspring for problematizations of this familiar background to the world as a whole; and it is from this source that basic philosophical questions draw the relation they have to the whole, their integrating and conclusive character.[276]

There is a reflective capacity to the lifeworld where cultural resources provide a reservoir of familiar, unproblematic understandings in tension with new and alien ones which allow questions of meaning to be articulated. In *Theory of Communicative Action*, it is contrasted with the "system imperatives" of political power and economics as its disruptive and invasive counterpart. The requirements they impose are identified by the evocative metaphor, "colonization";[277] instrumentalization for foreign purposes and the one-sided benefit of a purely technical and strategic rationality lead to impoverishment and homogenization. His address at the Stuttgart Hegel-Congress on the revised status of philosophy, held the same year as *Theory of Communicative Action* was published, enlisted philosophy to counter the threatening loss of the lifeworld's ability to provide the conditions in which the competencies of agents can be fostered; in its interpretive role, philosophy mediates between different rationalities.[278] It is to strengthen the "everyday communicative practices" of the lifeworld by putting the encroachments of the system to "the subversive power of reflection and of

---

275 Habermas, "Israel or Athens: Where does anamnestic reason belong?", trans. P. Dews, in *Religion and Rationality. Essays on Reason, God and Modernity*, ed. E. Mendieta (Cambridge: Polity, 2002), 129–138, 132–33. In "Neues Interesse der Philosophie?" in *Nachmetaphysisches Denken II*, 102, the examples given are: "The long process of translating essential, religious contents into the language of philosophy began in late antiquity; we only need to think of concepts like person and individuality, freedom and justice, solidarity and community, emancipation, history, and crisis."
276 Habermas, "Metaphysics after Kant", in *Postmetaphysical Thinking*, 16–17.
277 Habermas, *Theory of Communicative Action*, vol. II, Chs. VI and VIII.
278 Habermas, "Stand-in and interpreter", in *Moral Consciousness*, 2–3.

illuminating, critical, and dissecting analysis".[279] Thirty years later, in an age of marketization at a global scale, the challenges to the indispensable function of the lifeworld to support the formation of moral personhood are judged to be no less damaging. The semantic potential of religions is invoked to help protect the required but endangered cultural resources for developing reason-led communicative identities. Mentalities of "solidarity" that religions are still seen as being able to nourish are needed to redress a market-led individualization:

> Especially since the rupture in the tradition of the labour movement and the weakening of all progressive movements, our hyper-capitalist societies – which reward only the exclusive focus on one's own success – are less and less sensitive to societal pathologies, to the failure of individual life plans, and to the deformation of life worlds... When it comes to clashes of values which have to be regulated politically, our religiously and ethically pluralistic societies are increasingly divided. This is why interpretative communities, which are at least still able to provide articulate contributions to repressed questions about a way to live together in solidarity, can resonate so strongly in them.[280]

It is seen as a strength typical of religions to keep open "an awareness of what is missing":

> Postmetaphysical thinking misunderstands itself if it fails to include the religious traditions alongside metaphysics in its own genealogy. On these premises, it would be irrational to reject those "strong" traditions as "archaic" residua instead of elucidating their internal connection with modern forms of thought. Even today, religious traditions perform the function of articulating an awareness of what is lacking or absent. They keep alive a sensitivity to failure and suffering. They rescue from oblivion the dimensions of our social and personal relations in which advances in cultural and social rationalization have caused utter devastation.[281]

Concretely, in a situation where societies have too few venues for exchanges regarding encompassing orientations and quests,[282] the role proposed for "com-

---

279 Habermas, "Themes", in *Postmetaphysical Thinking*, 38 – 39.
280 Habermas, "Again religion and the public sphere: a response to Paolo Flores d'Arcais". Online: www.the-utopian.org/2009/02/000063.html (last accessed October 15, 2013).
281 This passage from Habermas, *Between Naturalism and Religion*, 6, ends with the line discussed above in 2.4.1.3: "Who is to say that they do not contain encoded semantic potentialities that could provide inspiration if only their message were translated into rational discourse and their profane truth contents were set free?" In *An Awareness of What is Missing*, the sources of the title quote are traced, one of them a radio conversation in 1964 between Th. W. Adorno and E. Bloch. Cf. M. Reder and J. Schmidt, S. J., "Habermas and religion", 1–14, and N. Brieskorn, S. J., "On the attempt to recall a relationship", 24 – 35.
282 Forst points out their relevance for the problem of justification in "Diskursethik der Moral", in *Habermas-Handbuch*, 234 – 240, 234. The need for "conversation" or "dialogue" prior to

munities of interpretation" is to offer a space that allows emerging issues to be explored dialogically in the light of basic convictions and attitudes; hosting such a forum can provide a counterweight to the increasing cultural tendencies towards self-objectification and submission to economic priorities. Having focused on the norms that guide practical discourses about the "right", that is, about goals and policies that have been justified as being in the interest of all affected, Habermas now agrees that the values, the personal and communal self-understandings in which such norms are embedded, also deserve attention, having taken on board the arguments of his philosophical and theological respondents. These processes of mutual elucidation on views of the "good" in their relevance for issues of the "right" happen in the informal public sphere. It is only recently that Habermas has used the category of "the political" to characterize such exchanges. They are not foreseen, indeed, actively discouraged in Rawls's outline of public reason, but key in Ricoeur's understanding of different traditions developing from their myths of foundation and co-creating the public space through their encounter. Now the discourse ethicist uses the term "the political" to denote a process where distinct positions engage with each other: a social integration that is *"consciously enacted"*[283] and that presupposes real differences in basic orientations.

"discourse" and the lack of venues to discuss issues in which the right and the good intersect were pointed out by David Tracy and Francis Schüssler Fiorenza in their contributions to the 1988 Chicago conference: D. Tracy "Theology, critical social theory, and the public realm" and F. Schüssler Fiorenza, "The church as a community of interpretation: Political theology between discourse ethics and hermeneneutical reconstruction", in Browning/Fiorenza (eds.), *Habermas, Modernity and Public Theology*, 19–42. 66–91. Institutions like churches and universities can provide such fora that are all the more relevant in contemporary democracies in which conceptions of the good are plural, and discourses on criteria of universalizability cannot be completely disconnected from these prior understandings.

283 In *Nachmetaphysisches Denken II*, 242, Habermas speaks of "das Reflexivwerden einer politisch, also *bewusst vollzogenen* sozialen Integration" which I have translated as "*consciously enacted*". In Habermas, "'The Political': The Rational Meaning of a Questionable Inheritance of Political Theology", in J. Butler/J. Habermas/C. Taylor/C. West, *The Power of Religion in the Public Sphere*, ed. and intro. E. Mendieta/J. VanAntwerpen, Afterword by Craig Calhoun (New York: Columba University Press, 2011), 15–33, 18, the same line is translated as follows: "Thus 'the political' means the symbolic representation and collective self-understanding of a community that differs from tribal societies through a reflexive turn to a *conscious* rather than spontaneous form of social integration."

2.4.2.2 The origin of "the political" in the encounter between religious and secular self-understandings

In the face of the self-destructive tendencies of a rationalization that spins away from the normative framework of equality and self-determination that modernity stood for at its inception, Habermas has rediscovered the not yet exhausted potential of religion. Against Rawls's proviso, he has called for a *mutual* effort in translating these intuitions into the language of reason. It serves the two goals of allowing to retrace the development of secular reason from its shared foundations with religion, and of setting religious motives free for reappropriation. The most recent stage of his thinking is to locate the democratic legitimation of the state in this encounter that forges a "collective self-understanding of all citizens" from different roots. I shall follow the stages he distinguishes in the rise of the idea of political legitimation and of the part religion plays in it because it illuminates the two poles that need to be linked by translation.

Transposing the category of "the political" from its meaning in Carl Schmitt's integralist programme for a state based on a religious justification, to society's conscious endeavour to integrate citizens in their diversity, he first explains its origin in the advent of the high cultures of antiquity. Their demand for legitimation revealed a new stage of awareness, namely that the use of political power needed justification:

> The emergent complex of law and political power gave rise to a new functional requirement – the legitimation of political authority. It is not a given that a person, or a handful of persons, can make decisions that are collectively binding on all.[284]

To fulfill the task of justification, the roots of religion needed to be distinct from the social bond. Habermas locates them in the orientation of religions towards "salvation" and its counterpart, loss of grace or "calamity":

> While the legal system is stabilized by the sanctioning power of the state, political authority in turn depends on the legitimizing force of a law, which has a sacred origin. It is in this symbolic dimension that the legitimizing alloy of politics and religion emerges, and the concept of the political refers to this alloy. "Religion" owes its legitimizing force to the fact that it draws its power to convince from its own roots. It is rooted, *independently of politics*, in notions of salvation and calamity (*Heil und Unheil*) and in corresponding practices of coping with redemptive and menacing forces.[285]

---

284 Habermas, "'The Political'", in Butler *et al.*, *The Power of Religion*, 17.
285 Habermas, "'The Political'", in Butler *et al.*, *The Power of Religion*, 17.

Having two frameworks to relate to, made it possible to advance to a new level where power became desacralized:

> We owe the first discursively elaborated *conceptions of "the political"* to the nomos thinking (*Nomosdenken*) of Israel, China, and Greece, and, more generally, to the cognitive advance of the Axial Age, that is to the metaphysical and religious worldviews that were emerging at that time... The reference to a divinity outside the world or to the internal base of a cosmic law liberates the human mind from the grip of the narratively ordered flood of occurrences under the sway of mythical powers and makes an individual quest for salvation possible. Once this transformation has taken place the political ruler can no longer be perceived as the manifestation of the divine but only as its human *representative*. From now on, he, as a human person, is also *subordinated* to the *nomos* in terms of which all human action must be measured. [286]

He concludes the history developing from these distinctions, away from a divinized ruler to a temporary head who is answerable to a cosmic law or to a creator God, with a remark that shows both the underlying rationale and the contingency of this process:

> What comes about finally in the West are those unlikely constellations that made possible both the ascent of Pauline Christianity to the Roman state religion and the productive confluence of theology with Greek metaphysics. It is only in these historical contexts that the thinking oriented by the concept of the political can be explained—a mode of thinking which Leo Strauss could link to the political philosophy of the Greeks and Christian natural law, and Carl Schmitt to a political theology that has left profound traces in the Christian West since the days of Augustine.[287]

An alternative to the consequences drawn by Leo Strauss on the one hand and Carl Schmitt on the other, under the conditions of a liberal, constitutional democracy, is to designate the "democratic process" as originating in the "interaction between religious and nonreligious parts of the population":

> the collective identity (*Selbstverständnis*) of a liberal community cannot remain unaffected by the fact of the political interaction between religious and nonreligious parts of the population, provided they recognize each other as equal members of the same democratic community. In this sense "the political," which has migrated from the level of the state to civil society, retains a reference to religion... In democratic discourse secular and religious citizens stand in a complementary relation. Both are involved in an interaction that is constitutive for a democratic process springing from the soil of civil society and developing through the informal communication networks of the public sphere. As long as religious

---

286 Habermas, "'The Political'", in Butler *et al.*, *The Power of Religion*, 18–19.
287 Habermas, "Neues Interesse der Philosophie", in *Nachmetaphysisches Denken II*, 116.

communities remain a vital force in civil society, their contribution to the legitimation process reflects an at least indirect reference to religion, which "the political" retains even within a secular state.[288]

To conclude: By spelling out the necessary part that religious self-understandings play in democratic legitimation, it is clear that no exclusion of religion from citizens' public use of reason is intended; on the contrary, it is "constitutive" for the democratic process.[289] But the price of this rehabilitation of the religious element in the collective self-understanding of all citizens is that the distinction becomes a complete disjunction. Citizens belong to either one or the other side, no matter how much they may disagree with others who are also either in the religious or in the secular camp. Habermas's previous reminder that the democratic public is "many-voiced" is not applied to believers' or agnostics' internal views which are more differentiated; despite the evidence, the possibility that more similarities and alliances may exist – for example, on questions of ecology, European unification, or genetic technology – across those camps, than within one of them is not explored. Since separate roots are needed for the religious and the social side to make up the dynamics of "the political", the distinction between the religious and the secular is in danger of being reified into opposite identities. When one looks at how the understanding of the "religious" has changed in the different stages, its continuity only seems to consist in its structural opposition to the emerging "secular": prior to the need of justification, a complex of magic, mythical and ritual elements; then the desacralizing effect both for nature and for human power structures of believing in God as creator; the gradual erosion of the idea of cosmic law through the monotheistic link of God to history, followed by the eschatological horizon of "Pauline Christianity". Thus, apart from its construction as counterpart, there is no unifying content; one could find "secularity" in the sense of desacralization just as much within biblical monotheism with its concept of nature not as a mythical power but as created, or its critique of kings from prophecy to apocalyptic thinking. Without

---

288 Habermas, "'The Political'", in Butler *et al.*, *The Power of Religion*, 24. 27.
289 In his "Reply to my critics" regarding his difference to Rawls on "The role of religion in the secular state" in J. G. Finlayson/F. Freyenhagen (eds.), *Habermas and Rawls. Disputing the Political* (London: Routledge, 2011), 283–304, 299, Habermas uses similar terms: "Because the liberal state expressly authorizes its citizens to conduct their lives in accordance with their religious faith, it must not strangle religious voices already at the roots of the democratic process in civil society...This liberal purpose does not justify restricting the polyphonic plurality of public voices already at the basis." The "roots" or the "basis" of the democratic process consist in the heterogeneous convictions from different traditions and life forms being articulated, not kept silent.

historical-critical and conceptual analyses of an era's intellectual engagement with the categories of its specific cultures it is hard to come to accurate assessments of this development. One may conclude that while the distinction between reason and faith or between the secular and the religious has more than heuristic value, they are also dialectical pairs with meanings that are co-dependent on each other.

In addition, the steeper the contrast made between them, the more difficult it will be to translate: "'monolingual' contributions of religious citizens then depend on the translational efforts of cooperative fellow citizens if they are not to fall on deaf ears."[290] The significance of the historical context, however, makes it clear that immediate, one-to-one translations of concepts will be misleading and that the horizons of their initial emergence and subsequent evolution have to be reconstructed. Instead, these translations of core terms of cultural and religious self-understandings, such as "salvation", have to reconfigure the horizon in which such quests were formulated.[291] This hermeneutical awareness is a precondition of translation. Before coming to the theological critiques of a hard and fast division between secular and religious and the concepts of reason and faith it implies, one area of agreement with most theological commentators on Habermas's work will be outlined: the limit he draws between postsecular society and the idea of a postsecular state.

2.4.2.3 Postsecular society or postsecular state?

The reasons for Habermas's opposition to the demand of Rawls's *proviso* to eventually translate religious arguments into ones of reason are normative, culture-diagnostic and practical. The normative foundations of democracy guarantee freedom of religion, and the relationship of citizens to each other has to be one of mutual respect. The self-destructive elements of modern rationalization that critical social theory highlights require the inclusion of all cultural resources as counterforces to marketization and self-instrumentalization. With discourses judging proposals for their universal acceptability by all affected, the opportuni-

---

290 Habermas, "'The Political'", in Butler *et al.*, *The Power of Religion*, 26.
291 Cf. Th. Pröpper, "Exkurs 2: Ist das Identische der Tradition identifizierbar? Zur Aufgabe und Hauptschwierigkeit einer historischen Rekonstruktion der Überlieferungsgeschichte des christlichen Glaubens", in *Erlösungsglaube und Freiheitsgeschichte*, 230–35. Argumentations in Christian Ethics that use the Bible as a quarry for norms which have already been established on different foundations, for example, on a classical interpretation of Natural Law, have been critiqued as circular and anachronistic; they privilege current interests over a genuine enquiry into historical differences.

ties to contribute and the burdens of argumentation have to be equal. Conflicts are pacified when these conditions are met:

> The other side of religious freedom is in fact a pacification of the pluralism of worldviews that distribute burdens unequally. To date, only citizens committed to religious beliefs are required to split up their identities, as it were, into their public and private elements. They are the ones who have to translate their religious beliefs into a secular language before their arguments have any chance of gaining majority support... But only if the secular side, too, remains sensitive to the force of articulation inherent in religious languages will the search for reasons that aim at universal acceptability not lead to an unfair exclusion of religions from the public sphere, nor sever secular society from important resources of meaning. In any event, the boundaries between secular and religious reasons are fluid. Determining these disputed boundaries should therefore be seen as a cooperative task which requires *both* sides to take on the perspective of the other one.[292]

Thus, new processes of learning are possible based on the capacity for mutual perspective taking; civic agency can be regained at least at this level, defeatism can be lifted with new self-understandings, and the reduction to the imperatives of a market that "cannot be democratized"[293] will find some resistance. The power of the "political", that is, the engagement with members of other worldviews, consists in generating new positions; it is a dynamic desired, not avoided by imposing in advance a limit to public reason. However, the line for the permissibility of religious contributions is drawn at the threshold of state institutions. While the "learning process" is to include the many voices of the public whose truth claims are being considered, the "outcome" has to be able to be expressed in generally accessible terms, in order to be "acceptable not just for the members of *one* religious community".[294]

This requirement is not couched in the terms of a triumph of reason but in a sober assessment of the ubiquity of ideological elements. The benchmark Rawls had established for proposals deemed acceptable for an overlapping consensus on disputed political issues, "common sense", is suspicious to the critical theorist:

> Considering the religious origins of its moral foundation, the liberal state should be aware of the possibility that Hegel's "culture of common sense" (*Kultur des gemeinen Menschenverstands*) may, in view of entirely novel challenges, fail to be up to the level of articulation which characterized its own origins. Today, the all-pervasive language of the market puts all interpersonal relations under the constraint of an egocentric orientation towards one's own

---

292 Habermas, "Faith and knowledge", in *The Future of Human Nature*, 109.
293 Habermas, "Prepolitical foundations", in *Between Naturalism and Religion*, 107.
294 Habermas, "Faith and Knowledge", in *The Future of Human Nature*, 105. 108.

preferences. The social bond, however, being made up of mutual recognition, cannot be spelled out in the concept of contract, rational choice, and maximal benefit alone.[295]

At this level, religions have the corrective capacity of reorienting towards solidarity, in view of human vulnerability, especially against induced pathologies which leave those who have been bypassed powerless to change their situation of suffering. The reflections drawn from the intellectual heritage of religions are also accorded a function of decelerating and interrupting mechanisms of transmission into law that may be too well-oiled to take concerns seriously:

> Secular majorities must not reach decisions in such questions before the objections of opponents who feel that these decisions violate their beliefs have been heard, they have to consider these objections as a kind of dilatory plea (*aufschiebendes Veto*) in order to examine what may be learnt from them.[296]

Yet, like Rawls Habermas insists on the need for the different institutional powers in a democratic state – the government, the parliament and the judiciary – to base their decisions on "general" reasons. It is this distinction and assumed devaluation of arguments based on religious terms that have drawn the criticism of philosophers like Nicholas Wolterstorff, Paul Weithman and Maeve Cooke. While Habermas has agreed with their objection to Rawls's *proviso*, that it would impose one-sided and unfair burdens on religious believers if they had to translate their positions in the informal public sphere in order to be heard, he rejects their demand to allow religious argumentations for decisions at the level of the state. At stake is therefore how the neutrality of the state is conceived.[297] Maeve Cooke, whose critique I shall focus on, admits that by permitting direct religious formulations only in the spontaneous and unregulated part of the public sphere where problems are voiced and developments commented on from many angles, his "insistence that religious reasoning should be prohibited in the democratic po-

---

295 Habermas, "Faith and Knowledge", in *The Future of Human Nature*, 110 – 11.
296 Habermas, "Faith and Knowledge", in *The Future of Human Nature*, 108 – 09.
297 In what follows, I am drawing on my discussion of Maeve Cooke's position in her article, "Säkulare Übersetzung oder postsäkulare Argumentation? Habermas über Religion in der demokratischen Öffentlichkeit", in Langthaler/Nagl-Docekal (eds.), *Glauben und Wissen*, 341– 65, in "Zwischen Integrität und Übersetzung. Christliche Überzeugungen in der Konstitution praktischer Freiheit im Bedingungsgefüge spätmoderner Gesellschaften", in N. Böhnke et al. (eds.), *Freiheit Gottes und der Menschen* (Regensburg: Pustet, 2006), 359 – 380.

litical process holds only for the formal public sphere."[298] Nevertheless, even if it applies "only for those who occupy public office (for example, politicians operating within state institutions) or who are candidates for such office", she agrees with Wolterstorff's critique that "the exclusion in principle of religious reasons from public law-making and decision-making is at odds with liberal commitments to equality and impartiality."[299]

Regarding Habermas's reason that "by opening parliaments to conflicts over religious certainties, governmental authority can become the agent of a religious majority that imposes its will in violation of the democratic procedure", she correctly observes that from "the essay as a whole it is clear that he wants to prevent not just conflicts over religious certainties, but any thematization of religious convictions in the formally organized, democratic public sphere."[300] In view of his defense of religious intuitions at one level, "the informal or 'weak' public sphere, which serves as a vehicle for public opinion and fulfils functions primarily of discovering and identifying problems", the question arises: Why is he so principally opposed to the same intuitions inspiring the "'arranged' public sphere, which serves to construct the will of the people and fulfils functions primarily of justification, decision-making and general problem-solving"?[301] The dispute, in my view, lies in whether his insistence on the level of universalizability is shared; he brings it to bear both against Rawls's restriction of public reason to "common sense", and to arguments that are tied to particular worldviews. Maeve Cooke observes astutely that "Habermas frequently uses the terms 'generally accessible' and 'secular' reasons as though they were synonymous".[302] In my reading, the "secular reasons" to which Habermas commits government officials, judges and civil servants and which he sees religious believers as able to take on board have to be interpreted in the sense of autonomous morality and not as arbitrary profane reasons. It offers a level of obligation that is justified

---

298 Cooke, M., "Violating Neutrality? Religious Validity Claims and Democratic Legitimacy", in C. Calhoun, E. Mendieta, and J. VanAntwerpen (eds.), *Habermas and Religion* (Cambridge: Polity Press 2013), 249–274, 249.

299 Cooke, "Violating Neutrality?", in Calhoun/Mendieta/ VanAntwerpen (eds.), *Habermas and Religion*, 249–50, quoting from Habermas, "Religion in the Public Sphere", in *Between Naturalism and Religion*, 128.

300 Cooke, "Violating Neutrality?", in Calhoun/Mendieta/ VanAntwerpen (eds.), *Habermas and Religion*, 249, quoting from Habermas, "Religion in the Public Sphere", in *Between Naturalism and Religion*, 134.

301 Cooke, "Violating Neutrality?", in Calhoun/Mendieta/ VanAntwerpen (eds.), *Habermas and Religion*, 429, n. 2, with reference to Habermas, *Between Facts and Norms*, 307–308.

302 Cooke, "Violating Neutrality?", in Calhoun/Mendieta/ VanAntwerpen (eds.), *Habermas and Religion*, 430, n. 7, with reference to *Between Naturalism and Religion*, 137. 139.

by reason, independently of worldviews; to be bound by it is not inappropriately coercive for political representatives. It is the basis for Habermas's insistence on the "discursive" character of political justification[303] in his negative answer to Paul Weithman's and Nicholas Wolterstorff's demand to permit religious reasons also in parliament and in the courts.

By contrast, Maeve Cooke considers the admission of not only moral, but also ethical and pragmatic reasons into the political process in *Between Facts and Norms* as a matter of principled enlargement. It constitutes the second, alternative reading to the main "epistemic-constructivist" conception with its "three core ingredients of construction, consensus, and (strong) cognitivism" which she wants to replace with one that is open to an argumentation-external understanding of truth:

> The proposed alternative conception retains the cognitive-consensual component of Habermas's epistemic-constructivist conception, but interprets it differently… whereas the epistemic-constructivist conception sees human beings as the makers of unconditional validity in the domain of practical reason, the alternative conception sees them as capable of *recognizing* truth in the practical sense. The relationship between consensus and (practical) truth is inverted: whereas in the epistemic-constructivist conception, a discursively achieved, rational consensus *produces* (practical) truth, in the alternative conception, truth *commands* a rational consensus. The intuition here is that if something is true, every rational person who had undergone the requisite shifts in perception would have to agree to it.[304]

Combining a variety of admissible reasons in political justification is found more promising since it does not endanger the political autonomy of religious believers:

> Thus, the alternative conception of legal/political validity is not only more consistent with Habermas's account of democratic deliberation as an interplay of ethical, moral, and pragmatic factors, but has a number of additional advantages: it avoids the objections of hubris, counter-intuitiveness, and finalism that I raised against his constructivist conception; it acknowledges the importance of the non-argumentative, experiential dimension of practical reasoning; it is congruent with the argumentation-external idea of truth to which many religious believers appeal; and it places no barriers in principle to the inclusion of religious arguments in processes of democratic legislation and decision-making.[305]

---

303 Habermas, "Religion in the Public Sphere", in *Between Naturalism and Religion*, 129.
304 Cooke, "Violating Neutrality?", in Calhoun/Mendieta/ VanAntwerpen (eds.), *Habermas and Religion*, 271–72.
305 Cooke, "Violating Neutrality?", in Calhoun/Mendieta/ VanAntwerpen (eds.), *Habermas and Religion*, 274.

From the perspective of this second reading based on the additional ethical and pragmatic factors admitted in *Between Facts and Norms*, Habermas' endorsement of the neutrality of the state appears as an unjustified limitation that makes one of two foundations the default position.[306] The counter-initiative of these philosophers to propose a "postsecular" state puts the accepted view into doubt that its neutrality is the condition for freedom of religion. So when is a state neutral, and when does it become secularist? For the advocates of a "postsecular state" it seems to lose its neutrality when moral validity is seen to be based on an independent autonomous foundation that is "constructed" rather than "discovered" or linked to a transcendent source called God or "truth". The legitimacy of the "institutional threshold" stands or falls with the capacity of practical reason to justify human rights and a constitution that is based on it.[307] It seems to me that what is underestimated in these argumentations against Habermas is the shared level of morality. The impression is given that the requirement of an autonomous justification was unilaterally extended only to members of religious communities rather than to all due to their shared capacity of reason. Habermas asks for this type of justification only in matters where a consensus based on shared reasons is needed. Ethical life projects and questions of authenticity that are not matters of conscience understood in its properly moral meaning are not candidates for arguments about justification. In Maeve Cooke's argumentation, however, the aim of the exchange is different:

---

306 Cooke points out that "(u)nlike Wolterstorff, who calls for impartiality rather than neutrality, Habermas tends to use the terms 'impartiality' and 'neutrality' interchangeably." (431, n. 27).

307 Kant does this with the concept of human dignity. For M. Cooke, theological and philosophical truth claims, such as that of human dignity, both rely on a "bedrock" experience that one cannot enquire into any further: "Habermas distinguishes religious validity claims from ethical claims (and other kinds of practical validity claims), on the basis of their reference to a "dogmatic" authority. To this, it can be objected that all fundamental insights of practical reason are *in a sense* dogmatic, including those that are not formulated in religious language. They are dogmatic in the sense that they are the fundaments – the "bedrock" – of processes of practical deliberation that, at any given time, in any particular socio-cultural context, cannot be challenged on the basis of good reasons. In *this* sense, the Kantian moral principle, which rests on the conviction that the dignity of every human being is inviolable, is as dogmatic as the Christian idea that human beings are made in the image of God." (251)

It seems to me that assigning the biblical and theological statement that the human being is "made in the image of God" to the same realm as Kant's concept of human dignity levels the limit between insights from faith and insights from reason; theologians defend this distinction together with the different origin of self-understandings from the self-communication of God in history, as testified to in the Bible, from the capacity of reason into which it might otherwise be dissolved.

it is about "transforming perceptions" which is less definite than a moral consensus. Her introduction of a level where cognitive and affective reasons and life experiences are considered supplies a much-needed bridge between ethical and moral self-understandings; but it cannot be in competition with or replace the level of morality to which Habermas's "Kantian republicanism" is committed. "Political autonomy" in this tradition relates to the possibility of understanding oneself as the author of laws which political representatives are then delegated to elaborate in detail. This autonomy is exercized between the poles of legality and legitimacy, in Kant's distinction, which safeguards the inner freedom to disagree with a law. The proposal to include religious foundations into the concept of "political autonomy" challenges the accepted position that specific religions and their ethos can no longer offer a public foundation for the validity of morality. It is one of the conditions that Habermas demands from religions in order to be able to participate in the democratic process. Recognizing the right to freedom of religion presupposes the neutrality of the state. In individual decisions, especially regarding the fluid border between positive and negative freedom of religion, the state might veer from neutrality to a secularist position; yet the outcome of these conflicts cannot be decided in advance, the decisions can be contested, and they do not invalidate the principle of state neutrality. Religious communities have subscribed to this principle and discovered its value in protecting religious freedom, as can be seen in the late Pope John Paul II's defense of it in marked contrast to Leo XIII's doctrine of state which was only left behind by the Second Vatican Council in 1965.[308] The demand for a postsecular state is not one that mainstream churches and academic theologians have put forward, apart from a new integralist movement[309] whose antimodern resentment she does not share. Quite on the contrary, systematic theologians have pointed out the origins of secularity in the Chalcedonian two-natures doctrine of Christ, and have worked out their understanding of the Christian faith in salvation within the modern history of freedom which has supplied the most adequate categories so far to explicate the message of the Gospel.[310]

---

308 E.-W. Böckenförde, "Religion im säkularen Staat", in *Kirche und christlicher Glaube in den Herausforderungen der Zeit* (Münster: LIT Verlag, 2004), 425–437, 427.
309 Habermas offers a critical response to John Milbank's claims in "Religion und nachmetaphysisches Denken", in *Nachmetaphysisches Denken II*, 120–182, 176–178.
310 G. Essen, "Autonomer Geltungssinn und religiöser Begründungszusammenhang. Papst Gelasius I. († 496) als Fallstudie zur religionspolitischen Differenzsemantik", in *Archiv für Rechts- und Sozialphilosophie* 99 (2013) 1–10; K. Wenzel, "Gott in der Moderne. Grund und Ansatz einer Theologie der Säkularität", in Wenzel/Schmidt (eds.), *Moderne Religion?*, 347–376; Th. Pröpper, "Zur theoretischen Verantwortung der Rede von Gott. Kritische Adaption neuzeitlicher Denkvorgaben", in *Evangelium und freie Vernunft*, 72–92.

Yet, the knowledgeable discussion of Habermas's argumentation that Maeve Cooke offers with characteristic clarity contains perceptive critiques which lead into its debate in theology. Domain-specific ethics offers numerous examples of the difficulty of drawing a clear-cut line between morality as marked by the test of universalizability, and worldview elements that inform concrete judgements where moral and ethical arguments, for example, on the concrete rights of children, are combined. Filling the concept of imperfect obligations needs input from historical self-understandings and standards achieved in historical struggles. She is correct in questioning some of Habermas's formulations that are in need of clarification and critique. Like Maeve Cooke, theologians have objected to the following problematic description, and Knut Wenzel has drawn the necessary distinctions:

> Religiously rooted existential convictions, by dint of their if necessary rationally justified reference to the dogmatic authority of an inviolable core of infallible revealed truths, evade that kind of *unreserved* discursive examination to which other ethical orientations and worldviews, i.e. secular "conceptions of the good", are exposed.[311]

Wenzel disentangles these concepts and locates them in the context of their original subdisciplines: dogmatic theology and its hermeneutics, the epistemological critique carried out in fundamental theology, and an ecclesiology that contextualizes the infallibility dogma, contested already at the First Vatican Council that passed it in 1870, in the history of the polarity between the primacy of councils and of the Pope. As an interdisciplinary enterprise, theology benefits from the complementarity and tension between these enquiries that are carried out by the critical powers of reason:

> The coupling of theology of revelation with infallibility... does not represent a continuous Christian consensus on these questions... According to the Second Vatican Council's Constitution on Revelation, *Dei Verbum*, the core of revelation does not consist in the divine communication of propositions... but in the self-giving of God which creates a relationship. Infallible statements which the church makes through its *Magisterium* are related back to this revelation which in its substance is not the giving of information but God's self-communication. The truth of these statements does not depend on their infallibility; declaring them infallible celebrates their truth, but does not make them "truer". Thus, their truth has

---

311 Habermas, "Religion in the public sphere", in *Between Naturalism and Religion*, 129, cf. Cooke, "Violating Neutrality?", in Calhoun/Mendieta/ VanAntwerpen (eds.), *Habermas and Religion*, 250.

to be able to be shown in a principally different way, namely corresponding to the discursive means of "natural reason".[312]

Similar to the final part of Maeve Cooke's counterposition, Knut Wenzel offers an immanent critique of Habermas's argumentation, and points out discrepancies between different propositions on religion. This mode of engagement was inaugurated in the work of Helmut Peukert. His ground-breaking, encompassing and elaborate setting of discourse ethics into the framework of the development of theories of science and of action in the 20th century movements of thinking, its comparison with questions of history and redemption pursued previously by thinkers within the Frankfurt School, and its theological discussion marked the starting point of a meanwhile longstanding theological debate.[313] Also in response to these insistent questions from theologians to the third stage of critical theory, Habermas's position has come a long way since the 1970s. My final section will treat theological comments on his understanding of the process of translation between faith and reason.

2.4.3 Theological critiques: Religion in the limits of postmetaphysical reason

The key theological objection to the task of translating concepts from a religious framework into secular reason is that the means required for this enterprise are not available within the confines of postmetaphysical thinking which Habermas sees as obligatory for a contemporary philosophy (1). Within these limits, the specific difference of religion can only be approached from external observations and comparisons such as cult practices, certainty, opacity and exterritoriality in keeping with a truth claim based on revelation, or an analogy to art (2). The limits of translatability as they appear in theological reflection will conclude Part Two (3).

---

312 Wenzel, "Gott in der Moderne", in Schmidt/Wenzel (eds.), *Moderne Religion?*, 353–54. "'Natural' reason" is a quote from Habermas, "Religion in the public sphere", in *Between Naturalism and Religion*, 120.
313 H. Peukert, *Science, Action, and Fundamental Theology: Toward a Theology of Communicative Action*, trans. J. Bohman (Cambridge/Mass.: MIT Press, 1984); –, "Enlightenment and theology as unfinished projects", trans. P. Kenny, in Browning/Schüssler Fiorenza (eds.), *Habermas, Modernity, and Public Theology*, 43–65; –"Nachwort zur 3. Auflage 2009", in *Wissenschaftstheorie – Handlungstheorie – Fundamentale Theologie. Analysen zu Ansatz und Status theologischer Theoriebildung* (Frankfurt: Suhrkamp, 3rd ed., 2009), 357–94.

2.4.3.1 The means of translation

From Habermas's interpretations of Jaspers and of the different stages of "the political" it has become clear that religion and reason are seen as co-original, but separate activities of the human spirit. Rather than extrapolate that religion is the "other" of reason *tout court*, it is important to specify what the respects and the contents are in which they differ. The philosopher of religion Thomas Schmidt points out the "conceptual tension" that leads to a discrepancy between the task of translation and the capacity to deliver it:

> How can a philosophy that remains "agnostic" in view of the principally hidden core of religious experience make its semantic contents generally accessible in the course of a salvaging translation? The idea of an "opaque core of religious experience" overemphasizes the difference between religious faith and rational knowledge and separates the area of the religious artificially from the continuum and the plurality of forms of human experience and their conceptual interpretations... In addition, it appears as a one-sided radicalization of such a postmetaphysical understanding to see authentic faithful existence precisely in the independence from general grounds of reason.[314]

The contradiction between the request to help translate and the lack of philosophical means to do so can be located precisely in the denial of postmetaphysical reason both to contemplate any abysses of reason, and to offer an analysis of the capacities of the self. The systematic theologian Saskia Wendel sees the shared aim of preventing modernity from destroying its own basis of normativity as inachievable

> with the means he makes available... Perhaps, greater trust in reason and in philosophy regarding religion is needed than Habermas shows when one asks for justification and translation, and objects at the same time to "Wittgensteinian fideism", to "reformed epistemology" as well as pragmatism... Habermas contradicts himself when, on the one hand, in line with postmetapysical thinking, he restricts the terrain of philosophy and does not want to extend the foundational reflection to the question for the reasons of the emergence and the determination of religion, yet, on the other hand, demands the effort to justify the validity claims of religious convictions; he breaks off this justification effort almost dogmatically when it threatens to become "metaphysical"..., when it enters a forbidden field and breaks a self-imposed taboo.[315]

---

314 Th. Schmidt, "Nachmetaphysische Religionsphilosophie. Religion und Philosophie unter den Bedingungen diskursiver Vernunft", in Schmidt/Wenzel (eds.), *Moderne Religion?*, 10–32, 25–26.
315 S. Wendel, "Religiöse Selbst- und Weltdeutung des bewussten Daseins und ihre Bedeutung für eine 'moderne Religion'. Was der 'Postmetaphysiker' Habermas über Religion nicht zu denken wagt", in Schmidt/Wenzel (eds.), *Moderne Religion?*, 225–65, 232. 230–31.

It seems that just like Rawls's concept of public reason limited practical reason, so does postmetaphysical thinking limit access to religion except as a social fact and as a part of modernity's intellectual heritage. It cannot show why religion is "not irrational", and can only point to the fallibility of reason to justify this claim. Philosophy of religion is disowned as a discipline within philosophy and classified as belonging to the internal clarification of a religious tradition.[316] Also in the realm of practical reason, Kant's idea of the highest good, the fulfillment of the striving for meaning, is criticized;[317] the scope of the "ought" is reduced to what is likely to be achievable. How can theologians translate and justify the truth claims of their religious traditions in the public realm if these questions of reason are not allowed to be kept open but are closed off? The expectations to religious resources are specified: hope for an "undamaged life", the heuristic capacity to spot social pathologies, resistance to the reductions of naturalism and hard scientism, and the unexhausted potential of the transcendence which religions are still able to keep available. But how can they become productive when their correspondence with reason's own question for the unconditioned is consistently avoided? When these bridges are blocked, a gulf separates religion from rationality. Its distinctive feature then has to be sought in a definitively alien core that is impenetrable by reason.

2.4.3.2 The specific difference of religion

There are several avenues in Habermas's work to capture the specific difference of religion: the certainty of its truth claims based on revelation, an experience of evidence similar to works of art, as well as its observable cultic practices. No sustained theory is offered to unite these elements which remain external. Regarding the first characteristic, revelation, the judgement that the "cognitively unacceptable imposition"[318] of a source of revelation precludes their compatibility with reason stands in contrast with other attempts by Habermas to characterize

---

316 "Certainly also philosophy of religion as the rational self-interpretation of a practiced faith with the means of philosophy is a worthy task (*verdienstvolles Geschäft*). But postmetaphysical thinking for which religious experience and the religious mode of faith maintain an opaque (*undurchsichtig*) kernel has to renounce to philosophy of religion. Habermas, "Einleitung", Studienausgabe, vol. V, 31.

317 Habermas, "Replik auf Einwände, Reaktion auf Anregungen", in Langthaler/Nagl-Docekal (eds.), *Glauben und Wissen*, 366–414, 376: "The problem how the realization of the highest good can be thought as possible speaks less for the postulate of God than against the prior and completely unjustified step to assume a problematic duty; it is this duty that generates the problem in the first place through an overextended (*überschwänglich*) goal."

318 Habermas, "Boundary", in *Between Naturalism and Religion*, 242.

religion which showed a more nuanced awareness that is already beyond an instruction theoretical understanding of revelation. By pointing to the "performative attitude" expressed in Schleiermacher's new approach of justifying religion after the anthropological turn,[319] he already relates the integrity of religious existence to the *fides qua*, the faith through which humans believe, not the *fides quae*, the particular elements they profess in historical religions. Yet Habermas turns away from Schleiermacher to Kierkegaard, and to a "very steep" interpretation that focuses on the polarity between faith and reason more in terms of the "early, 'dialectical' Barth"[320] than of contemporary philosophical and theological readings of his analysis of human subjectivity. Thus, the opportunity to link up with Schleiermacher's and Kierkegaard's reflections on freedom in the facticity of human existence is bypassed. This juncture, however, is exactly the place where Saskia Wendel locates the specific distinction of religion. By using a transcendental analysis of human subjectivity, critically modelled on Schleiermacher's "Introduction" to *The Christian Faith*, it becomes possible to trace the emergence of religion in self-reflection to the "feeling of absolute dependence". Her critical discussion of Dieter Henrich's reflections on "conscious life" concludes with proposing as the *differentia specifica* of religion the consciousness of owing one's existence to the unconditioned.[321] Despite his recognition of the need to distinguish transcendental from metaphysical thinking, Habermas steers clear of this alternative philosophical method because the framework of the philosophy of consciousness is considered to be solipsistic and in need of replacement with the "intersubjective" one of language. The existing possibility of a discursive explication is thus not used; instead, the analogy to art is chosen, placing religion in opposition to "discursive thought": the core of religious faith "remains as profoundly alien to discursive thought as the hermeneutic core of aesthetic experience, which likewise can be at best circumscribed, but not penetrated, by philosophical reflection".[322]

As Thomas Pröpper comments, the analogy to visual art is misleading when a content can only be expressed verbally; the testimony from which a religion in its particularity develops is mediated by language, which is exactly not the case with art. The difference between faith and knowledge has to be sought else-

---

319 In "Boundary", in *Between Naturalism and Religion*, 232, he refers to Schleiermacher's analysis "of what it means in a performative sense to have faith".

320 Pröpper, *Theologische Anthropologie*, vols. I and II (Freiburg: Herder, 2011), vol. II, 765, n. 127.

321 Wendel, "Religiöse Selbst- und Weltdeutung", in Schmidt/Wenzel (eds.), *Moderne Religion?*, 243–47.

322 Habermas, "Religion in the public sphere", in *Between Naturalism and Religion*, 143.

where, in a content that cannot be deduced from reason, and in the response of faith as a practical option:

> It is much less a "discursive exterritoriality" of infallible truths of revelation than the heterogeneity, that is, the origin of its own of the truth of faith in the contingent event of revelation that justifies the irreducible difference between knowledge (*Wissen*) and faith (*Glauben*)... It is true that faith [in contrast to aesthetic intuition (*Anschauung*)] refers to cognitive contents, but it is in its core also an act of decision, thus gaining an assuredness (*Gewissheit*) of its own... this does not imply that the truth of faith would become incommunicable... Part of the disclosing work of theology is the *reasoned insight* that the link between the truth of faith and its origin cannot be sublated without damaging its content.[323]

Pröpper opens up a different framework to the cognitive contrast between faith and knowledge by transposing the otherness that faith engages with into categories of freedom: "Why should there be only potential for reason in what is completely out of its reach (instead of what is not at its disposition because of its freedom)?"[324]

The analogy to the experience of art is also questioned by the philosopher of religion Thomas Schmidt:

> Religion, in contrast to art, *eo ipso* contains cognitive elements. In contrast to aesthetic intuition, religious experience also functions as a validity basis of convictions. At least this relationship between convictions and their basis of justification seems to have to be accessible to philosophical analysis.[325]

This internal connection to convictions requires further reflection on criteria of what makes an experience a religious one:

> In order to appropriate the store of religious heritage, secular reason needs to avail of an autonomous concept of religious experience, at least of a formal structural concept. It has to know which convictions can be counted as candidates for the content of genuine religious experience... an aesthetic theory can be expected to distinguish conceptually between authentic and merely claimed aesthetic experience, between art and kitsch... this is even more true in the case of religious experience, since religious convictions raise cognitive claims that are linked with justifications of validity."[326]

---

323 Pröpper, *Theologische Anthropologie*, vol. II, 766.
324 Pröpper, *Theologische Anthropologie*, vol. II, 765, n. 127.
325 Th. M. Schmidt, "Der Begriff der Postsäkularität", in Manemann/Wacker (eds.), *Politische Theologie – gegengelesen*, vol. 5, 251.
326 Schmidt, "Der Begriff der Postsäkularität", in J. Manemann/B. Wacker (eds.), *Politische Theologie – gegengelesen*, vol. 5, 251.

Religious experience is therefore not as impenetrable and closed to analysis as Habermas thinks. From the comparison with aesthetic experience that also secular persons share, Habermas moves further into a non-verbal direction when he identifies "cult" as the unparalleled property of religions. They provide a service by keeping access to "archaic roots" open. In my view, this definition risks identifying religion with a fiction of immediacy that ignores the mediated character of its initial revelation as well as the reflective and interpreted character of worship. Translation from such archaic grounds will have to go through several levels of re-verbalisation before it can reach the consciousness of the "sons and daughters of modernity". Taking the practice of worship as the ultimate manifestation of religion, focuses on a performative activity that only receives its meaning from the different reinterpretations a faith tradition gives it in its ongoing renewal in different cultural settings. The willingness of postmetaphysical reason to learn from religion is not helped by such attempts to define what is distinctive for religion by its otherness to reason. Then the diagnosis of "opacity" is not surprising. While the German term "*Gewissheit*" (certainty) has Lutheran resonances of the new existence of the justified sinner, the opposition of "certainties" over against "criticizable validity claims" is still indicative of a dichotomy that pits fallible reason against infallible truth claims:

> Can postmetaphysical thinking which has lost Hegel's strong concept of theory exclude that religious traditions carry semantic potentials with themselves which unfold an inspiring power for *all of* society, when they offer (*preisgeben*) *profane* contents of truth? Without detriment to its secular self-understanding, postmetaphysical thinking can relate to religion in a way that is *at the same time* agnostic and ready to learn. Faith retains something opaque for knowledge which can neither be denied nor just ignored. Secular reason insists on the difference between certainties of faith and publicly criticizable validity claims, yet abstains from a theory which judges the rationality or irrationality (*Vernunft oder Unvernunft*) of religion as a whole.[327]

It is doubtful whether "certainties" captures the sequence of critical reinterpretations, for example, from Anselm to Thomas Aquinas and Duns Scotus, of their different understandings of the core of the biblical message of salvation within the cultural constellations they found themselves in and inaugurated. If all they had done was to reassert certainties, the break-throughs that Habermas refers to would have been unthinkable. Herta Nagl-Docekal's philosophical assessment highlights the similarity between successful religious and other cultural transmissions through different eras:

---

327 Habermas, "Revitalisierung der Weltreligionen", in *Studienausgabe*, vol. 5, 407.

we need to consider that religious truths – as they are expressed in narrative language – are tied to history. From this perspective, Habermas's way of referring to "dogmatic authority" seems over-simplified. What hermeneutic research on "tradition" has found in general, does apply to religious traditions: They can only persist through centuries if the believers manage – over and over again – to re-interpret the core convictions of their faith in a way that renders them accessible, and convincing, in view of their respective contemporary condition.[328]

2.4.3.3 The limits of translatability

Aware of the history of translations that constitutes theological thinking, Habermas distinguishes between the translations achieved with theological intentions that produced key terms of Western self-understanding, and new postmetaphysical appropriations.

> From its beginnings and into the early modern period, Christian theology drew upon the conceptual apparatus of Greek metaphysics to make explicit the contents of the faith and to subject them to discursive treatment. This labor of dogmatization must not destroy the core of faith... Here the internal rationalization of the transmitted doctrines (*Lehre*) serves the need to justify a religion to itself and to the world. Something completely different is meant when secular reason tries to use the means of postmetaphysical thinking to assimilate contents from the Christian tradition in accordance with its own standards... Philosophical concepts such as those of the person, freedom, and individuation, history and emancipation, community and solidarity, are infused with experiences and connotations which stem from the biblical teaching and its tradition... What counts on the philosophical side is the persuasiveness which philosophical translations acquire for the secular environment.[329]

Yet the question remains whether the content that gets translated can keep its "inspiring potential" alive without its religious foundation. Is there a constitutive limit to the translatability of concepts that depend on faith in God for their meaning? Their relevance for human agency and self-reflection can be reconstructed, but the assumption has to be questioned that all of this heritage could be salvaged without its constitutive link to a God whose existence and nature remain contested. Its as yet "unexhausted" cognitive potential may depend on it: self-understandings such as being made in the image of God and called as a partner for the intentions of creation; human life and the earth as gift; agency encompassed by prior forgiveness; hope despite failure; resurrection against the

---

328 Nagl-Docekal, "'Many Forms of Nonpublic Reason'?" in H. Lenk (ed.), *Comparative and Intercultural Philosophy*, 85.
329 Habermas, "A reply", in Habermas et al., *An Awareness*, 79–80.

finality of death; rescue for the victims of history. These understandings are emptied of their meaning when they are secularized and turned into moral expectations which cannot be granted by human powers. Habermas's response to this insight was to abandon the horizon of Kant's solution to the antinomy of practical reason. While religious faith is intelligible and open to unreserved debate as an option of practical reason, it is the concept of God that resists translation in the sense of a transfer out of its original framework of faith. If this premise is left out, the logic unravels. The secular appropriation of a ground of all being that reason can reconstruct, but did not and cannot itself produce, fails.

In her analysis of the possible senses of "translation" into secular reason, the systematic theologian Gesche Linde rules out that the term "God" can be "substituted" by any secular term; yet she sees Habermas's examples as indicating "explication" rather than "substitution". The designation of humans as being made in the image of God, or that "biodiversity belongs to God's creation", can be explicated as expressing the need to protect them: against interference by fellow-humans into their created specificity, or as the task of counteracting damaging uses of nature. She argues that on the level of such explicative complementary propositions, there is no problem of communicability since they are not directed to the premise, but to the conclusions within a secular context which can be replaced by other, secular ones. She reminds theology that "God-statements" need an accompanying "worldly, secular explication" in order to have meaning. The questions to secular reason, however, are whether

> all statements or demands that can be justified by "God-statements" can also be justified on a different, namely a "secular" basis,... and whether without the "religious initiation" (*Anregung*) "secular", "god-less" reason would have discovered those statements and demands that are put forward by the "religious" side.[330]

These perceptive clarifications move the discussion away from a fruitless exchange on religious certainties versus self-critical reason, and reopen the question about the relation between the starting-points and the multiple inheritances of traditions. To capture this dimension sufficiently, the framework of enquiry has to include more than the history of reception of individual terms. If some of these designations and demands cannot be detached from their religious context of discovery, reason will find itself faced with an alternative: either to shed these intuitions and their context, or to allow itself to be receptive. For a postme-

---

330 G. Linde, "'Religiös' oder 'säkular'? Zu einer problematischen Unterscheidung bei Jürgen Habermas", in Schmidt/Wenzel (eds.), *Moderne Religion?*, 153–202, 198–200.

taphysical reason that has disconnected itself from previous overextended foundational claims, this is an option that should not be dismissed.

3 Religions as co-foundational of the public space in Paul Ricoeur's hermeneutical philosophy

In the work of Paul Ricoeur, the relationship between religion and reason in its practical and its public uses is a theme embedded into more encompassing enquiries: in a philosophical anthropology, in a hermeneutics of texts, of agency and of the self, and, in his final masterpiece, a treatment of the human historical condition.[331] Spanning more than fifty years, his work has reacted to and influenced questions of contemporary intellectual and political debate by clarifying key terms, distinguishing approaches, identifying perspectives of possible convergence, and by giving the task to the readers as citizens to work out a practical response of their own.

Ricoeur is the only one of the three authors studied to offer an analysis of subjectivity, using the methods of French philosophy of reflection, of phenomenology, hermeneutics and of antique and modern ethics. Thus, the problems of justice and of recognition are reached on a journey beginning with an investigation of the human will in its dual structure of what it has to presuppose and cannot control – the involuntary –, and the ways in which it can realize itself – the voluntary.[332] Expressed in myths, dramas, religious scriptures and practices that call for the move to a hermeneutics of symbols and their comparison within distinctive cultures, is the human striving for existence.[333] This core concept that

---

331 Ricoeur, *Memory, History, Forgetting*, trans. Kathleen Blamey and David Pellauer (Chicago: University of Chicago Press, 2004). Trans. of *La mémoire, l'histoire, l'oubli* (Paris: Editions du Seuil), 2000.

332 Ricoeur, *Freedom and Nature. The Voluntary and the Involuntary*, trans. E. Kodak (Evanston: Northwestern University Press, 1966)

333 In "The hermeneutics of symbols and philosophical reflection II", trans. Ch. Freilich, in *The Conflict of Interpretations. Essays in Hermeneutics*, ed. by D. Ihde (Evanston: Northwestern University Press, 1966), 315–334, 328–29, Ricoeur refers both to the Platonic link of knowledge to *eros* and to the Spinozistic term *conatus* to explain the roots of reflection: "reflection is ethical before it becomes a critique of morality. Its goal is to grasp the ego in its effort to exist, in its desire to be (*effort pour exister, désir pour être*). It is here that a reflective philosophy rediscovers and perhaps preserves both the Platonic idea that the source of knowledge is itself *eros*, desire, or love, and the Spinozistic idea that it is *conatus*, effort... Effort and desire are the two aspects of this positing of the self in the first truth: I am." (329) Beyond the cognitive and critical aspect, there is a vital aspect to reflexivity: "I maintain, along with Fichte and his French successor Jean Nabert, that reflection is less a justification of science and duty than it is an appropriation of our effort to exist... We must recover the sense of existential activity, the positing of the self within all the density of its works." (328) The self can only be grasped through its manifestations: "*reflection is the appropriation of our effort to exist and our desire to be by means of works which testify to this effort and this desire.*" (329)

stems from his phenomenological approach later leads into an Aristotelian foundation for ethics as originating in a capacity prior to the Kantian focus on moral obligation, namely in the human "striving to live well".[334] It also shapes his political ethics in the attention given to the "energy of founding" which leads to conceptualizing the public sphere as a space of which citizens and their traditions are "cofoundational".[335] His interest in historical origins and processes of formation in which cultural self-understandings are moulded is accompanied by an appreciation of language as a faculty that can open up worlds to be inhabited, and create new avenues towards reality. This power, as manifested in the tension between two semantic fields that a metaphor forges together, needs an interlocutor able to glimpse the new meaning. While Ricoeur gives a place to structuralist and analytical approaches in his hermeneutical, ethical and subject theoretical investigations, his treatment of language goes well beyond an examination of propositional truth claims; it uncovers the sources of an intersubjective constitution of meaning based on language as an already creative reservoir. From the evident and primordial plurality of languages follows the appreciation of the diversity of cultures in their original and uniquely creative cores that enable their continued development and renewal.[336] This position, together with his emphasis on the "hospitality of language", operative in the translations that have made encounters with strangers and other worldviews possible,[337] gives a specific foundation to the project of an intercultural ethics.

In addition to the anthropological and historical depth provided by the format of his studies, and to the precision with which he accounts for his methodological moves, it is Ricoeur's utter familiarity with the Bible that makes him such a valuable philosophical conversation partner. From his interpretations of biblical texts, to his discussion of the traditions that have given rise to modernity, his contributions stem from his own exploration of the sources that have shaped the normative heritage latent in Western intellectual and political culture. The encounter of biblical thinking with antique philosophy made possible through the seminal translations into Greek and Latin and into the nascent European lan-

---

334 Ricoeur, *Oneself as Another*, 172.

335 Ricoeur, "The paradox of authority", in *Reflections on the Just*, trans. D. Pellauer (Chicago: University of Chicago Press, 2007), 91–105, 105.

336 In *Dogmatik interkulturell* (Nordhausen: T. Bautz, 2007), 71–73, Margit Eckholt summarizes the position developed in *History and Truth*, trans. Ch. Kelbley (Evanston: Northwestern University Press, 1965) of each culture being animated by a "noyau créateur", a creative core that is activated and renewed in its values by the faculty of imagination. Cf. also Eckholt, *Poetik der Kultur. Bausteine einer interkulturellen dogmatischen Methodenlehre* (Freiburg: Herder, 2002), 108–171.

337 Ricoeur, *Reflections on the Just*, 3.

guages has made epochs and launched new cultural departures. Before exploring religion as a source of self-understanding, the role of religious traditions and the possible contribution of Christianity to the contemporary public sphere (4), his analysis of conceptions of authority, legitimation and foundations of democracy (3) will be discussed. I shall begin by presenting the approach used in his first monograph and in his ethical works since 1990, a phenomenology of the human being in its capability that includes its fallibility (1), and then the ethics designed on this basis (2).

3.1 The normative framework: A phenomenology of desiring, capable and fallible human beings

Major interpreters of Ricoeur's work have identified the conceptual framework of his thinking as "phenomenological", a designation that does not exclude, however, an understanding of key terms, for example of his ethics, as drawing on Aristotelian and Kantian thought. What he develops in distinction from its original focus on perception is a "phenomenology of acting".[338] His enterprise enters new territory by expanding and further developing the tradition of thinking founded by Edmund Husserl. I shall begin by characterizing the specific perspective Ricoeur takes on action which gives it the fruitful, encompassing and versatile character that allows other approaches to be accommodated within it. With its focus on "intention", phenomenology offers a method of thinking about the connection between agent and act. It develops a theory of action in which motivation (1) and self-understanding (2) become central, yet not through direct introspection but by an analysis of what is intended, and of why, and how this takes place.[339] It is here that Ricoeur saw the need for a first expansion by "grafting" a hermeneutics of symbols onto the phenomenological stem.[340] It

---

338 F. Dosse, *Paul Ricoeur. Un philosophe dans son siècle* (Paris: Armand Colin, 2012), 45–69. In his conclusion, Dosse summarizes the diverse philosophical influences on Ricoeur's basic understanding of the "power to be" that pushes the self, a "cogito brisé", from an original affirmation to an identity that is always beyond the current stage, such as Spinoza's concepts of life and *conatus*, Gabriel Marcel's "being en route", and Kant's outline of the power and the limits of reason (247–50).

339 J. Greisch, *Fehlbarkeit und Fähigkeit* (Münster: LIT Verlag, 2009), 134. Cf. in its application to memory, Greisch, "Vom Glück des Erinnerns zur Schwierigkeit des Vergebens", in S. Orth/P. Reifenberg (eds.), *Facettenreiche Anthropologie. Paul Ricoeurs Reflexionen auf den Menschen* (Freiburg: Alber, 2004), 91–114, 94.

340 Ricoeur, "Existence and hermeneutics", trans. K. McLaughlin, in *The Conflict of Interpretations*, 3–26, 6.

complements his examination of the basic structures of human existence in the first volume of his philosophy of the will by a study of the cultural mediations that constitute the material out of which concrete historical self-interpretations are formed. Their myths, narratives and utopias require an interpretation of their symbolism; yet the process of identifying their meaning gives rise to antagonistic perspectives which remain irresolvable (3). They continue to mark the complexion of the self in its creativity and fragility. The following subsection will treat the final shape of his hermeneutics of the self within cultural traditions that demand analysis (4), before the new insights made possible through Ricoeur's chosen course of enquiry are summarized (5).

3.1.1 Theory of action based on "desire and effort to exist"

By developing his understanding of human action from an analysis of the will, the French phenomenologist is able to account for two elements: on the one hand, the sense of being able to begin, of an initiative expressive of the self, that locates the basic relation to oneself in the affirmation of one's own power to act; on the other hand, placed against the backdrop of the involuntary, while uncovering the origin of the productive responses of humans to the challenges they encounter, its character as a desire equally indicates a lack and a disproportion: its contingent origin from a force it does not control, and a constitutive gap between the depth of the well of wishes, and the actualizations attainable. This view remains in force throughout his work. The "capabilities" specified from the 1990s onwards are the basis of renewed attempts at actualization, but they are not portrayed as robust, unquestionable, or demonstrable properties. The "fallibility" from which the analysis began is not withdrawn in a subsequent optimistic philosophical anthropology of the "I can", but remains as an accompanying feature of the human condition;[341] the limit set by the "tragic" continues to be accounted for.[342]

One consequence of the phenomenological starting-point is that the body comes into view as the original and individual medium of encountering and responding to reality, integral to the perception of self and other; it is not a collection of empirical features which a rational assessment can turn into assets that conform to the changing market needs of competitive economies, or that can be

---

341 For an in depth analysis of Ricoeur's work in its unity, cf. J. Greisch, *Fehlbarkeit*, and his discussion of this point in "Glück des Erinnerns", 93.
342 Ricoeur, *Oneself as Another*, 241–249.

made subject to optimizing interventions. In a phenomenological approach that undercuts the subject-object dichotomy by conceiving of the subject as "being in the world", it is not possible to distanciate oneself from the bodily basis of subjectivity in the way Rawls's approach tries to. The type of objectivizing judgement at work in Rawls's approval of genetic intervention, in order to improve the launching platform for society's attempts to ensure distributive justice, as discussed in Part One, is not possible if the basic approach is that a person's being is always already within a world.[343]

The possibility for distanciation comes in at a different point. The subject's turn to reflection presupposes a prior force that is given and operative, towards which it can take a stance. Regarding the works produced by cultural activity, distanciation describes the second stage of the movement of interpretation. At the same time, it is part of the orientation towards creating meaning which belongs to the foundational desire of the human being to be. As Ricoeur summarizes half a century after his first book:

> It is important that the word "life" appears within the framework of a philosophy of action. It recalls that human action is borne by desire, and correlatively, by a lack, as well as that it is in terms of these words "desire" and "lack" that we can speak of the wish for a full life. The connections among life, desire, lack, and accomplishment constitute the basis of morality, for which I reserve, as a convention of language, the term "ethics." This is why I define ethics as the wish for a good life.[344]

On the basis of this anthropology, ethics acquires a different role than in the approaches of Rawls and Habermas. It is inscribed into a dynamics of striving and part of the desire for a meaningful, fulfilling life.

3.1.2 Self-understanding as a result of appropriation

Decisive for being able to understand actions at the concrete historical level is their link to a person's self-conception. They originate from a projection of self which is realized by adjusting to circumstances and expectations, but which remains the energizing factor. Actions are elements within a projected unity and make sense in relation to the "telos of an entire life in quest of what human

---

343 In *Fehlbarkeit*, 118–9, Greisch points out how the analyses of the capability to act and that of one's own body go together, even though an "ontology" of one's own body can only be reached at the end when it is united with the "phenomenology of the 'I can' to give birth to a true ontology of the self".
344 Ricoeur, *The Just*, Preface, xv.

agents can consider as an accomplishment, a crowning achievement".[345] In comparison with the eagerness owed to this vital striving for existence, the concept of a "life plan", as it features in Rawls's *Theory of Justice*, appears rationalistic.

By relating actions back to the self that is invested in them, they become interpretable for others. But equally, the self needs the sequence of these expressions to take hold of itself. Thus, as commentators on this stage of Ricoeur's work agree, "the subject is not the starting point but the target of the hermeneutical movement".[346] At the same time, besides having to get to know itself through its works, it is already active as the authorizing moment of reflection that qualifies them as its own, by performing what Ricoeur describes as "the task of appropriating to itself the originary affirmation through the signs of its activity in the world or in history".[347]

Thus, self-understanding is reached via "works", "expressions", "signs, symbols and texts", yet at the same time, a prior familiarity with oneself is presupposed that allows for the "appropriation" of the originary striving for existence captured as "*effort pour exister, désir pour être*". The self-presence that *Oneself as Another* develops as "attestation" is linked to this original reflexivity. The material contents of the "works which testify to this effort and this desire" are constituted by the self's productive response to the multiple views of the world contained in the past and the present of one's own culture. As the systematic theologian Margit Eckholt sums it up, "from its origin, thinking is inserted into manifold forms of alterity".[348] The hermeneutical appreciation of a plurality of avenues towards reality has to do with the many "worlds" it allows the recipient to test and "inhabit".[349] The self can rejoice in their existence as long as it

---

345 Ricoeur, *The Just*, Preface, xv.
346 V. Hoffmann, *Vermittelte Offenbarung. Paul Ricoeurs Philosophie als Herausforderung der Theologie* (Ostfildern: Matthias Grünewald Verlag, 2007), 92.
347 Ricoeur, "Nabert on signs and acts", in *Conflict of Interpretations*, 211–222, 219. In "On interpretation", trans. K. Blamey, in *From Text to Action. Essays in Hermeneutics II* (Evanston: Northwestern University Press,1991), 1–20, 15, Ricoeur concludes: "there is no self-understanding that is not *mediated* by signs, symbols and texts; in the last resort, understanding coincides with the interpretation given to these mediating terms." Greisch interprets these instructive quotes in *Fehlbarkeit,* 106.
348 Eckholt, *Poetik der Kultur*, 30.
349 In articles such as "Philosophical hermeneutics and biblical hermeneutics", in *From Text to Action*, 89–101, 96–97, Ricoeur outlines the interpretation of a text as "projecting" a world, opening up "the reality of the *possible...* 'the kingdom of God is coming'... calls upon our ownmost possibilities". In different texts, Ricoeur refers to another scholar of Husserl, Wilhelm Schapp who is quoted by Hille Haker: "That what is interpreted in a text is the suggestion of a world in which I live and which could create my most personal possibilities." Cf. Haker, "Narrative and moral identity", in M. Junker-Kenny/P. Kenny (eds.), *Memory, Narrativity, Self, and the*

can trust in its integrating competence on the "more roundabout, more arduous path" of interpretation that Ricoeur proposes as an alternative to the "short route" taken by an "ontology of understanding" such as Heidegger's.[350] Yet, the encounter with multivalent and competing types of access is also confronted with a "conflict of interpretations" that erupts when these aspects and symbols provoke the counter-assessment of not being liberating, but deluding.

3.1.3 Symbols and conflicts of interpretation

On the one hand, the encounter with the mediating signs, symbols and texts opens up new purviews and broadens the range of perception and response; on the other, the interpreter gets caught in the antithesis of two types of assessment: one, a hermeneutics of trust, the other, a hermeneutics of suspicion along different lines of critique by the "three masters, seemingly mutually exclusive, that dominate the school of suspicion: Marx, Nietzsche, and Freud".[351] The *Symbolism of Evil* had already made the move to a level other than theoretical analyses of human faculties.[352] Faced with the extreme end of human fallibility, evil in its simply factual, contingent existence that mocks the attempt to make sense of it, Ricoeur had turned to examine and compare the great cultural expressions of reflection on this experience in different literary genres.[353] These texts provide

Challenge to Think God (Münster: LIT Verlag, 2004), 134–152, with reference to W. Schapp, *In Geschichten verstrickt. Zum Sein von Mensch und Ding* (Frankfurt: Klostermann, 1985, 3ʳᵈ ed.), 127.

350 Ricoeur, "Existence and hermeneutics", in *Conflict of Interpretations*, 6.

351 Ricoeur, *Freud and Philosophy: An Essay on Interpretation*, trans. D. Savage (New Haven: Yale University Press, 1970), 32.

352 Ricoeur, *The Symbolism of Evil*, trans. E. Buchanan (New York: Harper & Row, 1967). In *Vermittelte Offenbarung*, 83, V. Hoffmann explains why a change of method was required: "While the principle of human fallibility can be reached in a philosophy of reflection, a gap is posed between it and a factual offense which is unavailable (*entzogen*) to the direct access of a philosophy of reflection... Evil – not as a possible but as a real offense (*Verfehlung*) can always only be reached through its symbolic articulations... after the fact (*nachträglicher*)."

353 *The Symbolism of Evil* (1960) was published in the same year as Hans-Georg Gadamer's *Truth and Method*, but develops its understanding of hermeneutics by focusing on literary expressions of the human experience of evil. In his comparison of both theorists in their different paths towards hermeneutics, Jean Grondin observes how this theme is a practical one for Ricoeur: "It is not by chance that the theme of evil reveals itself as one of the outstanding constants in Ricoeur's work whereas it tends to be absent in Gadamer's philosophy. Even if evil remains incomprehensible in its ultimate foundation and thus inaccessible from a theoretical standpoint, it can be fought against through the subject's practical initiative which is certainly limited, but nevertheless real: 'Evil is a category of action and not of theory; evil is what one

the receiver with multiple possibilities for identification, for being attracted by other attitudes, insights, ways of solving conflicts, and models of life, an array of scenes to inhabit, try out, and learn from. Yet the interpretations of such texts remain contestable at a fundamental level. The failure of reason to produce a reflective solution to the abysmal mystery of evil is replicated; now, it is stymied in front of two equally strong alternatives. Ricoeur indicates the direction of a productive engagement with the conflict between a trusting reading that enriches the subject, and one in which the subject is taken apart and reduced to the illusions of consciousness over being, of reason over an anonymous will to power, or over the unconscious. Again, it is a movement of appropriating the critique into a self-conception that becomes more aware of the ambivalence of interpretation and of its own limits: "'Symbols give rise to thought,' but they are also the birth of idols. That is why the critique of idols remains the condition of the conquest of symbols."[354]

At the same time, since no attempt at refuting the dissolution of the presumed subject of action can succeed with demonstrable and conclusive certainty, it remains undermined as a foundational position. Alternative descriptions of the centre of agency continue to be possible. By recognizing these fundamental critiques, the hermeneutical approach has been lifted out of a predominantly receptive mood, a position into which it had been placed by the primacy of belonging in Hans-Georg Gadamer's emphasis on the history of reception in his concept of *wirkungsgeschichtliches Bewusstsein*. Valuing the different challenges beginning with Marx as comprehensive counter-positions means that hermeneutics has to rise to them and argue against them for the validity of still relating to a subject able to act, reflect and create meaning. I shall analyse its core capabilities as they are set out in *Oneself as Another* (5), and conclude by naming the differences that Ricoeur's elaborated anthropology makes for the concept of ethics (6). First, however, one further dimension of symbolic frameworks has to be

---

fights against when one has given up on explaining it.' Therefore, the historical determination of consciousness in Ricoeur marks not only the limit of a philosophy of reflection; it is also a reminder of the *initiative* which nevertheless belongs to the subject... Without a doubt, it is a 'passive' ability (I can suffer; I am the inheritor of a tradition; I have to 'suffer' mortality); yet it is inhabited by an inalienable (*unveräusserliche*) spontaneity which can be expressed in a – very simple – sentence that Gadamer doubtlessly would never have written: 'I am able to effect change.'" J. Grondin, "Von Gadamer zu Ricoeur. Kann man von einer gemeinsamen Auffassung von Hermeneutik sprechen?", in B. Liebsch (ed.), *Bezeugte Vergangenheit oder Versöhnendes Vergessen. Geschichtstheorie nach Paul Ricoeur* (Berlin: Akademie-Verlag, 2010) (*Deutsche Zeitschrift für Philosophie*, Sonderband 24), 61–76, 72, with reference to Ricoeur, "Le scandale du mal" (1989), in Ricoeur, *Anthologie*, ed. by M. Foessel and F. Lamouche (*Paris*: Seuil, 2007), 281.
354 Ricoeur, *Freud and Philosophy*, 543.

accounted for: the particularity of cultures, as well as their utopian and ideological aspects.

3.1.4 Cultural uniqueness, utopia and ideology

From Ricoeur's focus on human agency, culture comes into view as an enabling reservoir of symbolic forms and practices that is organized around a "creative nucleus on the basis of which we interpret life" which involves a "fundamental conception of time, space and interhuman relations".[355] The diversity of cultures testifies to the plurality of rational approaches to reality.[356] Their particularity expresses their originality; they derive their strength from their "ethico-mythical core" which is also their source of renewal. This "integration of the common world by means of symbolic systems immanent in action"[357] is the most elementary and inescapable level of ideology. Before discussing its other two levels, and distinguishing the manipulative and hidden nature of ideology from the open message of utopia (2), Ricoeur's view of diversity as a good to be protected from forces of uniformity and his warning against a historicist aestheticising relativism need to be explained. By anchoring concrete agency in the productive power of imagination, ethics as a will-directed expression of striving is not given a foundational, but a constituted status. There is a level prior to the will that evokes action.[358] This is why the major written sources of a culture, among them the Bible, are considered first of all as literary texts that open up a world, before the symbols and stories they offer engender specific evaluations and orders of living (1). Utopias and biblical texts are portrayed in similar terms: both project alternative worlds and social relations. By linking utopias to the founding hopes and promises of a culture, the hermeneutical philosopher offers a distinctive conception that is critical of attempts to sever the connection between tradition and utopia, as his comments on Habermas's objections to Gadamer will show (3). It is necessary to outline these foundational categories in

---

355 Ricoeur, "Universal civilization and national cultures", in *History and Truth* (Evanston: Northwestern University Press, 1965) (ET of *Histoire et vérité* (Paris: Éd. du Seuil, 1st ed. 1955, 2nd enlarged ed. 1964), 271–284, 276. 279.

356 In *Poetik der Kultur*, 29, Eckholt points out that the "other of reason" is not the "wholly Other" that cannot be mediated to reason, but an awareness of the "alterity" of rational approaches (*Zugänge*) to reality.

357 Ricoeur, *Memory, History, Forgetting*, 82.

358 In *Vermittelte Offenbarung*, 209, in the context of discussing the connection between metaphor and productive imagination, V. Hoffmann points out the priority of imagination over the will.

order to understand Ricoeur's configuration of the factors and layers operative in the public space of political communities.

3.1.4.1 Particularity versus homogenization and historicist relativism

Ricoeur calls the productive capacity of a culture its "poetics" which is specified in a foundational originating imagination. This "poetics" expresses itself in "the most varied symbolic forms, in myths, narratives of origin, poems, dreams".[359] The attention of the hermeneutical philosopher is drawn to what is different and distinct, an interest not unlike Romanticism's move against a shallow notion of universality taught by some Enlightenment positions. Similar to Friedrich Schleiermacher's emphasis against a Deist "natural religion" on the unique "intuitions of the universe" received by different religious believers within their particular historical faith traditions,[360] Ricoeur highlights the original alterity of cultures and of the civilizations they give rise to. Their future as a tradition depends on their ability to "activate their own specific cultural core" and "reorient themselves in order to become universal... from the unkept promises of the past, of what has been forgotten and blocked out".[361] The original intuition at the core gives rise to different formations in a multiplicity of genres. For Ricoeur, the problem is not that their particularity would preclude access to universality; each culture harbours its own "inchoative universalism".[362] His concern, voiced already in 1961 in an article that welcomes recent moves from colonization to democratic self-government, is that the homogenizing factors of modern life will result in a loss of the cultural uniqueness needed to replenish motivational and imaginative powers. Examining under "what conditions this creativity (may) be pursued", his judgement is that the prospect of an incremental integration into the uniformity of a consumer civilization poses a threat: "We have the feeling that this single world civilization at the same time exerts a sort of attrition or wearing away at the expense of the cultural resources which have made the great civilizations of the past."[363]

His enquiry into the conditions of the possibility of continued creativity in the face of new encounters and challenges identifies the locus of productivity as being at a level prior to consciousness. The symbolic worlds that can be interpreted and compared express an intangible depth dimension: "Images and sym-

---

359 Eckholt, *Poetik der Kultur*, 613.
360 Schleiermacher, *On Religion*, 236–37.
361 Eckholt, *Dogmatik interkulturell*, 78.
362 Ricoeur, *Oneself as Another*, 289–90.
363 Ricoeur, "Universal civilization", in *History and Truth*, 276.

bols constitute what might be called the awakened dream of a historical group" that call for a "methodical interpretation... like symptoms or a dream to be analysed".[364] Differences at this deeper level are the reason for the fact that humanity only exists in the shape of distinct cultural formations: one may think that the enigma

> of human diversity lies in the structure of this subconscious or unconscious. The strange thing, in fact, is that there are many cultures and not a single humanity. The mere fact that there are different languages is already very disturbing and seems to indicate that as far back as history allows us to go, one finds historical shapes which are coherent and closed, constituted cultural wholes. Right from the start, so it seems, man is different from man; the shattered condition of languages is the most obvious sign of this primitive incohesion. This is the astonishing thing: humanity is not established in a single cultural style but has "congealed" in coherent, closed historical shapes: *the* cultures. The human condition is such that different contexts of civilization are possible.[365]

Two conclusions for contemporary debate can be drawn from this analysis, offered more than five decades ago, of factors that were then beginning to emerge: (1) Global developments can only be judged as progress if cultural diversity is recognized as a good and its erosion resisted. Only a cosmopolitanism that is sensitive to such original plurality will have the necessary depth, complexity and circumspection to identify the directions theoretical enquiries and policy proposals should take. (2) From a hermeneutical perspective, it is clear that in contrast to "a set of tools which accumulates, sediments, and becomes deposited, a cultural tradition stays alive only if it constantly creates itself anew".[366] For Ricoeur, it is decisive to keep open the possibility of the "movement of reinterpretation begun by these texts from the heart of their own culture".[367]

This chance is threatened, however, not only by global factors, but also by an attitude that has become possible in the sequence of alternative positions internal to the development of Western philosophy. The aestheticizing, contemplative mood that Ricoeur describes and critiques as feeding into a skeptical and relativist view disinterested in human action and distanciated from the exigencies of life, can be linked to a school that became prominent in the modern history of thinking after the demise of the Hegelian system: Historicism.[368] By giving

---

364 Ricoeur, "Universal civilization", in *History and Truth*, 280.
365 Ricoeur, "Universal civilization", in *History and Truth*, 280.
366 Ricoeur, "Universal civilization", in *History and Truth*, 280.
367 Ricoeur, "From the moral to the ethical and to ethics", in *Reflections on the Just*, 45–57, 54.
368 In *Philosophie in der veränderten Welt* (Pfullingen: Neske, 1972), 469–522, the late Tübingen philosopher Walter Schulz sees the programmatic split proposed by Wilhelm Dilthey between

up on the possibilities of its own culture to engage with current global challenges, it retreats from the demands and risks of responsible action. It is a mindset influencing lifestyles in affluent Western societies that Ricoeur judges to be as pernicious as the nuclear threat: the

> discovery of the plurality of cultures is never a harmless experience. The disillusioning detachment with respect to our own past, or even self-criticism... reveals rather well the kind of subtle danger which threatens us... when we acknowledge the end of a sort of cultural monopoly, be it illusory or real, we are threatened with destruction by our own discovery. Suddenly it becomes possible that there are just *others*, that we ourselves are an "other" among others. All meaning and every goal having disappeared, it becomes possible to wander through civilizations as if through vestiges and ruins. The whole of mankind becomes a kind of imaginary museum: where shall we go this weekend – the Angkor ruins or...Tivoli of Copenhagen? We can very easily imagine a time close at hand when any fairly well-to-do person will be able to leave his country indefinitely in order to taste his own national death in an interminable, aimless voyage. At this extreme point, the triumph of the consumer culture, universally identical and wholly anonymous, would represent the lowest degree of creative culture. It would be skepticism on a world-wide scale, absolute nihilism in the triumph of comfort. We have to admit that this danger is at least equal and perhaps more likely than that of atomic destruction.[369]

3.1.4.2 Between foundational hopes and strategies of legitimation: Utopia and ideology

From the backdrop of Ricoeur's theory of culture, which unlike some current constructivist approaches posits a unique and unexchangeable core intuition, it is

---

the natural sciences and the humanities as the origin of the latter's loss of relevance for the reality of everyday life and for shaping the future (cf. 471). By divorcing themselves from the exigencies of life and by leaving economics, technology and science to themselves, they withdrew into a sphere of interiority (cf. 510), turning to an enriching but ineffective contemplation of the treasures of past cultural productivity. Schulz sees it as revealing that history is regarded in a similar way to the appreciation of visual art. While both counted as activities of the world spirit for Hegel, after this metaphysical premise was removed and his system collapsed, the analogy breaks down. What observers enjoy in museums and streetscapes are past productions of other people (cf. 521). The idea of history, however, should also include the contribution of one's own agency to the historical development of contemporary society, not just a review of what others have achieved. Ricoeur's critique of the dichotomy between "explaining" and "understanding" in Dilthey's division between the natural sciences and the humanities questions this epistemological alternative and orients both modes towards agency. Ricoeur, "What is a text? Explanation and understanding", in *Hermeneutics and the Human Sciences*, ed. and trans. by J. Thompson (Cambridge: CUP, 1981), 145 – 64.

369 Ricoeur, "Universal civilization", in *History and Truth*, 278.

clear that the concept of utopia will be expounded as sharing in the particularity of its context of origin. It will be connected to the founding promises of a culture, reinvigorating its unrealized hopes, drawing on possibilities marginalized by contingent historical circumstances, and holding up a mirror to the power arrangements of the current stage. By imagining a different world, utopias reveal a critical, reflective capacity. Against the canvas they provide, past and present actions can be seen in their contingent nature, and the social organization they produced as merely the existing order, which is by no means necessary:

> The "nowhere" of utopia, which is also an "elsewhere", casts a new light on the social world in which the reader is immersed, which thus acquires a degree of strangeness that paves the way for the recognition of its contingent character and therefore of the human possibility to change it through action.[370]

While utopia invites the reader's imagination to re-envisage life in the gap between promise and fulfillment, ideology is a process that intends to cover up this gap. It is "opaque in two ways", first, by remaining "hidden, unlike utopia,... unacknowledged"; secondly, through the different levels at which it works. At the deepest level of "symbolic synthesis", it belongs to a "semiotics of culture" where it is a "guardian of identity, offering a symbolic response to the causes affecting this identity". Only at the subsequent two levels does ideology become "manipulative" when it functions in the "legitimation of systems of power" and, "grafted" onto this, "distortion of reality". In *Memory, History, Forgetting*, these two levels become connected to instrumentalized, self-serving uses of history.[371]

The political philosopher Vicky Iakovou summarizes how ideology as a steered exercise of gaining a legitimacy that necessarily becomes contested is constructed as the counterpart to utopia:

> This sense is further enriched because utopia has the status of an imaginative variation on power, which corresponds to ideology's legitimating function. According to Ricoeur, every system of authority raises claims to legitimacy that are not entirely met with a corresponding belief on the part of the citizens. Precisely this gap between the claim and the belief is filled by ideology's legitimating function. By trying "to deal with and make sense of hierarchy"... by proposing alternative ways of exerting power, utopia renders this function of

---

370 V. Iakovou, "To think utopia with and beyond Paul Ricoeur", in T. Mei/D. Lewin (eds.), *From Ricoeur to Action* (London/New York: Continuum, 2012), 113–135, 122.
371 Ricoeur, *Memory, History, Forgetting*, 82–83.

ideology manifest; it exposes ideology as a kind of surplus-value added to the lack of belief in a given structure of authority.[372]

This analysis opens up interesting questions regarding the types of utopian visions that have the capacity to unmask ideological rationalizations of power, and that may retrieve utopia from its own pathology, namely that of remaining ideal and unconnected to the realm of action where definite, limited steps have to be identified and risked.[373] In what light do biblical texts appear from the examination of the roles of ideology and utopia? Section 3.4.3 will discuss some of Ricoeur's interpretations of biblical monotheism under the aspect of what the task emerging from his concept of culture could mean for religious traditions: the charge of remembering complex histories of foundation and of creatively writing them forth.[374] It will become clear from his discussion of concepts of democracy in section 3 that such texts will belong to the sphere of "enunciative authority", as distinct from "institutional authority".

3.1.4.3 Tradition and emancipation: Ricoeur's comments on Habermas's critique of Gadamer

By connecting utopias to the unrealized aspirations of the past, history and identity have been introduced as relevant dimensions. In this framework, to assume a radical and normative disjunction between modern and premodern approaches seems misplaced; this is all the more so since Ricoeur, in distinction from Ernst Bloch, emphasizes the continuity between the reality experienced as it is, and the alternative vision of what it should be like, which is developed in culture-specific utopias. Equally strong is the French philosopher's orientation towards agency, its connection with self-understanding, its reconstitution after failing, and the cultural and political conditions of its exercise. From here, a first question to Habermas arises, regarding the subject on whose behalf the critique is announced. Ricoeur's second correction concerns what he perceives to be a

---

372 Iakovou, "To think utopia", in Mei/Lewin (eds.), *From Ricoeur to Action*, 123, with reference to Ricoeur, *Lectures on Ideology and Utopia*, ed. by G. H. Taylor (New York: Columbia Press, 1986), 310.
373 Iakovou, "To think utopia", in Mei/Lewin (eds.), *From Ricoeur to Action*, 125, refers to this possible limit of an imagination that wants to steer clear of dilemmas of action: "At one point Ricoeur maintains that utopia's pathology amounts to escaping from the always plural and often incompatible goals of action. He speaks of this aspect of utopia in terms of the 'magic of thought'", quoting from Ricoeur, *Lectures on Ideology and Utopia*, 296.
374 Cf. Eckholt, *Dogmatik interkulturell*, 85 – 86.

false dichotomy within a unitary concept of "Tradition" with which Habermas tries to secure the possibility of self-reflective action against Gadamer's overwhelming insistence on the receptive role of inheritors of traditions. While the French and the German commentator agree on the necessity and the possibility of ideology critique and of engaging with the crisis of legitimation of the power of governance, they differ in their presuppositions. Ricoeur enquires about the starting point of ideology critique: "(F)rom where do you speak when you appeal to *Selbstreflexion*, if it is not from the place that you yourself have denounced as a non-place, the non-place of the transcendental subject?" Since Habermas has rejected philosophies of subjectivity as philosophies of consciousness that have been superseded by the linguistic turn, he has to find a different point of departure. If this point is the normative position of the Enlightenment critique of reason, then, Ricoeur concludes, he has inscribed himself into a tradition, and is no longer able to contrast "tradition" as something discredited with "Enlightenment" as the normative basis of critique. He continues:

> It is indeed from the basis of a tradition that you speak... *Aufklärung*... is a tradition nonetheless, the tradition of emancipation rather than that of recollection. Critique is also a tradition. I would even say, it plunges into the most impressive tradition, that of liberating acts, of the Exodus and the Resurrection... nothing is more deceptive than the alleged antinomy between an ontology of prior understanding and an eschatology of freedom... As if it were necessary to choose between reminiscence and hope!"[375]

This argument against false dichotomies, especially against disconnecting critique from the prior aspirations, hopes and intuitions of a cultural formation, is also significant for the role of religion in the public realm. Ricoeur is reacting to a position that Habermas has since then nuanced substantially when he points out that the need to distinguish between traditions does not coincide with the difference of modern from earlier understandings of self and world.[376] The critique illustrates that different directions can be taken from the shared starting-point of modernity's anthropological turn to human freedom. Instead of opposing modern and premodern, postmetaphysical and metaphysical,

---

375 Ricoeur, *Hermeneutics and the Human Sciences*, 99–100. The restatement of this critique in *Oneself as Another*, 286–7 was quoted above in 2.2.3.
376 It is remarkable that Habermas now points to the "origins of modernity in the thinking of the Middle Ages", although his brief remarks on the consequences of Nominalism for the Protestant doctrine of grace and voluntarist concept of God, for the development of the experimental natural sciences, for Renaissance Humanism and for Christian Natural Law would need further differentiated debate. Habermas, "'Das Politische'", in *Nachmetaphysisches Denken II*, 245–46, n. 8.

there is a need to establish criteria that allow one to distinguish between elements of worldviews and argumentations that negate freedom and those that affirm and empower freedom. Religious traditions could well have supplied elements for the latter; they are not to be excluded from the public realm on the basis of being movements with roots in antiquity and with a truth claim about a transcendent creator.[377] Their specific utopias of hope in redemption from suffering and guilt, and their histories of reception which deepened the concept of individual agency by an analysis of interiority and responsibility *coram Deo*, cannot be discounted in advance.

3.1.5 A hermeneutics of the self as *idem* and *ipse*, and as self and other

In *Oneself as Another*, the positions that Ricoeur had previously dealt with under the inventive label, "masters of suspicion", are condensed into just one voice: The "Anti-Cogito" stance is now represented by Nietzsche, against which Descartes' "Cogito ergo sum" is not defendable. Answers at the level of the "What" of a general anthropology miss the crucial sense of the "Who".[378] This is what the new turn to the problem of the subject after the three volumes of *Time and Narrative* sets out to investigate: the constitution of the self in its duality and in its internal relation to an "other". The enquiry concludes not by regaining any type of certainty, but with a new term for the self's presence to itself between an awareness of its capabilities, and ineradicable doubt: attestation.

The final stage of an analysis of subjectivity that began with distinguishing the forms of the "involuntary" from what remains open and available to the human will is thus reached forty years later in a hermeneutics of the self that is still composed of receptivity and activity. One of the forms of the "involuntary"

---

377 On the consequence of contrasting specific concepts of modernity and tradition for his view of religious belief at this earlier stage of Habermas's thinking, cf. *Oneself as Another*, 287, n. 79: "The same observation can be made about Habermas's continually pejorative use of the idea of tradition, following his long-standing confrontation with Gadamer... We touch here, as in connection with the idea of convention, on a sensitive point of the ethics of argumentation, namely its tendency to overevaluate the break of modernity, to confirm secularization not only as a fact but as a value, to the point of excluding from the field of discussion, either tacitly or openly, anyone who does not accept as a prior given the Nietzschean profession of the 'death of God.'"
378 Ricoeur, *Oneself as Another*, 1–25. Greisch illustrates the point in *Fehlbarkeit*, 114: "'I think therefore I am' does not necessarily mean: 'I, René Descartes, is the one who is thinking!'" V. Hoffmann, *Vermittelte Offenbarung*, 156, explains the Cogito from which the tradition of the philosophy of the subject developed as Descartes "clarifying what he is: a thinking being, not who he is... the momentary, unhistorical identity of an I, of a sameness".

returns as an element in the new distinction of the self into two aspects, *idem* and *ipse:* "character", as an unchosen heritage, is now one of the factors of the *idem* that stands for the sameness component which allows re-identification over time.[379] The part previously played by exercising the active function of appropriation is now transformed into the spontaneous, self-directed initiative of the *ipse.* The fact that its constancy is experienced in the offering and keeping of promises points to a new stage of analysis of the human constitution: it discovers within itself a dimension that is other, which appears in three manifestations. In the first instance, it is the experience of being a body, rather than having a body;[380] in the second, it is the internal presence of another person, and in the third, it is the voice of conscience to which the self is in a position of receptivity.

With the second manifestation of otherness, the role of another person within the self's consciousness, the stage is set for following its pursuits within the realms of ethics. In addition to the first two capabilities of the self named in *Oneself as Another*, "acting" and "speaking", two further capabilities that belong in this sphere are investigated: being able to narrate, and being imputable which bring into view two different levels of ethics, the teleological and the deontological. Before going into Ricoeur's architecture of ethics, however, I want to profile the dimensions of the framework opened up so far by his enquiries.

3.1.6 Insights from Ricoeur's philosophical anthropology as a framework for ethics

Even before turning to the aspects which Ricoeur's theory of self acquires in the field of ethics, the new openings offered by the angles and breadth of his reconstruction can be summarized as including the following:

1. The subject of agency, left unthematized in Rawls's and Habermas's analyses of the citizen and of communicative reason, is no longer presupposed

---

379 An original application of this distinction to the New Testament concept of discipleship is given in Seán Freyne's exegetical comparison of its use in Luke and John in "In search of identity. Narrativity, discipleship and moral agency", in *Moral Language in the New Testament,* ed. by R. Zimmermann/J. Van der Watt, in cooperation with S. Luther (Tübingen: Mohr Siebeck, 2010), 67–85.

380 Haker, "Narrative and moral identity", in Junker-Kenny/Kenny (eds.), *Memory, Narrativity, Self,* 135, speaks of the "physically immediate certainty of self which makes it impossible to treat oneself as an external object of consideration. We are our bodies, even though we have bodies about whose nature we can communicate directly with others."

but examined for its true capabilities after critiquing both the "exalted" and the "humiliated subject" of Descartes' and Nietzsche's positions.[381]

2. Action originates from the self-motivation to reach out to one's very own possibilities; such interest in one's own initiative provides a different starting-point from the material orientation of self-interest considered as the only motivation in the rational choice theory borrowed from by Rawls.

3. The significance of a person's self-understanding, recognized by Habermas only in the context of his engagement with the debate on genetic programming since 2000, allows one to locate actions on a trajectory aspiring towards the horizon of a fulfilled life accomplished "with and for others, in just institutions".[382] Its explication requires a differentiation of levels that only a philosophy of reflection can offer. For Habermas, this type of thinking belongs to a "philosophy of consciousness" deemed to be superseded by the linguistic turn. By turning to the tools of individual social sciences instead, both his and Rawls's theories leave the question of self unexplored. Individual agency remains underdetermined as that of abstract, and possibly idealized, inhabitants of lifeworlds and polities.

4. The mediating role of the collective self-understandings that have arisen in the sequences and turns of particular cultural histories has been highlighted. They provide a cultural store of symbols which individual imagination draws on in its perception of reality and in envisioning a world in which it can devise projects.

5. Against the larger backdrop of the philosophical position of skepticism, recognized as a major counterplayer already by Kant, but reinforced in 20th century cultural trends of a defeatism or even cynicism of reason, philosophical effort has to be invested in the faculty of imagination; this task includes analyzing the role of utopia within a culture. Projecting different futures in the shape of utopias is neither sinister nor immature; while having to be distinguished from steered levels of ideology, and from a pathological refusal to identify steps of action, it expresses human striving by envisaging a social order beyond the status quo.

6. Symbolic worlds and cultural memories of the promises contained in their foundational writings are not closed, but are open to be compared and exchanged. Recognition of such plurality and its tensions expands the horizon of one's own culture of origin and creates chances for new departures.[383]

---

381 Ricoeur, *Oneself as Another*, 16.
382 Ricoeur, *Oneself as Another*, 172.
383 Cf. Eckholt, *Dogmatik interkulturell*, 60–61.

7. Literary works as expressions of conflict and longing are given a place of significance as an integral part of what philosophy needs to reflect on.
8. It is recognized as a task for philosophy itself, not only for individuals in their personal lives, to explore both the tragic and the role of hope for human action.
9. The reflections on the human constitution offered by religious traditions are taken seriously as texts for philosophical consideration and conversation.
10. Ethics, as the following section will establish, begins with a philosophical anthropology in which the good is more foundational than the experience of evil.

3.2 The self and its agency: Three types of ethical reflection

Having identified the duality of *idem* and *ipse*, as well as the co-constitutive presence of the other, to be examined next are the different ways in which the self relates to its agency; they give rise to a threefold structure of ethics (1). Subsequently, I shall discuss Ricoeur's engagement with the ethical theories proposed by Rawls and Habermas and highlight the differences that his phenomenology of the self and its capabilities makes in relation to the outlines of ethics (2). The consequences of this approach for how life in a democracy, culture, and religion are to be accessed will conclude this section (3).

3.2.1 A phenomenological reconstruction of the three dimensions of ethics

It is through the same method of analysis that is operative already in his philosophy of the will that Ricoeur brings together two hitherto opposed approaches to ethics. In his architecture of ethics, what previously seemed to be self-contained units are converted into communicating chambers. His examination of starting-points and categories that appeared to be radical alternatives discovers shared insights; what Aristotle expressed as "striving for a good life" can be found in Kant's foundational concept of the "good will".[384] In turn, Aristotle's virtue, so

---

384 Since *Oneself as Another*, the relationship between the two levels has been further elaborated in *The Just, Reflections on the Just*, and in the article "Human Capability: A Response," in J. Wall/W. Schweiker/W. D. Hall (eds.), *Paul Ricœur and Contemporary Moral Thought*, New York/London 2002, 279–290. In "From the moral to the ethical", in *Reflections on the Just*, he specifies: "Kantian moral philosophy can be taken... for an exact account of our common moral experience, one which holds that the only thing that can be taken as obligatory are maxims of

often taken as the basis of a unitary and complete counterpart to modern deon-tological ethics, is reinterpreted as a "pre-imperative".[385] The orientation towards *eudaimonia* is rescued from possible misunderstandings by translating it into the active verbal form of "living well", and specifying this aim by the inclusion of co-subjects and by necessary conditions: "with and for others, in just institu-tions".[386] Thus, both striving and obligation are released out of the grips of the antithesis between Aristotle and Kant and turned towards each other as two independent operations of reflection that can be related as dual stages of an overall enterprise. A third stage is given the Aristotelian-sounding title of "practical wisdom" and explained as the search for "equity" in the face of the inevitably multi-faceted, new and unique cases that the "law can never cover in its generality".[387] Yet it can equally be understood as the faculty of judgement that Kant analysed in his Third Critique, namely the reflective judgement that seeks a rule for a case marked by a set of factors that remain individual.[388]

From his starting point, the acting subject, Ricoeur reconstructs the different perspectives that emerge in attestation as the root of ethics in its three forms: to be able to act, to be obligated, to decide responsibly.[389] I shall investigate its tel-eological expression and the role of narrative in forming identity (1), the need for and the difficulties of its deontological formulation (2), and the function and sta-

---

action that can satisfy a test of universalization. Still, for all that, it is not necessary to take duty as the enemy of desire." (46–47). Regarding the relation between Aristotle and Kant, he states: "Not only are the two approaches, which for didactic reasons get encapsulated under the labels of teleology and deontology, not rivals inasmuch as they belong to two distinct planes of practical philosophy, but they overlap at some significant points." (50) Aristotle is preferred in terms of theory of action which begins with the "realm of desires... in the opening chapters of Aristotle's Nicomachean Ethics... we find a discourse structured in terms of *praxis,* something sorely lacking in Kant". (49) It is a lack he addresses with introducing a third level, that of practical wisdom for exactly this mediation. He finds the "lineaments of such a fundamental ethics", encompassing all the dimensions of "living well... most clearly outlined... in Aristotle", although he does "not renounce the idea of finding something equivalent in Kant himself". (50)
385 Ricoeur, "Ethics and human capability. A response", in J. Wall/W. Schweiker/D. W. Hall (eds.), *Paul Ricoeur and Contemporary Moral Theory,* 288.
386 Ricoeur, *Oneself as Another,* 172.
387 Ricoeur, "Justice and truth", in *Reflections on the Just,* 58–71, 63, with reference to Aristotle, *Nichomachean Ethics,* 1137b12–13.
388 In *Oneself as Another,* 262–73, Ricoeur uses Kant's recognition in his *Critique of Judgment* of the artist's singularity that creates the rule as a basis of an internal critique of his ethics where this idea is absent. He points out the possible conflict between the "universal" and the "plu-ralist" forms of the Categorical Imperative; Kant's insistence on the universality of the law does not leave room for the need to make exceptions "on behalf of the other" in order to do justice to a person's singularity.
389 Cf. Ricoeur, "Who is the subject of rights?", in *The Just,* 1–10, 4.

tus of practical wisdom (3). Finally, I shall illustrate the "wish" from which this tripartite structure receives its motivating force with an example both relevant for democratic life, and enabled by a religious perspective: memory and its relation to forgiveness. From this concluding perspective to ethics in which the power to act is restored to a subject who has failed in his moral responsibility, two points become especially clear: the "Who" of agency can only be found progressively by passing through the different levels of ethics;[390] yet the freedom to distinguish the agent from his acts equally has to be kept open, to allow for reversals and renewal (4).

3.2.1.1 The wish to "live well, with and for others, in just institutions"

When analysed under the aspect of ethics, the "wish," "desire" or "striving" identified phenomenologically as the source of action becomes a teleological orientation towards a fulfilling life. It has found its classical formulation in the Aristotelian conception of ethics which serves Ricoeur as the entry point and as the irreplaceable benchmark for individual judgements. The most striking feature of this programmatic formula is that all the components relevant for the moral level are already there: "Self, others, city", the directions identified in the different formulations of Kant's Categorical Imperative are all considered as relevant co-players.[391] It is already at the level of striving for the good life that others, both as near and as distant fellow-human beings, are recognized as significant. In addition to relatives and friends to whom a relation of "solicitude" exists, anonymous others, "third persons" beyond the I and the Thou, are

---

390 At the end of his perceptive reconstruction of Ricoeur's "implied theory of ethics" in *Ethische Identität und christlicher Glaube. Theologische Ethik im Spannungsfeld von Theologie und Philosophie* (Mainz: Grünewald, 2002), 216, the theological ethicist Christof Mandry asks about its status: "Phenomenology of the ethical, theory of the ethical subject, meta-ethics?" He points to Ricoeur's "reiterated intention to develop a theory of the self to which the perspectives on its ethical and moral dimensions are subordinated". Mandry concludes that "the question about the Who of ethical action and of moral obligation has been reversed in favour of enquiring what the ethical identity of the acting self consists in, how the good and the obligatory are connected and how practice has to be thought in ethical and moral regard".

391 In *Reflections on the Just*, 62, the phenomenological analysis anchors these three dimensions in expanding horizons: "The internal progression of what is one's own, what is near, and what is distant rejoins the three formulations of the Kantian imperative, which Kant presents in the *Groundwork*. When so transposed to the plane of the norm, this basic triad becomes that of the autonomy of the self, respect for the humanity in the person of oneself and others, and the projection of the city of ends in which everyone would be both subject and legislator."

equally counted in.[392] By locating the orientation towards justice at the very level of the individual desire to be, Ricoeur takes a position not only against Hobbes, but also against communitarian as much as against liberal ethics. In distinction from a naturalist foundation of political theory on the fear of the other, recognition is taken as a marker of basic human relationality.[393] Both the restrictions of the ethical perspective to one's own community of origin and liberalism's bounded society are ruled out by the inclusion of the distant other. Conceptualizing the social link as "contract" is in danger of missing and denying the deep foundation of human sociability that Hannah Arendt has expressed as "the will to live together". Thus, Ricoeur's strong assertion, "only as citizen is the person fully human",[394] is not meant to entail a restriction and reduction of the three dimensions of ethics to the legal, but will appeal to all of them, bringing together striving, morality and the orientation of institutions towards justice.

The first connection to be examined is that of the first to the second level of ethics. How does the "thesis of the primacy of the teleological approach in the determination of the idea of the just"[395] relate to Kant? On the one hand, it is a corrective to seeing inclination only as the counter-position to duty:

> Justice, in this reading, is an integral part of the wish to live well... the wish to live in just institutions arises from the same level of morality as do the desire for personal fulfillment and the reciprocity of friendship. The just is first an object of desire, of a lack, of a wish. It begins as a wish before it is an imperative.[396]

---

392 J. Greisch, *Fehlbarkeit*, 128, exemplifies this orientation also of the good life towards the anonymous other with the situation of "excluded third persons... who desperately try to find a secret entry (*Schlupfloch*) into 'Fortress Europe'... The faceless and anonymous 'anybody'... has to be thought as an 'included'... third, belonging to the social institution as such which is supported by the wish of the members of a historical community to live together."

393 *The Course of Recognition*, trans. D. Pellauer (Cambridge: Harvard University Press, 2005), 148–49, shows the need to take a stance regarding this alternative and to clarify the philosophical foundations on which productive proposals, such as A. Sen's focus on capabilities, can be developed, rather than taking for granted a framework of recognition.

394 In *The Just*, Preface, xv-xvi, Ricoeur argues together with Aristotle and H. Arendt for the inclusion of "just institutions" into the original wish to live well: "Aristotle had already indicated that... the goal of happiness did not reach the end of its trajectory in solitude – to which I would add, friendship – but in the setting of the city. Politics... thus constituted the architectonic of ethics. I would say the same thing in a language closer to that of Hannah Arendt: it is within the *interesse* that the wish for a good life finds its fulfillment. It is as citizens that we become human. The wish to live in just institutions signifies nothing else."

395 Ricoeur, *The Just*, Preface, xvi.

396 Ricoeur, *The Just*, Preface, xv.

Yet the dimensions in which Kant unfolds his ethics are kept and defended against any shrinking of its domain; the unconditional character it has uncovered is upheld. The "good will" is specified as being directed towards others. They appear as co-agents in the narratives through which the self seeks to achieve a sense of unity of its life. Here, it is important to see that the capability to narrate is linked to the quest for an identity that is "fragile";[397] it is not without effort, as Jean Greisch points out in his reconstruction of the lines of continuity from "fallibility" to "capability" in Ricoeur's work.[398] A further indication of the intention to investigate the moral ought from below, in continuity with striving, is the repeated reference to Charles Taylor's term, "strong evaluations". For a phenomenological analysis that is interested in the self-reflective references accompanying action it is a fitting perspective. It also allows to understand "identity" first of all not in an adversarial sense of defining the self against others but as seeking continuity in the realization of its ethical wish for a fulfilled existence; actions are chosen in keeping with the priorities of the values to which a self is attracted. This discourse is not about the sociological question of external identity markers or about identity politics; it is a philosophical enquiry into how a subject's self-esteem that is based on the capability to act is unfolded in the turns of a life, and recapitulated in stories, creating a "bridge between description and prescription".[399]

3.2.1.2 The deontological level as the "sieve of the norm"

This "self-esteem" can become "self-respect" when an intention pursued in ethical striving is subjected to a critical examination against the moral claim of universality, is reconsidered and discontinued. The moral level allows a new relationship to oneself, as a subject responsible for one's acts. This capability is distinguished as the one to which the others – speaking, acting, and narrating – are oriented as the "highest": "imputability" receives a new application when it turns from theoretical to practical reason.[400] Being an agent who can initiate courses of action in the world is now qualified as a power for which the self is morally accountable. The need to progress to this level is justified with the reference to human violence. It is because of human vulnerability that an autonomy is needed which submits maxims to a law valid for every subject: "violence con-

---

397 Ricoeur, *Reflections on the Just*, 79.
398 Greisch, *Fehlbarkeit*, 142–46.
399 H. Haker, "Narrative and moral identity", in Junker-Kenny/Kenny (eds.), *Memory, Narrativity, Self*, 140.
400 Ricoeur, *Reflections on the Just*, 82.

stitutes the primary circumstance in the transition from a teleological to a deontological point of view".[401]

On the one hand, the analysis of this transition stresses the break that occurs in the expansion of striving when it encounters the other as a limit:

> the transition from the wish to the imperative, from desire to interdiction appears to be inevitable. Why? For the fundamental reason that action implies a capacity to do something that gets carried out on the interactive plane as the *power* exercised by an agent on another agent who is the recipient of this power. This *power over* others offers the permanent occasion for violence in all its forms: from the lie, where only the instrument of language seems to be misused, to the imposition of suffering, culminating in the imposition of a violent death and in the horrible practice of torture, where the will to humiliate exceeds that of merely imposing suffering. In short, it is owing to the wrong that one person inflicts on another that the moral judgment... has to add the predicate of the obligatory to that of the good, usually under the negative figure of what is prohibited.[402]

On the other hand, Ricoeur underlines the fundamental theory decision in which Kant emphasizes the only factual, not necessary character of moral evil. Foundational in his anthropology and ethics is the good will, and evil is only a "penchant" or "propensity" (*Hang*).[403] Thus, the self-experience of moral obligation is as original and distinct as that of striving, but both are related in that the "enabling and protective function of morality"[404] can connect with the level of Aristotelian virtues as "pre-imperatives".

The authority of this level is based on the position that the attitude of impartiality to which it commits is something that can be expected from humans. Ricoeur examines Thomas Nagel's claim that this insight is possible:

> "Since the impersonal standpoint does not single you out from anyone else, the same must be true of the values arising in other lives. If you matter impersonally, so does everyone... every life counts and none is more important than any other." Is this an assertion stemming from the order of truth or from that of the just? An assertion or an obligation? I would say that it is a mixture of the orders of fact and right. But the fact here is nothing other than the capacity to adopt the impersonal point of view, better, the capacity to negotiate between the personal and the impersonal points of view.[405]

---

401 Ricoeur, *The Just*, Preface, xvii.
402 Ricoeur, *The Just*, Preface, xvi- xvii.
403 Kant, *Religion Within the Limits of Reason Alone*, Book One, II.
404 Mandry, *Ethische Identität*, 193.
405 Ricoeur, "Justice and truth", in *Reflections on the Just*, 67, quoting from Th. Nagel, *Equality and Partiality*, 11. Cf. also his summary of Nagel's argument in "Autonomy and vulnerability", in *Reflections on the Just*, 72–90, 88–89.

At the same time, the formality of the Kantian Categorical Imperative can equally be a source of injustice. This is why a third level has to be added, where "practical wisdom" is entrusted with finding solutions between impartiality, and a justified concern for a person's singularity.

3.2.1.3 "Practical wisdom" as a "heartfelt conviction"

In contrast to Kant, Ricoeur's identification of the types of ethical reflection does not end at the summit of imputability as the final level. Faced with the thicket of applications of the formal rule to specific persons, goods and situations, the faculties of the will and of autonomous reason are complemented by a resource that makes it possible to find mediations: the power of imagination. Between exceptionless universality and the "perspectivism of personal singularity",[406] directions have to be discovered that can find agreement as being "equitable". This function of creating new situation-adequate rules is identified as *"poetic"*; it constitutes an "innovation" and actualizes a category used, but by no means exhausted by Kant: The "invention of an appropriate solution to the unique situation stems from... productive imagination (Kant)".[407]

Unprecedented as these creative suggestions of finding a "fit" are,[408] they are discovered from the symbolic stocks of a culture. Here the further realm in which "practical wisdom" is rooted is indicated: it draws not only from the agent's personal experience of moral life, but also from the accumulated insights of value orientations, structures and institutions. In his discussion of the complex questions posed by Hegel's critique of Kant, Ricoeur takes care to distinguish the resources offered in the existing ethical life of a polity, from Hegel's understanding of *Sittlichkeit* as a counter-proposal to a Kantian morality which in its radically personal conscientious quality Hegel ultimately denounces as "terrorist". In

---

406 Ricoeur, "Autonomy and vulnerability", in *Reflections on the Just*, 88.

407 Ricoeur, *The Just*, Preface, xxii.

408 Ricoeur, *The Just*, 113. Interpretation becomes "the way the productive imagination follows once the problem is no longer to apply a known rule to a presumably correctly described case, as with determinative judgment, but to 'find' a rule *under* which it is appropriate to place a fact that itself must be interpreted." (126). Mandry, *Ethische Identität*, 195, summarizes the difficulty of relating practice and norms as follows: "In his analysis of the conflicts of moral life Ricoeur unites the problem of the mediation of general norms with the singularity of the situations under decision, and the problem of the complexity of practice. 'Onesidedness of norms' thus means that the formality of the moral norm cannot be brought together with the multivalence (*Vieldeutigkeit*) of practice simply in a procedure of subsumtion. The illusion of an 'easy' applicability of morality itself leads to conflicts that cannot be solved in a moral-deontological way since they demand a different avenue (*Zugang*) to practice."

his defense of the "beautiful soul" against its dismissive review by Hegel,[409] Ricoeur moves the innovative conclusion represented by the term "conviction" away from the pole of given cultural value systems, to the pole of individual conscience.[410] It figures both as emerging from a shared *Sittlichkeit*, and as taking a reflected stance against it in conscientious objection. The concluding formulation for the achievement of this level thus highlights the internal validation, as opposed to a structurally conservative use of *phronesis* as mediating in a closed cultural framework:

> The search for justice ends with a *heartfelt conviction*, set in motion by the wish to live in just institutions, and ratified by the rule of justice for which procedural formalism serves to guarantee impartiality.[411]

With the three distinct, but related levels of ethics as discovered in self-reflection, Ricoeur steers clear of neo-Aristotelian interpretations that emphasize receptivity and continuity at the expense of critique and new departures. The break that occurs through the second level, interrupting striving by exposing it to an impartial judgment on its universalizability, shows the distance of his thinking from an understanding of life merely in forms of unfolding an already given ethos. The philosopher Herbert Schnädelbach has pointed out the ideological tendencies of contemporary returns to this model; similarly, Otfried Höffe has commented on the difference between a self-contained worldview oriented towards a continual unfolding of virtue within the limits of reason, and biblical monotheism.[412]

---

409 Ricoeur, *Oneself as Another*, 256.
410 Mandry, *Ethische Identität*, 194–196, points out this dual orientation, but also judges that the short shrift Ricoeur gives to Hegel's concept of the state in *Oneself as Another*, 256, may be unjustified: "In his interpretation, the philosophy of the spirit leads to a hypostatization of the state, which cannot be upheld in view of the crimes committed in the 20th century. What Ricoeur criticizes are, in my view, slanted interpretations [*Verzerrungen*] of Hegelian philosophy which, however, were powerful in the history of reception, but cannot be charged to Hegel." While it is always true that a thinker's new approach needs to be distinguished from its history of reception, Hegel's characterization of conscience also speaks for itself.
411 Ricoeur, *The Just*, Preface, xxi.
412 H. Schnädelbach, "Was ist Neoaristotelismus?" in *Zur Rehabilitierung*, 205–230. In *Ethik und Politik* (Frankfurt: Suhrkamp, 1979), 329–332, Höffe points out that this framework has no provision for radical critique and reform based on moral reasons; both the prophets and the idea of a "new law" would be unthinkable. The "concept of striving lives off an unproblematized presupposition: the (individual-spontaneous) finality of human agency. Interpreted as striving, human praxis is always already assigned a goal... In phenomena such as moral criticism out of morality or ethical-political protests, in the giving of a "New Law" (cf. New Testament), in

What Ricoeur achieves in his hermeneutical enquiry into the structural features and performances of the self as *idem* and *ipse* is to anchor justice twice as the endpoint of two types of reconstruction: one horizontal, the other vertical.

> I propose two intersecting readings of the structure of morality. A horizontal reading will lead me derive the constitution of the self from the following threefold structure: the wish for a good life, with and for others, in just institutions. A vertical reading will then follow the ascending progression that, starting from a teleological approach guided by the idea of living well, traverses the deontological approach where the norm, obligation, prohibition, formalism, and procedures dominate, to find its end on the plane of practical wisdom, of prudence as the art of a fair decision in situations of uncertainty and conflict, hence in the tragic setting of action... Justice finds itself situated at the intersection of two axes, since it first figures in third place in the threefold structure..., and it remains the third category named when this threefold structure is transposed from one plane to another... Justice can thus be taken as the highest category of the practical field if we can show that there is a progression on the horizontal plane from the first to the third term of the basic threefold structure, and equally on the vertical axis where the idea of justice culminates in that of fairness.[413]

In carrying out this design, the extent and the depth of moral life have been outlined and a conclusion reached in which "fairness" is another name for the divinatory ability of proposing an equitable mediation of rule and singularity. A paradigmatic case for the attempt to bring together all the factors recognized in their vitality and their validity can be found in the role of memory for agency.

3.2.1.4 The wish for a reconciled memory and the status of forgiveness in a theory of agency

Spelling out the wish to "live well" in all its dimensions with regard to memory concretizes several aspects: the self's sense of continuity through personal and family memories connecting with cultural memory, its moral identity, and its hope for fulfillment. The narrative in which the self evolves its self-understand-

---

constitutional reforms, political revolutions or in an explicit renewal of personal and political value priorities, aims are no longer pursued in the framework of a lived ethos. Rather, the ethical-political basic framework itself is up for decision. An inherited system of institutions and patterns of behaviour and the activities of striving that correspond to them is put up for disposition with regard to the principles themselves. Such a process can no longer be conceptualized as agency due to internalized basic orientations, as a spontaneous affirmation and pursual of ends, i.e. as an act of striving. It is rather a case of a distance of striving within itself, i.e., an act of the will... due to which ends are not only pursued but first of all posited."
413 Ricoeur, "Justice and truth", in *Reflections on the Just*, 60.

ing selects and compares shared memories and provides a personal lens on the historical events that form the objective timeline against which its subjective experience takes place.[414] A community's interpretation of such events forms its cultural memory and affects individual self-understanding. The teleological unity of life aspired to in the originating wish to live well reappears under the title of a "reconciled" memory.[415] But this concept of unity is ambiguous: on the one hand, it just denotes a formal idea and labels as a "good" something that is composed both of good and of questionable actions; on the other hand, if it is meant as a qualitative assessment of an agent's life, this "good" has to include the moral level.[416] Then the memory of harmful and evil acts needs the counterpart of a freely offered and accepted forgiveness to be able to become "reconciled". Its analysis thus allows one to plumb the depths of a self-experience that can no longer progress from the self-esteem based on the affirmation of its own power to act, to morally acquired self-respect, since it has already failed the other by contravening this level. The transition from the "structure of the ethical self" relating to self, known other and anonymous other in self-esteem, solicitude, and sense of justice, to the "faces of the moral self... autonomy, respect and procedural justice/social contract" has been halted.[417] Which analyses are offered in *Oneself as Another* and in *Memory, History, Forgetting* when the problem of evil becomes personalized in the identity of a perpetrator?

One answer to be drawn from the discussion of "conflicts" arising at the moral level in *Oneself as Another*, is that it makes evident the limits of a purely moral judgement. In an internal critique of Kant who recognizes that a singular stroke of aesthetic genius has the power to create a new paradigm of rules, but who keeps this realization tied to the sphere of art, Ricoeur makes singularity the measure and the limit of moral universalization. It is not as an exchangeable bearer of reason but as a singular case that the subject of morality counts. In the dilemma between solicitude and norm, it is singularity that justifies making an exception to the rule "on behalf of the other": the "exception takes on a different countenance, or rather, it becomes a countenance, a face, inasmuch as the

---

414 In *Memory, History, Forgetting*, the category of family memories is inserted between personal and collective memory as a mediation between the poles of an individual and a sociological level that abstracts from agents. Cf. Greisch's comments on Ricoeur's difference to Halbwachs in "Vom Glück des Erinnerns zur Schwierigkeit des Vergebens", in Orth/Reifenberg (eds.), *Facettenreiche Anthropologie*, 104.

415 Ricoeur, Epilogue, *Memory, History, Forgetting*, 457–506.

416 In *Ethische Identität*, 146, n. 9, Mandry points out the distinction between the two.

417 Greisch, *Fehlbarkeit*, 126. 129.

genuine otherness of persons makes each one an exception."[418] In another text, written as a contribution to the *Festschrift* for the theologian Jürgen Moltmann, the need to go beyond morality is linked with a view of the human person inspired by religion: Since there is "no absolutely constraining moral reason why the difference in persons should be in itself an object of obligation", what is needed is the "pressure of love on justice".[419] At the same time, while the "univocity" of the imperative needs to be challenged, the other extreme to be avoided is "arbitrariness", a "decisionism" without criteria that is in "complicity" with the "rigidity" of the first.[420] It is here, facing the "gaping tear... so carefully concealed by Kant between respect for the rule and respect for persons" that practical wisdom is called for:

> Practical wisdom consists in inventing conduct that will best satisfy the exception required by solicitude, by betraying the rule to the smallest extent possible... Practical wisdom consists here in inventing just behavior suited to the singular nature of the case.[421]

Also regarding the process of legal decision-making against an offender, the emphasis is on wisdom in judgement. From a reflection on the internal connection between "Autonomy and Vulnerability", judges are asked to include "into the very act of judging... the degree of the accused's capacity to situate him- or herself in relation to a symbolic order" and to "take into account deficits at the very level of the figuration of obligation".[422]

While *Oneself as Another* already referred to Kant's designation of religion as the potential to "restore" the capability for agency by opening up again the sour-

---

418 Ricoeur, *Oneself as Another*, 265.
419 Ricoeur, "Theonomy and/or autonomy", in M. Volf/C. Krieg/Th. Kucharz (eds.), *The Future of Theology. Essays in Honor of Jürgen Moltmann* (Grand Rapids: Eerdmans, 1996), 284–98, 294.
420 Ricoeur, *Oneself as Another*, 264. Concerning "the dialectic of moral judgment in a situation" in the legal sphere, *The Just*, 152–3, states: "To apply a norm to a particular case is an extraordinarily complex operation that implies a style of interpretation irreducible to the mechanism of the practical syllogism." Ricœur underlines the need to respect the dignity also of the offender, and everyone's accountability to the social bond. The distance the law institutionalizes and the role of the judge as a third party between the perpetrator and the victim are to create space for a just sentence that does not turn into revenge. The unconditional respect for the person who is more than what she has done has to be safeguarded in the course of coming to a sentence. In *Memory, History, Forgetting*, 493, the formula that honours singularity is addressed to the offender: "You are worth more than your acts." (trans. changed from: "You are better than your acts.")
421 Ricoeur, *Oneself as Another*, 269.
422 Ricoeur, *Reflections on the Just*, 72–90, 86.

ces of the good,[423] it is the Epilogue of *Memory, History, Forgetting* that works out the question of forgiveness from the link between agent and action. How can an agent who has done wrong, diminished the other, and lost his moral identity, relate to himself? For Ricoeur, the possibility to be restored to one's capacity for agency depends on the availability of a perspective that sees in the self more than the doer of his deeds. Two separate acts have to be initiated: the free offer of forgiveness, and the free acceptance of that offer. These are not just generic human abilities, as in Hannah Arendt's analysis, which he critiques for only considering agency in its temporal directions towards the future and the past, putting promising and forgiving on the same level. For forgiveness to occur for a past deed which cannot be undone, one has to believe that it exists: "Il y a le pardon".[424] What status this "voice" and "hymn" of forgiveness has, is left in suspense; but quotes from the Bible include it in what St. Paul's Letter to the Corinthians states of the theological virtues faith, hope and love that will "remain", and what the Song of Songs asserts of the power of love, that it is "as strong" as death.[425] The origin of forgiveness is kept open, while both the freedom of the act of forgiving and the need for it to restore agency are made clear.

By identifying "forgiveness as the eschatology of memory" in the Epilogue, it is proposed as a "horizon" for the preceding studies into the role of memory in the phenomenology of the self, the epistemology of history and the historic condition of humans. It is a presupposition for accessing the betrayed hopes of the past for which history and the cultural memory of it function as a "graveyard of unkept promises".[426] The possibility of a reconciled memory thus relates beyond the individual to the sources of renewal within a culture; it has to begin with what did not come to pass of the energy, themes and motifs harboured in its creative core. Before outlining the context in which the persistence of original promises reappears as a theme, namely in religious and cultural traditions seen in their function as co-founders of the public sphere, I shall summarize the differences of Ricoeur's theory of action, self and ethics to those of Rawls and Habermas.

---

423 Ricoeur, *Oneself as Another*, 216.
424 Ricoeur, *Memory, History, Forgetting*, 466: "There is forgiveness."
425 Ricoeur, *Memory, History, Forgetting*, 506.
426 Ricoeur, *Das Rätsel der Vergangenheit. Erinnern – Vergessen – Verzeihen* (Göttingen: Wallstein, 2000), 128.

3.2.2 Differences to Rawls and Habermas in the outline of ethics

The differences to Rawls (1) and Habermas (2) concerning the theory of action that were stated at the end of the previous section can now be specified and expanded regarding the anchoring of ethics in a hermeneutics of the self.

3.2.2.1 Questions to Rawls

They relate to the understanding of the subject, the interpretation and scope of the ethical sense of justice, of moral self-determination and proceduralism, the realm of goods for equal distribution, the role of convictions, and responsibility in all its temporal dimensions.

1. The lack of a deeper analysis of the subject and its capabilities leaves out aspects that are presupposed in key terms, such as "life plan". Missing are several factors: the self- interpretation required for it which needs to be articulated in narratives, the aspiration for the unity of a life, and the self-relation expressed as "attestation". A sense of authorship has to be regained and reclaimed over the ongoing possibility of "suspicion" since it is not at the level of facts that can be proved.

2. While the overall direction of Rawls's theory that at "each degree of complexity, justice presents itself... as 'the first virtue of social institutions'",[427] is welcomed by Ricoeur, its orientation towards systems rather than selves leaves the necessary connection between them underexplored.

3. Rawls assumes a "sense of justice" as one of the two ethical faculties of the individual, together with an idea of his own good. As we have seen in Part One, Ricoeur distinguishes two alternative directions which the sense of justice can take as a "reasonable sentiment": one at the "lower level", which is "atomistic" used in the "contractualist conception from Hobbes to Rousseau to Kant to Rawls", and marked by "mutual disinterest", the other directed towards mutuality at the "higher level", a "desire for mutual dependence, mutual indebtedness".[428] This difference in destination will have an effect on how society, global justice, intercultural relations, and the ability of religious comprehensive doctrines for outreach and dialogue can be conceived.

4. The "sense of justice" is one basis for the contract concluded in the "original position". For Ricoeur, the move from the ethical to the moral level requires its formalization into a procedural form of justice, but not its replacement. It vi-

---

427 Ricoeur, *The Just*, Preface, xiv, with reference to Rawls, *Theory of Justice*, 3.
428 Ricoeur, "Theonomy", in *The Future of Theology*, 291.

olates the level of striving if this sense no longer continues to be "presupposed",[429] but is taken over by the contract. This move poses the question of how the relation of ethical reflection and philosophy as a whole to pre-theoretical foundations is conceived. In phenomenology, the level prior to reflection, in short, "life", has to be recognized by philosophical thought. More specifically, in ethics, the material to be considered is not neutral but imbued with the original ethical capacity of humans. This is why Ricoeur formulates the doubt that was already quoted in Part One: Does the invention of the original position effectively bypass the existing basis of ethics in the striving and the morality of agents and make it superfluous?[430]

5. Not only does the "contract" take the place of continued reliance on and reinvigoration by the ethical energy that exists prior to its philosophical clarification; it is also based on an anthropology of rational choice which strips agents of their original benevolence and assumes self-interest as their principal motivation. Ricoeur has interpreted the maximin rule as an "ethical argument disguised as a technical argument" against Utilitarianism, but he has equally wondered "how it can be possible to maintain simultaneously the recognition of an ethical presupposition and the attempt to free the procedural definition of justice from every presupposition concerning the good and even the just".[431]

6. From Ricoeur's reconstruction of the different levels of ethics, the scope of the sense of justice should be cosmopolitan. It also covers those outside one's own culture of belonging who need to be included if institutions are to be just. Jean Greisch has explicated its extent in Ricoeur's proposal in the following terms: "Equality in relation to living in institutions requires the consideration not only of fellow-citizens, but of fellow-humans".[432] In Rawls, neither the ethical nor the procedural levels extend to this horizon.

7. A moral orientation appears in Rawls as a commitment to "civility" and "tolerance", but no change of level from a sense of justice to self-determination is outlined in which the self puts itself under a law of reason. Law is mainly char-

---

429 In "Is a purely procedural theory of justice possible?", in *The Just*, 36 – 57, 37 – 38, Ricoeur points out "that a moral sense of justice founded on the Golden Rule... is always presupposed by a purely procedural justification of the principle of justice".

430 Ricoeur, "Purely procedural theory of justice", in *The Just*, 56: "In the final analysis, this ambiguity has to do with the role of rational arguments in ethics. Can they be substituted for prior convictions thanks to the invention of a hypothetical situation of deliberation (or a transcendental argumentation?) Or is their function instead to clarify in a critical way such prior convictions?"

431 Ricoeur, "Purely procedural theory of justice", in *The Just*, 52 – 53.

432 Greisch, *Fehlbarkeit*, 128 – 129, with reference to *Oneself as Another*, 194.

acterized as "coercive", rather than also as enabling.[433] The experience of human evil that is the motivational force behind the positing of the Categorical Imperative is not followed up into its origin in the freedom of the agent, although the existence of evil is acknowledged and the violation of urgent human rights is the basis on which "outlaw states" are defined in *The Law of Peoples*.

8. Practical wisdom can be seen to be at work in the "considered convictions", much quoted by Ricoeur, which form the second, contextual foundation of *Theory of Justice*. They relate both to the individual basis of judgement, and to the collective store of practices in democratic institutions. The appeal to a sense of fairness inherent in the values operative in liberal polities is effective as a reminder of a shared motivation. Yet the difference between Rawls's and Ricoeur's use of the term "considered convictions" is that for the latter, convictions are forged in the encounter of deontological principles and biographically acquired moral experience; in Rawls, the "principles" are already mediated and fall short of the Categorical Imperative both in their conditionality and in their content. They only apply as long as they are being reciprocated, in contrast to the Categorical Imperative of respecting and not instrumentalizing the other that holds even in situations where it is not requited, indeed, where enmity is continued. Rawls's principles are also tempered by "political values" that consist in liberal interpretations of what "liberty" and "equality" signify: a "liberty" that is distinguished from a "republican" orientation towards building a participative democracy from the resources of its members, and an "equality" within the walls of each constitutional state. A "duty of assistance" was assumed but restricted to the case of severely disadvantaged states in which the survival of people is threatened; it did not put into question structural disadvantage, such as global trade relations, as Rainer Forst observed in his critique. For Ricoeur, these are matters for "practical wisdom" but based on more ambitious definitions of what the "sense of justice" and what "principles" entail. While Rawls uses them loosely, they belong to two different levels in Ricoeur's analysis; they need to be mediated in a practical wisdom that is situation-adequate but not prematurely modest or defeatist.

9. The meanings conveyed by the worlds of culture and by past and present works of literature play no role in Rawls's model. Different types of access to reality are not investigated, and the openings they offer for the imagination of a self that seeks to realize itself anew is not considered in their vital function of

---

433 Cf. B. Laux, "Welche Geltungsansprüche, welche Gründe?" in B. Laux (ed.), *Heiligkeit und Menschenwürde. Hans Joas' neue Genealogie der Menschenrechte im theologischen Gespräch* (Freiburg: Herder, 2013), 144–167, 158.

being a bridge to ethics. Yet, as Hille Haker observed in the context of her discussion of Habermas, it is a perspective that (theological and philosophical) social ethics should be interested in if it wants to link up with the sources and self-conceptions that motivate or limit the actions of citizens of different ages and subcultures.[434]

10. A further source in need of a differentiated treatment in its plurality is addressed with a unitary rationale in Rawls: "Primary goods" are all situated at the same level, to be subjected to a unitary concept of distribution. Ricoeur frames the critique of Michael Walzer and others that distinct criteria of justice obtain in different "spheres" and "cities", as only an "extension", not a "refutation" of Rawls;[435] yet, he draws attention to the crucial need to demarcate and protect spheres from one another. Above all, there is a historical and a categorical dimension where the distinction between the commercial and the priceless is drawn. Rawls presupposes this distinction in his opposition to slavery; it is a historical turning point for which he has also acknowledged the contribution of religious convictions. But the ongoing challenge to stop the encroachment of the market even on primary human relationships is not identified in its current forms, as his comments on the goal of genetic improvement show.

11. While Rawls includes in the concept of justice between generations the task to "preserve the gains of culture and civilization, and maintain intact those just institutions that have been established",[436] it does not include the unfulfilled promises of the past. The idea that unfulfilled and thwarted breaks for freedom that occurred in history beckon the present to live up to its debt to the past is missing.[437] The cultural debt owed to previous eras is also not mentioned. The break that modernity constitutes with pre-enlightened eras is even more pronounced than in Habermas who explicitly states the originating role of biblical monotheism for the modern understanding of justice, individuality, and other core ideas of modern ethics.

12. The question of the capability and the limits of the will, of the sources of its renewal and of the significance of forgiveness for restoring the self towards new action are only discussed in a critical dismissal of Kant's postulates of practical reason. They are recommended to be transformed or replaced by a meas-

---

434 Haker, *Moralische Identität*, 27.
435 Ricoeur, "Purely procedural theory of justice", in *The Just*, 38.
436 Rawls, *Theory of Justice*, 285.
437 On the threefold horizon of time in Ricoeur's concept of responsibility, including "the past that is not completely our work but that makes us what we are", cf. Greisch, *Fehlbarkeit*, 134, with reference to *Oneself as Another*, 295.

ured hope for gradual progress.[438]Against this firmly established median line of aspiration, tied to "common sense" in *Political Liberalism*, the idea that there can be more than fairness, justice, and even more than equity, namely generosity, love, or superabundance in a dialectical relationship with justice, is not glimpsed as a question appearing at the upper limit of procedural ethics.

3.2.2.2 Questions to Habermas

Ricoeur recognizes Habermas's and Apel's proposal of a discourse ethics as "exemplary" for "the universalist thesis".[439] Some of the questions he poses to it are the same as to Rawls: its proceduralism, the goal of consensus, the failure to engage with the plurality of persons expressed by their striving and their singularity. Others are specific: the role of argument in discourse; the view of tradition as convention; the guiding perspective on language. Some of the causes defended by the German and the French theorists through their choice of approach are similar: the need to take seriously the theorists of suspicion, Marx, Nietzsche, and Freud; to rescue self-reflection, critique and distanciation from being submerged into a hermeneutics of belonging; a lively public sphere of citizens engaging with each other; the insistence on the integrity of different spheres against their "colonization", and the task posed to relate the segments back to a unity of action, or the flourishing life of the self; the opposition of what is priceless to the sweep of a relentless commercialization; advocacy for Europe as a political project of peace, justice and cultural exchange. Yet the question remains whether the theory decisions made in the outline of the discourse theory of ethics allow these concerns to be adequately represented.

1. As a proceduralist form of deontology, it is equally in danger of detaching morality from its pre-imperative expression in the wish for a good life. While it does not replace the good will by a contractual account, as Rawls does in the original position, it draws a sharp line between the universalistic level of discourse, and all the particularities of its participants, which do not enter into the material questions to be discussed. It is true that Habermas admits that such an insight can become a universally sharable one,[440] but what counts for Ricoeur is whether the connection to the level of ethical striving to live well in just institutions is kept alive or severed. By not identifying an ethical sense of justice, as Rawls does, and by going straight to the moral level, the possibility

---

438 Cf. Rawls, *Lectures on the History of Moral Philosophy*, 317–25.
439 Ricoeur, *Oneself as Another*, 284.
440 Habermas, "Discourse ethics", in *Moral Consciousness*, 104.

of anchoring responsibility in a "hermeneutics of the self" is excluded. In her comparison of the approaches of Hans Krämer, Jürgen Habermas, Charles Taylor and Ricoeur, Hille Haker distinguishes between an "extrinsic," an "intrinsic" and a "complementary" relationship of ethical striving to morality. She identifies Habermas's as an "extrinsic" model with no connections, indeed, a "radical gap", to personal identity. Thus, it offers a "moral theory", but has nothing to say on "moral identity" defined precisely as arising from life story and responsibility taken on for the present, the future, and the past.[441]

2. Although Ricoeur endorses the need for universalistic arguments and the place they are given by Habermas, he deplores that they are not entered as "convictions" that can be tested for their universalizability. Here, two different comments of his can be brought together. Discourse ethics raises the claim that it has taken the step from Kant's "monological" procedure of testing maxims against the Categorical Imperative, to communicative rationality with its "intersubjective" platform. Ricoeur sees the reproach to Kant as unfounded.[442] A separate remark relates to the plurality of persons who are more than exchangeable bearers of reason. For "safeguarding its dialogical vocation from slipping back into the solitude of monologue", convictions have to be taken seriously:

> If subjects called to argumentation must lay aside everything that our moralists hold for simple conventions, then what remains of the singularity and otherness of the partners in the discussion? If their convictions are only conventions, then what distinguishes the partners from each other, apart from their interests? Only a vivid sense of the *otherness* of persons can safeguard the dialogical dimension against any reduction to a monologue conducted by an undifferentiated subject.[443]

Thus, by not taking claims to validity first of all as convictions arising from personal reflection on principles and their intention, Habermas misses the dialogical part of intersubjectivity which exchanges reasons and their motivations, rather than just strict universality claims.

3. For Habermas, the universalistic level of morality is reached in the rational consensus of discourse participants on what is justifiable for all, not just those present. Ricoeur strongly endorses the approach of discourse ethics for its universalistic scope; yet he also insists, in view of the tension between the universalistic and the pluralist versions of the Categorical Imperative, that such a consensus is only justified if it takes singularity into account, which is the task of

---

441 Haker, "Narrative and moral identity", in Junker-Kenny/Kenny (eds.), *Memory, Narrativity, Self"*, 143–152.
442 Ricoeur, "Interpretation and/or argumentation", in *The Just*, 109–126, 118.
443 Ricoeur, "Theonomy", in *The Future of Theology*, 296.

practical wisdom. At the political level, Ricoeur prefers to emphasize the reality of abiding disagreement and to set in motion a search for equity, including, at times, the finding of compromises and provisional solutions. He points out that at the concrete level, it is more often a question of deciding between "gray and gray", and, in tragic situations, between "worse and worst".[444] Habermas's principled consensus formulates high expectations towards citizens and requires sacrifice for the sake of ensuring everyone's basic rights, but it leaves all concrete historical matters of dispute to discourses of application between participants. For Ricoeur, this concrete level needs to be included as a matter for philosophy, as it decides on what is equitable and has to take into account the tragic.

4. One root of Habermas's focus on argument, rather than on conviction with its personal element, is the "postconventional" level of morality identified with Lawrence Kohlberg as the sixth stage of moral development towards autonomy. From Habermas's debate with Gadamer, the critical view of tradition as convention and as a basis from which emancipation is needed still makes itself felt. Although, as we have seen, Habermas has inscribed his project into a framework much enlarged by Karl Jasper's concept of an "axial age" of the joint origin of the great philosophical systems and the world religions to which we are still heirs two-and-a-half millennia later, the distance of critical reason from life forms in their particularity is still maintained. Having diagnosed the threat that system imperatives pose to the lifeworld, Habermas has identified the need to protect the processes of understanding in which communicative reason is operative. Ricoeur's hermeneutical approach goes beyond this in pointing to the enabling power of cultural traditions. They form a reservoir of already articulated precedents for current quests for meaning, much more than being restricting conventions.

5. Since the foundation for discourse ethics is not a presumed sense of justice, but language in its ability to express the orientation towards mutual agreement between subjects in their autonomy, Ricoeur enquires into this guiding perspective. He values the questioning of the purposive rationality privileged by

---

444 Regarding "the way in which the passage from the deontological point of view to that of practical wisdom leads to an ultimate transformation in the idea of justice", Ricoeur describes the dilemma that arises "with the difficult decisions that have to be made in circumstances marked by incertitude and conflict under the sign of the tragic dimension of action, whether it be a conflict among norms of apparently equal weight, of a conflict between respect for a norm and solicitude for the persons involved, of a choice that would not be one between black and white but between gray and gray, or finally, of a choice where the line between the bad and the worst is not clear." Ricoeur, "Justice and truth", in *Reflections on the Just*, 62–63.

Max Weber: "the Frankfurt School will rush into this gap",[445]endorsing the alternative concept offered, communicative reason. Yet, by treating language in the singular as the defining characteristic of the human species, and analyzing it mainly in regard to argumentation to which it contains the "presuppositions", its creative, its dialogical and its culture-bridging potentials are missed, such as the ability to connect to the stranger through the "hospitality" present in the capability for translation. A much more promising starting-point for the interest in the potential of language to forge agreement would be the plurality of languages and their translatability.

6. Moving from capacity to the limits of ethics, Habermas joins Rawls in dismissing the significance of the limit questions posed by Kant within his ethics as a challenge to its foundations. Actions against the odds are recognized in their strength, but are seen as heroic and supererogatory deeds that do not allow for theory. Also in the third phase of engaging with religion since 2000, the postulates of practical reason are moved out of philosophical ethics and into a philosophy of religion that is no longer part of philosophy but of faith traditions. These corrections of the philosophical origin to which both Neo-Kantian thinkers relate their own theory proposals will curtail their view on concrete historical religions and will influence how they see them engage with the public realm.

3.2.3 Conclusions from perspectives on ethics

Issues for the following two enquiries into the framework of democracy and into religion will be how the social bond, the problem of domination, and the role of traditions are conceived. Rawls privileges "considered convictions", Habermas "argumentation", and Ricoeur gives a place to both as related projects. In his own analysis of religious, especially biblical texts, he pays attention to the history of reception and the question of translation.

Regarding the understanding of the role of reason, it is relevant how each of the three social ethicists conceives of philosophy. In *Political Liberalism*, Rawls moves to a culturalist position in the sense that an overarching realm of discourse in which each school of thinking can be discussed is no longer assumed. As has been noted, they are no longer considered as philosophical approaches, namely to reason, but as "doctrines", indeed, as "comprehensive" ones. The only mediating power lies in "public" reason which is the reason embedded in con-

---

445 Ricoeur, "The fundamental categories in Max Weber's sociology", in *Reflections on the Just*, 133–148, 141.

stitutional democratic states. For Habermas, the role of philosophy in a civilization analysed by individual sciences had to be adjusted to those of "interpreter" and "stand-in", yet the critical and uniting function of reason is retained. Does its interpretive ability also extend to religions, or does the strict separation of particularity from universality in ethics also affect what can be understood about them? Ricoeur puts philosophical thinking in the position of a subsequent, reflective activity of articulating, clarifying and critiquing, but remaining dependent on what is prior to thinking. Does this starting point offer a path into the understanding of religion? When approaching religion from the perspective of ethics, how is the autonomous subject posited between its capabilities and its failures which call for the restitution or reopening of the sources of goodness? Where is the ability and power of being affected by the divine located? For example, is it in conscience, or in the imagination that precedes the will? Since all three thinkers agree that religion can be reasonable, are any criteria named for a religious commitment in comparison with other options?

3.3 Co-founding the public space: Types of authority, legitimation, and citizens' convictions

From the architecture of ethics just presented, it is already evident that the French mediator between antique and modern philosophy will offer a view on a democratic framework of political existence that will spell out more precisely the interconnection between Aristotle and Kant. The task of living together with anonymous others in a political formation is reached from a hermeneutics of the self in which rational striving for a fulfilled life "with and for others in just institutions" meets a moral obligation to test maxims of action for their universality in the deontological "sieve of the norm".[446] The positions of Rawls and Habermas will be given specific places. The public space will include Rawls's contextual anchoring of justice in "considered convictions", reinterpreted as belonging to the foundational level of striving for justice in all its dimensions; the "reflective equilibrium" into which they are to be brought with principles requires the testing that discourse ethics will carry out. Together, these two approaches are identified as the two parts which practical wisdom seeks to relate to each other.[447] The

---

446 Ricoeur, *Oneself as Another*, 170. It is interesting that Rainer Forst comes up with the same image of a "deontological justice filter" in *Right to Justification*, 118.
447 Ricoeur, *Critique and Conviction. Conversations with F. Azouvi and M. de Launay.* trans. K. Blamey (Cambridge: CUP, 1998), 128–29.

meaning of justice which conserves its rootedness in the wish for a good life and finds its most ascetic rational formulation in procedural formalism, does not attain concrete plenitude except at the stage of the application of the norm in the exercise of judgment in some situation.[448]

In keeping with his theory of action, however, political rule is not just accepted as an existing order, but is reconstructed in its origins. Models of legitimation are compared: authority issuing from foundational myths, the self-authorization provided by contract theory, and a third model that takes the self-understandings of traditions seriously as resources for the democratic project (1). A subsequent analysis of the concept of "domination" (*Herrschaft*) from a sociological and a phenomenological perspective will widen the framework in which citizens' convictions can play a role. If "credit" and "belief" are factors for their cooperation, then the counterpart to domination cannot simply be obedience; it has to include initiative, and an "enunciative" authority speaking to citizens' motivations has to be distinguished from an "institutional" one based on power. A distinguishing feature of Ricoeur's analysis of the civic and political spheres is their relation to the "social bond" which is ethical (2). With major attention given to the role that the act of foundation of states plays for its citizens, a problem appears in view of the violence that has often accompanied their origins: a specific debt to the past arises in view of suffering inflicted on others. It calls for a memory that reflects on this heritage to reopen the path in which the unfulfilled and betrayed promises of the past might still find a future, and the social bond be renewed. This task, however, draws on resources that are reflected in a philosophy of religion; it will have to be discussed in the context of the subsequent section on religion (3.4).

3.3.1 Democracy between foundational myths and self-authorization

A guiding insight of Ricoeur's anthropology is that the self acquires its "capabilities" by cultural and institutional mediations, and that the analysis of its receptivity and agency has to take the long way of "detours", rather than shortcuts such as introspection or abstract definitions. There is always already a mediating framework between individuals and states. When one speaks of a "subject of rights", institutions are being presupposed.[449] In order to understand the inter-

---

448 Ricoeur, *The Just*, Preface, xxii. Realms in which practical wisdom carries out its assigned task to concretize the moral norm include cultural memory, biomedical ethics and criminal law.
449 Ricoeur, "Who is a subject of rights?", in *The Just*, 1–10.

action and the responses of the subjects, it is necessary to reflect on the genealogy of symbolic orders that have shaped them. Part of Ricoeur's critique of the liberal "contract" tradition is that it replaces foundations that differ historically with a construct placed in a void. His enquiry into the origin of authority begins at a level prior to the question about how to legitimate the coercive nature of law; it takes its starting point in the analysis of foundational myths and narratives that form part of the social bond. They offer a "paradigmatic case of recounting the foundational story of a community which is disclosed from its end" in the present age, and critically appropriated by the participating audience for its contemporary self-understanding. Building on Hannah Arendt's analyses, Ricoeur illustrates the generative power of a foundational myth with the difference between Greece and Rome and with the French Revolution (1);[450] he discusses the adequacy of the narrative model of foundation over what he designates as an alternative, namely democratic "self-authorization" (2). The solution he proposes is the exchange between heterogeneous traditions, taken as co-foundational of the public space, and sent to search both for a critical consensus and for a watchful capacity for tolerance when disagreements endure (3).

3.3.1.1 The narrative model: Myths of foundation, *potestas* and *auctoritas*

The starting point of the diachronic comparison is the problem already noticed in antiquity that political authority constitutes a "paradox" by "establishing a hierarchy among free people" while "the city is a community of equals".[451] The need for government arises in order to provide "a factor of stability, of durability, capable of exceeding the transitory existence of individuals and supervising the replacement of generations"; this requires the institution and the justification of law: the "*politeia* was to be such a source of stability,... capable of giving validity to the laws." Yet, the question of the split between those giving and those following the law remains: "the origin of the power to command remained the enigma of political life", and it was pursued in reflection "to its most virulent point in Greek political philosophy". Ricoeur observes that in Aristotle, the idea of being equals in its relation to "potentially the best life" was not reconciled with the distinction between those who govern and those who are governed, put forward in his *Politics*. Greek thinking offered metaphors for this paradox, such as the "helmsman in his ship, the master of slaves,... the

---

450 For an illuminating précis of Arendt's position, see Dosse, *Paul Ricoeur. Un philosophe dans son siècle*, 168–69.
451 Ricoeur, "The paradox of authority", in *Reflections on the Just*, 91–105, 98, for this quote and the following quotes.

head of the household,... all inappropriate". The reason for this failure is located, with Arendt, in the lack of "immediate political experience" of the idea of authority which Roman political thinking conceptualized and based the city's rule on: *ab urbe condita*, invoking its myth of foundation.[452] The "founding event" brings governed and governors together and gives *potestas* to the first, *auctoritas* to the latter. The distribution summed up by Cicero, "while power [*potestas*] resides in the people [*in populo*], authority [*auctoritas*] rests with the Senate [*in Senatu*]," links authority with the task of transmitting "this founding energy. The *auctoritas majorum*, the authority of the ancients, gives the present condition of ordinary people its weight, its gravitas."[453]

The paradoxical structure now consists of founding events and figures combining "anteriority, exteriority, and superiority", and subjects who are linked to this originating myth or story of which they are still part; their connection to those who claim authority to protect this tradition is a "fiduciary" one.[454] The paradigmatic character of appeal to founding figures is traced through to the French Revolution's revival of such founders from the republican and imperial ages of Rome, to make up for its own lack of precedent. Ricoeur concludes the review of ports of call in the political quest for creditability since antiquity by applying Cicero's distinction between the people's power and the Senate's authority to two possible interpretations of the "unclear... message" left by the French Revolution. On the one hand, epitomized in the new revolutionary calendar it established, it can be read as a complete new beginning after the ending of all authority prior to the will of the people itself:

> On the one hand, we have a strong vow to admit just one source of power, that of the people... taken as one indivisible, unified will, that of a sovereign people... Pierre Nora was right to begin the volumes he edited entitled the *Lieux de mémoires* with their mad idea of starting the calendar over again at year zero. Everything is wiped away and one starts again from nothing. In Arendt's vocabulary, this is the power of the people without the authority of the ancients. Or we could say, it is authority as stemming from power, where this power is itself identical with the general will.[455]

---

452 Ricoeur, *Reflections on the Just*, 99: By contrast, "there could exist many Greek cities and even a whole *diaspora* of cities, but there was only one Rome, whose singular, unique holiness Virgil and Titus Livy celebrated."

453 Ricoeur, *Reflections on the Just*, 99, quoting Cicero, *De Legibus* 3:12–28.

454 Ricoeur, *Reflections on the Just*, 105. As will be shown in subsection 2, the pairing of "credence" and "accrediting" with "creditability" is continued in his discussion of Max Weber's analysis of domination; Ricoeur will again underline the contribution of those governed, namely the element of "belief".

455 Ricoeur, *Reflections on the Just*, 103.

Alternatively, its subsequent history can be seen as an example of power legitimizing itself eventually through its age and the tradition it inaugurated. Already Rousseau is seen as having to conceive of a bridge between the principle, here in the form of the social contract, and the realm of concrete historical conditions, by making "recourse to the figure of a founding legislator". In order to legitimate a specific system of political power, the Roman model of an origin prior to the current exercize of political life is drawn on:

> It is as though the history of authority was functioning as a distinct, cumulative source, one capable of giving a then-current, momentary, fragile, and perishable power the aura that its novelty could not ensure but that the great age of the past history of authority alone could confer on power in the present... In fact, a revolution that outlived its wars of conquest became established and has endured because it was able to transform its own age into an argument for authority".[456]

This double heritage, one of political self-foundation, the other of pre-political foundations, can still be recognized in current theories of democracy. The résumé Ricoeur draws from this survey before outlining his own normative proposal is that he is "pretty willing to believe that no power is assured of stability and endurance unless it succeeds in capitalizing on the earlier history of authority for its own benefit".[457]

The different levels of ideology outlined in *Memory, History, Forgetting* illustrate some aspects of such attempts of "capitalizing" on authority from history. At the first level, the inescapable role of symbolic mediation enables humans to partake in their culture. It is at the subsequent levels that the conscious use of power begins and that "ideology" as an invention of the ruling class acquires the quality of producing "false consciousness" that the master of suspicion, Marx, has analysed. The legitimating role of history-writing in a state's education system and in the commemorative events it organizes for its citizens is subjected to a similar ideology critique by Ricoeur in the same book. Thus, it becomes clear that the forms of justifying state power by appeal to symbolic worlds and narrative continuities, which encompass the differential between those ruled and those who exercize this power, still need scrutiny. Yet also in the second model to be discussed in the following subsection, it is not the case that authority has simply disappeared. Against the assumption quoted from Hannah Arendt, that it has "vanished" in modernity, Ricoeur specifies the task to follow in its transformations the dual parts of claiming and of giving credit. If "author-

---

456 Ricoeur, *Reflections on the Just*, 104.
457 Ricoeur, *Reflections on the Just*, 104.

ity is a thing of the past, then a mixture of violence and, more or less fraudulent, persuasion seems to have replaced it".[458] For him, authority is a persistent feature, and giving up on the task of diagnosing its current shapes is not an option.

3.3.1.2 The model of self-authorization

One alternative to a mythical or narrative foundation on something prior to the power of the people, as in deriving authority from the act of founding *auctores*, is offered by the French theorist of democracy, Claude Lefort who states that there are no foundations. From Ricoeur's perspective which presupposes cultural mediations in his theory of action, and a striving for just institutions already as part of the wish for a good life in his ethics, this counts as a "more radical solution... Claude Lefort and his school... assume the lack of a foundation as the fate of democracy along with all the weaknesses inherent in what we have called self-authorization".[459]

Ricoeur outlines the problem in the terms of Rousseau's distinction between an assumed *volonté générale* against the sum of individual wills. When the "one indivisible, unified will... of sovereign people" becomes supreme, the distinction between *potestas* and *auctoritas* is levelled; "authorization" becomes "self-referential... the 'people' authorizes itself." In Ricoeur's view, this condition of a unitary will "for the exercize of a self-grounding of sovereignty" is "draconian". As an example of the "inerrant" and "infallible" status this will assumes he points to the fact that in the French legal system, no possibility existed "until recently" to "appeal beyond our criminal courts whose decisions were held to be made in the name of an infallible people".[460] One can summarize his critique as introducing a universalistic normative level: once the distinction between *potestas* and *auctoritas* is collapsed, there is no other instance left to appeal to and challenge decisions in the name of an authority that does not coincide with the people's power, such as human dignity, upheld by a transnational court of justice. Spelt out in terms of concrete democratic decision making, the assumption of a unitary will is totalizing:

> We might think that it is only within a unanimous group that constraint would be absent. In reality, such a group may be the most coercive of all. The law of unanimity is more dan-

---

458 Ricoeur, *Reflections on the Just*, 94.
459 Ricoeur, *Reflections on the Just*, 105.
460 Ricoeur, *Reflections on the Just*, 103–4.

gerous than that of majority rule, which alone allows the minority to be identified and its rights to be defined.[461]

These serious limitations arise from a model that dispenses with a social bond prior to the contract concluded between individuals, and with the narratives of diverse religious and cultural communities of the founding events they trace themselves back to. For Ricoeur, it is akin to the gigantic effort of creating a world when it is left

> up to a contract and procedures to take on the difficult task of making up for this missing foundation ... even those who charge democracy with this demiurgic task, once they move to the phenomenological level, cannot avoid situating themselves beyond such a founda-tion and assuming the phenomenon of authority, with its threefold structure of antece-dence, superiority and exteriority.[462]

Having identified as an alternative the two models of having to choose either a foundational myth, or a self-authorization in which democracy is given the role of a demiurge, he ends his analysis with an aporetic conclusion:

> Can we rest with this? Can we allow foundational myths, myths of great age, to replace the rational need for legitimation? Can we resign ourselves to eliminating from the definition of "authority" the factor of recognition, by virtue of which the creditability of power is dialec-tically balanced by that act of accrediting it? If it is this fiduciary connection that makes the ultimate difference between authority and violence at the very heart of the hierarchical re-lation of domination, to what then do we finally give credit? To authority per se, to the great age of power, to the authority of tradition weighed against the tradition of authority?[463]

The two models portrayed so far do not exhaust the possibilities; a third combi-nation of *potestas* and *auctoritas* is identified which does justice both to citizens in the plurality of their self-understandings, and to changed political conditions.

3.3.1.3 The model of recognizing heterogeneous traditions as co-foundational
The deficit pertaining to legitimation by an anterior act of founding, that recog-nition is not an act that can be withheld, and the totalizing danger inherent in the ambition of the contract model to do without a separate basis of foundation and "to reabsorb authority into power",[464] can be contained by turning to the

---

461 Ricoeur, *Reflections on the Just*, 139.
462 Ricoeur, *Reflections on the Just*, 85.
463 Ricoeur, *Reflections on the Just*, 104–105.
464 Ricoeur, *Reflections on the Just*, 103.

multiple sources and traditions that co-exist in a pluralist society. I see Ricoeur's reference to worldviews, initiatives and religions as fitting into what recent debates have named "the pre-political foundations of democracy",[465] the manifold backgrounds from which the democratic project is revived and its future co-determined. In view of the multiple supporting motivations for a democratic framework for living together, Ricoeur thinks it more adequate

> to admit a plurality of foundations... Rather than a lack of foundation, we should acknowledge an acceptable form of plurality..., a pluralism made viable by an overlapping consensus concerning moral sources compatible in this way with those reasonable practices which Rawls speaks of in terms of reasonable disagreements.[466]

The reason to refer to the American theorist of public reason, interpreted through a category of the hermeneutical philosopher Charles Taylor, is Rawls's admission of plural "moral sources"; among them, those considered "reasonable" are allowed into the recognized sphere of supportive worldviews that contribute to public reason. One could summarize its value in Ricoeur's view in the insight that their very variety already constitutes an advantage over the unitary origin of one foundational myth, as well as over Rousseau's unitary *"volonté générale"*. They articulate the different perspectives that may eventually feed into a possible "sum of individual wills", if such a sum can be drawn. What is clear is that Ricoeur considers the "overlapping consensus" as constituting a major piece of work, as arising from an active effort at forging agreements, and not as a geometric segment in which mainly distinct circles coincide that can only be viewed by an observer from above the scene. While it is Ricoeur's practice to relate to proposals of other theorists by giving their distinctive categories a place, this does not mean that the meaning of these terms is identical in both systems of argumentation. I see four additional factors typical of Ricoeur's enterprise that are lacking in Rawls's:

(1) The premise of an "effort and desire to exist" of the French phenomenologist's theory of action makes him conceive of ancient and modern political spheres as ones of foundational energies. The question of "authority" was addressed in terms of the transmission of the effects of such originating acts. Thus, contemporary groups and traditions are thought of as forces; this is dis-

---

465 This broad heading encompasses quite different proposals, once one has agreed that this level exists. Cf. the debate on the 1960 thesis of Ernst-Wolfgang Böckenförde in J. Habermas/J. Ratzinger, *The Dialectics of Secularization. On Reason and Religion* (San Francisco: Ignatius Press, 2005).
466 Ricoeur, *Reflections on the Just*, 85.

tinct from conceiving them, as Rawls does, as "comprehensive doctrines" complete in themselves and only in need of bringing themselves up to the level of public reason by developing "political conceptions" agreeable to the shared values of "liberty" and "equality". For Ricoeur, one cannot say in advance what such communities might contribute and whether there is any such overlap, but he sees their diversity as promising for the joint enterprise.

(2) They are asked not only to co-exist, nor to relate to an intermediate platform drawn by a non-participant, but to recognize each other directly in their capability of being cofounders and contributors. His reference to the Rawls of *Political Liberalism* is made in the context of having taken his position firmly against the model of self-foundation, declaring "[h]ere I resist and refuse to yield":

> Or ought we, taking advantage of the very idea of credit, like the later Rawls, admit a multiple foundation, a diversity of religious and secular, rational and Romantic traditions, that mutually recognize one another as cofoundational under the double auspices of the principle of "overlapping consensus" and the "recognition of reasonable disagreements"?[467]

(3) Each of the founding partners is in a relation of debt to their own origin, being "reinvigorated and driven by their unkept promises", and in "competition with other, heterogeneous traditions" to give account of their own. For example, as a religious tradition that has been liberated from its early inheritance of Rome's imperial authority only in modernity, thereby setting also politics free from its previous amalgamation with the ecclesiastical practice of authority,[468] Christian churches and initiatives are asked to take their place alongside other cofounders:

> Within such a framework with this double principle [cf. consensus and disagreement] a role might be found for the authority of the Bible and that of ecclesiastical institutions – but not in such a way as to give rebirth to the lost paradigm of Christendom. It would be a question, rather, of Christian communities taking up, without any hang-ups, their part in this cofoundation in open competition with other, heterogeneous traditions, which themselves are reinvigorated and driven by their unkept promises.

(4) The goal of these efforts is not sufficiently described as keeping a liberal and just society stable under conditions of pluralism; it is marked by engaging in

---

467 Ricoeur, *Reflections on the Just*, 105.
468 Despite the duality of the temporal and the religious powers in Latin Christianity, Ricoeur highlights the close mutual support of "unction plus sanction" in the history of Christendom. *Reflections on the Just*, 101.

a quest for authority that is inherently linked to risk. With no power to force the other to extend recognition, the shared enterprise is built on a "credit" that can only be given freely, or withheld; it is a condition which Ricoeur defends as a necessary limit case to underline the voluntary level of cooperation.

> Finally,... a place has to be reserved for dissensus and for the right to respond to the offer of creditability on the part of any authorities in place by a refusal to grant credit to them. This calculated risk, which should be recognized as having a supporting marginal role, is, after all, part of the very idea of "credit," of accrediting.[469]

In view of the "fragility of the symbolic order",[470] the risk is real when authority is spelt out as an offer that has no power but only the hope of convincing others. When public space is generated and regenerated by the political action of all co-founders, the outcome of actually engaging with the convictions and energies from different moral sources cannot be predicted. It is a model that seeks universality from recognized diversity by making each tradition accountable to its own origin; it trusts in the continuing strength of these sources to allow for new interpretations of the promise contained in their writings and practices. Thus, the public sphere is revealed as consisting of a multiplicity of movements and initiatives in which historical self-understandings play a role in detecting problems, redirecting fellow-citizens' attention and seeking solutions by actively engaging with state institutions. This analysis of sources of authority and legitimation is carried further by subjecting Max Weber's influential position to the criteria developed in Ricoeur's dialogues with other thinkers: the capacities for initiative and trust that are distinctive of human agency.

3.3.2 Domination and obedience, or initiatives in plural spheres of negotiation?

One feature revealed in the discussion of the possibility of multiple foundations has been a positive outlook on plural symbol systems: far from undermining a willingness for cooperation that the state seeks to foster in its citizens, they are credited with resources that renew the motivation to work out divergences and conflicts. A crucial element already in the justification of rulers in antiquity was the "fiduciary" connection to them as guardians of their polity's source of origin. How is this element captured in modern sociological analyses of social action and domination? By engaging with Max Weber and his critics, the interest

---

469 Ricoeur, *Reflections on the Just*, 105.
470 Ricoeur, *Reflections on the Just*, 85.

of a phenomenological analysis in the intentions of agents will again add factors excluded by other approaches (1), and critique explicit and implicit assumptions which have shaped the terms of debate in a history of reception that is still on-going (2). This critique will restore the importance of self-understandings for po-litical practice, and allow a nuanced view on the interplay between "enuncia-tive" and "institutional" authority in the sequence of constellations of legitimation in European history (3).

3.3.2.1 Pluralizing the category of *Herrschaft* in Max Weber's theory of social action

In his reconstruction of the "fundamental categories" of Weber's approach and in his review of the 1995 study of his work by Pierre Bouretz,[471] Ricoeur begins with the productive elements of Weber's theory: its combination of interpretation and explanation, against their opposition in Wilhelm Dilthey; a concept of action directed by its meaning for the individual,[472] with the possibility of devising a typology of "ideal types" based on the meanings attached;[473] a social orientation that includes the expectations of others; the continual pairing of domination and legitimation as the context in which the state gets defined by its power to com-mand. The motives for extending validity to the political order on the part of those governed are supplemented by a factor at the level of ideas, intuitions, and imagination: "belief" (*Vorstellung*) is added as a "fact" encountered in expe-rience.[474] For Ricoeur, this is the starting point from which the self-understand-

---

471 Ricoeur, *Reflections on the Just*, 133–148, and 149–155, "Bouretz on Weber", review of *Les promesses du monde* (Paris: Gallimard, 1995).

472 Weber's definition in *Economy and Society. An Outline of Interpretive Sociology*, ed. by G. Roth/C. Wittich (Berkeley and Los Angeles: University of California Press, 1978), 4, is quoted: "We shall speak of 'action' insofar as the acting individual attaches a subjective meaning to his behaviour." Ricoeur, *Reflections on the Just*, 134.

473 Ricoeur, *Reflections on the Just*, 135: The "notion of an ideal type... consists of a reflective concept applied to the notion of meaning as constitutive of the object under study, meaningful action. What is meaningful for agents is also what makes sense for the sociologist's reflection, that is, the possibility of constructing types. These are methododological constructs,... but not arbitrary ones... it is a question of a means of identifying, inventorying, classifying forms of action and, at the same time, of a procedure that makes room for a typology."

474 Ricoeur, *Reflections on the Just*, 142: "What is most interesting and perhaps finally asto-nishing... is that the belief by means of which agents respond to the claim of legitimacy is presented as a supplement...To what? To known forms of motivation: 'custom, personal ad-vantage, purely affectual or ideal motives of solidarity, do not form a sufficiently reliable basis for a given domination. In addition, there is normally a further element, the belief in *legiti-macy.*'" For Ricoeur, this quote from *Economy and Society*, 213, reveals that the typology does not

ings of the subjects can be explored more extensively than the simple polarization of "domination" and "obedience" allows for. Several others of Weber's distinctions, such as the famous one between rational, traditional, and charismatic forms of *Herrschaft*, are equally released from their grid as alternatives and are set in motion as elements that can enter into different balances.

What is found missing in Weber's concept of domination is the inextinguishable factor of human initiative; it is this element that turns the direct correlation of command and obedience into a space of productive negotiations with conditions set by the system where the plural self-understandings of citizens make a difference. With reference to authors who explore microhistory, a sociology of action from below,[475] and the formation of collective identity, the unitary direction is broken up by the interest in the different strategies pursued by agents in response to expectations in the various spheres where identities are worked out and defended:

> We should next bring into play a crisscrossing of such top-down and bottom-up readings. We would then encounter strategies of negotiation and appropriation, whereby a decisive power of initiative is restored to social agents... agents pursue the legitimation of their action in a plurality of cities or worlds, which call for a typology of a new type, no longer in terms of a model of obedience to authority but in types of arguments for legitimacy exercised by social agents themselves, when acting in the city of renown, or that of inspiration, or those of commercial exchange, of industry, of citizenship. In Walzer we find the same plurality of orders of legitimation and an equal interest granted to strategies of negotiation and compromise, irreducible to the mere relation of domination to obedience. We could

---

cover the whole phenomenon, but is itself devised to contain the "enigma" in a rational classification: "the whole typology we are about to consider has to do with this something extra... It is experience, we are told,... as though we could not derive this factor from the basic categories that had been elaborated with such precision. Belief in legitimacy is a supplement that has to be treated as a pure and simple fact resulting from experience. Perhaps this fact is destined to remain enigmatic." (142) This interpretive clue is followed through the categories devised and brought to its conclusion: "(A)re not the hidden stakes here the mastering by sociological rationality of the residual irrationality attached to the very phenomena of the exercising of power?... Does the work of rationalization not work... in an opposite way, or as a countereffort, to the increasing opacity of the concepts considered, up to this ultimate residue of belief?" (146) I read this as a comment on the limit that an all-too clear-cut classification meets in the forces interacting in political life. Its origin in a constructivist method will be further discussed in 3.3.2.2.

475 He mentions Carlo Ginzburg, *The Cheese and the Worms: The Cosmos of a Sixteenth Century Miller*, trans. by J. and A. Tedeschi (Baltimore: Johns Hopkins Univ. Press, 1990); Giovanni Levi, *Le pouvoir au village: Histoire d'un exorciste dans le Piémont du XVIIe siècle*, trans. M. Aymard (Paris: Gallimard, 1989), as well as Luc Boltanski and Laurence Thévenot, *De la justification: les economies de la grandeur* (Paris: Presses universitaires de France, 1987).

even expand the space of the constituting of the social bond and the search for collective identity further by exploring with Michel de Certeau and Bernard Lepetit the many strategies for appropriating norms used by social agents. All these works have in common a concern for the constitution of the social bond, thanks to a great variety of procedures of appropriation and identification.[476]

Do the contours of this research programme still fit into what Weber outlined? Ricoeur answers the concluding question of whether we have "moved completely beyond Weber" with a "No". We have "simply situated his analyses in a social space traversed by a multitude of strategies appropriate in each instance to transactions of different kinds".[477] By recognizing different logics at work in the various spheres, cities or segments, which need to be distinguished and protected, the inadequacy of a unitary approach is overcome. The main problems of Weber's proposal are identified as threefold: its constructivist stringency which offers grand-scale interpretations with no space for alternative readings; a claim to offer "value-free" scientific analyses; and finally a framework in which, due to a neo-Nietzschean nihilist bent, reason loses its power of critique and of instigating new departures.

3.3.2.2 Explicit and implicit theory decisions in Weber's approach

By tying rationality to a purposive, instrumental understanding, and by failing to differentiate between the spheres in which rationalization occurs, major factors are excluded from view, and a reductive interpretation is facilitated. Among the types of social action, what dominates is the first: *zweckrational*, instrumentally directed action towards purposes set by the individual who is the starting point of Weber's sociological theory.[478] So while social action is the object of analysis, it comes into view as action between individuals. Prior cultural mediations and inter-group relations do not belong to the framework of the analysis. Its "methodological individualism... authorizes a reduction of collective entities to constructs derived from human interactions".[479] While other types of action are

---

476 Ricoeur, *Reflections on the Just*, 147.
477 Ricoeur, *Reflections on the Just*, 147–8.
478 Ricoeur, *Reflections on the Just*, 136: "We have to start from the fact that what is real for Weber is always the individual. The ideal types must not be dissociated from what we can call his methodological individualism. We are always dealing with individuals who orient themselves in relation to other individuals, once the notion of social action implies intersubjectivity."
479 Ricoeur, *Reflections on the Just*, 155.

specified, their possible strengths are not exploited.[480] Together with the "convergence" assumed between economic, political, and juridical paths of rationalization, this leads to an underestimation of the potential of each of these spheres for critical and innovative responses, and subsequently to a unitary reading of religious motives as they influence economic life.

Equally in the sphere of politics, different links could have been pursued. Rather than culminating in bureaucratic administration, rationalization could have been explored in its "liberating" potential leading to a state bound by law. The second orientation of action towards values espoused for non-instrumental reasons, could have been given greater significance, and could have led to an interpretation at the level of ethics, in terms of recognition, rather than remaining at the level of analyzing violence in its different forms:

> A new series of questions is posed by the degree of convergence between what are called here "ways of disenchantment"— that is, the economic, political, and juridical spheres. In truth, these ways of rationalization remain quite disparate... The political realm poses quite specific problems, once we admit the prevalence of the problematic of domination. It is clear that for Weber, the moment of violence is first, last, and always. We find it at one extreme as the generating matrix of power, in the middle as a force appropriated by the state, and it appears again at the other end of political history as a kind of arbitrary decision. As for legitimation, it lies only in the motives for obedience. But it never rises to the rank of Hegelian recognition".[481]

By invoking Habermas's critique in this regard, a different understanding and weighting of rationality, legitimation and value-led action of citizens becomes conceivable:

---

480 In *Reflections on the Just*, 136, Ricoeur quotes them in full from *Economy and Society*, 24–25: "Social action, like all action, may be oriented in four ways. It may be:

(1) *instrumentally rational* (*zweckrational*), that is, determined by expectations as to the behavior of objects in the environment and of other human beings; these expectations are used as 'conditions' or 'means' for the attainment of the actor's own rationally pursued and calculated ends;

(2) *value-rational* (*wertrational*), determined by a conscious belief in the value for its own sake of some ethical, aesthetic, religious, or other forms of behavior, independently of its prospects of success;

(3) *affectual* (especially emotional), that is, determined by the actor's specific affects and feeling states;

(4) *traditional*, that is, determined by ingrained habituation."

Ricoeur points out that "it is not by chance that the first one named is the one called *zweckrational*, to which later the bureaucratic type of system will correspond" (137).

481 Ricoeur, *Reflections on the Just*, 153.

> With Habermas, we may regret that from one end to the other the analysis of "rationality in terms of ends" – instrumental reason – should cover over the "rationality of values," which alone could have given rise to a distinct problematic of legitimation. The result is that the rationalization of power and the turning of this into its contrary are concentrated on the bureaucratic phenomenon alone... directly grafted to the "logic of objectifying constraint," hence to domination, and not to the rationalizing aspects of legitimacy, which we would expect to see identified with the resources of liberation offered by the state ruled by law.[482]

Thus, it is clear that theory decisions of great range pre-structure the outcome of the analysis which gives no counterweight to reason as a resource of correction and resistance.

A final example of the danger of overdrawing results from analyses obtained by a prior reduction of alternative readings is seen in the role accorded to Protestantism for the genesis of the capitalist system. Ricoeur begins by questioning the accuracy of the selection of biblical motives regarding the origin of rationalization. "Was theodicy really the most important question attached to Jewish prophetism?" And regarding the shape rationalization took in the economic sphere, where a number of different motives could have equally been specified, the question is whether there are other aspects of a religious motivation that are underestimated and sacrificed for one overarching thesis. According to Weber, the problem posed first by the theodicies of the Ancient Near East allowed for two responses, "either flee the world, or worldly asceticism",[483] the latter solution being taken by English Puritanism. Ricoeur questions each of these factors, and how they are linked by Weber:

> Was the concern to find a guarantee and a reassurance against the risk of damnation the exclusive motivation behind Christianity, and more specifically Puritanism? What happens to salvation by grace, and a faith with no guarantee, in relation to the perhaps overemphasized theme of predestination?... On the side of economics, we could pose symmetrical questions... What about the virtues attached to exchange and commerce and to the connection Montesquieu caught sight of between these virtues and what he called "English liberty"?[484]

Each of these factors can be construed differently, and so can their connection, by which the "rational motive", capital accumulation, is translated into the "religious motive of investing religious faith in a terrestrial vocation". Doubting whether this motive can be "the sole generating focal point of economic ration-

---

482 Ricoeur, *Reflections on the Just*, 153.
483 Ricoeur, *Reflections on the Just*, 150–1.
484 Ricoeur, *Reflections on the Just*, 151–2.

ality", Ricoeur concludes: "The recurring question about plurivocity can thus be posed about both terms of the equation: the Protestant ethic and the spirit of capitalism".[485]

What is at stake in his critical dismantling of a thesis which continues to enjoy some resonance, is the method of enquiry into cultural worlds that shape agents' motivations, and the concern to venture interpretations that can be tested: "It would be interesting to know if in his work... Weber ever encountered the problem of the equivocity in the interpretation of cultural phenomena on a grand scale." To this general objection I would like to add a suspicion from a theological and a hermeneutical perspective: admitting, as Weber does, to being religiously unmusical may not predestine a theorist to venture accurate appreciations of the components of the symbolic world of a historical religion, such as the ideas of creation, election and covenant, incarnation, redemption and eschatology.

Ricoeur is in a good position to put these questions, having compared the very same "great Ancient Near Eastern" texts that Weber interprets as unequivocal cases. Ricoeur's studies from *The Symbolism of Evil* onwards offer insights into the nuances of developments in religious self-understanding that might disturb the construction of great systematizations; yet, they have the advantage of being closer to the historical and literary sources by which one has to justify in detail the line of interpretation proposed. Ricoeur's insistence on offering a hermeneutics based on texts, rather than one of existence, as Heidegger and Gadamer do, takes seriously the resistance that such written documents offer against a generalizing sweep by interpreters of later eras. The willingness to concede the possibility of misinterpretation is part of such scholarly practice. Misconstruals can be discovered more easily when there is a counterpart in the shape of a body of texts; the origins, dating, authors, communities, redactions, functions, meanings, and histories of reception can be discussed between experts in the area. Two more problems are linked to Weber's grand-scale procedure: the label of "value-free" enquiry, and the implicit philosophy or perhaps "inverted theology of history" operative in its course and outcome.[486]

The objections formulated against the "value-free" status put forward for his sociological theory are instructive for what Ricoeur considers to be required of theories of human agency and its political framework. Weber's claim is judged to be at odds with its very theme, human social action, even if it can be read as an attempt at "immunizing itself" against the draw of the philosophical

---

485 Ricoeur, *Reflections on the Just*, 152; the following quote, 151.
486 Ricoeur, *Reflections on the Just*, 143.

neighborhood he has chosen, which Ricoeur identifies as nihilism;[487] in addition, Weber fails to name a normative goal of the whole conceptual and diagnostic effort. The neutral position assumed contradicts its theme: the nature of human action which requires a normative, not a "value-free" analysis:

> Turning back from the royal gate of the sociology of religions toward the servants' entrance of the epistemology of the social sciences we can ask if things are really as clear on this epistemological plane... How are we to hold together the *wertfrei* posture, claimed by Weber, with having to make recourse to the meanings experienced by social actors in the identification of the object of the social sciences? To be sure, one can give an impartial account of what seemed to be laden with meaning for these actors. But is the same impartiality tenable once these meanings reveal themselves to be what Charles Taylor... calls "strong evaluations"? It is a question of such strong evaluations when the meanings in question have to do with the whole historical process of the rationalization of the world. It is also such strong evaluations that are at issue in the economic world of work, wealth, and enjoyment. Even more so, they are at issue in the political register, under the figure of the large-scale motives for obedience, which contribute to the legitimation of domination.[488]

The scientistic framework of a research into objects that Weber inscribes his sociology into misjudges that the issues explored belong to the realm of practical reason.[489] Ricoeur appreciates that other writings of his show a concern with the social bond.[490]But especially in view of a diagnosis given at a world historical scale, a process of "disenchantment" that ends in an "iron cage", and that offers no starting points for renewed departures, the failure to provide an explanation of the reversal of rationalization into its opposite is serious:

---

487 Ricoeur, *Reflections on the Just*, 143: "[W]e can ask whether interpretive sociology itself, given its epistemological stance, is safe from this presumed disenchantment which would be a presupposition as well as a result... the question will remain how well Weber's epistemology really succeeds in immunizing itself by means of such axiological neutrality against the bite of nihilism."

488 Ricoeur, *Reflections on the Just*, 152.

489 Ricoeur, *Reflections on the Just*, 151: "From the perspective that will finally be that of Pierre Bouretz, that of a resistance to the nihilism implied by the thesis of the rationalization of the world's turning against itself, one can ask if Weber did not systematically avoid the question of the univocity of his overall interpretation of the religious phenomenon, and whether he usurped the qualifications of the scientist's axiological neutrality to the benefit of a highly problematic overall interpretation".

490 Ricoeur, *Reflections on the Just*, 148: One can "even rediscover... Weber's other contributions to the exploration of the formation of the social and political bond, as in his 'Politics as Vocation'. What we might have to give up in the process is the axiological neutrality so proudly claimed by the theory of fundamental sociological categories presented in *Economy and Society*."

No interpretation of this phenomenon is proposed, which is called sometimes a paradox, sometimes an enigma, sometimes a reversal...What then does this exact superimposition of rationalization and a loss of meaning signify? Is it a question of a phenomenon of inertia in virtue of which a process, once begun in history, outlives its initial motivation and produces perverse effects beyond the control of the original justification? Bouretz comes back to Weber's... "silence" regarding the overall sense of his enterprise.[491]

For Bouretz, the "univocity" of the analysis amounts to "complicity" since it "reinforces the phenomenon being described".[492] The question for Ricoeur is, whether "this presumed disenchantment...would be a presupposition as well as a result",[493] stemming from an implicit philosophy of history that is uncovered as neo-Nietzschean.

The scale of disagreement reaches its summit when the "nihilistic contamination engendered by the rest of his work"[494] is openly declared; yet Ricoeur's concern has been the same from the beginning of his analysis. There is a normative interest in opening up alternative views and plural interpretations of cultural developments, and in defending the different spheres in which rationalization would have to be followed up, with equal attention to the negotiating capability it meets in agents: to protect the limit that each person poses to the other, as well as to the system. Ricoeur's diagnosis that the reversal of rationalization into its opposite occupies the same place as Hegel's "cunning of reason" is instructive since it reveals how Weber inscribes a destructive turn where Hegel located the activity of reason. Against such overbearing negativity, Ricoeur wants to chart a path able to "save a noninstrumental reason, a rationality based on values". He welcomes the philosophical "line of resistance"[495] Bouretz sets up by

localizing the moments where the Weberian analysis of modernity sacrifices the capacity of rationality to still be an instrument of liberation today to a kind of speculative discouragement – whence the pathetic tone of a scrupulous, analytic work, which reveals a thinker personally struck by the... disenchantment of the world and seeking good reasons not to despair about reason.[496]

---

491 Ricoeur, *Reflections on the Just*, 154.
492 Ricoeur, *Reflections on the Just*, 154.
493 Ricoeur, *Reflections on the Just*, 152.
494 Ricoeur, *Reflections on the Just*, 152–3, excepting his "essays on the theory of science."
495 Ricoeur, *Reflections on the Just*, 154.
496 Ricoeur, *Reflections on the Just*, 150. Regarding the "Habermasian side of Bouretz's book", his view is that it could have taken more of the defense of reason on board that is contained in his "moral cognitivism", over "the skeptical diagnostic that Bouretz seems to take for granted" (155).

For Ricoeur, the question is from what point onwards Weber's theory decisions, explicit and implicit, have to be reconceived, to allow for a less unidirectional interpretation of a process ending in modernity that is conceived of as a loss of meaning:

> The question remains open: to what point must we withdraw in order to open up such plurivocity? This question seems essential to me, if we want to resist the dazzling effect created by Weber's metaphors: the "iron cage," the "battle of the gods," the "last man," enchantment and disenchantment.[497]

Dazzling just like the rhetoric of Nietzsche, but not conducive to understanding the persistence of creative human agency which requires categories that are able to render the motivation expressed in its resistance to a sapping of meaning. The following discussion of two types of authority will complete the review of authors on matters pertaining directly to how the presence of religion in the contemporary public sphere will be conceived by a thinker who has been intent on defending access to personal and civic agency under changing historical, political and intellectual conditions.[498]

3.3.2.3 Enunciative and institutional authority

In Ricoeur's overview of the origins and of the structural counterparts identified in the process of legitimizing political rule since antiquity, a study by Gérard Leclerc, *Histoire de l'autorité*, is credited with posing the problem correctly: it distinguishes "two foci of legitimation:... one... enunciative authority; the other institutional". Legitimation proceeds from two places of origin: "on the one side, discourse, as the source of symbolic power; on the other, the institution as the source of legitimacy for those who exercize authority within it." The first consists in the "symbolic power, either of an enunciator or of an 'author,' to engender belief, to persuade", the second in the "'legitimate power... to impose obedience'".[499] By charting their interaction and conflict at focal points in European

---

497 Ricoeur, *Reflections on the Just*, 155.

498 F. Dosse, *Philosophe dans son siècle*, 164–175, offers instructive background analyses to Ricoeur's interventions in public debates. For example, the events to which the *Esprit* article, "The political paradox" (1957) responds, namely the Soviet crackdown in Budapest in 1956 against moves for Hungarian autonomy, 164–168, and the critical defense of the concept of free agency in his dialogue with neuro-scientist J.-P. Changeux, 172–175.

499 Ricoeur, *Reflections on the Just*, 94, quoting Gérard Leclerc, *Histoire de l'autorité* (Paris: PUF, 1986), 7.

history, Ricoeur treats what can be called the precursors of the public sphere, diagnosing the current situation as resulting from these turning points.

What has to be noted first, however, is how the idea of an "enunciative authority" fits into his framework. One can see that the term Leclerc has chosen as the counterpart to "institutional authority" connects well with Ricoeur's interest in symbolic mediations and with the structure of his ethics that emphasizes the continuous elements between the levels of striving and of morality. It prepares for a different understanding of the factors at work in the public sphere than, for example, Habermas's conception. "Enunciative" is more than discursive in the sense of a universalizing debate aiming for the consensus of participants as moral subjects: it appeals to their self-understandings, shaped by cultural traditions and anchored in their individual life projects; morality only appears as the "sieve of the norm"[500] for maxims arising at this foundational level. Discourse about their universalizability is one necessary area of argumentation, but it needs to be linked to prior exchanges on motivations; otherwise the universality consented to is at risk of remaining disconnected from the self-motivated pursuits of agents in the public sphere. Understanding the non-institutional focus of authority as comprising an appeal to the symbolic worlds in which self-understandings are constituted, helps to conceive of discourse in the public realm as being directed towards working out identities that will include also the moral dimension. In comparison with Habermas's understanding of discourse as the procedure of attaining legitimacy, it connects the binding force of moral insight to an earlier level. While Habermas spells out the presuppositions at work when citizens use their moral capability in debates on conflicts arising within their lifeworlds, his disregard and separation of the ethical level as irretrievably particular works against the embedding of morality in life projects. It is only recently, in his writings since 2000, that he has taken the need for ethical appropriation seriously by calling for the level of a "species ethics" at which this self-understanding can be worked out, albeit again at a universal, not at a culturally specific level.

How has authority in European history been produced through the interplay of the enunciative and the institutional forms, and how has religion been involved in this? Ricoeur's thesis is that it is necessary to follow their different combinations, rather than assume that one type ended and was superseded by the other:

> What has taken place is not the replacement of an authority that was largely enunciative by one that is only institutional, but rather the replacement of one historical configuration de-

---

500 Ricoeur, *Oneself as Another*, 170.

termined by a pairing of enunciation and institution by another configuration of the same two terms. What is true about Leclerc's thesis is that in the authority that has disappeared there was a prevalence of heralded authority. But there has never been a purely enunciative authority with no institutional authority, and today there is no purely institutional authority without the contribution, the symbolic support, of some enunciative order.[501]

Thus, the role of belief, of a fiduciary connection of those governed has to be taken into account; the stories and myths of foundation discussed before clearly belong to the enunciative side. However, the move from a transcendent to a secular foundation for the political community is not simply one from an enunciative to an institutional authority. The Enlightenment as epitomized by Denis Diderot's and Jean D'Alembert's *Encyclopédie* is seen as being on "the same enunciative terrain" as the "ideal type of a dominantly enunciative authority,… medieval Christendom".[502] Yet, at the same time, the church was also drawing on a heritage of political origin. It was the "beneficiary of an origin distinct from this scriptural authority", namely of Roman law, which in Ricoeur's account it had incorporated not only since the fourth century but even earlier, since

> Peter was brought to Rome, the seat of the *imperium* and of the political origin of institutional authority. This episode of historical Christianity… makes sense as a fusion of the *auctoritas* of the Roman foundation and the authority of the instituted church, held to be founded in the scriptures. It was thanks to this conjunction that the Roman church could, over the course of its history, reign in the antipolitical and anti-institutional tendencies of primitive Christian faith. What is more, once the Roman Empire collapsed under the blows of the barbarians, the Roman church could save the heritage of the *imperium* and perhaps, without knowing it, preserve it for adventures other than the ecclesiastical one beyond the age of the Enlightenment and for the time of decline we see today as the relentless foe of the ideal type of Christendom …the suggestion of a double origin of this ideal type of Christendom clarifies the fate not only of this ideal type but also of its ferocious adversary, the French Lumières, who proclaimed themselves through the *Encyclopedia* as a kind of anti-Bible.[503]

Equally, the challenge of the Enlightenment in the shape of the *philosophes* on the enunciative plane had a sequence in the shape of the revolutionaries on

---

501 Ricoeur, *Reflections on the Just*, 95.
502 Ricoeur, *Reflections on the Just*, 95. With the *Encyclopedia*, "a new figure of enunciative authority takes shape, one that does not authorize itself on the basis of the absolute transcendence of a sacred text in relation to other utterances and to public opinion, but which is based on the creditability of the author … To the medieval hierarchy of the sciences, dominated by theology, stands opposed the dispersion of articles in dictionaries arranged in terms of an anarchical alphabetical order" (101–2).
503 Ricoeur, *Reflections on the Just*, 100.

the institutional one.[504] Thus, both in the Middle Ages and in modernity, one side became linked to the other.[505] The contemporary situation is explained as marked by a crisis that is

> double (or if you will, doubly dense, doubly staged): we are reexperiencing in a way the crisis of the deaccrediting of the ideal type of medieval Christendom by way of the crisis of the delegitimizing of what followed from this loss of creditability... the ideal type of the French Enlightenment thinkers has itself lost much of its creditability, as contemporary talk about postmodernity bears witness.[506]

The problem Ricoeur highlights is not simply that of an age superseded, that one formation inspired by a specific motivating goal is followed by another, but that each seems to run out of energy, resonance, and convocation power. The analysis just treated, Max Weber's theory of rationalization, can be seen as an example of reason giving up on a previous hope and turning defeatist. It is not a crisis that can be solved by the institutional side, since it is located in the symbolic resources of a society. It is deeper than the level rational governance and management can reach. The question to the sphere of public discourse then is, what forces of renewal can it draw on, to foster identities motivated and capable of facing challenges of global proportions in its discourses on policies that stand the test of universalizability?

A first step on the way is to clarify the level of the problem: that it is located at the most elementary stage and consists in the need to replenish the enunciative-discursive side; the question that follows immediately from this is whether the founding energy of each original vision can be tapped into again, or whether the diagnosis has to be one of an impulse having ended in "inertia" and "perverse effects".[507]In contrast to Weber's proposition of a reversal of reason, Ri-

---

504 Ricoeur, *Reflections on the Just*, 100: "The *philosophes* shared the illusion of the defenders of Roman Catholic orthodoxy ... that the authority to be combated was par excellence one of a discourse and that it had to be fought against principally on this ground. It was left to the thinkers of the French Revolution to attack the institutional authority of the Ancient Régime on the properly political plane."

505 Ricoeur, *Reflections on the Just*, 100 – 1: "What justifies this hypothesis of a double root to institutional authority is the fact that despite the medieval dream of a unity of authority, the duality of monarchical and ecclesiastical power remained insurmountable. At best the two powers and the two corresponding authorities mutually supported each other, the ecclesiastical one offering its unction to the monarch, while the political realm offered the sanction of the secular arm in return. Unction plus sanction could ensure the practical functioning of an internally divided theological politics."

506 Ricoeur, *Reflections on the Just*, 95.

507 Ricoeur, *Reflections on the Just*, 143.

coeur identifies a double chance for both society and for Christian communities opened up by the end of the period of amalgamation between religious and political sources of authority:

> [W]e can... ask whether this part of authority... issuing from the Roman *imperium*, once freed of its union with the properly religious authority of the church... was not thereby made available for other durable investments, owing to which we now find ourselves situated today at the end of the theological-political age.[508]

Regarding the religious side, any nostalgia for the Christendom stage is dismissed and described in terms of ideology:

> Christianity... has not exhausted its specific religious creditability, in the production of the particular historical configuration of what we call Christendom. I would say of this latter that its ideal type was as much a dream as an actual reality... it never was historically what it claims to have been.[509]

Hope is attached to the "reserves of meaning" that are still fresh in the original sources:

> [W]ithout injustice, we can present the enunciative and institutional authority that together make up the largely nostalgic ideal type of Christendom as a fossilized model, which... erased the history of its own genesis while also repressing its original creative aspects, which were capable of resurfacing after the calling into question of this ideal type by the *philosophes*. In fact, some of these resources were actually liberated by this critique: for example, reserves of meaning connected with the very formation of the New Testament and the birth of the early church, or the riches linked to a buried pluralism, sometimes tributary to deviances of all sorts[510].

Thus, for Ricoeur, the way forward is the way back to a purely "enunciative" authority prior to the half-borrowed "institutional" authority. For Ricoeur, the sources of Christianity that were buried in the stage of institutional amalgamation, can now be freely availed of again, and so can the political after being untied from the religious.

What needs to be questioned, however, about his portrayal of the "ideal type" in the Middle Ages is that it stays at a generalizing level and neither goes into the intellectual debates between theologians at universities, with "Rome" and at councils, nor the religious movements and the microhistory,

---

508 Ricoeur, *Reflections on the Just*, 98.
509 Ricoeur, *Reflections on the Just*, 95–6.
510 Ricoeur, *Reflections on the Just*, 97.

for example, of the individualization of piety in medieval mysticism. Its broad strokes offer a unitary view of Christianity in the Middle Ages which borders on what Ricoeur admits may be a "caricature".[511] The struggles within the Catholic church and between church and princes should be recognized, even when they were not successful, especially since they evoked the original vision of the Gospels, as well. Yet Ricoeur's point is significant that there were translations of its message into the symbolic worlds of different eras that were inadequate, and that a democratic age provides a realm in which the aspirations of freedom, equality and brotherliness at a universal scale offer a congenial cultural backdrop. Current theological movements that advocate religious testimony either in purely countercultural or in integralist terms ignore these achievements, and fail to identify the factors in their own traditions that obstruct the attraction of the original source for contemporary searchers. Ricoeur's analysis can be further developed into a critique of recent theological attempts to portray Christianity as being countercultural in principle. One of their typical features is that they only wish to "witness" but decline to enter into a forum where impulses, visions and arguments are exchanged; thus, they equally refuse to be corrected by other sources, and so give up on the social bond that is wider than any single communitarian allegiance. Insights from the comparison of the three social philosophical approaches for theology will be drawn in the Conclusion that follows this third part.

In relation to the civic engagement that contributes to the public sphere of democracies, however, a feature that Rawls and Habermas both fail to highlight can be derived from Ricoeur's understanding of ethics: the social bond is constituted and nourished by a level prior to moral obligation, that of solicitude which becomes concrete in an invitation to trust. This is what the "fiduciary" connection drawn on before to explain the attachment to a joint foundational myth means. It is a "political capability", a "political concept in the most fundamental sense, concerning the establishment of the social bond".[512] It is therefore a capability of human beings in the social sphere that turns their factual plurality into an ethical endeavour. The philosopher Andreas Hetzel points out what role the

---

511 Ricoeur, *Reflections on the Just*, 96–97: "I have emphasized to the point of caricature the aspect of being already instituted that made the idea of tradition the favoured target of the *philosophes*." Current research offers a more differentiated view of the plural expressions of Christianity in the Middle Ages, for example, D. Mieth/B. Mueller-Schauenburg (eds.), *Mystik, Recht und Freiheit. Religiöse Erfahrung und kirchliche Institutionen im Spätmittelalter* (Stuttgart: Kohlhammer, 2012).
512 A. Hetzel, "Bezeugen, Vergeben, Anerkennen", in Liebsch (ed.), *Bezeugte Vergangenheit*, 217–231, 226, quoting from *Memory, History, Forgetting*, 60.

unvouched-for character of testimony plays for lifting the "social" up to the "ethical":

> Here, Ricoeur speaks of a "fiduciary" principle of social integration that is based on trustworthiness. In the act of giving testimony we experience an essential *lack of foundation* (*Unbegründetheit*) of the social which we can equally describe as the innate sense (*Eigensinn*) of the ethical. "More and more, this bond of trustworthiness" which relies only on the given word and on trust in this word, "extends to include every exchange, contract and agreement, and constitutes assent to others' word, the principle of the social bond, to the point that it becomes a *habitus* of any community considered, even a prudential rule. First, trust the word of others, then doubt if there are strong reasons for doing so. In my vocabulary, it is a question of competence of the capable human being. The credit granted to the word of others makes the social world a shared intersubjective world."[513]

This "ethical moment within the social" turns out to be not only the necessary step beyond Weber. It also adds an element that is missing in Rawls's and even in Habermas's social philosophies: the willingness to take the risk of initiatives with regard to others who might not respond. The theme of the gift, developed in Ricoeur's final publications, stands for this unsecured opening. It belongs to an anthropology that offers an alternative to a merely conflictual view of the human struggle for freedom. Recognition is explored in terms of a gift that is free, not owed, rather than in terms of a competition for an ever-greater range of rights. It thus becomes clear that an anticipatory act of trust is elementary for the constitution and renewal of the social bond.

It is a category that belongs to the "logic of superabundance" typical for religious sources, yet it is foundational for general processes of understanding. The philosopher Inga Römer explores the theme of the individual initiative of testimony by linking the introduction and the tenth chapter of *Oneself as Another* to the Epilogue of *Memory, History, Forgetting*. She highlights the "risk" of a "hermeneutically necessary basic trust", a "credence without any guarantee" on which "Ricoeur's critical hermeneutics depends in its foundations: 'To my mind, attestation defines the kind of certainty that hermeneutics may claim... credence (*créance*)... and trust (*confiance*)..., as credence without any guarantee'". She links the forgiveness treated in the Epilogue to this advance trust:

---

513 Hetzel, "Bezeugen, Vergeben, Anerkennen", in *Bezeugte Vergangenheit*, 226, quoting from *Memory, History, Forgetting*, 165.

Forgiveness and gift can thus be understood as higher grades of a hermeneutically necessary basic trust; yet in their unconditional risk they cannot trust in something that is already testified to; they trust in the mere possibility of a new beginning in history.[514]

Ricoeur's discussion of origins of authority, of different theories of democracy, of
political governance and of civic action from different cofoundational traditions
has spelt out a basic anthropology in which religions appear alongside other historical sources for self-understandings. It has also given a role to them on the
enunciative level of the public sphere where they can offer a perspective that
is relevant not only to their own communities, but for the future of the democratic project since it concerns basic questions of selves and their capability to act.

3.4 Religion and agency: Fallibility, hope, and translation

As a consequence of his hermeneutical starting point with selves who express
their striving through the symbolic resources of a culture, religion and reason
are equally seen as symbolically mediated. Worlds of meaning at this level fulfill
the elementary and non-manipulative definition of ideology as integrating a
community.[515] From his use of George Herbert Mead's Symbolic Interactionism,
Habermas would agree that all action is symbolically mediated. For the French
philosopher, however, this insight calls for a change of methodology; reconstructing the stages of development of his own thinking, he points to the
move it required of "grafting" a hermeneutics onto a phenomenological analysis.[516] His correction of a philosophy of consciousness consists in turning from
abstract to concrete freedom by examining the genetic aspect of consciousness:
the self needs to acquire its capacities by a "detour" through the appropriation of
the symbolic worlds expressed in texts and actions. The hermeneutical horizon
of expectation arising from the particularity of cultural symbols shapes what
these selves consider as meaningful. Not only are life plans culturally mediated;
the whole idea of a "plan" owes itself to a particular conception of history, of the
task of a community, and of the role of the self within both. By adding the dimension of historical reflection that is missing in Rawls's analyses of contemporary liberal society and only sketched, sometimes polemically, by Habermas, as

---

514 I. Römer, "Eskapistisches Vergessen? Der Optativ des glücklichen Gedächtnisses bei Paul
Ricoeur", in Liebsch (ed.), *Bezeugte Vergangenheit*, 291–309, 304–5, quoting from *Oneself as
Another*, 21–23.
515 See above, 3.1.4.
516 Ricoeur, "Existence and hermeneutics", in *The Conflict of Interpretations*, 6.

in his contrasting of modernity to metaphysics, Ricoeur gives access to the formative forces of Western thinking. I shall first treat his interpretation of different narrative encodings of the human experience of fallibility in texts from antiquity, and compare the emerging understanding of freedom in biblical monotheism with his reception of Kant's reflections on evil (1). I shall then turn to the classical modern treatment of the experience of good moral action failing that led Kant to complement his dialectic of practical reason with a philosophy of religion. It is on the shared ground of the original philosophical foundation of all three theorists of public reason, namely Kant's critical work, that differences in direction will become obvious. How the scope of reason and the role of hope are determined, will affect the question of the rationality of religion and its place in the public sphere (2). Thirdly, his interest as an interpreter of texts in shifts in thinking has drawn his attention to the translations that have created Western culture by making encounters, cross-fertilization and new syntheses possible. The "hospitality of languages"[517] is a presupposition for these achievements. Yet by examining also the limits of translation, he identifies crucial turning points that can be uncovered retrospectively as sources of meaning that feed into individual and cultural aspirations. Whether and how these sources shape the contours and scope of public reason, will depend on their continued ability to relate to contemporary challenges (3).

The argumentation in all three subsections, but especially in the first two, concerns basic capacities of the human person. It raises a truth claim about anthropological structures that can be found in reflection on existence. It thus makes the case that it is still meaningful to speak about the human person; the quest to make sense of elementary human experiences, such as birth, facticity, finitude, others, guilt and evil, that takes different historical and literary shapes is an anthropological constant. Neither suspending this question nor leaving it to the individual social sciences to investigate aspects of it in sequences of enquiries, Ricoeur makes the case for supplying a coherent, methodologically reflected anthropology.

Against the backdrop of the option that was sketched previously, namely the historicist observer's attitude content to float between the different cultures inspected, Ricoeur's analysis of the self in its capacity and incapacity thus has to be seen as taking a stance in the interest of the individual ability to act. Instead of remaining paralysed in the contemplation of an unending relativism between meaning-providing goals across the ages and cultures of humanity, it is

---

517 Ricoeur, "Reflections on a new ethos for Europe", trans. E. Brennan, in R. Kearney (ed.), *Paul Ricoeur: The Hermeneutics of Action* (London: Sage Publications, 1996), 3–13.

directed towards the future, intent to initiate and change conditions; it does so by actively investigating the potential of its own cultural resources to deal with global threats to the foundational human desire to flourish with others in just institutions. Translation is part of the work to discover the inchoative universalisms of other languages and cultures.

Ricoeur's setting of the original basis for ethics in the human desire for a flourishing life contains criteria for the interpretation of what is to count as "meaning". In Hegel's system, truth and meaning consist in the whole, in the completion of the stages in which reason is realized by the world spirit. In Kierkegaard's critique of this perspective, meaning is approached from the point of view of the individual subject. His proposed solution in the face of the unresolved polarities, dialectics and antinomies of human life is to ground one's existence in God: "by relating itself to its own self and by willing to be itself the self is transparently grounded in the Power which posited it."[518] In Ricoeur's phenomenology of agency, it is not primarily the facticity of existence that leads to the question of an absolute foundation, but the problem of how the capacity of the agent can be renewed and reopened after failure and guilt. Therefore, one major perspective for the question of meaning is about the possibility of forgiveness. Ricoeur argues against Hannah Arendt's understanding of it as a generic human capability, and insists on it as already existing, prior to the actions of individuals, there to be availed of: "Il y a le pardon".[519] It is a theme that needs to be put back on the agenda of philosophical thinking, as part of the moral agent's quest for meaning; this is an integral part of ethics, affecting its foundations for Kant and not delegated, as Habermas does, to the private attempts of individuals to cope with contingency. It is the originality, depth and integrating capacity of Ricoeur's anthropological reflections as much as his engagement with biblical texts that have provided instructive points of connection and reception for theological anthropology and ethics.

3.4.1 Fallibility and freedom in religious experience and in philosophical reflection

It has become clear that for Ricoeur, the material for philosophical reflection is to be found in the experiences of conscious life expressed in the symbolic forms of

---

518 S. Kierkegaard, *Fear and Trembling* and The *Sickness Unto Death*, trans. and intro. by W. Lowrie (Princeton: Princeton University Press, 1968), 147.
519 Ricoeur, *Memory, History, Forgetting*, 466.

a culture. Reflection takes its "starting-point with pre-philosophical experiences, intuitions and motives".[520] The network of symbols forms the basis from which concrete self-understandings are developed: The "self turns out to depend on such symbolism and constitutes itself through something like a spontaneous interpretation of it".[521] In a process of critical appropriation of these symbolic understandings of world contained in literary writings, practices and institutions, the self acquires its own specific outlook. This "detour" cannot be replaced by any shortcut, neither of introspection nor of a claimed immediacy of life. Its experiences, including those of the divine, are encountered in an already mediated form which calls for interpretation: "(B)oth philosophy and theology have to learn starting from what he expresses through his well-known motto that 'the symbol gives rise to thought'."[522] The mediating structure of the symbol remains operative even after it has been interpreted conceptually. The great questions for human reflection, about origin and destiny, finitude and failure, do not lose their enigmatic character. Veronika Hoffmann locates the first realization of Ricoeur's philosophy of mediations in his achievement to

> refute the illusion of an immediate point of departure, that symbolic thinking with philosophical appropriation opens up access to the mystery of evil. However, symbolic-hermeneutical mediation is not a bridge that one crosses only once but an abiding structure of access. It is impossible to completely encompass evil in reflective thinking.[523]

Symbolic expressions, such as myths and narratives, thus help the self to articulate and make sense of its own experiences. By reconstructing the question of meaning from the perspective of the individual, criteria for speaking of meaning are established: the reality of human life is taken seriously; its finitude, its capability and, as part of this, its fallibility are problems for reflection, not reason as such and its history of transformations. Ricoeur's analysis identifies three different stages in the symbolic forms of expressing the experience of the discrepancy between a person's striving and the reality of failing to carry out the good intended. At the first stage, evil appears as a stain, an impurity affecting the self like a destiny coming over it from the outside; at the second stage, it appears as the

---

520 V. Hoffmann, *Vermittelte Offenbarung*, 79. Cf. Greisch, *Fehlbarkeit*, 21: "borne by what is not philosophy, it lives off the substance of what has already been understood unreflectedly."
521 D. Pellauer, *Ricoeur: A Guide for the Perplexed* (Continuum: London/New York, 2007), 34–35.
522 Pellauer, *Guide for the Perplexed*, 40. This Kantian motto is the title that Ricoeur has given to the Conclusion of *The Symbolism of Evil*, trans. E. Buchanan (Boston: Beacon Press, 1967), 347–358.
523 Hoffmann, *Vermittelte Offenbarung*, 88.

breach of a relationship, as failing to respond to God's expectation.[524] Here, sin is experienced both as a deed, a factual act of human freedom, and as a power existing prior to human action. The third stage is the complete interiorization of failure as individual guilt faced with the forum of conscience.

Agency, self-consciousness and sin or guilt are thus connected: the awareness of the freedom of agency arises from knowing that one could have acted differently. This is where the anthropological relevance of the Genesis account of Adam's and Eve's move from innocence to failure appears. It shows fallibility as a human structure, but the act of sinning as a contingent, not a necessary event.

It is only at the second stage that evil can become an ethical problem as an act committed, not an event suffered. As Thomas Pröpper explains in his comment on Ricoeur's reconstruction, evil becomes a matter for ethics "due to a dual relationship: to the consciousness of freedom, and to the phenomenon of obligation."[525] Regarding the first, what the biblical account achieves is that evil is "not treated in the shape of a substance, as in dualist ontologies like Manicheism…, but as an act of freedom". Without trying to explain the mystery of its origin, the starting point of the analysis is a "performative act,… a confession" which accepts the implication and authorship of one's own person.

The second aspect, obligation, specifies evil as acting counter to what one *should* have done. The person's moral identity becomes aware of a temporal dimension to the past and to the future. Imputability, the sense of authorship, now turns into a moral evaluation not only of what one could have done, but should have done. Freedom is thus recognized as the capability also for evil. The background from which this personalized understanding becomes possible is religious: a deeper experience of God expressed by the prophets.[526] The systematic perspective which directs the interpretation of the Genesis narratives is the promise received by Abraham of a blessing for all peoples, Genesis 12:1–3. It is this blessing for all of humanity in which the narratives of the creation and of the Fall of the human person as made in God's image are seen as culminating.[527]

In a third round of enquiry, Ricoeur looks for a philosophical equivalent for the biblical story of the Fall and finds a similar status of the enigma of evil in Kant's treatment of "radical evil" in his *Religion within the Limits of Reason*

---

524 Pröpper, *Theologische Anthropologie*, vol. II, 684–692, 685, with reference to P. Ricoeur, "Guilt, ethics and religion", in *Concilium* 5 (1970) 11–27.
525 Pröpper, *Theologische Anthropologie*, vol. II, 687.
526 Pröpper, *Theologische Anthropologie*, vol. II, 686.
527 Cf. Pröpper, *Theologische Anthropologie*, vol. II, 936.

Alone. Kant's answer is threefold: (1) Evil is inscrutable (*unerforschbar*) in its radicality. (2) Yet, it is not foundational at the level of a predisposition (*Anlage*), but secondary as a penchant (*Hang*). Humans remain open to the call of conscience.[528] (3) The role and the capacity of religion is to restore the actual power to act according to the good principle in each human being.

Thus, evil is encountered as only factual.[529] Reflection on it hits a double limit, one of knowledge, the other of freedom itself which finds itself incapable of unconditional good. Ricoeur calls it "the greatest paradox of ethics"[530] that freedom is both responsible and not available to itself, and thus in need of liberation. Regarding human fallibility, the symbolic story of the Fall has given rise to thought in the following points that summarise the link of the Genesis account to Kant's modern reflection on evil:

– it has its origin in human agency, but also precedes individual action;

– its origin remains inscrutable, which is why the act of admission and confession of guilt is the starting point;

– the awareness of human freedom arises from realizing that one could have acted differently; the experience of obligation makes it clear that one should have;

– evil is not as primary as the human disposition towards goodness, as expressed in the state prior to the Fall in Genesis, and in taking "good will" as foundational in Kant's ethics;[531]

---

528 Cf. Ricoeur, "A philosophical hermeneutics of religion: Kant", in *Figuring the Sacred*, 75–92, 80: "evil cannot bring it about that we cease being open to the appeal of conscience. In this sense, evil remains contingent, albeit always already there."

529 In "Da ist keiner, der nicht sündigt, nicht einer..." Analyse und Kritik gegenwärtiger Erbsündentheologien und ihr Beitrag für das seit Paulus gestellte Problem, in Th. Pröpper, *Theologische Anthropologie*, vol. II, 1092–1156, 1156, G. Essen summarizes: "(S)ince sin is in its essence enacted by freedom, the qualitative difference between the disposition towards sin and the fact of sin cannot be eclipsed (*übersprungen*)."

530 Ricoeur, "Guilt, Ethics and Religion", in *Conflict*, 425–439, 436.

531 In "A philosophical hermeneutics of religion: Kant", in *Figuring the Sacred. Religion, Narrative, and Imagination*, trans. D. Pellauer, ed. by M. Wallace (Minneapolis: Fortress Press, 1995), 75–92, 81, Ricoeur recognizes "Kant's intellectual honesty while facing the question of evil, of giving it a merely factual status by declaring it unexplainable: 'There is then for us no conceivable ground from which the moral evil in us could originally have come.' (38) Ricoeur then points out how Kant can draw on a symbolic parallel, the role of the devil, in the Genesis account: "Again, Kant can claim for this philosophical meditation a certain affinity with the biblical narrative in that it assigns the origin of the origin of evil to 'a *spirit* of an originally loftier destiny' (39). 'Thus is the *first* beginning of all evil represented as inconceivable by us (for whence came evil to that spirit?); but man is represented as having fallen into evil only *through seduction.*' (39)" Ricoeur concludes: "It is noteworthy that Kant glimpsed, beneath this theme of

– yet the experience of freedom is that it is in need of liberation or renewal – a perspective of forgiveness or grace against the burden of moral self-accusation.

Both in the biblical and in the philosophical self-reflections of stages two and three is evil linked to an understanding of human freedom. In the experience of sin and guilt, it appears as a capacity of both good and evil. In the following analysis, a different limit is explored, at the higher end of what freedom intends but cannot achieve by its own means. Ricoeur's high evaluation of the role of hope in Kant's philosophy, with its radical analysis of the antinomy of practical reason, is rare in comparison with his philosophical colleagues, not only with Rawls and Habermas. His interest in the conditions for human agency also directs his attention towards diagnosing its constitutive limits, and how they feature in philosophical conceptions of reason and action.

3.4.2 A dialectic that gives a place to hope: Kant's concept of the "highest good"

Regarding the connection between religion and agency, the previous section has shown that the stage of evil as "sin" that follows the mythical stage of "stain" has been a break-through in the consciousness of human agency. The personal relationship to God in the context of a Covenant led to an individual sense of responsibility. Similar conclusions to the Genesis account are reached in philosophical reflection: Evil is already there as a factor, and individual action freely continues and reinstates it. A different link between religion and agency from the genetic aspect appears when the best intentions of freedom are being realized. The limits to be discussed in this section concern a constitutive inability at the higher level where agents would be "worthy" of happiness due to the purity of their motives, but cannot accomplish this "synthesis" by themselves. The fact that they cannot make it happen reveals that they are caught in an antinomy between a justified orientation towards a happiness commensurate with virtue, and the experience of moral effort spent in vain.

I shall follow Ricoeur's argumentation in four steps: First, he shows that the question of the completion of reason belongs to the remit of philosophy (1). Con-

---

seduction, a connection between the hermeneutics of evil and that of hope. If humankind became evil through seduction, then it was not basically corrupt. In releasing humankind from the full weight of the origin of evil, the theme of seduction indicates the point where the culmination of radical evil coincides with the first glimmer of hope." The quotes refer to the edition used above: Kant, *Religion within the Limits of Reason Alone*, trans. Th. M. Greene and H. H. Hudson (New York: Harper & Brothers, 1960).

trasting two types of solution, Hegel's and Kant's (2), he discusses the status of the hope offered by Kant in response to the antinomy of practical reason which he has stated so sharply (3). Ricoeur ends with the perspective of Kant's *Religion within the Limits of Reason Alone* on evil and on the renewing power of religion; he thus turns the analysis towards the perpetrator and the problem of forgiveness, rather than focusing on what the Dialectic in the *Critique of Practical Reason* explores: namely the perspective of the moral person who is left at a loss when the legitimate striving for happiness ends in failure (4). I shall conclude with a summary of the points which Ricoeur endorses in relation to the concept and the scope of reason, and examine where Habermas and Rawls stand in relation to them (5).

3.4.2.1 Reason as structurally oriented towards completion

While philosophy in Ricoeur's view finds its material in what is prior to it, namely the symbolically mediated understandings of reality in conscious life, this renunciation to an absolute status does not entail a diminishing of the scope of reason. In contrast to Habermas whose proposal of a postmetaphysical concept of reason leads to philosophy losing its own method by assuming only a structuring and mediating role as "stand-in" and "interpreter", Ricoeur fully supports the dynamic outreach of reason, as the faculty of principles, to ultimate questions. As a philosopher in dialogue with biblical studies and theology, he sees his task as engaging in

> nothing else than a more complete and more perfect activation of reason; not more than reason, but *whole* reason... for it is this problem of the integrality of thinking which will prove to be the core of the whole problematic.[532]

With Kant and Hegel he assumes that reason is structurally directed towards "completion", aspiring towards a totality which has a "function of horizon" for cognition and will. Quoting from the beginning of the Dialectic of Kant's second *Critique*, reason "demands the absolute totality of conditions for a given conditioned thing".[533] The same "completion structure of pure reason" that was analysed in the first *Critique* is now "transposed" to the will. That is, in the context of

---

532 Ricoeur, "Freedom in the light of hope", trans. R. Sweeney, in *The Conflict of Interpretations*, 402–424, 403.
533 The following quotes are from Ricoeur, "Freedom in the light of hope", in *Conflict*, 416, quoting Kant, *Critique of Practical Reason*, trans. L. W. Beck (New York: Liberal Arts Press, 1956), 117.

the *Critique of Practical Reason* it is the will that is assumed to be extended to-wards an ultimate goal; as Ricoeur observes, it is designated with the "old name" the "highest good", which, however, "should not hide the novelty of his move". Comparing both approaches structurally, he locates the "highest good" at the position that "absolute knowledge" will occupy in Hegel's outline of reason. Having clarified their parallel architectural place, he then goes on to explain the distinction between the two. Before following the steps of enquiry that show Kant's definition of the "highest good" as leading into a new antinomy, Ricoeur's evaluation of the two distinct enterprises of reason needs to be ex-plored. Both classical modern thinkers offer an analysis and an endpoint of rea-son, but one in the shape of a critique, the other of a system. The fact that the goal of practical reason "does not permit knowledge, but only a demand" in Kant's setting, gives it a different outlook: "something to do with hope". The pur-pose of this limit idea, as the Kant scholar Rudolf Langthaler points out in his critique of Habermas's reconstruction of Kant's argumentation, is not to "pro-duce" the highest good, but to show the "rational demonstrability (*vernünftige Aufweisbarkeit*) of the justice- and meaning oriented final aim (*Endzweck*) of practical reason for 'rational, finite beings'".[534] It belongs to reason to ask the question of unconditional meaning, even if it cannot meet its challenge by its own means.

3.4.2.2 The endpoint of reason in Kant and Hegel: Demand of unconditional meaning versus absolute knowledge

Ricoeur has treated the differences between Kant and Hegel in many places under a number of perspectives. The question what his "post-Hegelian Kantian-ism"[535] entails and what it rejects has received different answers. In the context

---

534 Langthaler, "Zur Interpretation und Kritik der Kantischen Religionsphilosophie bei Jürgen Habermas", in Langthaler/Nagl-Docekal (eds.), *Glauben und Wissen* , 32–92, 53–54.

535 Ricoeur, "Freedom in the light of hope", in *Conflict*, 412: "But the Kantianism that I wish to develop now is, paradoxically, more to be constructed than repeated; it would be something like a post-Hegelian Kantianism, to borrow an expression from Eric Weil... we are as radically post-Hegelian as we are post-Kantian... it is this exchange and this permutation which still structure philosophical discourse today. This is why the task is to think them always better by thinking them together – one against the other, and one by means of the other." (412) What he esteems in Hegel's "philosophy of the will" is the "diversity of problems it traverses and resolves: union of desire and culture, of psychology and politics, of the subjective and the universal... an inex-haustible reservoir of descriptions and mediations (414)... I abandon the ethics of duty to the Hegelian critique with no regrets" (413)... This new classification and critique in essays from 1960–1970 of core terms of Kant's ethics anticipate the reinterpretation of the deontological

of an enquiry into ideas of "public reason", I see the following aspects of how the underlying concept of reason is determined as relevant: the definition of its endpoint; the conception of time and history; the role of negativity, suffering, and evil; and the open or closed character of an approach that reflects on reason in its achievements, powers and limits.

Regarding its structural orientation towards completion, together with Kant, Ricoeur distinguishes between "supreme", and "whole" or "complete". If the highest good is understood as the "supreme" good, it could be fulfilled by being moral since it realizes duty; if, however, "highest" means realized in the integrity of both of its components, virtue and happiness, then the idea of completion as "*bonum consummatum*" is constitutively outside of what is achievable by human forces. If one does not want to give up on this direction of reason, then an adequate cause is required. This sequence of steps of argumentation demonstrates the analytical capacity of reason but equally its limits. It gives a critique of (practical) reason by reason and concludes by outlining the sufficient condition for achieving the *bonum consummatum*: reason has to "postulate" a benevolent author of the universe who has created the world in such a way that it is receptive to the best moral endeavours of humans. Whether this function of a guarantor for a hospitable rather than hostile or absurd context for moral agency is accepted, is left to the individual as a matter of "subjective faith". Ricoeur does not go into the details of this line of reasoning, nor does he quote the consequences Kant draws for the foundations of ethics if the synthesis of moral effort and fulfillment cannot be brought about; he concludes:

> No one as much as Kant has had a sense for the transcendent character of this connection, and this against the whole of Greek philosophy to which he is directly opposed, rejecting Epicurean and Stoic equally: happiness is not our accomplishment: it is achieved by super-addition, by surplus.[536]

It thus remains a hoped-for synthesis, not one that can be "produced by... will". It is a connection relating to attitudes and acts of freedom that risk one-sided initiatives which leave their authors vulnerable. What kind of outlook and actions he has in mind becomes clear through his reference to the Beatitudes –

---

level of ethics with its replacement of "duty" by the "sieve of the norm" and the translation of "obligation" into "indebtedness" in *Oneself as Another*. But there is a reason to return to Kant: "And yet, Kant remains... he surpasses Hegel from a certain point of view... which is precisely essential for our present dialogue between a theology of hope and a philosophy of reason. The Hegel I reject is the philosopher of retrospection, the one who... reabsorbs all rationality in the already happened meaning." (414)

536 Ricoeur, "Freedom in the light of hope", in *Conflict*, 417.

the peace-makers, the meek, those pure of heart, those who hunger and thirst after justice: "Thus the meaning of the Beatitudes is approached philosophically only by the idea of a nonanalytic liaison between the work of man and the contentment susceptible of satisfying the desire which constitutes his existence."[537] He concludes: "Kant explicitly brings religion to the question 'What can I hope for?' I do not know any other philosopher who has defined religion exclusively with that question."[538]

Hegel offers a different construction of what the completion of reason consists in: the sum of knowledge achieved in all the mediations it has effected in reconciling opposites. Instead of a Critique, it offers a view of the sought-for totality in terms of necessity. Fulfillment consists in being able to look back at the distance covered from the summit reached. This position implies a specific conception of the time of history: It looks backward in affirmation, but not forward towards a future beyond the present stage. In

> Hegelian thought, the horizon of the system is called absolute knowledge... represent(ing)... (n)ot at all a sense to come, an unexplored field of meanings, but the philosophical repetition of antecedent mediations. There is nothing new in absolute knowledge; it merely concludes the reconciliation already at work in the successive phases of the philosophical process between certitude and truth... it is this development itself as absolutized... The Hegelian system is a system written from the end toward the beginning, from the standpoint of the totality toward the partial achievements of the system. And this end is not something that could be awaited or expected – it is the eternal present of thought that sustains the history of thought... a recapitulative summary of all the intermediary mediations... the Hegelian system represents the contrary to a philosophy of hope. It is a philosophy of reminiscence, for which rationality belongs to the whole as present".[539]

Ricoeur objects to the lack of distinction between philosophical reflection and reason itself that appears in Hegel's statement at the end of the Preface of the *Philosophy of Right*, with its "totem animal... well chosen: Minerva's owl".[540]

> 'Philosophy always comes too late!' Philosophy, without a doubt. But what about reason? It is this question which sends me from Hegel to Kant... the Kant of the two Dialectics... instituting the tension which makes of Kantianism a philosophy of limits and not a philosophy of system.[541]

---

537 Ricoeur, "Freedom in the light of hope", in *Conflict*, 417.
538 Ricoeur, "Freedom in the light of hope", in *Conflict*, 417–18.
539 Ricoeur, "Hope and the structure of philosophical systems" (1970), in *Figuring the Sacred*, 203–216, 208.
540 Ricoeur, "Hope and the structure of philosophical systems", in *Figuring the Sacred*, 210.
541 Ricoeur, "Freedom in the light of hope", in *Conflict*, 414–15.

A stance that posits rationality as present and realized in the whole implies a structurally conservative endorsement of the present order; a critical position, by contrast, would set out to analyse whether principles that have been historically reached and established as guiding norms for political, legal and social life are being put into action.[542] The sharpest expression of his motives for distancing himself from Hegel's edifice of reason is reserved for the complete absence of regard for individual suffering, the existence of evil, and the continuing discrepancy between promise and achievement: negativity plays a role only as already countered and contained. This conceptual negation of the negation marginalizes the reality of human suffering. An awareness of the gaping difference between hopes and piecemeal achievements that would lead to identifying ongoing tasks is left behind by a "bold extrapolation to totally realized reason". The alternative between Kant's and Hegel's outlook is identified by comparing Hegel's "painful but victorious 'work of the negative'" with its "rational hubris" to Kant's twofold answer to evil: both at the levels of action and of reflection on how the human predisposition (*Anlage*) to the good, countered by a penchant (*Hang*) towards evil, can be restored by religion.

> On every level, negativity is what constrains each figure of the Spirit to invert itself into its contrary and to engender a new figure that both surpasses and preserves the preceding one, in the twofold sense of the Hegelian concept of *Aufhebung*. This conclusive dialectic makes the tragic and the logical coincide at every stage. Something must die so that something greater may be born. In this sense, misfortune is everywhere, but everywhere it is surpassed, to the extent that reconciliation always wins out over what is torn apart.
>
> The question is whether this triumphant dialectic does not reconstitute, with logical resources unavailable to Leibniz, another form of optimism issuing from the same audacity, with perhaps an even greater rational hubris. Indeed, what fate is reserved for the suffering of victims in a worldview where the pan-tragic is constantly covered over by a pan-logicism? We may say that the scandal of suffering is overlooked in two ways. First, it is diluted and defused by the very expansion of negativity beyond the human predicament. Second, it

---

542 Ricoeur, "Hope and the structure of philosophical systems", in: *Figuring the Sacred*, 203–216, 210: "The concept of actualization of freedom by which we defined the field of practical reason has two dimensions: that of fulfilled achievement and that of unfulfilled claim. And these two implications belong to the structure of actualization as such. On the one hand, human action makes sense because we may discern in some places adequation between rationality and reality… the contractual law of exchange, the acquisition of penal law, the conquest of civil rights, and some aspects of the modern state… But, … do those cases cover the whole field of human action? Are they not rather sorts of islands of rationality, surrounded by irrationality? Is not the Hegelian philosophy of action a kind of extrapolation based on the limited experience of the fulfilled achievements of humankind?… Hence the question: Has not Hegel destroyed the spring of action by excluding the second dimension of action, that of unfulfilled claim, which counterbalances the first one, that of fulfilled achievement?"

is silenced by the substitution of reconciliation (of contradictions) for consolation addressed to human beings as victims. The famous motto of the 'cunning of reason' in the introduction to the *Lectures on the Philosophy of History* is the well-known stumbling block of this post-Kantian theodicy. [543]

By contrast, Kant's analysis of practical reason and of its limits becomes aporetic by insisting on the question of happiness as unrelinquishable. A philosophical system that seeks to ensure meaning by giving up on the hope for happiness discredits itself, especially when it is viewed from the history of the twentieth century:

> The irony of the Hegelian philosophy of history lies in the fact that, assuming that it does give a meaning to the great currents of history,... it does so to the extent that it abolishes the question of happiness and unhappiness ... But if the great actors in history are frustrated as concerns happiness by history, which makes use of them, what are we to say about its anonymous victims? For we who read Hegel after the catastrophes and the sufferings beyond number of our century, that dissociation that his philosophy of history brings about between consolation and reconciliation has become, to say the least, a source of great perplexity. The more the system flourishes, the more its victims are marginalized. The success of the system is its failure. Suffering, as what is expressed by the voices of lamentation, is what the system excludes.[544]

It is clear, then, to which of the two projects religious self-understandings can align themselves: not to a "system" that is closed and in no need of further realization, but to a critical analysis also of the limits of reason that leaves room for imagination and hope, and that is open for a fulfillment from beyond human powers after moral action has achieved as much at it can: "if we act as well as lies in our power, what is not in our power will come to our aid from another source, whether we know in what way or not".[545]

3.4.2.3 The epistemological status of hope

Since the remit of public reason depends on the properties and the scope given to reason – for example, whether it is allowed to go beyond current common sense, or how its relationship to the individual sciences is seen –, it matters how Ricoeur argues for a philosophy that leaves space for hope. He traces two

---

543 Ricoeur, "Evil, a challenge to philosophy and theology", in *Figuring the Sacred*, 249–261, 256.
544 Ricoeur, "Evil, a challenge to philosophy and theology", in *Figuring the Sacred*, 256–7.
545 Kant, *Critique of Practical Reason*, 132, n. 2, quoted by Ricoeur, "Freedom in the light of hope", in *Conflict*, 421.

decisive theory moves of Kant's: the distinction between "thinking" (*Denken*) and "knowing" (*Erkennen*) which is paralleled in how reason (*Vernunft*) differs from understanding (*Verstand*), and the connectedness of the three basic human pursuits linked to the three modalities can, must and may. He emphasizes that "hoping" does not belong to the sphere of "knowing", which pertains to empirically verifiable objects, but is characterized by terms such as "extension", "opening", or "disclosure" (*Eröffnung*).[546] It is not on the level of what can be proved when disputed. What can, however, be established in an analysis of the capability and the illusions of reason are its specific limits which show that it is not absolute:

> Such is the first step of a philosophy of hope: it consists in an act of renunciation by which pure speculative reason gives up its claim to fulfill the thought of the unconditioned along the line of the knowledge of empirical objects; this repudiation by reason of its absolute claim is the last word of theoretical reason.[547]

The critical self-analysis of pure reason on the one hand curtails the claim of knowledge to what can be established through the cooperation of understanding (*Verstand*) and sensibility (*Sinnlichkeit*); on the other, it leaves open the possibility to "think" beyond them, in the shape of postulates such as freedom, or a transcendent synthesis. It is not irrational to assume them to be possible. And it is the "interconnection between knowing, doing and hoping" that defines the human being, as Kant's *Opus Postumum* states. Regarding the status of hope, Ricoeur summarizes that "we cannot separate the third question raised... from the two others that precede it... Knowledge is what we can, doing is what we must, hoping is what we may, or are allowed to."[548]

At the same time, the content of this hope is tied closely to morality's demand for meaning. The beginning of the Dialectic of Kant's second *Critique*

---

546 Ricoeur, "Hope and the structure of philosophical systems", in *Figuring the Sacred*, 214: The "famous 'postulates of practical reason'... speak of an 'extension,' of an 'increasing,' of an 'opening'... They speak of God, of immortality, and of freedom only in a practical way, that is, as the existential implications of the structure of action, as the existential conditions for the actualization of freedom. They speak of the reality thanks to which freedom may exist. This reality can only be postulated... the modality of belief remains that of hypothesis and not that of evidence... the necessity of hope is not epistemological, but practical and existential... The God of the postulates is not an entity about which we could speculate; God is intended as the origin of a gift, the gift of this reconciliation... between the purity of heart and the need for happiness."
547 Ricoeur, "Hope and the structure of philosophical systems", in *Figuring the Sacred*, 212–213.
548 Ricoeur, "Hope and the structure of philosophical systems", in *Figuring the Sacred*, 211–212.

which was quoted before, that reason "demands the absolute totality of conditions for a given conditioned thing", has revealed itself to be unachievable. When "the absolute totality of conditions" is not at the disposition of any, not even the most intent human will, practical reason's orientation towards completion is frustrated. Kant does not hide the significance of this failure; it affects the meaning of ethics as a whole: it becomes "null and void".[549] By treating both the power and the limits of practical reason, the reality of life is taken seriously and allowed to challenge philosophical reflection. The validity of obligation can be shown, but the realization of morality is not only confronted with the lower limit when "inclination" gets in the way of a pure, not self-interested orientation towards respect for the moral law and for others in their equally original freedom; the crucial aporia that affects the meaning of ethics arises at the upper limit where the realization of the best moral intentions is stopped by contrary forces. Thus, the problem here is not one of inclination or a heteronomous will, but one that autonomy is confronted with in its prime:

> it is important to repeat, after Kant, that the "Dialectic" does not undo what the "Analytic" has constructed: it is only for an autonomous will that the career is opened for this new problematic of the highest good and of happiness.[550]

In view of the constitutive limits of the human ability to realize even the most ardent good intention, an alternative arises: the question is whether one reduces one's expectation to what humans can achieve on their own, or whether the idea of a God whose existence cannot be known, but only postulated,[551] allows to keep open the possibility for a support beyond human powers. This question belongs to autonomous morality:

> the first origin of the question, "What may I hope for?"... is situated again at the heart of moral philosophy, itself engendered by the question, "What should I do?" Moral philosophy engenders the philosophy of religion when the hope of fulfillment is added to the consciousness of obligation.[552]

This argumentation is not speculative, nor does it venture audacious extrapolations from accepted particular achievements, such as equality before the law, to

---

549 "If... the highest good is impossible according to practical rules, then the moral law which commands that it must be furthered must be fantastic, directed to empty imaginary ends and consequently inherently false." Kant, *Critique of Practical Reason*, trans. L. W. Beck, 118.
550 Ricoeur, *Oneself as Another*, 212, n. 18.
551 Ricoeur, "Hope and the structure of philosophical systems", in *Figuring the Sacred*, 214.
552 Ricoeur, "Freedom in the light of hope," in *Conflict*, 421.

the whole course of history;[553] it marks out clearly the foundations and para-meters of its claims and their place in the architecture of reason: "Dialectic in the Kantian sense is to my mind the part of Kantianism which not only survives the Hegelian critique but which triumphs over the whole of Hegelianism."[554] It accounts for alternatives, and choices to be made, such as the priority of practi-cal reason which allows us to decide the antinomy of pure reason between free-dom and natural determination in favour of freedom, based on moral conscience as a "fact" of self-experience.[555] This interest in human agency and in hope, de-scribed with Kierkegaard's designation for faith, as the "passion for the possi-ble",[556] is what turns Ricoeur back to Kant: "Hope is not a theme that comes after other themes, an idea that closes the system, but an impulse that opens the system, that breaks the closure of the system; it is a way of reopening what was unduly closed."[557]

3.4.2.4 Kant's treatment of evil in *Religion within the Limits of Reason Alone*
In his analysis of the structure of Hegel's philosophical system, Ricoeur notes a correspondence between its position regarding the completion of reason, its in-difference to suffering, and its sublation of evil into a negativity that is already dialectically contained. In contrast, in his treatise on religion Kant offers an an-thropological reflection on the human capacity to make others suffer, and on the problem of how the sources of goodness can be reopened.

> We have an important reason to think that a horizon of unfulfilled claim belongs to the most genuine experience of action. This reason relies on our experience of evil. All of us have some hint of this experience and the difference between evil and failure... there is something broken in the very heart of human action that prevents our partial experience of fulfilled achievements from being equated with the whole field of human action.

---

553 Ricoeur shares Hegel's interest in concrete realizations of freedom: "from that point of view [the whole process of history, thanks to which freedom becomes real] the history of contract and that of penal law and the kind of rationality at work in economic and political life are more significant for the actualization of freedom than any morals of mere intention, deprived of all impact on individual desires or on collective institutions... But,... (a)re they not... islands of rationality, surrounded by irrationality?" (Ricoeur, "Hope and the structure of philosophical systems", in *Figuring the Sacred*, 209–10).
554 Ricoeur, "Freedom in the light of hope", in *Conflict*, 413.
555 Ricoeur, "Freedom in the light of hope", in *Conflict*, 419: "Freedom is the true pivot of the doctrine of the postulates; the other two are in some sort its complement or explication".
556 Ricoeur, "Freedom in the light of hope", in *Conflict*, 407 and in "Hope and the structure of philosophical systems", in *Figuring the Sacred*, 206.
557 Ricoeur, "Hope and the structure of philosophical systems", in *Figuring the Sacred*, 211.

It is that breach, that brokenness, that is denied by the Hegelian claim to absolute knowledge and its bold extension from partial rationality to total rationality. For Hegel, the philosopher can speak only about negations that can be mediated, that is, overcome by a negation of a negation. Evil is only a case among nonmediated negations, and forgiveness of sins is merely a case of mediation in process...The blindness to the reality of evil and to the specificity of the experience of humankind concerning evil cannot be separated from that other blindness that we just denounced, the blindness to the experience of unfulfilled claim that is the counterpart of that of fulfilled achievements on which the Hegelian philosophy of action relies.[558]

If such a cushioning by reason of the adversity between humans and in their finite lives is ruled out as a solution, then the questions of agency and its regeneration return as a task for philosophy. In contrast to Rawls and Habermas who both assume the human capacity for action as unbroken and unproblematic, Ricoeur identifies the problem of how the agent's capability can be regained, after becoming culpable, as an inescapable question of individual hope. In Kant's treatise on religion he finds the attempt to "elaborate the condition of the possibility of this regeneration, without alienating freedom either to a magical conception of grace and salvation or to an authoritarian organization of the religious community".[559] The need for regeneration becomes evident once it is no longer a question of freedom at the theoretical level but of an "effective freedom, a freedom that *can*".[560] Since freedom "has from the beginning always chosen badly", not as a matter of necessity, but of fact, what needs to be restored is its "actual reality". Its renewal is "the very content of hope".[561] Religion can offer regeneration by a forgiveness which frees the wrongdoer from the legacy of the past and reopens actual agency to a new start: "What is at stake in the whole process of religion... is the effective liberation of the bound will."[562] It is necessary to distinguish between an analysis of freedom at the theoretical level of a philosophical anthropology, and of its actual capability to live up to its moral calling that is a matter for ethics. Ricoeur's insistence on "effective" freedom and its liberation shows an interest both in individuals and their subjective experience, and in the two levels of enquiry needed for an adequate analysis of freedom. It is instructive that the distinction between formal and concrete,

---

558 Ricoeur, "Hope and the structure of philosophical systems", in *Figuring the Sacred*, 211, with reference to the 6th chapter of Hegel's *Phenomenology of the Spirit*.
559 Ricoeur, "Hope and the structure of philosophical systems", in *Figuring the Sacred*, 215.
560 Ricoeur, "Freedom in the light of hope", in *Conflict*, 419.
561 Ricoeur, "Freedom in the light of hope", in *Conflict*, 422.
562 Ricoeur, "A philosophical hermeneutics of religion: Kant", in *Figuring the Sacred*, 75–92, 85.

actualized freedom is unparalleled in the reconstructions of Habermas and Rawls.[563]

3.4.2.5 Comparison of the three Kantian argumentations on the scope of reason

The enquiries above have revealed substantial differences in how the three social philosophers interpret and continue their Kantian heritage. While Habermas has also pointed out the debt owed by modern ethics to biblical monotheism, Ricoeur offers some striking insights into the difference the history of reception of biblical thinking has made in comparison with antique ethics.

> This closeness to a kerygmatic thought provokes, it seems to me, "effects of meaning," on the level of philosophical discourse itself, which often take the form of dislocation and recasting of systems. The theme of hope has precisely a *fissuring* power with regard to closed systems and a power of *reorganizing* meaning... I therefore see as converging toward the idea of a post-Hegelian Kantianism the spontaneous restructurings of our philosophical memory and those which proceed from the shock effect of the kerygma of hope on the philosophical problematic and on the structures of its discourse.[564]

Concretely, the biblical orientation towards the future in hope for the God who is coming against an emphasis in antique philosophies on what is given in the present, has encouraged historical "exchanges and permutations"[565] and introduced an outreach beyond the present order:

> ... the "He is coming" of Scripture must be opposed to the "It is" of the *Proem* of Parmenides. This dividing line is henceforth going to separate two conceptions of time and, through them, two conceptions of freedom. The Parmenidean "It is" in effect calls for an ethics of the eternal present... Stoicism is doubtless the most developed expression of this ethics of the present; the present, for Stoicism, is the unique time of salvation; the

---

563 On the need for an analysis of freedom both at the transcendental and the historical levels, cf. Th. Pröpper, *Erlösungsglaube und Freiheitsgeschichte*, 183–85. Ricoeur's discussion of Kant's concept of freedom and his endorsement of Kant's position that sin is only factual presupposes the distinction between formal and actualized, historical freedom that can only be made in a transcendental enquiry into the condition of the possibility of concrete realizations of freedom. Ricoeur has consistently referred to the need for maintaining both a transcendental and a historical level of analysis. I take the distinction introduced in *Oneself as Another* between *ipse* and *idem* as an indication of this approach in which the *ipse* stands for the transcendental level of freedom in its spontaneity, exemplified in its ability to promise, and the *idem* for the concrete, given and historically realized elements.
564 Ricoeur, "Freedom in the light of hope", in *Conflict*, 412–13.
565 Ricoeur, "Freedom in the light of hope", in *Conflict*, 413.

past and the future are equally discredited... hope is rejected for the same reason as fear, as a disturbance, an agitation... But hope is diametrically opposed, as passion for the possible, to this primacy of necessity. It is allied with the imagination insofar as the latter is the power of the possible and the disposition for being in a radical renewal. Freedom in the light of hope... is nothing else than this creative imagination of the possible.[566]

Modern self-conceptions and ethics have been shaped profoundly by the monotheistic understanding of history as the time given by God to fulfill the calling to be God's created image and partner in establishing an order of justice and compassion in which the fruits of creation are shared. This drive beyond a "consent without reservation to the order of the whole" as one strong motif in antique ethics[567] is also reflected in Kant's conception of morality as never totally completed; the fulfillment of its hope for meaning depends on a world which a good creator has intended to be accommodating and responsive to the best moral efforts. On the basis of Ricoeur's inclusion of the biblical heritage of both divine summons and promise as sources of origin and renewal for the cultures inspired by it, how do Rawls and Habermas compare on the four aspects of reason treated in this section?

Regarding the first aspect, reason's structural orientation towards completion, neither of their concepts of philosophy allows for this strong claim. Rawls's culturalist argumentation as manifest in *Political Liberalism* keeps its distance from any universalistic truth claim about reason as such. Habermas considers it necessary to climb down from philosophy's role as queen of the sciences and "usher" who allocates places, to the serving role of interpreter between the different discourses of individual sciences. The completion of reason is thus turned into a non-ending empirical task.

In view of this reticence, it is clear that the alternative between Kant and Hegel regarding the second aspect, the endpoint of reason, will only appear in a diminished version, too. Neither of the two twentieth century theorists backs the idea of a summit attained in absolute knowledge; but equally, the orientation for finite freedom offered by Kant in his demand for unconditional meaning no longer appears on the agenda of philosophical questioning. The problem of meaning is taken out of the remit of reason and is privatized; it will depend on citizens' biographical roots and the resources of their lifeworld whether it will continue to be a matter for reflection, or disappear. Habermas refers to reli-

---

566 Ricoeur, "Freedom in the light of hope", in *Conflict*, 407–08.
567 Ricoeur, "Freedom in the light of hope", in *Conflict*, 408. It is offset in a "continual contradiction" by "a detachment, an uprooting from passing things, a distancing and an exile in the eternal" (407–08).

gious resources regarding the question of suffering and of sensitivity to social pathologies of reason. An "awareness of what is missing" is what religions can represent as open questions in a culture's public sphere. But if their core is at the same time considered as inaccessible and "opaque" to communicative rationality, what does this imply for the concept of reason? Such questions remain outside of its tasks, and they are not seen as affecting the foundations of ethics.

If neither the American nor the German theorist defend the full-blown claim of the presence of realized reason in the Hegelian system, are there any signs of a historicist diminution after its collapse? Both Rawls's and Habermas's approaches are nowhere near an aestheticizing contemplation of the world's colourful array of cultures as an escape from the task to configure future-oriented action; yet the problem of sources for renewing motivation rarely appears, and if so, most often in response to questions from theologians. For Habermas, the lifeworld is capable of reproducing communicative reason, if it can be protected from colonization by system imperatives. Equally, Rawls's turn to the existing ethos of democratic societies in *Political Liberalism* can be seen as softly Hegelian; but it seems unaware of the crisis symptom of the historicist response once only the backward gaze towards already accomplished works remains of the Hegelian dialectic-driven élan of realizing reason by working through negativity.

Regarding the third aspect, Kant's incisive account of the defeat of motivation in the experience of the antinomy of practical reason is analysed as too demanding by Rawls. His solution is a measured trust in incremental progress; the main goal remains stability in a society oriented towards just structures, in view of competing claims and interests. Happiness is a question for private life, and negative freedoms need to be protected to enable its pursuit.

While the analysis of the antinomy of practical reason already belongs to philosophy of religion (itself seen as theological) for Habermas, thus downplaying its virulence for ethics, he keeps the discrepancy between is and ought alive in the early distinction of a factual from a true consensus. His recent critique of the naturalistic reduction of reason to determinism[568] shows his awareness of cultural factors, such as scientism, that threaten the self-understanding of citizens as authors responsible for the moral conduct of their lives.

Due to the lack of a theory of self in both social philosophers, motivated in the case of Habermas by his dismissal of philosophies of consciousness, there is

---

568 Naturalism presents itself as the "legitimate successor of the old utopias" in Th. Assheuer's critique, "Ich war es nicht!" in DIE ZEIT, No. 42, October 11, 2007, 57, quoted by Th. Pröpper, *Theologische Anthropologie*, vol. II, 840.

no systematic reflection on the place of evil in selfhood: neither as equally elementary as goodness, nor as only a "penchant" and thus subordinated to the
original orientation towards the good will. In conclusion, Ricoeur is the only author to take evil, finitude, and unintended consequences as challenges to the
quest for meaning and happiness seriously, leading him to identify in the
hoped-for synthesis the philosophical equivalent of the religious category of
the gift: the

> postulate of the existence of God manifests existential freedom as the philosophical equiv-
> alent of the gift. Kant has no place for a concept of gift, which is a category of the Sacred.
> But he has a concept for the origin of a synthesis which is not in our power. God is "the
> adequate cause of this effect which is manifested to our will as its entire object, namely,
> the highest good."[569]

With Ricoeur's exploration of limit questions of ethics in the framework of a
theory of self, religion has been established not only as a conversation partner
on a par with other symbolic resources within a culture; in view of the profound
effects of biblical monotheism on the making of Western concepts of self and
other, community and humanity, individual agency and history, the encounters
and interactions themselves become a matter of analysis in their particularity,
including epoch-making translations. My final section will treat Ricoeur's discussion of exemplary cases in the history of translation and reception of biblical
texts and impulses.

3.4.3 Translations, particularity and plurality of religious traditions

Before investigating epoch-making translations and the terminological decisions
that had to be made in the history of reception of the Hebrew Bible and the New
Testament (3), the possibility of translations has to be clarified first (1); also, the
particularity of a religious or cultural formation which translation aims to do justice to, needs to be explained in relation to other recent attempts at interreligious
exchanges, such as the project of a global ethic (2). One of the resources of the

---

569 Ricoeur, "Freedom in the light of hope", in *Conflict*, 421, quoting from Kant, *Critique of
Practical Reason*, trans. L. W. Beck, 132, n. 2. In "Hope and the structure of philosophical
systems", in *Figuring the Sacred*, 213–14, he summarizes: "Kant teaches us that the reconciliation between purity of motives and the requirement of happiness is not at our disposal, as
something that we could acquire and possess. This connection – this *Zusammenhang* – must
remain a transcendent synthesis between the work of humankind and the fulfillment of the
desire that constitutes human existence."

particularity emphasized by Ricoeur is the plurality of interpretations emerging from the "movement of reinterpretation begun by these texts from the heart of their own culture"[570]; they show the fecundity of a tradition and enrich theology as the second order reflection on the primary symbols and foundational narratives of a historical religion (4).

3.4.3.1 The possibility of intercultural understanding

Before discussing translations as concrete engagements with and investments into other cultures, some brief remarks on the condition of their possibility should help clarify Ricoeur's specific angle in comparison with Rawls and Habermas. To an interpreter of texts, distinguishing between different eras, authors, genres, and perspectives is a matter of subtle judgement; exploring continuities and shared horizons is as central for understanding as is identifying epoch- and culture-specific boundaries. The French philosopher's inclusion of different avenues and disciplines as well as otherwise oppositional approaches also shows his interest in uncovering a multiplicity of viewpoints before attempting to mediate their truth claims at a higher level of theory into an enriched and more complex account. This methodologically reflected style of enquiry steers a middle course between a simply culturalist track that renounces the task of investigating any features of shared reason, and a theory that stays at the level of rationality, language or culture in the singular. The first direction can be seen in Rawls's assumption that philosophy just like worldviews disassembles into an array of comprehensive doctrines that do not communicate with each other; the second in the foundation of Habermas's discourse ethics on the presuppositions of argumentation at the level of a universal pragmatics. Ricoeur's hermeneutics arises from the basis of a phenomenological anthropology; dealing with the plural historical manifestations of language, it asks and answers the question of how cross-cultural comparisons are possible.

Discussing whether Max Weber's concept of "ideal types" claims an "at least transhistorical, if not ahistorical" validity for the types of domination (*Herrschaft*) across cultures, such as "pre-Columbian, Asiatic, or other societies", Ricoeur argues for the possibility of understanding in terms of "analogy". His "provisional reply" is:

> For a perspective that would remain historicist, it would be simply impossible to speak of a different organization than our own if we could not identify it on the basis of analogical

---

570 Ricoeur, "From the moral to the ethical", in *Reflections on the Just*, 54.

concepts, capable of making sense in our linguistic universe of what explains itself to itself in terms of another cultural field.[571]

There is thus, an underlying assumption of the unity of human nature that justifies such analogy. A similar turn is taken in relation to "the religious", of going back to a unity behind the differences of their original core intuitions and the plurality of perspectives between and within religious confessions. In a posthumously edited book, the name given to this unity is capitalized: "the "Essential". The

> religious is like a fundamental language that exists only in natural, historically limited languages. Just as everyone is born into a language and accedes to other languages only by a second apprenticeship, and most often, only through translation, the religious exists culturally only as articulated in the language and code of a historical religion; language and code articulate only on the condition of filtering, and in this sense limiting the amplitude, that depth, that density of the religious that I am here calling the Essential.[572]

The following subsection will focus on particularity as the concrete appearance of the universal: "I have said it often enough, I do not scorn what I call, to put it quickly, 'codes.'" Yet, as this text written around 1996 makes clear, these "codes" are not the endpoint; one needs to go behind or beyond them to what they testify to, what Ricoeur calls "the mobilization of the deepest resources of life in the coming to light of the Essential, fracturing the limitations of the confessionally religious."[573]

3.4.3.2 The goal of translation between a search for equivalents and engagement with particularity

The task of translating between different languages and cultures is outlined in dimensions that encompass more than the linguistic search for nearest equivalents; they include problems of social and political ethics. Having marked these cornerstones, I shall discuss the contrast that emerges between the herme-

---

571 Ricoeur, "The fundamental categories", in *Reflections on the Just*, 141. A similar question about the transhistorical status of Charles Taylor's assumption of "inescapable frameworks" and his concept of "strong evaluations" is put in "The fundamental and the historical: Notes on Charles Taylor's *Sources of the Self*", in *Reflections on the Just*, 168–184.
572 Ricoeur, *Living Up to Death*, trans. D. Pellauer (Chicago: University of Chicago Press, 2009), 15.
573 Ricoeur, *Living Up to Death*, 14–15.

neutical philosopher's interest in difference, and Hans Küng's theological project of a "global ethic" that identifies shared values among the world religions.

In her lucid analysis of the depth dimensions of intercultural exchange that translation leads into, Margit Eckholt outlines the "triad of translation, exchange of cultural memory and reconciliation as a model of intercultural hermeneutics".[574] The lexical and grammatical tasks are accompanied by historical memories of previous encounters. For a successful series of responses one could think of the fruitful literary and artistic, philosophical and theological interchanges in the history of European culture; for memories that pose the difficult task of reconciliation, it is a history of annexations and subjugations that forms a backdrop which reveals translations not as a merely technical matter, but as a cause of renewed and sustained engagement after prior enmity. Eckholt points to the "histories of foundation of cultures with their burden of betrayed hopes" which call for a "creative, plural re-reading."[575]

Thus, an ethical quality can be found in language at a different level than Habermas's enlisting of presuppositions of argumentation for discourse ethics. It is operative in what Ricoeur calls the "hospitality" of language, aimed at dialogue, not first of all discourse, and its changing and innovating character as the site of historical mediations, exchanges, and new syntheses; some of these will be examined in the following subsection. This "hospitality" presupposes a shared human nature and the possibility of empathy with another person's perspective.[576] In view of the effort of surfacing multiple angles and narratives of historical encounters between linguistically and culturally diverse communities,

---

574 Eckholt, "Übersetzung – Erinnerung – Versöhnung. Frauen in Europa auf der Suche nach Gestalten einer verbindenden Spiritualität", in P. Hünermann/J. Juhant/B. Zalec (eds.), *Dialogue and Virtue. Ways to Overcome Clashes of Our Civilization* (Münster/Berlin: LIT Verlag, 2007), 57–68, 60.
575 Eckholt, "Übersetzung – Erinnerung – Versöhnung", in *Dialogue and Virtue*, 60–61.
576 Ricoeur, "Universal civilization", in *History and Truth*, 282: "yet the strangeness of man to man is never total... one has to raise it (this feeling) to a wager and a voluntary affirmation of man's oneness... There is no reason or probability that a linguistic system is untranslatable. The belief that the translation is feasible up to a certain point is the affirmation that the foreigner is a man, the belief, in short, that communication is possible. What we have just said about language – signs – is also valid for values and the basic images and symbols which make up the cultural resources of a nation. Yes, I believe it is possible to understand those different from me by means of sympathy and imagination, just as I understand a character in a novel or at the theatre or a real friend who is different from me... To be a man is to be capable of this projection into another center of perspective."
Regarding the term "hospitality", David Pellauer points out that it is "echoing Kant's requirement of hospitality in his essay on perpetual peace." Pellauer, *Guide for the Perplexed*, 143, n. 12.

and the position articulated already in 1961 regarding the distinctive cores of cultures, it is not surprising that Ricoeur takes the side of religions in their difference. In a 1996 television discussion on religions, violence and peace,[577] Hans Küng explains his global ethic project that led to the "Declaration of the Parliament of the World's Religions" in 1989. Predating the events of September 11, 2001, it demonstrates how efforts at reaching agreement across distinct and often oppositional understandings of the divine can bear fruit; a facile identification of religion with the will to defend strong truth claims with, if need be, violent means, does not capture the reality of different religions' interest in each other and their exchanges on their distinctive avenues towards God. The fact that a joint Declaration was possible as the outcome of intricate discussions already puts into question the view that religions are mainly a cause of division and will only ever compete with each other. The disagreement between the two experts on intercultural exchange does not relate to the possibility of dialogue, but to the question of whether the declaration of a global ethic shared by religions is the most promising path out of histories of violence. Küng's argumentation proceeds from the theses, "no new global order without a new global ethic", and, "no peace without peace between the religions". This peace is built on their internal resources, which, as Küng shows in four "irrevocable directives", overlap or can be mutually understood. They can be retraced to "four broad ancient guidelines…, (1) a commitment to a culture of non-violence and respect for life, (2) to a culture of solidarity and a just economic order, (3) to a culture of tolerance and life of truthfulness, (4) to a culture of equal rights and partnership between men and women."[578]

Küng's proposal for the process of agreeing on a manifesto of world religions is to set aside doctrinal differences, and to identify shared practical orientations at the level of virtues. An alternative process to searching for common ethical or moral convictions is to indicate the path of each historical religion towards their own source of depth. Ricoeur's questions to Küng suggest a way that keeps their diversity alive and visible, and draws on the well of their particularity which is not moral but religious. To him, what should be of interest is not a shared expres-

---

577 "Les religions, la violence et la paix". Entretien Hans Küng – Paul Ricoeur autour du "Manifeste pour une éthique planétaire" (Ed. du Cerf), ARTE, April 5, 1996, Redaction: Laurent Andres, cf. www.fondsricoeur.fr, under "texts on line" (last accessed October 27, 2013). All quotes in this section that do not have a book reference are taken and translated from pp. 2–9 of the transcribed text of this television debate which has also been published in *Sens. Revue de l'Amitié judéo-chrétienne de France* 5 (1998) 211–230.
578 Cf. H. Küng/K.-J. Kuschel (eds.), *A Global Ethic. The Declaration of the Parliament of the World's Religions* (New York: Continuum, 1993), 24–34.

sion in ethical values, but the distinctive paths of arriving at this ethic from a *"fond"* of convictions which is more than ethical. The same metaphor as in the task of translation is used, presupposing and honouring the difference between home and temporary guest position, host and visitor: The goal should be an "ecumenism as a hospitality of convictions" that does not make the difference between vernacular and foreign language, or that of one's own and another religious tradition, disappear but explores it for mutual enrichment. Indicative of his dialectical thinking is his plea to keep productive tensions in play, rather than produce a superficial agreement. For the interpreter and translator of texts, it is important to understand from the core of each faith the dogmatic differences that Küng wants to leave behind in a practical consensus. Küng's position that "how we live together does not depend on our conception of mystery" is countered with a critique of its rationalism and distance from the roots of its own motivation. To translate the different intuitions of the divine into terms such as "fundamental" or "ultimate reality" is an "abstract... rationalistic" move for Ricoeur. Taking the side of the "foundational religious energy" over a "poor, uprooted morality", he argues, effectively with Kant, that "ethical principles do not need a religious foundation", whereas "religions can go back into the depth of their traditions, to the unsaid". The source of their vitality is not originally expressed in a verbal manifesto, but addressed in a "prayer of thanks". The task is to find out what it is in a religion that leads to "respecting life, the word, social justice" which can then be conceptualized in ethical values. Going back to the *"fond* of convictions" which can never be completely articulated, it is possible to discover parallels, as between compassion in Buddhism and in other religions, or a message that reinforces an element of one's own, as does Buddhist "detachment" with the "insouciance" of the Sermon of the Mount. As already intimated 35 years earlier in his reflection on national cultures and global civilization, "harmony" or agreement between singular entities is not something that can be constructed but that emerges at a foundational level:

> I think that among all creations, there is a kind of harmony in the absence of all agreement... When one has penetrated to the depths of singularity, one feels that it is harmonious with every other in a way that cannot be put into words.[579]

The work of ecumenical dialogue is the opposite of merging the expressions of different faiths. This is not what the global ethic intends, nor what it would lead to, since it is about agreements at the ethical level; yet, Ricoeur's early arguments against syncretism are helpful as a backdrop to the counterposition he

---

579 Ricoeur, "Universal civilization", in *History and Truth*, 283.

takes in this television exchange. It is about being true to one's own roots and to be open to encounters from that position: "Then the question of fidelity is raised: what happens to my values when I understand those of other nations? Understanding is a dangerous venture in which all cultural heritages risk being swallowed up in a vague syncretism".[580] His "frail and provisional reply" in 1961 was:

> only a living culture at once faithful to its origins and ready for creativity on the levels of art, literature, philosophy and spirituality, is capable of sustaining the encounter of other cultures – not merely capable of sustaining but also of giving meaning to that encounter. When the meeting is a confrontation of creative impulses, then it is itself creative.[581]

The way to create, sustain and renew motivation is not to be found in an overlapping section of values between religions, but in a process of reaching understanding from one's own resources:

> I am convinced that a progressive Islamic or Hindu world in which old ways of thinking would inspire a new history, would have with our European culture and civilization that specific affinity that all creative men share. I think that scepticism ends here. For the European, in particular, the problem is not to share in a sort of vague belief which would be acceptable to everyone; his task is expressed by Heidegger: "We have to go back to our own origins," that is, we have to go back to our Greek, Hebrew and Christian origins so as to be worthy participants in the great debate of cultures. In order to confront a self other than one's own self, one must first have a self. [582]

Only between different partners who are ready to risk exposing their specific perspectives, is "authentic dialogue" possible:

> Hence, nothing is further from the solution to our problem than some vague and inconsistent syncretism. At bottom, syncretisms are always residual phenomena; they do not involve anything creative; they are mere historical formations. Syncretisms must be opposed by communication, that is, a dramatic relation in which I affirm myself in my origins and

---

580 Ricoeur, "Universal civilization", in *History and Truth*, 282.

581 Ricoeur, "Universal civilization", in *History and Truth*, 283.

582 Ricoeur, "Universal civilization", in *History and Truth*, 283. Regarding Heidegger's position, in "From interpretation to translation", in A. LaCoque/Ricoeur, *Thinking Biblically. Exegetical and Hermeneutical Studies,* trans. D. Pellauer (Chicago: University of Chicago Press, 1998), 331–361, 357, Ricoeur points out the "marginalization of our Judeo-Christian heritage, which is referred back to its Near Eastern place of origin and divested of any universalizing intention its marriage with Hellenism might have conferred on Hebraic thought or on newly born Christianity." What Ricoeur identifies as an "expulsion of Judaism and Christianity from the sphere of Western culture" stands in marked difference to Habermas's appreciation of the presence of this heritage, even in the second stage of his thinking, on the historical links between communicative reason and biblical monotheism.

give myself to another's imagination in accordance with his different civilization. Human truth lies only in this process in which civilizations confront each other more and more with what is most living and creative in them... this encounter has not yet taken place at the level of an authentic dialogue.[583]

Ricoeur's insistence on the core of each religious formation as its irreplaceable source of renewal also gives a different explanation to violence motivated by religious difference. For him, the problem does not originate with the truth claim, for example, of monotheism,[584] but exactly in what makes the *"fond* of conviction" unrivalled by other doctrines: when the "force of norms" comes from "being affirmed (*approbation*) by a religious conviction", it means that this "anteriority" and "superiority of the Word" consists in the fact "that I have not posed this rule myself, but that it has been entrusted to me". When Küng points out that religions have inspired and legitimated wars, Ricoeur goes to the source of this violence which is not simply the general human penchant for evil, as discussed by Kant: it is "from the *fond* itself of a strong conviction" that the threat of violence arises. Yet, it also carries the source of its own remedy, a self-critique motivated by "its attachment to a word that surpasses and precedes it". The task therefore, is to look for such an internal standard in each religion itself, and to accept being called to the "self-purification" of "discovering "truth that is not as much expressed in my language" or faith since each confessional identity only offers a limited perspective.

Ricoeur's differentiated attention to religious outlooks in their particularity offers a way beyond both the religious and the historicist danger, namely the "dogmatism of a single truth", and "scepticism".[585] The great translations, such as the Septuagint, and the ensuing theological reflections, as well as influential recastings of biblical narratives into dogmatic concepts such as original sin, are analysed as points of new cultural departures and reception histories that have marked subsequent self-understandings.

---

583 Ricoeur, "Universal civilization", in *History and Truth*, 283.
584 Cf. the thesis put forward by J. Assmann in *Moses the Egyptian. The Memory of Egypt in Western Monotheism* (Boston: Harvard University Press, 1998) and its revisions since then, for example, in *The Price of Monotheism* (Stanford: Stanford University Press, 2010) after its debate by biblical and theological scholars, such as in P. Walter (ed.), *Das Gewaltpotential des Monotheismus und der dreieine Gott* (Freiburg: Herder, 2004).
585 Ricoeur, "Universal civilization", in *History and Truth*, 283.

3.4.3.3 Epoch-making translations of biblical texts

The "alterity" present in the foundations of European culture[586] with its two contributory streams of the thinking and ethics arising from Jewish and Christian monotheism and from Greek philosophy is studied in an exemplary case of the Septuagint translation of Exodus 3:14: the revelation of God's name to Moses at the burning bush. The final version of Ricoeur's repeated treatment of this narrative and its history of reception offers a differentiated discussion of philosophy of religion and historical revelation, concretized in the positions developed by Anselm and by Thomas Aquinas.[587] The encounter of the biblical experience of God as creator and liberator with the ontological thinking of the Greeks presents the intercultural challenge of finding a fitting translation especially of the Hebrew verb *'ehyeh*, the self-naming of God at the request of Moses, translated inadequately with the Greek verb *einai* as "I am who I am." Ricoeur refers to the translation offered by the exegete Hartmut Gese as the "most convincing...: *ich erweise mich als der ich mich erweisen werde*"[588] (I disclose myself as the one as whom I shall disclose myself). The lack of complete congruence and the discrepancy between terms filled with their own history of connotations and resonance in each culture is turned into an occasion of pushing boundaries and enlarging horizons of meaning:

> Why not formulate the hypothesis that the Hebraic verb *'ehyeh* proposes a "gap in meaning" that enriches the already broad, albeit culturally limited, polysemy of the Greek verb *einai*, which was all that was available during the period of the LXX for translating Exodus 3:14? Being, Aristotle says, is said in many ways. Why not say that the Hebrews thought being in a new way?[589]

Having thus moved onto ontological territory with the use of the Greek verb *einai* and the Latin *esse*, a history of effects begins in which philosophical and theological thinkers probe each others' limits. Despite his misgivings about "theological speculation" against which he sees the biblical testimony as in need of defense, Ricoeur now offers a subtle argumentation in favour of a faith seeking

---

586 Eckholt, *Dogmatik interkulturell*, 77.
587 For an in depth treatment of how Ricoeur's position changes from an ontotheological reading of Aquinas to defending him against this charge, in the context of exploring the fruitfulness of Aquinas's concept of analogy for Ricoeur's intercultural hermeneutics, cf. Amy Daughton, *Toward an Intercultural Hermeneutic in a Global World*. PhD thesis Trinity College Dublin, 2011.
588 Ricoeur, "From Interpretation", in *Thinking Biblically*, 361, n. 48, translated as "I shall show myself in that I shall show myself, as the one who will show himself."
589 Ricoeur, "From Interpretation", in *Thinking Biblically*, 360.

understanding. In view of Emmanuel Levinas's and Jean-Luc Marion's critiques of linking God with ontology, he notes: "This attempt to think God apart from being poses a problem for theologians concerned to preserve a link with philosophy."[590] While he is equally intent to safeguard the distinctive biblical "logic of the gift" from being levelled into what reason could produce by its own means, he also wants to avoid the opposite danger of an "irrational" or fideist privileging of religious truth over a philosophically defensible general consciousness of truth:

> The logic of superabundance of love... certainly appeals to a logic of paradox, to a rhetoric of hyperbole. But it still needs to be shown that neither this logic nor this rhetoric contribute to reinforcing the current vogue for irrationalism. In short, it still needs to be shown that thinking in terms of love does not demand a new *sacrificium intellectus*, but rather another reason... Without this pact (with Western reason), declaring themselves totally foreign to Greek thought, identified globally with the metaphysics of being, do Jewish and Christian thought not "disenculture" themselves and consent to their marginalization?[591]

His perceptive interpretation of Thomas Aquinas concludes that "convergence without fusion between the biblical verse and the ontologism inherited from the Greeks"[592] is the result of an argumentation that counters Anselm's attempt to demonstrate existence as a necessary predicate of God.[593] "Fusion" in this case indicates an illegitimate levelling of the distinction between thought and history, by turning an insight that could only be gained through the religious experience of God's self-revelation in history into a necessary conclusion of reason:

> (P)rogress in the affirmation of the intelligibility of Being tended to render superfluous the self-affirmation of the Being of God according to Exodus 3:14. Recourse to this verse tended to become an extrinsic confirmation, once *doctrina sacra* was raised to the rank of a science and once the divorce was consummated between theological speculation, governed by the *quaestio* and its logical order, and the hermeneutic interpretation of the biblical text, governed by its *lectio* and the order that the text imposes.[594]

---

590 Ricoeur, "From Interpretation", in *Thinking Biblically*, 358.
591 Ricoeur, "From Interpretation", in *Thinking Biblically*, 359.
592 Ricoeur, "From Interpretation", in *Thinking Biblically*, 352.
593 Ricoeur, "From Interpretation", in *Thinking Biblically*, 348: "It goes without saying that such an argument renders superfluous any recourse to the self-designation of God according to Exodus 3:14. And, in fact, the great scholastic thinkers indicated a great distrust of this short way".
594 Ricoeur, "From Interpretation", in *Thinking Biblically*, 348.

Despite this negative qualification as "theological speculation" of what systematic theology offers as the reconstruction of the implications and anthropological
presuppositions of God's self-revelation, his final judgement on the Scholastic
efforts is that of a "deep kinship" between reading the biblical text, and analyzing the conceptual tasks it posed. Even

> the most independent theological speculation... continued to be intimately bound to this
> interpretation as regards its inquiry into the concept of Being, as though the question
> *quid est?* (what is God?) were still driven by the question *qui est?* (who is God?)... In this
> sense, the Christianization of Hellenism is secretly more powerful than the Hellenization
> of Christianity.[595]

Thus, a history of effects was put into motion by the challenging task faced by
the translators of the Septuagint of what Wilhelm von Humboldt described as
"'raising the distinctive spirit of... (one's) own language to the level of that of
the foreign language'".[596] It created a new synthesis with the tension between
the two origins maintained, rather than collapsed to one side. His defense of
Thomas against Heidegger's critique, that "genuine Thomist ontology does not
correspond to the defaming criterion of ontotheology",[597] makes a case for the
new ground opened up by the classical antique translations; they made the ven-
tures of thought and self-understanding possible which came to shape the intellectual as well as the institutional history of Europe.

A different case of an innovative use of biblical motifs is Augustine's concept
of original sin. Ricoeur's astute critique of this late antique move beyond the biblical texts in the context of the fight against Manicheism is well-known and has
had great influence especially in Continental systematic theology. With the concept of a hereditary original sin Augustine goes far beyond the Pauline understanding of sin. His move from biblical images like "captivity" and "Fall" to "hereditary sin" which "tries to be a concept"[598] had a profound and extensive
history of effects in Western religious self-understanding. Ricoeur does not use
the term "speculative theology" here, but it would be apposite in view of its departure both from biblical narratives and from the Pauline theological reflection
that, in effect, nobody is without sin (Rom 5:12). The categories that come to replace those of the New Testament are, in Ricoeur's analysis, a combination of
"quasi-juridical" and "quasi-biological" thinking: As the theory of a hereditary

---

595 Ricoeur, "From Interpretation", in *Thinking Biblically*, 348.
596 Ricoeur quotes W. v. Humboldt in "Reflections on a new ethos for Europe" in R. Kearney
(ed.), *Paul Ricoeur: The Hermeneutics of Action*, 5.
597 Ricoeur, "From Interpretation", in *Thinking Biblically*, 356.
598 Ricoeur, "'Original sin': a study in meaning", in *Conflict*, 269–286, 269.

sin that one has not committed and that still is one's own, it is "false knowledge" that "compresses in an inconsistent notion a juridical category of debt and a biological category of inheritance".[599] The reason for Ricoeur's insistence on the need to distinguish "radical evil from the intolerable idea of original sin"[600] is Kantian. Sharing this critique, Thomas Pröpper enquires from a systematic theological perspective about the "decisive point that went beyond everything before: a guilt before God from birth onwards, passed on by conception... Can there be guilt before God *without* free action – *before* all free action? Do we have the right, and which right, to insist on a personal, that is non-transferable, attribution of guilt?"[601]

3.4.3.4 Plurality of interpretations in foundational scriptures and histories of effect

For a theology with an interest in the thought forms in which the biblical message of salvation was articulated in the contexts of their eras, Ricoeur's critical perspective on innovations that are so steeped in the controversies of their time that they leave the biblical texts behind is helpful.[602] His hermeneutical awareness of a plurality of readings already in the biblical texts themselves is liberating in view of the task of cultural and religious traditions to remember and creatively continue their histories of foundation: "The problem is not simply to repeat the past but rather to take root in it in order to ceaselessly invent."[603] There are productive tensions and responses in the New Testament's accounts and reflections on the person and work of Jesus Christ and the understanding of the reign of God he proclaimed and practiced. Thus, the fecundity of a tradition appears in the plurality of interpretations already in its own foundational texts even before their translation into new cultural horizons. Examples for this richness and the possibilities of correction can be found in the different New Testament interpretations of Jesus' death and their conceptions of atonement. This diversity in the sources, for example, between Paul, the Synoptics, and Hebrews offers different motifs to the histories of reception. In view of the

---

599 Ricoeur, "'Original sin': a study in meaning", in *Conflict*, 269–286, 270, quoted in Th. Pröpper, *Theologische Anthropologie*, vol. II, 982.
600 Ricoeur, "From the moral to the ethical", in *Reflections on the Just*, 51.
601 Pröpper, *Theologische Anthropologie*, vol. II, 982.
602 Ricoeur, "'Original sin': a study in meaning", in *Conflict*, 271: "Although clearly anti-Gnostic, the theology of evil let itself become engaged on the very ground of Gnosticism and hence elaborated a similar conceptual structure."
603 Ricoeur, "Universal civilization", in *History and Truth*, 282.

accumulated systematic weight of the history of theological thinking, historical critical approaches to the Bible have been a source of renewal for soteriology. Another example, relevant for the relationship between faith and action in Christian life, is the letter of St. James as a New Testament corrective to the Pauline emphasis on the role of faith alone. The continuing vitality of a tradition depends on being able to return to sources that are not univocal but themselves present different outlooks on the meaning of the events they testify to. It makes the role of Scripture as *norma normans* over the ecclesial reception history as *norma normans normata* more complex and more difficult to ascertain; but as a hermeneutical insight it makes it clear that the events at the basis of the biblical testimonies, while being accessible with degrees of objectivity through external sources, cannot be isolated as pure facts; they are mediated through a self-interpreting tradition with its internal elucidations and corrections.[604]

As the only hermeneutical philosopher among the three authors treated, Ricoeur has sharpened the awareness of biblical and theological scholars on the processes of interpretation involved in the task of judging the development of a religious tradition against its foundational Scriptures. As the only one of the three who has studied antique literary, philosophical and religious sources in depth, he has also provided enlightening and fruitful comparisons; his analysis and classification of symbolizations of evil has provided a productive and influential backdrop to conceptions of human flourishing and of salvation as well as a reconstruction of the original experience of freedom as the power to act towards good or evil. He has thus uncovered the foundations of ethics as the capacity for moral reflection and elaborated in detail the resources that have contributed to producing guiding concepts of Western self-understanding; it is a heritage that is open to the thought of an "economy of superabundance", as the biblical promise is summed up, which, in his view, is still needed to direct and correct present visions of living together. The dimension of reason it speaks to is not first of all the cognitive and verbal one of an overlapping consensus, nor a practical discourse on norms of action, but the faculty of productive imagination that responds to images of liberation and visions of an unfailed life.

---

604 Cf. Th. Pröpper, "Exkurs 1: Zur theologischen Relevanz und Begründung der Frage nach dem 'historischen Jesus'", in *Erlösungsglaube und Freiheitsgeschichte*, 226–230.

4 Conclusion of the comparison of the three positions

The three social philosophers investigated in this study have been relevant for the development of Christian Ethics since the 1970s: one as the author of an influential approach to justice, the other two also as dialogue partners with biblical exegetes and theologians. I shall sum up their differences in their understandings of reason (1) and of religion (2), and draw conclusions from their comparison on the role ensuing for religion in relation to public reason.

As has become clear in the investigation of each approach, the contours of "public reason" depend on which general concept of reason has been espoused: What makes it "general", accessible, neutral, or communicative? Is it differentiated into distinct dimensions, and if so, what is their relationship? What is its scope? Is it universal, or culture-bound? Does it have a history? What is its "other"? Is it, for instance, distinguished from natural chance, from metaphysics, from cultural conventions, from comprehensive doctrines, or from religion in its opacity? The content and scope, ambition and inclusiveness of reason will determine how religion is conceived of.

4.1 Reason in its three dimensions

Since all three thinkers see themselves as at least partly continuing the heritage of Kant, I shall use the dimensions of reason he distinguished as pure (1), as practical (2), and as the faculty of judgement (3) as points of comparison.

4.1.1 Theoretical reason

Rawls's move in *Political Liberalism* to the convictions embedded in democratic cultures and to citizens' and theorists' comprehensive doctrines implies a position regarding the possibility of pure reason: it only exists in cultural formations and in the division into philosophical schools, with no power of analysis, communication or evaluation across different schools. With this turn to completely embedded forms of reason, the history of mutually aware, critically responsive and innovative sequences of philosophical approaches risks being left behind. Contemporary controversies fall into predictable schools of thought, each of them counting as a comprehensive doctrine. At the same time, they are credited with the ability to supply a translator into the language of public reason, which presupposes some ability to go beyond their tradition of origin. There are also areas of common ground to be found in the contingent spaces of overlapping consensus, even if the reasoning itself is not shared. Yet pure theoretical reason is divested of its culture-transcending and mediating claim; the ability for translation that would have to rest on some universalistic premise is implied but not accounted for.

Habermas's early attempt to found a critical social theory takes its starting point in an epistemological analysis that is anchored in a naturalizing philosophy of history of the human species directed towards emancipation. Reason exists at a universal, culture-transcendent level in three anthropologically based epistemological interests: an *empirical-analytical* capacity which finds expression in the subject-object relationship of labour and displays an instrumental form of reason; *interactive* reason that realizes the intersubjective constitution of humans in symbolic interaction and exemplifies the hermeneutic, interpretive capability of reason; thirdly, the interest in *emancipation* elaborated by critical individual sciences such as psychoanalysis and a corresponding sociology that uncovers social pathologies.[605] Reason's power of self-critique, implied in Kant's critiques of reason by reason, is endorsed, although it is linked to the natural history of the human species. As Dirk Jörke points out, after *Knowledge and Human Interests*, Habermas takes a different path to found his theory of communicative reason, closer to Kant's *Critique of Practical Reason*; yet he still anchors the deontological dimension in the natural human endowment with language. Philosophy as the discipline that carried out the organizing and place-allocating role of theoretical reason is given a more modest position; critically dismantling its "metaphysical" heritage that is seen as incompatible with modernity, it realizes itself instead in the different individual sciences for which it can only supply the functions of placeholder for universalist questions, and of interpreter. The changed role of philosophy in a world investigated by the sciences is reflected in its task of translator between these academic enquiries and the lifeworld, but it keeps its universalistic orientation within the sciences and the humanities.

For Ricoeur, at the historical level where pure reason is encountered concretely, it appears in the categories of its symbolic world. But it displays an independent reflective capacity that operates in a dialectical search for truth at a level which mediates contrasting positions. Not content, as Rawls is, to leave doctrines side by side without further effort of analysis and identification of both opposite and shared elements, he clearly endorses the critical power of the-

---

605 Cf. D. Jörke, "Kommunikative Anthropologie", in Brunkhorst *et al.* (eds.), *Habermas-Handbuch*, 331–32.

oretical reason. Its self-reflective capacity, emphasized also by Habermas, is linked by Ricoeur to a concept of self. Unlike Habermas who retraces the I to the pole of intersubjectivity, thus undermining its own original reflexivity, Ricoeur, as David Pellauer summarizes, "will always argue for a more interactive theory, one where neither the ego nor the other takes precedence but also where there is something singular about the self that is not reducible to intersubjective relations".[606]

By combining a phenomenological enquiry into the self's intentionality with a hermeneutic of the cultural symbols in which it expresses itself, Ricoeur draws on two approaches in the philosophy of subjectivity which Rawls does not consider and which Habermas dismisses as the superseded paradigm of consciousness; for the discourse ethicist, it is to be replaced by the prior intersubjective mediation provided by language. Both Rawls and Habermas fail to explore the question of the author or the self behind the acts and their reflection. Ricoeur's ongoing inclusion of this issue into the agenda of philosophy does not imply the thesis that the self is transparent to itself, nor that the *Cogito* supplies a foundation at the level of the concrete self. He just makes the case that if the critically reflective power of reason is claimed, then it has to be anchored in the capabilities of the self which need to be accounted for, rather than reduced to the other pole, intersubjectivity.[607]

4.1.2 Practical reason

It could be argued that rather than looking for the strength of the three approaches in analyses of reflexivity, it should be sought in their accounts of practical reason on which their commitments to justice, communication and discourse as equals are founded. Rawls's greatest achievements in his Anglophone context have been to replace Utilitarianism as the guiding paradigm for social ethics with a defense of individual basic rights within a structural

---

606 Pellauer, *Guide for the Perplexed*, 142, n. 8, with reference to his discussion of Levinas and Husserl at the end of *Oneself as Another*, and to *The Course of Recognition*.

607 This is one of the main points of Henrich's critique of Habermas with which Ricoeur would agree. A related point is the function of reason to mediate between and unify the different worlds to which the self belongs and relates. Dirk Jörke sees Habermas's return to the question of "authorship", which implies reflective selfhood, in the context of the controversy on genetic enhancement as a "specific admission that makes this text [*The Future of Human Nature*] so remarkable... The possibility of positive eugenics... points to unthematized presuppositions of deontological conceptions of morality". "Kommunikative Anthropologie", in Brunkhorst *et al.* (eds.), *Habermas-Handbuch*, 332.

framework of justice; to highlight the role of consensus between different world-views in a pluralist democracy; and to supplement his reinterpretation of contract theory by the device of the "veil of ignorance" with the level of "considered convictions", that is, already shared normative presuppositions which have emerged within the history of a political culture. However, if not his programme, then core features of his argumentation are marked by deficits in relation to practical reason:

(1) The rational choice foundation brought into the contract part of *Theory of Justice* compromises its ethical credentials; it undermines morality from the start by establishing as the guiding motivation a self-interested calculation of risks. How this extraneous import into a theory of ethics – which is dropped in subsequent essays – relates to the sense of justice that is equally assumed remains unresolved in this work.

(2) The empirical understanding of autonomy as self-determination in the tradition of J. S. Mill does not allow for a conception of dignity as respect for oneself and the other as ends-in-themselves in equally original freedom; by definition, these concepts are beyond empirical demonstrability. This theory choice has consequences for the view of and the level of relating to the other. By submitting the relationship between self and other only to the criterion of reciprocity, the possibility and risk of innovative and one-sided action[608] are left out. Without the concept of the Categorical Imperative with its unilateral commitment to morality even if the active interest in the other's freedom goes unrequited, only a version of negative rights remains. Its direction is ambiguous and can be interpreted as protecting individuals, yet as promoting a polite form of disinterest with no desire for realizing the social bond. This is the opposite assumption to Ricoeur's inclusion of the wish to live together in just institutions already at the level of initial striving. The communal and participative dimensions of working out the project of cosmopolitan peace and justice are not taken over from Kant. The contract motivation portrays agents as only accepting the need to include the others' perspectives for self-serving reasons. There is no actual engagement with one another as ethically desiring and morally conscious beings, but only as legally equal fellow-citizens. In comparison with the position his work argues against, Utilitarianism, it achieves its goal; yet, compared to the other two approaches, as a social anthropology it lacks the detail provided by the social sciences engaged by Habermas, and the depth of the different human-

---

608 Cf. H. Peukert, "Beyond the present state of affairs: *Bildung* and the search for orientation in rapidly transforming societies", in *Journal of Philosophy of Education* 36 (2002) 421–35.

ities' disciplines employed by Ricoeur to trace the dialectics of evolving historical self-understanding as the sources of current positions.

(3) Missing from reflection are the dimensions of evil, of alienation, of powers constraining the self, or frustrated attempts at liberation. Contrast experiences to the wish for a flourishing life or, in Rawls's term, a successful life plan, are rarely considered; this backdrop to human attempts of creating meaning remains undeveloped. The question of a reflective relationship to oneself, more complex and tenuous than a straight-forward realization of plans, is left unexplored.

(4) The departure from the Kantian heritage of a universalistic concept of reason comes at the price that the replacement term, "reasonable", is fluid and empty, thus waiting to be filled with unexamined and possibly ideological assumptions. If one wanted to take seriously the Hegelian critique of Kant's universal concepts as "abstract", the answer would be to deepen and concretize the analysis by including questions of the priority of goods and their evaluation. Since Rawls treats all primary goods as being at the same level of distribution, this chance is missed; insights that might have arisen from exploring the history of concrete struggles for rights, thereby overcoming the abstractness and equal validity of goods, have no place in the theory.[609] "Rational" as a predicate would have to meet criteria that can be argued for and justified; the move to "reasonable" loses the possible gain of more concrete parameters obtaining in specific cultural contexts to a generalized concession that claims to universality must be replaced by areas of overlap between different traditions.

Habermas has been the most prominent critic of this lessening of standards of practical reason caused by giving up on a justifiable measure for rationality which a universalizing test of its criteria in a practical discourse could supply. The two problems of his theory, however, from the perspective of Kant's foundation of ethics, are:

(1) it naturalizes morality by investing language (in the shape of the presuppositions of argumentation) and the interactive capability of perspective-taking

---

609 Mandry points out with reference to *Oneself as Another*, 233, that this is due to the "'formalist nature of the contract'" that abstracts from the "'diversity of goods'". For Ricoeur, it is no longer possible to "'neutralize'" the qualitative differences between goods once the political level of "concrete social conflicts of distribution" (*Ethische Identität*, 190) is included. The evaluation of these political struggles will differ according to what conception of society guides the analysis. In *Ethische Identität*, 189, Mandry summarizes the alternative Ricoeur depicts in *Oneself as Another*, 250: "Behind the question of the status of justification of the contract and of the maximin argument lies the question about the coherence of the community (*Gemeinwesen*) itself, of a cooperative enterprise whose bonding power must be strengthened, or a connection of mutually disinterested individuals oriented towards their self-interest?"

with a moral dimension, thus founding equal regard for the other on properties of language and of the species, rather than the good will of the individual agent; (2) in its critique of the "highest good", it curtails practical reason to what is likely to be achievable. On the other hand, the discourse ethicist shares many of Ricoeur's concerns: his insistence on the critique of instrumental reason; his new discovery of the role of a person's self-understanding in the genetic enhancement debate; the primacy of practical reason and a participative format of public reason; his critiques of positivism and scientism and of the new pathologies of commercialization affecting the lifeworld, as well as his interest in translation between different worldviews and cultures.

It is only the French theorist, however, who both endorses Kant's analysis of the antinomy of practical reason, and takes the question of suffering inflicted by fellow-humans and of sustained but failing moral intentions as a challenge to the foundations of ethics. Ricoeur also marks out clearly that Rawls's rational choice insertion into a theory of justice is an instance of radical evil, enacting the human "penchant" to act in a self-serving way.[610] Unlike the first two authors, he puts the emphasis on judgement or "practical wisdom" where universal principles and the respect for singularity have to be mediated and concrete solutions to conflicts worked out. It is here that cultural and religious resources for public reason come into play.

---

610 The only considerations that redeem it from this devastating critique is that it forms part of an argument against Utilitarianism's "sacrificial principle", and that the prior convictions owed to a history of religious and cultural formation provide a distinct motivational context of pre-understanding. See above, 1.1.2.3. By contrast, John Wall in his treatment of "The economy of the gift. Paul Ricoeur's significance for Theological Ethics", in *Journal of Religious Ethics* 29 (2001) 235–260, 244–45, sees the reason for Ricoeur's distanciation from Rawls's argumentation in that it fails "to grasp the depth of this fallen human incapacity to overcome our utilitarian tendencies... According to Ricoeur, Rawls's project does not succeed because no such 'original position' is humanly possible... the problem... is that human beings are radically and unalterably finite. We are simply not capable, by our own powers, of imagining all the relevant goods (particularly, but not only, those that conflict with our own) that should be considered from an impartial perspective." It seems to me that this interpretation of Ricoeur's objection to Rawls misses his critique of any contract foundation on account of its "centrifugal forces" that promote an atomistic concept of individuality at the expense of the social bond; in addition, it seems to identify epistemological and existential finitude with a moral lack of impartiality and thus to naturalize guilt and sin; it also downplays human capacity apart from its religious fulfillment, thus theologizing Ricoeur's phenomenological account of the intentionality to live well with others in just institutions from the outset. With these corrections, I find the focus of Wall's interpretation of Ricoeur's significance for Christian Ethics on the imaginative and creative task of morality in linking the good and the right as the particular and the universal an attractive project. See also his *Moral Creativity. Ricoeur and the Poetics of Possibility* (Oxford: OUP, 2005).

4.1.3 Judgement

With Kant's third *Critique*, the question of the relationship between the universal and the particular is posed in the contexts both of aesthetics and of a teleology that also relates to hopes of history. With Hannah Arendt, Ricoeur argues for an "extension" of Kant's use of judgement: "The epistemology of judicial debate may constitute another of these extensions beyond Kant's own framework, alongside, for example, historical judgment and medical judgment."[611] Judgement is a decisive level for the exercise of public reason which has to apply the test of universalizability conducted by practical reason to domain-specific issues and cases. For example, the question of including children's rights into national Constitutions which has been on the agenda in several countries, requires exchanges on how to spell out the human dignity of children in areas such as the family, in medical and in criminal law, in education and in the generational contract of a society. It is here that convictions shaped by particular traditions enter into debate in the public sphere; they support and concretize universal moral principles by bringing to the forum of public reason the different values and priorities of goods that each of them stand for. While these values, their order and their relevance are under debate in each tradition – for instance, the relationships between faith, freedom, reason and praxis in different Christian denominations –, they form one distinctive position when viewed against other traditions for which the relationship to a transcendent God is not essential. Thus, the capacity of reflective judgement is operative within a tradition as well as in its contribution of points to consider in a public debate that deals both with principles and their concretization in ethical criteria.

In Habermas's framework, the need for discourse arises when differences and dissent make previously shared assumptions problematic. The cooperative search for truth is lifted to this level, charged with offering justifications which are achieved by arguing successfully that a norm or demand is universalizable; yet, domain-specific debates themselves and the judgements they offer are not

---

611 In "Interpretation and/or argumentation", in *The Just*, 126, n. 19, Ricoeur supports H. Arendt in her attempt to move its remit beyond examples from aesthetics and teleology. The "Kantian theory of reflective judgment illustrated in the third Critique by the analysis of the judgment of taste and that of the teleological judgment can receive other applications than those proposed by Kant, by following the way opened by Arendt in her unfinished work on judging." He argues that "for Kant himself (the problematic of reflective judgment) encompasses, beyond the judgment of taste, the teleological judgment and, by way of it, the whole Kantian philosophy of history" (*The Just*, xxi).

part of this level.[612] There is a marked difference between norm and application. One of the concrete fields the theorist of communicative action has attended to himself has been the controversy about the permissibility of genetic enhancement; the moral reason advanced against it is the demand of symmetry in the future parents' relationship to their child, to safeguard its ethical authorship over its life.

Rawls, on the other hand, has shown an awareness of the need to link the levels of principles and of values in their particularity through his term, "reflective equilibrium". In Rawls's theory, it originates at the level of the individual but it also offers the chance to bring in the plurality of agents and self-understandings that do not simply co-exist but engage with each other on the future of their polity.

It is the Rawlsian concept of "reflective equilibrium" that Ricoeur refers to repeatedly since it indicates the necessity of including the third dimension of reason, judgement, specifically in its "reflective" operation.[613] In his architecture of ethics, it is "practical wisdom" that carries out this work in professional settings such as law and medicine, as well as in the political setting of cultural memory as a civic resource. He explains its mediating and innovating character in the process of legal judgement in terms of the comparative and the divinating

---

612 In his article, "Diskurs", in Brunkhorst et al. (eds.), *Habermas-Handbuch*, 303 – 306, 305, K. Günther points out that practical discourses have to alternate between justificatory and domain-specific discourses (*Begründungs- und Anwendungsdiskurse*) "since when justifying a norm one cannot foresee all the cases of its application". He refers to the variety of discourses envisaged by Habermas, which can be oriented towards theoretical or towards practical truth, as well as "ethical and political discourses directed towards the appropriateness (*Angemessenheit*) of individual or collective self-understandings".

613 In *Ethische Identität*, 312, Mandry interprets Ricoeur's use of this term as relating to the "contextualization of universalism as well as to the universalization of contexts. Morality finds its goal in leading to morally right actions in concrete situations. From the conception of reflective equilibrium it follows on the other hand that communitarian particular convictions can 'potentially' be universally valid, if it emerges from their discursive examination that they transport a moral content whose significance reaches beyond the historical situation." He concludes with reference to *Oneself as Another*, 289, that "convictions incorporated in concrete forms of life" have to be submitted to discourse as carried out in the ethics of argumentation. By carrying the term "reflective equilibrium" to the level of intersection between "universality and historicity", Ricoeur lifts existing life forms to the rank of "inchoate universals" and allocates complementary functions to Rawls's and Habermas's approaches: the second foundation of TJ and subsequent foundation for PL, "considered convictions", and the crucial, correcting role of Habermas's discursive tests of universalizability (*Oneself as Another*, 288 – 290).

moments of hermeneutics.[614] Thus, it is not a case of adding further specifying or "supplementary rules", as the legal theorist Robert Alexy, relevant also for Habermas's discourse rules, proposes, but of a double process of interpreting case and rule. As a process of "mutual adjustment between the interpreted norm and the interpreted fact",[615] it appeals both to logic and to the imagination. It is "poetic" in that it creates a new understanding beyond the elements given before.[616] What has been shown in relation to law, applies whenever the universal level of principles is concretized: a crucial role falls to productive imagination in its innovative, conflict-solving capacity of finding a "fit" between singular persons and circumstances and general norms. The role entrusted to "practical wisdom" is thus both inventive and critical, working out how the initial striving to live well in just institutions can be actualized or regained, also, as the following section will show, with the resources of religion.

Of the three, Ricoeur has the most appreciative view of the enabling power of the symbolic resources from which public reason operates. For Rawls, these cultural particularities only figure as a private background of comprehensive doctrines but not as historical formations of self-understandings in encounters with others that have shaped imaginations, aspirations and concrete realizations of the social bond in specific life forms. Habermas privileges the deontological moment of universalization in moral decision-making; he trusts in the resources of the lifeworld, itself a phenomenological concept, but does not explore them for their guiding ideas, since they are also suspected of being mere conventions that are obstacles to universality. Having outlined the strength of the ethical level of self-understanding as depending on "the prior *telos* of a conscious conduct of life", he then goes on to contrast its "embedded" nature with the requirement of moral-practical reason to "break with" and of "distancing oneself" from these contexts of life.[617]

---

614 Ricoeur, "Conscience and the law", in *The Just*, 146–155, 153: "Argumentation and interpretation are inseparable, the argumentation constituting the logical framework and the interpretation the inventive framework of the process ending in the making of a decision."
615 Ricoeur, "Interpretation and/or argumentation", in *The Just*, 122.
616 The practice of legal reasoning involves what Kant calls "reflective" as opposed to "determinative" judgement which subsumes a known case under an evident rule. When neither the specific case nor the general rule are already known, then reflective judgment comes in. Interpretation becomes "the way the productive imagination follows once the problem is no longer to apply a known rule to a presumably correctly described case, as with determinative judgment, but to 'find' a rule *under* which it is appropriate to place a fact that itself must be interpreted." (Ricoeur, "Interpretation and/or argumentation", in *The Just*, 126).
617 Habermas, "On the employments of practical reason", in *Justification and Application*, 1–17, 12.

In contrast, for the French hermeneutical philosopher, cultural heritages in their particularity have at least the potential for universality within themselves. A recognition that "potential universals" are contained in all cultures, including "so-called exotic" ones,[618] is the goal, and this needs the interest of its own members in its renewal, as well as the bilingual, hermeneutical and imaginative capacities of current and future translators. Habermas's recent specification of the "community of communication as a community of translation"[619] takes a step in the direction of the plurality of languages and traditions with their still "unexhausted force".[620]

Regarding the three dimensions of reason in its Kantian understanding, the French theorist is the only one who distinguishes and avails of the properties of each. The primacy of practical reason translates into a primacy of the will and of an imagination able to discover analogies in foreign life forms. Only Ricoeur's understanding of the moral level recognizes the step needed between naturalizing explanations, like Aristotle's and Habermas's in his universal pragmatics, and Kant: morality is a matter of the will, not a natural orientation towards the good, nor a language-based orientation towards cooperation. It is a decision taken in view of the possible alternative direction towards only serving one's own interests. To liberate the will from this penchant, however, requires resources that engage the power of imagination; this poetic level, not morality, is where he sees the originary contribution of religions.

4.2 Religion and public reason

The epistemological status accorded to religion by the three thinkers, and the parameters for its exercise in a pluralistic society (1) indicate the framework in which its relation to public reason is set (2). To each of these, points of debate have been raised by theologians.

4.2.1 Three views of religion in relation to reason

Due to Rawls's theory decision to regard philosophy in its different schools as on a par with worldviews, religious traditions have the same status as secularism,

---

618 Ricoeur, *Oneself as Another*, 289.

619 Habermas, "Wie viel Religion verträgt der liberale Staat?", in *Neue Zürcher Zeitung*, August 4, 2012.

620 Habermas, "An awareness", in Habermas *et al.*, *An Awareness*, 16.

Aristotelianism, Kantianism or other "doctrines" that pass the criterion of being "reasonable". What may look like a positive theory decision, that religions can qualify as not irrational but as reasonable, is thus owed to the levelling of the distinction between particular worldviews, and different philosophical approaches to reason; a faculty still deemed autonomous enough by the other two authors to be credited with constituting a general consciousness of truth. Turning all approaches, also philosophical analyses of truth claims, into self-contained doctrines, implies in addition that no specific capacity or unique contribution of religions as distinct from other worldviews to the project of a just society can be identified. Comprehensive doctrines in general supply their members with orientation and motivation. Once the unreasonable ones have been sorted out from those that qualify as reasonable due to their endorsement of liberty and equality, they are protected as their members' home conviction and as part of citizens' privacy. The expectation to them is to contribute to stability by eventually translating their religious responses to current issues into the categories of the political conceptions related to them.

While Habermas defends religion as not a priori irrational and as harbouring resources of solidarity and reflectiveness that can be inspirational for society in its current pathologies, he also emphasizes its counterpart position to reason and the "opacity" of its core. He has specified three stringent conditions for religious traditions to recognize as criteria for their compatibility with the self-understanding of modern polities: the distinction between state and religion as dual independent orders, which also rules out new integralist theologies; the autonomy of reason in the enquiries of the natural and social sciences; and the plurality of religions with which each of them has to be able to co-exist. Religions that meet these criteria will engage in the dialogues that are needed to jointly translate their distinct intuitions.

For Ricoeur, the core of religions like that of any other symbol system is hidden and mysterious but is also the source of their renewal. He highlights their difference from philosophical reason in a number of respects: at the literary level of the genres of their texts that include narratives of responsiveness and betrayal, lamentations, beatitudes, poems and parables; in the sense of time, exemplified with the orientation of biblical monotheism towards the future; and in a conception of life from the promise of superabundance, gift and hope in new beginnings. Discussing with Hans Küng the roots of violence, he argues that this general human feature is intensified when it becomes connected to religion. Apart from being an ordinary human propensity, it is the unconditional claim to which religious believers feel committed that can bring forth a self-understanding of being the executor of God's will. A remedy for such lack of distinction between God's intention and one's own interpretation is to be found by turning to the very same texts that have been used to justify violence against those who hold competing revelations of God to be true. Inspired by a faith in which each creature is unconditionally affirmed, these texts also express the power of religion to turn indifference into "love", generic equality on the moral plane into appreciation of another person's singularity, and condemnation of evil into forgiveness. Religions that express the hope for forgiveness hold a key to human agency, especially when the present is considered as a heritage of hopes that have been partially realized and partially betrayed. The debt and obligation to history are present in the current issues that are under consideration in the public realm. Hegel's overlooking of the victims of history is the moral reason for Ricoeur to depart from his solution and to seek analyses and expressions that are more adequate to the task of taking up the unkept promises of the past. Distinct traditions and movements are held to their original founding intuitions.

All three thinkers thus have expectations of religious traditions. The principle that religions have obligations to reason is accepted by theologians, but exactly how they are answerable to it needs specification from both sides. The systematic theologian Hans-Joachim Höhn points out that "the other of reason is required to seek a reasoned (*vernunftgemäßes*) relationship to reason if it wants to be distinguishable from irrationality and willfulness. The debt (*Bringschuld*) which representatives of religious traditions have to deliver consists in a cognitive reorganization of their faith convictions". In return for being reckoned with as continuing factors in society, they have to be "compatible with modernity".[621]

It is in response to Habermas that the task to define the difference between religion and reason has been articulated most clearly. Höhn sums it up in the term "heterogeneity": "religion claims 'heterogeneity' to reason, that is, an origin of its own. The independence (*Eigenständigkeit*) of religion is to stand for something that is underivable from the means of reason."[622]

On the other hand, this does not mean "opacity". Habermas overinterprets the "specific boundary (*Sperre*)" between the two forms of the human spirit as a complete disjunction between reason and religion. He has to base this view on emphasizing as the key non-cognitive element of religion that it expresses itself in ritual, and not only as an intellectual and practical tradition: "Religion itself cannot survive without being rooted in ritual praxis. This circumstance is

---

621 H.-J. Höhn, "Rettende Aneignung? Die Vernunft und die Logik der Religion", in Manemann/Wacker (eds.), *Politische Theologie – gegengelesen*, 255–262, 258.
622 Höhn, "Rettende Aneignung?", in Manemann/Wacker (eds.), *Politische Theologie – gegengelesen*, 259.

what separates religion – even more stringently (*unerbittlicher*) than the authority of revelation – from all secular formations (*Gestalten*) of the spirit."[623] The decisive theological argument, quoted in 2.4, from a position that elaborates the Gospel message of salvation in modernity's categories of freedom, remains: "Why should there only be potential for reason in what is completely out of its reach (instead of what is not at its disposal because of its freedom)?"[624] Pröpper concludes:

> It is much less a "discursive exterritoriality" of infallible truths of revelation than the heterogeneity, that is, the origin of its own of the truth of faith in the contingent event of revelation that justifies the irreducible difference between knowledge (*Wissen*) and faith (*Glauben*)... It is true that faith [in contrast to aesthetic intuition (*Anschauung*)] refers to cognitive contents, but it is in its core also an act of decision, and as such gains an assuredness (*Gewissheit*) of its own... this does not imply... that the truth of faith becomes incommunicable... Part of the disclosing work of theology is the *reasoned insight* that the link between the truth of faith and its origin cannot be sublated without damaging its content.[625]

Thus, the abiding difference between religion and reason, or, in the Hegelian terms Habermas employs, between faith (*Glauben)* and knowledge (*Wissen*), is not that religion is "rooted in ritual" while reason is not; it is that the *origin* of its knowledge can only be expressed in *religious* terms as distinct from having been *generated* by reason. It is this what the term "revelation" stands for, not for an "infallible" content imposed on humans, which would indeed remain opaque and unintelligible. Both God's self-revelation in history and the human capacity for self-reflection that it presupposes and invites do not belong to the objectifiable type of knowledge; yet, they are "generally accessible" if reason is understood as the capacity of enquiring towards the unconditioned, and if it accepts its dimension of receptivity. Only if reason is aware of its outreach beyond what it can secure with its own means, and if the possibility of God's self-communication – that could not be anticipated in its freedom – is not rejected, can religious resources be appropriated in a way that does not restrict their unexhausted potential.

If the parameters of cooperation are to be defined in a way that does not lead to curtailing the content to be translated, the role of particularity in shaping generic structures and concretizing universals has to be acknowledged. In his probing analysis of the changes in Habermas's thinking on religion in the framework

---

623 Habermas, "Einleitung", *Studienausgabe*, vol. V, 32.
624 Pröpper, *Theologische Anthropologie*, vol. II, 765, n. 127.
625 Pröpper, *Theologische Anthropologie*, vol. II, 766, with reference to Höhn.

of postmetaphysical reason, the sociologist Austin Harrington assesses how the idea of a religious genealogy of reason is carried out. Regarding the way in which this "contingently received historical heritage" is traced back to a joint origin, he observes that by tying all secular enquiries to "methodological atheism", Habermas arrives at "fixed framework positions" for religion and reason. Harrington explains this allocation of separate territories which he considers as "alien to Kant" with metaphors taken from international relations: Contact between the two is seen in terms of mediation between two countries, rather than faculties connected by their joint origin in reflection. The model for this division is the political sphere, not the internal connection between two forms of the spirit:

> Habermas may be attempting to transfer too much from the political relation of the religious and the secular to the existential relation of the philosophical and the theological. Legal and political norms of good diplomacy between people do not seem an entirely appropriate model for our understanding of the conflict between knowledge and faith and its prospects of resolution. A clash of different religious and non-religious groups, or even a "clash of civilisations", is not the same as a clash of aspects of the life of the mind, and the modes, idioms and possibilities of resolving these clashes are different... despite his advocacy of a "religious genealogy of reason", Habermas tends to prioritize diplomacy between religion and reason as if from two relatively fixed points in conceptual space.[626]

What is missing, although it should be part of the conceptual programme, is a "historically concrete account of how the two countries came into being over time, of how they eventually seceded from one another, and what kind of shared continent or land-mass they once held in common". Harrington's judgement is that instead of holding "'talks about talks'" and in the end "immunizing itself against a challenge from something more profoundly outside itself", reason needs to engage with the particularity of religions. He concludes:

> Only when his thinking regains a commitment to expose itself to something more one-sided, something more dangerously particularistic, decisive or excessive – perhaps with the consequence of failing, disappointing or even antagonizing certain people or parties – only then, one might suggest, will it have a chance of acceding to the universality it so passionately desires.[627]

In his response to Habermas at the panel discussion published under the title, *An Awareness of What is Missing*, the systematic theologian Friedo Ricken explains how genealogy and translation go into two opposite directions. The first

---

626 A. Harrington, "Habermas's theological turn?", in *Journal for the Theory of Social Behaviour* 37 (2007) 45–61, 59.
627 Harrington, "Habermas's theological turn?", 59.

is the condition for the latter by moving from abstract concepts to a different register, the original context of an experience, as expressed in narratives of situations of decision and response from which these terms emerged. The originally religious framework of experience can be recaptured at the abstract level of philosophical anthropology and moral theory, but its memorable, heuristic, sensitizing, disclosing and motivating qualities arise from its original articulation:

> But how can a changed perspective on the genealogy of reason make good the motivational deficit of practical reason and awaken a consciousness of the worldwide violation of solidarity? The return to the prehistory of the emergence of reason (*Entstehungsgeschichte*) can be understood as the reverse process to that of translation. Translation leads to abstract concepts, the study of genealogy leads us back to the lifeworld context, to the anthropological phenomena, on which this abstraction is based. Religions perform a maieutic function in the sense that they enable us to see these phenomena, force us to confront them, and trigger our responses.[628]

The example already quoted of such a narrative is the experience of guilt as in the Genesis story of the Fall. God's question to Adam induces the self-reflection of knowing that he could have acted otherwise which then makes it possible to develop a concept of freedom in its dual aspects: a transcendental aspect, capturing the formal condition of the possibility of agency, and a concrete aspect, its empirical realization.

> Thus the abstract concept of transcendental freedom, for example, has its origins in the concept of guilt, and what guilt means in lifeworld terms and how we experience it are shown by the corresponding religious narratives. Only through the encounter with the latter, therefore, can an "awareness of what is missing, of what cries out to heaven" be awakened and kept awake.[629]

Both the theological and the sociological comments highlight the irreplaceable role of the particular. It remains to be shown what contents such particular traditions can contribute to the principles of public reason, and in what way.

4.2.2 Co-founders of the public sphere

Religious traditions are already present in the public sphere by virtue of being part of the symbolic worlds from which the categories and life forms of a culture

---

628 F. Ricken S. J., "Postmetaphysical reason and religion", in Habermas *et al.*, *An Awareness*, 51–58, 52–53.
629 Ricken, "Postmetaphysical reason and religion", in Habermas *et al.*, *An Awareness*, 53.

emerge; in the cultural and religious history of the West, the interaction of intellectual currents in the Mediterranean and Europe created self-understandings that produced the idea of a self-governing *polis* of equals. The theological ethicist Duncan Forrester points out the theological heritage of the "difference principle as originally derived from the Judaeo-Christian tradition and now so deeply embedded in western culture that it is regarded as more or less self-evident". He also quotes Rawls's comment on the second foundation of justice, considered convictions: "given our history and the traditions embedded in our public life it is the most reasonable doctrine for us".[630]

Beyond the dimension of a latent normative heritage, Ricoeur has developed the most dynamic conception of the public space of which distinct traditions are co-founders. They are themselves made up of various accentuations, extremes and counterpositions in different eras; in their histories, subdued elements re-emerge, and the contemporary situation receives a strong impetus from the unkept promises of their origins. His distinction of "institutional authority" from "enunciative authority" is not unlike Habermas's "formal public sphere" beyond the "institutional threshold" of democratic office over the "informal" or "wild" public sphere. It creates space for motivations, political causes espoused by different citizens, and overarching visions that orient current day-to-day management by aspirations that can be realized if the political will is summoned for them; the Millenium Development Goals would be one example for directing politics by a horizon beyond the status quo. Forrester points to the origins of social change in such encompassing visions, rather than in an "overlapping consensus": "measured consensualism... has little in common with the visionary accounts of justice which have motivated most great movements for social transformation and reform".[631] The public sphere is about capturing the hopes and evidences of citizens and their traditions of thinking in their assessments of current policy regarding the future directions a society should take.

For both Ricoeur and Habermas, it belongs to the role of public reason to engage with other positions in the public sphere. They have already taken on board the questions the theological ethicist David Hollenbach has put to Rawls. He calls for the "intellectual solidarity" needed in "societies of difference" for "reviving the common good", to listen to each other's visions, and to "understand discrepancies as positive", since they will lead to an "enriched understanding of the common good". [632] This intellectual exchange enlarges every-

---

630 D. Forrester, "Fairness is not enough", in *Christian Justice and Public Policy* (Cambridge: CUP, 1997), 113–139, 129, with reference to Rawls, "Kantian Constructivism", 519.
631 Forrester, "Fairness is not enough", in *Christian Justice and Public Policy,* 128.
632 Hollenbach, *The Common Good and Christian Ethics* (Cambridge: CUP, 2002), 137.

one's horizon: A "predominantly on-guard posture towards those who are different will diminish one's overall intellectual and social possibilities".[633] In view of the structural transformations of contemporary societies, the option not to communicate with the diversity within and beyond one's own borders is dwindling. In view of the "thickening technological and economic interconnections among people... living in non-intersecting parallel worlds is not enough". He sees the "method of avoidance" advocated by Rawls as a "solitary form of freedom" in which citizens are "insulated from each other by tolerance".[634] It is a task in itself to create a receptive environment of mutual interest prior to any debate. A society's development depends on the resources its traditions bring to it, which need to be articulated in mutual exchange on their understandings of the good life. Reinterpreting "civility" as "the political face of intellectual solidarity – the virtue that creates a community of freedom in the midst of diversity",[635] he envisages a field of interaction between the comprehensive doctrines that Rawls identified as crucial for bringing citizens' self-understandings into dialogue.

Each of the three social philosophers recognizes the level of discourse or of principles to be drawn from reason, though with a different standing in each approach. Both Habermas and Ricoeur avail of the moral evidence of the experience of obligation that the test of universalization presupposes. Rawls invokes the normative evidence of the "inviolability" of each person. All three equally assume a counterpart in "comprehensive doctrines", in the semantic heritages, values and accommodating life forms co-existing in the lifeworld, or in distinct traditions re-energizing themselves from the enunciative authority of their origins.

How can these particular heritages influence future directions in a struggle with other, powerful forces that claim a hearing in the public sphere? Forrester enquires how to construct an "account of justice robust enough to face real conflicts of interest and of understanding, and visionary enough to evoke a passionate commitment capable of calling forth self-sacrifice and challenging self-interest". He draws attention to the difficult task of deliberation and compromise that will be involved in what Rawls refers to as a seemingly unproblematic balance of principles with individual judgements which are to be "duly pruned and adjusted". What is at stake in this task is to create a fruitful intersection between the

---

633 Hollenbach, *The Common Good*, 139.
634 Hollenbach, *The Common Good*, 140.
635 Hollenbach, *The Common Good*, 146. It "leads to a deeper understanding of how to live well together."

particular and the universal, rather than a reduction of unique semantic and pragmatic potentials to a lowest common denominator:

> Principles emerge "which match our considered judgements duly pruned and adjusted". But on what basis does this pruning and adjustment take place? What makes the theory after pruning more fruitful than before? And what if the branches that are removed are essential to the continuing health of the main stem?... what if it degenerates into a reshuffling of prejudices and nothing more?... it is not easy to see how such a theory of justice can indeed be more than a refinement of the conventional wisdom of the age.[636]

For Ricoeur, the tension between the particular, that is, the religious, and the universal, that is, the moral dimension, is concretized as the tension between love and justice, compassion and strict reciprocity, regard for singularity and moral responsibility. His biblical examples illustrate how this specific determination happens concretely:

> Would it not be the role of love, then, to contribute to the reduction of the gap between this universalism ideally without restriction and the contextualism in which cultural differences prevail? The biblical world – first the Jewish, then the Christian – offers examples, since then become paradigmatic, of this extension of culturally limited spheres outward toward an actually universal acknowledgment. The Old Testament's repeated call to the people to include in their hospitality "the alien, the orphan, and the widow among you" (Deut. 16:11, etc.) – in other words, the "other" beneficiary of hospitality – presents us with a first example of the pressure exerted by love upon justice.[637]

At their best, religions address the plurality of subjects in their uniqueness and personal response. Habermas has identified this personal relationship of the believer to the biblical God as the root of the moral concept of "responsibility". For Ricoeur, a religious outlook can "contribute to the preservation of the irreplaceability of persons in all exchanges of roles":

> The each is still distributive: To "each his own," to each his or her just portion, with a validity even to unequal distribution. "One" is anonymous: he or she congeals into an indistinct mass. Does it not fall to love's imagination, then, and to its singularizing glance, to extend the privilege of the one-on-one, the face-to-face, to all relationships, even to those with the faceless other or others? The case is like that of a love for enemies, which denies the validity of the political difference between friends and enemies.[638]

---

636 Forrester, "Fairness is not enough", in *Christian Justice and Public Policy*, 116–17, with reference to TJ, 20.
637 Ricoeur, "Theonomy", in Volf/Krieg/Kucharz (eds.), *The Future of Theology*, 293.
638 Ricoeur, "Theonomy", in Volf/Krieg/Kucharz (eds.), *The Future of Theology*, 295.

Thus, if one of the co-founding traditions brings the religious injunction to love one's enemy into the public sphere, the plausibility of Carl Schmitt's definition of the political by the distinction between friend and enemy will be challenged. The Hobbesian relationship of fear of the other can be transformed into a readiness to extend recognition also to those whose response cannot be predicted. However, it cannot be taken for granted that the public sphere is one of genuine exchange, and not of antagonism, staged identities and polarities, and amplification of vested interests. The theological ethicist Robert Gascoigne points to the potential of symbolic traditions with their world structuring, formative and enabling orientations to keep a participative democracy inspired towards goals beyond stability:

> What are the visions of humanity, the sources of life, which can inspire social discourse to become a genuine forum of civil respect, a community of justice and generosity – even of willingness to sacrifice interests for the sake of the need of others?... Understandings of the human person are formed by historical traditions, so that any commonality must be the result of a dialogue between traditions.[639]

Distinguishing between the particular and the universal – rather than seeing as "universal" the average of what reasonable particular traditions can agree on – allows for a dialectic in which one can correct the other and drive it to a higher level. On the one hand, cultural and religious traditions need to stretch to this horizon. For Habermas and Ricoeur, cultures in their particularity have it within themselves to be open to a universalistic morality. On the other hand, they supply not only conceptions of the good, but also a pre-understanding of the moral. For the theological ethicist H. Schelkshorn, this is an indispensable function and contribution of worldviews or life forms in their distinctiveness:

> discourse norms qualify a discourse as practical only in combination with a pre-understanding of morality as such. The consensus theory does not supply a criterion of the good or the just but guides as a regulative idea the search for possible moral criteria. If these two points are correct, then practical discourses depend on substantive life forms that express and argue for their basic understandings of morality and of the criteria of the good respectively the just, instead of bracketing them as far as possible, as Habermas insinuates.[640]

---

639 R. Gascoigne, *The Public Forum and Christian Ethics* (Cambridge: CUP, 2001), 40. 42.
640 H. Schelkshorn, "Christliche Ethik im Sog argumentativer Vernunft. Diskurstheoretische Bemerkungen zur moraltheologischen Debatte um eine 'autonome Moral im christlichen Kontext'", in a. Holderegger (ed.)., *Fundamente der Theologischen Ethik. Bilanz und Neuansätze* (Freiburg i. Ue./Freiburg i. Br.: Freiburger Universitätsverlag, 1996, 237–260, 249, quoted in Th. Pröpper, *Theologische Anthropologie*, vol. II, 744.

If the above descriptions express some of the intuitions religions can offer to the process of citizens developing their self-understandings and their political judgements, the question remains, how each of the authors envisions religion in delivering this task. I see Rawls as focusing on the question of the "who", Habermas on the "what", and Ricoeur on the question "from where" they affect the public realm. Rawls takes religions seriously as communities nourished in their contemporary vitality by deep historical roots. They are factors to be reckoned with in the social and political life of a pluralist democracy, even if, against Kant's antinomy of practical reason, the faith they confess is not seen as responding to a demand of reason. As comprehensive doctrines, they are thus taken as external social facts with great motivating power that can support the democratic values of liberty and equality.

For Habermas, the potential of religions is viewed from a diagnosis of the colonizing, self-objectifying and self-instrumentalizing tendencies of modern rationalization. It is not who they are as institutional factors, but their practices, intuitions and theological concepts that are of interest. They create mentalities of solidarity and reconciliation and can help "mobilize modern reason against the defeatism lurking within it".[641] They can be allies for reinvigorating the universalistic horizon of responsibility they co-created, and they take on questions posed by individual suffering. As the "other" of reason, they enjoy recognition and are defended against over-secularizing political demands.

For both political ethicists, religions, while having a life of their own, can have a direct functionality for the project of democracy. Ricoeur approaches them from a different starting-point. By making it clear that there is no direct route, but only an unavoidable detour through symbols located between experience and concept, the relation of religion to the life of a social community is taken to be indirect. His methods of analysis – phenomenological, transcendental, hermeneutical – are not concerned with objects or sequences that the empirical sciences are best placed to investigate, but with self-understandings and the condition of their possibility. Symbolic worlds are not the "other" of reason, they give rise to thought, but they resist attempts to translate them into equivalents, secular or other, as the dialogue on a global ethic with Hans Küng shows. The most fruitful avenue of understanding them is to interpret their spontaneous expression in different genres: images of liberation, exhortations, hymns, prayers of thanks, narratives that engage the response of the listener. What they contribute to their societies is not a segment to an overlapping consensus but something more foundational: they re-ignite the sense of the possible, enlivening a source

---

641 Habermas, "An awareness", in Habermas *et al.*, *An Awareness*, 18.

of productivity that manifests itself in unpredictable creations and renewals from its own depth.[642] Jesus' re-imagining the restitution of the people of the Covenant not in terms of territory but in the shape of a banquet,[643] the miraculous effect when the plenitude of creation is shared, restoring the power of forgiveness from the priests to the believers – all these openings exemplify a criterion by which Ricoeur has measured the *oeuvres* of philosophers: remembering lost causes, re-committing to unkept promises, redeeming individual agency from guilt, lifting practical reason to a source of hope. Reading Ricoeur, religions seem to be especially endowed to be agents of the sense of the possible.

In one of her memorable formulations, Onora O'Neill has stated: "Ethics and politics are not spectator sports."[644] It is a position shared by the discourse ethicist and by Ricoeur; in his work on *Memory, History and Forgetting*, not the experts and scholars, but the citizens based on their own reflection between the "intellectual honesty of the historian" and "the fairness" of the judge "remain the ultimate arbiter".[645] They decide which version of history to reject or continue as their own contribution to the project of humanity's hopes. It is decisive which resources they will be able to avail of. The three philosophers compared here have contributed remarkable orientations:

"Justice is the first virtue of social institutions, as truth is of systems of thought... Each person possesses an inviolability founded on justice that even the welfare of society as a whole cannot override."[646]

> The human interest in autonomy and responsibility (*Mündigkeit*) is not mere fancy, for it can be apprehended a priori. What raises us out of nature is the only thing whose nature we can know: *language*. Through its structures, autonomy and responsibility are posited for us. With the first sentence the intention of a universal and unconstrained consensus is unmistakeably expressed.[647]

> ... the wish to live in just institutions arises from the same level of morality as do the desire for personal fulfillment and the reciprocity of friendship. The just is first an object of desire, of a lack, of a wish. It begins as a wish before it is an imperative.[648]

---

642 As his reflections on the abuses of memory show, trying to enlist a faculty like this endangers and may destroy memory as a "matrix": Ricoeur, *Memory, History, Forgetting*, e. g., 57–58. 87.

643 Freyne, "The Galilean Jesus and a Contemporary Christology", in *Theological Studies* 70 (2009) 281–297.

644 O'Neill, *Bounds of Justice*, 49.

645 Ricoeur, *Memory, History, Forgetting*, 295. 333.

646 Rawls, *Theory of Justice*, 3.

647 Habermas, *Knowledge and Human Interests*, 314.

648 Ricoeur, *The Just*, Preface, xv.

The evidence of the human capacity for morality is the Kantian heritage they share in their understanding of justice or practical reason. The biblical heritage bases its trust on a history that anchors the attestation of the self in God's promise of loyalty. It links "eschatology" to "acts of deliverance from the past" and resists as a "false antinomy" the idea of having to "choose between reminiscence and hope".[649] Religious faith is less than a certainty, it is a practical "wager" on the goodness of creation and God's universal salvific will. Even before they appear in contemporary social theories as moral agents and as citizens in the public sphere, humans are invited to hear the message about themselves that they are images of a God who hopes on them.[650]

---

649 Cf. Ricoeur, *Hermeneutics and the Human Sciences*, 100.
650 Pröpper, "Gott hat auf uns gehofft... Theologische Folgen des Freiheitsparadigmas", in *Evangelium und freie Vernunft*, 300 – 321, 321, with reference to Charles Péguy.

Bibliography

Abeldt, Sönke/Bauer, Walter *et al.* (eds.), *… was es bedeutet, verletzbarer Mensch zu sein. Festschrift H. Peukert* (Mainz: Grünewald, 2000)

Ansorge, Dirk, *Gerechtigkeit und Barmherzigkeit Gottes* (Freiburg: Herder, 2009)

Anzenbacher, Arnold, *Einführung in die Ethik* (Düsseldorf: Patmos, 1992)

———, *Einführung in die Philosophie* (Freiburg: Herder, 2002, 8th edn)

Apel, Karl-Otto, "Normatively grounding 'critical theory' by recourse to the lifeworld? A transcendental-pragmatic attempt to think with Habermas against Habermas", in Rasmussen/Swindal (eds.), *Jürgen Habermas*, vol. III, 344–378.

Assmann, Jan, *Moses the Egyptian. The Memory of Egypt in Western Monotheism* (Boston: Harvard University Press, 1998)

———, *The Price of Monotheism* (Stanford: Stanford University Press, 2010)

Biggar, Nigel and Hogan, Linda (eds.), *Religious Voices in Public Places* (Oxford: OUP, 2009)

Böckenförde, Ernst-Wolfgang,"Religion im säkularen Staat", in *Kirche und christlicher Glaube in den Herausforderungen der Zeit* (Münster: LIT Verlag, 2004), 425–437.

Böhnke, Michael/Bongard, Michael/Essen, Georg/Werbick, Jürgen (eds.), *Freiheit Gottes und der Menschen. Festschrift Th. Pröpper* (Regensburg: Pustet, 2006)

Boltanski, Luc/Thévenot, Laurent, *De la justification: les economies de la grandeur* (Paris: Presses Universitaires de France, 1987)

Brieskorn S. J., Norbert, "On the attempt to recall a relationship", in Habermas *et al.*, *An Awareness*, 24–35.

Browning, Don S./Schüssler Fiorenza, Francis (eds.), *Habermas, Modernity, and Public Theology* (New York: Crossroad, 1992)

Brunkhorst, Hauke/Kreide, Regina/Lafont, Christina (eds.), *Habermas-Handbuch. Leben – Werk – Wirkung* (Stuttgart: J.B. Metzler'sche Verlagsbuchhandlung/C.E. Poeschel Verlag und Darmstadt: Wissenschaftliche Buchgesellschaft, 2009)

Brunkhorst, Hauke, "Platzhalter und Interpret", in Brunkhorst et al. (eds.), *Habermas-Handbuch*, 214–220.

Buchanan, Alan/Brock, Daniel/Daniels, Norman/Wikler, Dan, *From Chance to Choice* (Cambridge: CUP, 2001)

Butler, Judith/Habermas, Jürgen/Taylor, Charles/West, Cornel, *The Power of Religion in the Public Sphere*, ed. and intro. E. Mendieta/J. VanAntwerpen, Afterword by C. Calhoun (New York: Columba University Press, 2011)

Cooke, Maeve, "Säkulare Übersetzung oder postsäkulare Argumentation? Habermas über Religion in der demokratischen Öffentlichkeit", in Langthaler/Nagl-Docekal (eds.), *Glauben und Wissen*, 341–366.

———,"Violating Neutrality? Religious Validity Claims and Democratic Legitimacy", in C. Calhoun, E. Mendieta, and J. VanAntwerpen (eds.), *Habermas and Religion* (Cambridge: Polity Press 2013), 249–274.

Daughton, Amy, *Toward an Intercultural Hermeneutic in a Global World*, PhD thesis Trinity College Dublin, 2011.

Dews, Peter (ed.), *Habermas – A Critical Reader* (Oxford: Blackwell, 1999)

Dosse, François, *Paul Ricoeur. Un philosophe dans son siècle* (Paris: Armand Colin, 2012)

Eckholt, Margit, *Dogmatik interkulturell* (Nordhausen: T. Bautz, 2007)

———, *Poetik der Kultur. Bausteine einer interkulturellen dogmatischen Methodenlehre* (Freiburg: Herder, 2002)

———, "Übersetzung – Erinnerung – Versöhnung. Frauen in Europa auf der Suche nach Gestalten einer verbindenden Spiritualität", in P. Hünermann/J. Juhant/B. Zalec (eds.), *Dialogue and Virtue. Ways to Overcome Clashes of Our Civilizations* (Münster/Berlin: LIT Verlag, 2007), 57–68.

Essen, Georg, "Autonomer Geltungssinn und religiöser Begründungszusammenhang. Papst Gelasius I. († 496) als Fallstudie zur religionspolitischen Differenzsemantik", in *Archiv für Rechts- und Sozialphilosophie* 99 (2013) 1–10.

———, "'Da ist keiner, der nicht sündigt, nicht einer...' Analyse und Kritik gegenwärtiger Erbsündentheologien und ihr Beitrag für das seit Paulus gestellte Problem", in Pröpper, *Theologische Anthropologie*, vol. II, 1092–1156.

Feder Kittay, Eva /Carlson, Licia (eds.), *Cognitive Disability and its Challenge to Moral Philosophy* (Chichester: Wiley-Blackwell, 2010)

Finlayson, James G./Freyenhagen, Fabian (eds.), *Habermas and Rawls. Disputing the Political* (London: Routledge, 2011)

Forrester, Duncan, "Fairness is not enough", in *Christian Justice and Public Policy* (Cambridge: CUP, 1997), 113–139.

Forst, Rainer, *The Right to Justification. Elements of a Constructivist Theory of Justice*, trans. J. Flynn (New York: Columbia University Press, 2011)

———, "Diskursethik der Moral. 'Diskursethik – Notizen zu einem Begründungsprogramm' (1983)", in Brunkhorst et al. (eds.), *Habermas-Handbuch*, 234–240.

Freyne, Seán, "In Search of Identity. Narrativity, Discipleship and Moral Agency", in *Moral Language in the New Testament,* ed. by R. Zimmermann/J. Van der Watt, in cooperation with S. Luther (Tübingen: Mohr Siebeck, 2010), 67–85.

———, *Jesus, a Jewish Galilean* (London/New York: T & T Clark International, 2004)

———, "The Galilean Jesus and a Contemporary Christology", in *Theological Studies* 70 (2009) 281–297.

Gascoigne, Robert, *The Public Forum and Christian Ethics* (Cambridge: CUP, 2001)

Greisch, Jean, *Fehlbarkeit und Fähigkeit* (Münster: LIT Verlag, 2009)

———, "Vom Glück des Erinnerns zur Schwierigkeit des Vergebens", in S. Orth/P. Reifenberg (eds.), *Facettenreiche Anthropologie. Paul Ricoeurs Reflexionen auf den Menschen* (Freiburg: Alber, 2004), 91–114.

Grondin, Jean, "Von Gadamer zu Ricoeur. Kann man von einer gemeinsamen Auffassung von Hermeneutik sprechen? ", in B. Liebsch (ed.), *Bezeugte Vergangenheit*, 61–76.

Grotefeld, Stefan, *Religiöse Überzeugungen im liberalen Staat. Protestantische Ethik und die Anforderungen öffentlicher Vernunft* (Stuttgart: Kohlhammer, 2006)

Günther, Klaus, "Diskurs", in Brunkhorst et al. (eds.), *Habermas-Handbuch*, 303–306.

Gula, Richard, "Natural Law Today", in Ch. Curran/R. McCormick (eds.), *Natural Law and Theology (Readings in Moral Theology No. 7)* (Mahwah: Paulist Press, 1991), 369–91.

Habermas, Jürgen, "A postsecular world society? On the philosophical significance of postsecular consciousness and the multicultural world society." Jürgen Habermas interviewed by Eduardo Mendieta, trans. M. Fritsch, in *The Immanent Frame* (February 3, 2010). German title: "Ein neues Interesse der Philosophie an Religion. Ein Interview von Eduardo Mendieta", in *Nachmetaphysisches Denken II*, 96-119.

———, *Between Facts and Norms. Contributions to a Discourse Theory of Law and Democracy*, trans. W. Rehg (Cambridge: Polity Press, 1996), ET of *Faktizität und Geltung. Beiträge zur*

Diskurstheorie des Rechts und des demokratischen Rechtsstaats (Frankfurt: Suhrkamp, 1992)

———, *Between Naturalism and Religion*, trans. C. Cronin (Cambridge: Polity Press, 2008), ET of *Zwischen Naturalismus und Religion* (Frankfurt: Suhrkamp, 2005)

———, *Communication and the Evolution of Society*, trans. Th. McCarthy (Boston: Beacon Press, 1979), ET of *Zur Rekonstruktion des Historischen Materialismus* (Frankfurt: Suhrkamp, 1976)

———,"Die Revitalisierung der Weltreligionen – Herausforderung für ein säkulares Selbstverständnis der Moderne?", in *Kritik der Vernunft, Studienausgabe, Philosophische Texte*, vol. 5 (Frankfurt: Suhrkamp, 2009), 387 – 407.

———, *Glauben und Wissen* (Frankfurt: Suhrkamp, 2001)

———, *Justification and Application. Remarks on Discourse Ethics*, trans. C. Cronin (Cambridge/Mass.: MIT Press, 1993), ET of *Erläuterungen zur Diskursethik* (Frankfurt: Suhrkamp, 1991)

———, *Knowledge and Human Interests*, trans. J. J. Shapiro (Boston: Beacon Press, 1971), ET of *Erkenntnis und Interesse* (Frankfurt: Suhrkamp, 1968)

———, *Moral Consciousness and Communicative Action*, trans. C. Lenhardt and S. Weber Nicholsen (Cambridge/Mass.: MIT Press, 1990), ET of *Moralbewusstsein und kommunikatives Handeln* (Frankfurt: Suhrkamp, 1983)

———, *Nachmetaphysisches Denken II. Aufsätze und Repliken* (Frankfurt: Suhrkamp, 2012)

———, "Nachwort", J. Rawls, *Über Sünde, Glaube und Religion* (Frankfurt: Suhrkamp, 2010), 315 – 336.

———, "Prepolitical foundations of the constitutional state?", in *Between Naturalism and Religion,* trans. C. Cronin (Cambridge: Polity Press, 2008), 101 – 113.

———, *Political-philosophical Profiles*, trans. F. Lawrence (Cambridge/Mass.: MIT Press, 1983), ET of *Politisch-philosophische Profile* (Frankfurt: Suhrkamp, 1971, extended eds 1981, 1987)

———, *Postmetaphysical Thinking. Philosophical Essays*, trans. W.M. Hohengarten (Cambridge/Mass.: MIT Press, 1992), ET of *Nachmetaphysisches Denken* (Frankfurt: Suhrkamp, 1988)

———, *Religion and Rationality. Essays on Reason, God, and Modernity*, ed. and intro by E. Mendieta (Cambridge: Polity Press, 2002).

———,"Replik auf Einwände, Reaktion auf Anregungen", in Langthaler/Nagl-Docekal (eds.), *Glauben und Wissen*, 366 – 414.

———, "Reply to my critics", in J.G. Finlayson/F. Freyenhagen (eds.), *Habermas and Rawls*, 283 – 304.

———, *Studienausgabe*, vol. V, *Kritik der Vernunft. Philosophische Texte* (Frankfurt: Suhrkamp, 2009)

———, *Texte und Kontexte* (Frankfurt: Suhrkamp, 1991)

———, *The Future of Human Nature*, trans. W. Rehg/M. Pensky/H. Beister (Cambridge: Polity Press, 2003), ET of *Die Zukunft der menschlichen Natur. Auf dem Weg zu einer liberalen Eugenik?* (Frankfurt, Suhrkamp, 2001)

———, *The Inclusion of the Other. Studies in Political Theory*, ed. C. Cronin/P. De Greiff (Cambridge: Polity Press, 1999), ET of *Die Einbeziehung des Anderen* (Frankfurt: Suhrkamp, 1996)

———, *The Liberating Power of Symbols*, trans. P. Dews (Cambridge: Polity Press, 2001), ET of *Vom sinnlichen Eindruck zum symbolischen Ausdruck. Philosophische Aufsätze* (Frankfurt: Suhrkamp, 1997)

———,*The Philosophical Discourse of Modernity. Twelve Lectures*, trans. F. Lawrence (Cambridge/Mass.: MIT Press, 1987), ET of *Der philosophische Diskurs der Moderne* (Frankfurt: Suhrkamp, 1985)

———, "'The political'. The rational meaning of a questionable inheritance of political theology", in J. Butler/J. Habermas/C. Taylor/C. West, *The Power of Religion in the Public Sphere*, 15 – 33.

———, *The Structural Transformation of the Public Sphere*, trans. Th. Burger (Cambridge, Mass.: MIT Press, 1989), ET of *Strukturwandel der Öffentlichkeit* (Neuwied/Berlin: Luchterhand, 1961)

———, *Theory of Communicative Action*, vol. I: *Reason and the Rationalization of Society*, trans. Th. McCarthy (Boston: Beacon Press, 1984)

———, *Theory of Communicative Action*, vol. II: *Lifeworld and System: A Critique of Functionalist Reason*, trans. Th. McCarthy (Boston: Beacon Press, 1987), ET of *Theorie des kommunikativen Handelns*, 2 Bde. (Frankfurt: Suhrkamp, 1981)

———, *Toward a Rational Society* (Cambridge: Polity, 1986), ET of *Technik und Wissenschaft als Ideologie* (Frankfurt: Suhrkamp, 1968)

———, "Transcendence from within, transcendence in this world", trans. P. Kenny/E. Crump, in Browning/Schüssler Fiorenza (eds.), *Habermas, Modernity, and Public Theology*, 226 – 250.

———, *Truth and Justification* (Cambridge: Polity Press, 2003), ET of *Wahrheit und Rechtfertigung* (Frankfurt: Suhrkamp, 1999)

———, *Vorstudien und Ergänzungen zur Theorie des kommunikativen Handelns* (Frankfurt: Suhrkamp, 1984)

———,"Wie viel Religion verträgt der liberale Staat?", in *Neue Zürcher Zeitung*, August 4, 2012

Habermas *et al.*, *An Awareness of What is Missing. Faith and Reason in a Postsecular Age*, trans. C. Cronin (Cambridge: Polity Press, 2010)

Habermas/ Ratzinger, Josef, *The Dialectics of Secularization. On Reason and Religion* (San Francisco: Ignatius Press, 2005)

Haker, Hille, *Moralische Identität. Literarische Lebensgeschichten als Medium ethischer Reflexion. Mit einer Interpretation der Jahrestage von Uwe Johnson* (Tübingen: Francke, 1999)

———, "Kommunitaristische Kritik an der Diskursethik", in *Ethik und Unterricht* 5 (1994) 12 – 18.

———, "Narrative and moral identity," in Junker-Kenny/Kenny (eds.), *Memory, Narrative, Self*, 134 – 152.

Harrington, Austin, "Habermas's theological turn?", in *Journal for the Theory of Social Behaviour* 37 (2007) 45 – 61.

Henrich, Dieter, "Was ist Metaphysik – was Moderne? Zwölf Thesen gegen Jürgen Habermas", in *Konzepte. Essays zur Philosophie in der Zeit* (Frankfurt: Suhrkamp, 1987), 11 – 43. ET "What is metaphysics – what modernity?", in Dews (ed.), *Habermas: A Critical Reader*, (Oxford: Blackwell, 1999), 291 – 319.

Henrich, Daniel C., *Zwischen Bewusstseinsphilosophie und Naturalismus. Zu den metaphysischen Implikationen der Diskursethik von Jürgen Habermas* (Bielefeld: Transcript Verlag, 2007)

Hetzel, Andreas, "Bezeugen, Vergeben, Anerkennen", in B. Liebsch (ed.), *Bezeugte Vergangenheit*, 217–231.

Höffe, Otfried, *Ethik und Politik* (Frankfurt: Suhrkamp, 1979)

———, (ed.), *John Rawls – Eine Theorie der Gerechtigkeit* (Berlin: Akademie-Verlag, 1998)

———, "Einführung in Rawls's Theorie der Gerechtigkeit", in Höffe (ed.), *John Rawls*, 3–26.

———, "Überlegungsgleichgewicht in Zeiten der Globalisierung? Eine Alternative zu Rawls", in Höffe (ed.), *John Rawls*, 271–293.

Höhn, Hans-Joachim, "Rettende Aneignung? Die Vernunft und die Logik der Religion", in Manemann/Wacker (eds.), *Politische Theologie – gegengelesen*, 255–262.

Hoff, Johannes, "German theology in contemporary society", in *Modern Believing* (Special Issue, ed. by J. Hoff) 50/1 (2009) 2–12.

Hoffmann, Veronika, *Vermittelte Offenbarung. Paul Ricoeurs Philosophie als Herausforderung der Theologie* (Ostfildern: Matthias Grünewald Verlag, 2007)

Hollenbach, David, "Civil society: beyond the public-private dichotomy," in *The Responsive Community* 5 (Winter 1994–95) 15–23.

———, "Contexts of the political role of religion: civil society and culture," in *San Diego Law Review* 30 (1993) 879–901.

———,*The Common Good and Christian Ethics* (Cambridge: CUP, 2002)

Huber, Wolfgang, *Gerechtigkeit und Recht. Grundlinien christlicher Rechtsethik* (Gütersloh: Gütersloher Verlag, 1996)

Iakovou, Vicky, "To think utopia with and beyond Paul Ricoeur", in T. Mei/D. Lewin (eds.), *From Ricoeur to Action*, 113–135.

Jaspers, Karl, *The Origin and Goal of History*, trans. M. Bullock (London: Routledge, 1953)

Jörke, Dirk, "Kommunikative Anthropologie", in Brunkhorst *et al.* (eds.), *Habermas-Handbuch*, 331–32.

John, Ottmar/Striet, Magnus (eds.), "… und nichts Menschliches ist mir fremd". Theologische Grenzgänge. Festschrift H. Peukert* (Regensburg: Pustet, 2010)

Junker-Kenny, Maureen, "Between postsecular society and the neutral state: religion as a resource for public reason", in N. Biggar/L. Hogan (eds.), *Religious Voices in Public Places*, 58–81.

———, "Der Gipfel des Schöpferischen. Das Jesuszeugnis als Quelle öffentlicher Vernunft", in O. John/M. Striet (eds.), "…und nichts Menschliches ist mir fremd", 59–75.

———, "Genetic enhancement as care or as domination? The ethics of asymmetrical relationships in the upbringing of children", in *Journal of Philosophy of Education* 24 (2005) 1–12.

———, "Genetic perfection, or fulfillment of creation in Christ?", in C. Deane-Drummond/P. M. Scott (eds.), *Future Perfect? God, Medicine and Human Identity* (London: T & T Clark, 2006), 155–167.

———, "Granting forgiveness: moral blackmail, or a free gift? Questions to the Epilogue of Paul Ricoeur's *Memory, History, Forgetting*", in *Annali di Studi Religiosi* 13 (2012) 149-158.

———, *Habermas and Theology* (London/New York: T & T Clark International, 2011)

———, "Jenseits liberaler öffentlicher Vernunft: Religion und das Vermögen der Prinzipien", in Schmidt/Wenzel (eds.), *Moderne Religion?*, 92–127.

———, "The pre-political foundations of the state", in E. Borgman/M. Junker-Kenny/J. Martin-Soskice (eds.), *The New Pontificate: A Time for Change?, Concilium* 2006/1 (London: SCM Press, 2006), 106–117.

———, "Witnessing or mutual translation? Religion and the requirements of reason", in L. Hogan/S. Lefebvre/N. Hintersteiner/F. Wilfred (eds.), *From World Mission to Interreligious Witness, Concilium* 2011/1 (London: SCM, 2011), 105–114.

———, "Zwischen Integrität und Übersetzung. Christliche Überzeugungen in der Konstitution praktischer Freiheit im Bedingungsgefüge spätmoderner Gesellschaften", in Böhnke et al. (eds.), *Freiheit Gottes und der Menschen*, 359–380.

Kant, Immanuel, *Critique of Practical Reason*, trans. L. W. Beck (New York: Liberal Arts Press, 1956)

———, *Religion within the Limits of Reason Alone*, trans. Th. M. Greene and H. H. Hudson (New York: Harper & Brothers, 1960)

Kierkegaard, Soren, *Fear and Trembling* and The *Sickness Unto Death*, trans. and intro. by W. Lowrie (Princeton: Princeton University Press, 1968)

Küng, Hans/Kuschel, Karl-Josef (eds.), *A Global Ethic. The Declaration of the Parliament of the World's Religions* (New York: Continuum, 1993)

Lafont, Cristina, "Hermeneutik und *linguistic turn*", in Brunkhorst et al. (eds.), *Habermas-Handbuch*, 29–34.

Langthaler, Rudolf/Nagl-Docekal, Herta (eds.), *Glauben und Wissen. Ein Symposium mit Jürgen Habermas* (Wien: Oldenbourg/Berlin: Akademie-Verlag, 2007)

———, "Zur Interpretation und Kritik der Kantischen Religionsphilosophie bei Jürgen Habermas", in Langthaler/Nagl-Docekal (eds.), *Glauben und Wissen*, 32–92.

Larmore, Charles, "Public Reason", in S. Freeman (ed.), *The Cambridge Companion to Rawls* (Cambridge: CUP, 2003), 368–393.

Laux, Bernhard, "Welche Geltungsansprüche, welche Gründe?" in B. Laux (ed.), *Heiligkeit und Menschenwürde. Hans Joas' neue Genealogie der Menschenrechte im theologischen Gespräch* (Freiburg: Herder, 2013), 144–167.

Liebsch, Burkhard (ed.), *Bezeugte Vergangenheit oder Versöhnendes Vergessen. Geschichtstheorie nach Paul Ricoeur* (Berlin: Akademie-Verlag, 2010) (Deutsche Zeitschrift für Philosophie, Sonderband 24)

Linde, Gesche, "'Religiös' oder 'säkular'"? Zu einer problematischen Unterscheidung bei Jürgen Habermas", in Schmidt/Wenzel (eds.), *Moderne Religion?*, 153–202.

Mack, Elke, *Gerechtigkeit und gutes Leben. Christliche Ethik im politischen Diskurs* (Paderborn: Schöningh, 2002)

Mandry, Christof, *Ethische Identität und christlicher Glaube. Theologische Ethik im Spannungsfeld von Theologie und Philosophie* (Mainz: Grünewald, 2002)

McCarthy, Thomas, "Kantian constructivism and reconstructivism: Rawls and Habermas in dialogue", in *Ethics* 105 (1994) 44–63.

Mei, Todd/Lewin, David (eds.), *From Ricoeur to Action* (London/New York: Continuum, 2012)

Mieth, Dietmar, "Autonomy of ethics – neutrality of the Gospel?" in *Concilium* 18 (Edinburgh: T & T Clark, 1982), 32–39.

Mieth, Dietmar/Mueller-Schauenburg, Britta (eds.), *Mystik, Recht und Freiheit. Religiöse Erfahrung und kirchliche Institutionen im Spätmittelalter* (Stuttgart: Kohlhammer, 2012)

Nagl-Docekal, Herta, "Eine rettende Übersetzung? Jürgen Habermas interpretiert Kants Religionsphilosophie", in Langthaler/Nagl-Docekal (eds.), *Glauben und Wissen*, 93–119.

———, "Moral und Religion aus der Optik der heutigen rechtsphilosophischen Debatte", in *Deutsche Zeitschrift für Philosophie* 56 (2008) 843–855.

———, "'Many forms of nonpublic reason'? Religious diversity in liberal democracies", in H. Lenk (ed.), *Comparative and Intercultural Philosophy* (Berlin/Münster: LIT, 2009), 79–92.

O'Neill, Onora, *Autonomy and Trust in Bioethics* (Cambridge: CUP, 2002)

———, "Bounded and cosmopolitan justice", in *Review of International Studies,* vol. 26 (2000) 45–60.

———, *Bounds of Justice* (Cambridge: CUP), 2000

———, "Kantian Ethics," in P. Singer (ed.), *Companion to Ethics* (Oxford: Blackwell, 1991), 175–185.

———, "The method of *A Theory of Justice*", in O. Höffe (ed.), *John Rawls,* 27–43.

———, *Towards Justice and Virtue. A Constructive Account of Practical Reasoning* (Cambridge: CUP, 1996)

Pellauer, David, *Ricoeur: A Guide for the Perplexed* (Continuum: London/New York, 2007)

Peukert, Helmut, "Beyond the present state of affairs: *Bildung* and the search for orientation in rapidly transforming societies", in *Journal of Philosophy of Education* 36 (2002) 421–35.

———, "Enlightenment and theology as unfinished projects", trans. P. Kenny, in Browning/Schüssler Fiorenza (eds.), *Habermas, Modernity, and Public Theology,* 43–65.

———, "Nachwort zur 3. Auflage 2009", in *Wissenschaftstheorie – Handlungstheorie – Fundamentale Theologie,* 357–94.

———, *Science, Action and Fundamental Theology. Toward a Theology of Communicative Action,* trans. J. Bohman (ET of 1st edn.) (Cambridge/Mass.: MIT, 1984)

———, *Wissenschaftstheorie, Handlungstheorie, Fundamentale Theologie,* 3rd German edition with a preface and postscript (Frankfurt: Suhrkamp, 2009)

Pröpper, Thomas, *Der Jesus der Philosophen und der Jesus des Glaubens* (Mainz: Grünewald, 1976)

———, *Erlösungsglaube und Freiheitsgeschichte. Eine Skizze zur Soteriologie* (München: Kösel, 3rd edn 1991)

———, *Evangelium und freie Vernunft* (Freiburg: Herder, 2001)

———, *Theologische Anthropologie,* vols. I and II (Freiburg: Herder, 2011)

Rasmussen, David M./Swindal, James (eds.), *Jürgen Habermas,* vols. I–IV (Sage Masters of Modern Thought) (London: Sage, 2002)

Rawls, John, *A Brief Inquiry into the Meaning of Sin and Faith. With "On my Religion",* ed. by Th. Nagel (Cambridge/Mass: Harvard University Press, 2006)

———, *A Theory of Justice* (Cambridge/Mass.: Belknap Press of Harvard University Press, 1971)

———, "Justice as fairness: Political not metaphysical", in *Philosophy and Public Affairs* 14 (1985) 223–51.

———, *Lectures on the History of Moral Philosophy,* ed. by B. Herman (Cambridge: Mass.: Univ. of Harvard Press, 2000)

———, *Political Liberalism* (New York: Columbia University Press, 1993)

———, "Reply to Habermas", in Rasmussen/Swindal (eds.), *Jürgen Habermas,* vol. II, 99–139.

———, "The basic structure as subject", in *American Philosophical Quarterly* 14 (1977) 159–65.

———, "The Idea of Public Reason Revisited", published first in 1997, repr. in *The Law of Peoples,* 129–180.

———, *The Law of Peoples* (Cambridge/Mass.: Harvard University Press, 1999)

Reder, Michael and Schmidt, S. J., Josef, "Habermas and religion", in Habermas *et al., An Awareness,* 1–14.

Ricken S. J., Friedo, "Postmetaphysical reason and religion", in Habermas *et al., An Awareness,* 51–58.

Ricoeur, Paul, *Anthologie,* ed. by M. Foessel and F. Lamouche (*Paris:* Seuil, 2007)

———, *Critique and Conviction. Conversations with F. Azouvi and M. de Launay.* trans. K. Blamey (Cambridge: CUP, 1998)

———, *Das Rätsel der Vergangenheit. Erinnern – Vergessen – Verzeihen* (Göttingen: Wallstein, 2000)

———, *Discours et communication* (Paris: L'Herne, 2005)

———, *Figuring the Sacred, Religion. Narrative, and Imagination,* trans. D. Pellauer, ed. by M. Wallace (Minneapolis: Fortress Press, 1995)

———, *Freedom and Nature. The Voluntary and the Involuntary,* trans. E. Kohák (Evanston: Northwestern University Press, 1966)

———, *Freud and Philosophy: An Essay on Interpretation,* trans. D. Savage (New Haven: Yale University Press, 1970)

———, *From Text to Action. Essays in Hermeneutics II* (Evanston: Northwestern University Press, 1991)

———, *Hermeneutics and the Human Sciences. Essays on Language, Action, and Interpretation,* ed. and trans. J. B. Thompson (Cambridge/Mass: MIT Press, 1981)

———, *History and Truth,* trans. and intro. Ch. Kelbley (Evanston: Northwestern University Press, 1965)

———, "Human capability: a response", in J. Wall/W. Schweiker/W. D. Hall (eds.), *Paul Ricœur and Contemporary Moral* Thought (New York/London: Routledge, 2002), 279 – 290.

———, *Lectures on Ideology and Utopia,* ed. by G. H. Taylor (New York: Columbia Press, 1986)

———, *Living Up to Death,* trans. D. Pellauer (Chicago: University of Chicago Press, 2009)

———, *Memory, History, Forgetting,* trans. K. Blamey and D. Pellauer (Chicago: University of Chicago Press, 2004). Trans. of *La mémoire, l'histoire, l'oubli* (Paris: Editions du Seuil), 2000

———, *On Translation.* trans. E. Brennan (London: Routledge, 2006)

———, *Oneself as Another,* trans. K. Blamey (Chicago: University of Chicago Press, 1992)

———, *Reflections on the Just,* trans. D. Pellauer (Chicago: University of Chicago Press, 2007)

———, "Reflections on a new ethos for Europe", trans. E. Brennan, in R. Kearney (ed.), *Paul Ricoeur: The Hermeneutics of Action* (London: Sage Publications, 1996), 3 – 13.

———, *The Conflict of Interpretations. Essays in Hermeneutics,* ed. by D. Ihde (Evanston: Northwestern University Press, 1966)

———, *The Course of Recognition,* trans. D. Pellauer (Cambridge: Harvard University Press, 2005)

———, *The Just,* trans. D. Pellauer (Chicago: University of Chicago Press, 2000)

———, *The Symbolism of Evil,* trans. E. Buchanan (New York: Harper & Row, 1967)

———, "Theonomy and/or autonomy", in M. Volf/C. Krieg/Th. Kucharz (eds.), *The Future of Theology. Essays in Honor of Jürgen Moltmann* (Grand Rapids: Eerdmans, 1996), 284 – 298.

———, "Les religions, la violence et la paix". Entretien Hans Kung-Paul Ricoeur autour du "Manifeste pour une éthique planétaire" (ed. du Cerf), ARTE, April 5, 1996, Redaction: Laurent Andres, cf. www.fondsricoeur.fr, under "texts on line" (last accessed October 27, 2013). Also in *Sens. Revue de l'Amitié judéo-chrétienne de France* 5 (1998) 211 – 230.

LaCoque, André, /Ricoeur, *Thinking Biblically. Exegetical and Hermeneutical Studies,* trans. D. Pellauer (Chicago: University of Chicago Press, 1998)

Römer, Inga, "Eskapistisches Vergessen? Der Optativ des glücklichen Gedächtnisses bei Paul Ricoeur", in B. Liebsch (ed.), *Bezeugte Vergangenheit,* 291 – 309.

Schapp, Wilhelm, *In Geschichten verstrickt. Zum Sein von Mensch und Ding* (Frankfurt: Klostermann, 1985, 3rd ed.)

Schelkshorn, Hans, "Christliche Ethik im Sog argumentativer Vernunft. Diskurstheoretische Bemerkungen zur moraltheologischen Debatte um eine 'autonome Moral im christlichen Kontext", in A. Holderegger (ed.), *Fundamente der Theologischen Ethik. Bilanz und Neuansätze* (Freiburg i. Ue./Freiburg i. Br.: Freiburger Universitätsverlag, 1996), 237-260.

Schleiermacher, Friedrich, *On Religion. Speeches to its Cultured Despisers*, trans. J. Oman, with an introduction by R. Otto (New York: Harper & Row, 1968)

Schmidt, Thomas and Wenzel, Knut (eds.), *Moderne Religion? Theologische und religionsphilosophische Reaktionen auf Jürgen Habermas* (Freiburg: Herder, 2009)

Schmidt, Thomas, "Der Begriff der Postsäkularität", in J. Manemann/B. Wacker (eds.), *Politische Theologie – gegengelesen*, vol. 5 (Münster: LIT Verlag, 2008), 244–254.

———, "Objektivität und Gewißheit. Vernunftmodelle und Rationalitätstypen in der Religionsphilosophie der Gegenwart", in F.-J. Bormann/B. Irlenborn (eds.), *Religiöse Überzeugungen und öffentliche Vernunft. Zur Rolle des Christentums in der pluralistischen Gesellschaft* (Freiburg: Herder, 2008), 199–217.

Schnädelbach, H., *Zur Rehabilitierung des animal rationale. Vorträge und Abhandlungen* 2 (Frankfurt: Suhrkamp, 1992)

Schüssler Fiorenza, Francis, "The church as a community of interpretation: Political theology between discourse ethics and hermeneutical reconstruction", in Browning/Schüssler Fiorenza (eds.), *Habermas, Modernity, and Public Theology*, 66–91.

———, "The works of mercy: Theological perspectives," in *The Works of Mercy: New Perspectives on Ministry*, ed. F. A. Eigo (Philadelphia: Villanova Press, 1992), 31–71.

Schulz, Walter, *Grundprobleme der Ethik* (Pfullingen: Neske, 1989)

———, *Philosophie in der veränderten Welt* (Pfullingen: Neske, 1972)

Schweitzer, Albert, *The Quest of the Historical Jesus. A Critical Study of its Progress from Reimarus to Wrede*, with a preface by F. C. Burkitt, trans. W. Montgomery (London: A. & C. Black, 1910)

Siep, Ludwig, "Moral und Gattungsethik", in *Deutsche Zeitschrift für Philosophie* 50 (2002) 111–120.

Storrar, William F. / Morton, Andrew R. (eds.), *Public Theology for the 21st Century. Essays in Honour of Duncan B. Forrester* (London/New York: T & T Clark, 2004)

Striet, Magnus, "Wissenschaftstheorie – Handlungstheorie – Fundamentale Theologie. Analysen zu Ansatz und Status theologischer Theoriebildung (Düsseldorf: Patmos, 1976)", in M. Eckert/ E. Herms/B. J. Hilberath/E. Jüngel (eds.), *Lexikon der theologischen Werke* (Stuttgart: Kröner, 2003), 812–813.

———, "Grenzen der Übersetzbarkeit. Theologische Annäherungen an Jürgen Habermas", in Langthaler/Nagl-Docekal (eds.), *Glauben und Wissen*, 259–282.

Tracy, David, "Theology, critical social theory, and the public realm", in Browning/Schüssler Fiorenza (eds.), *Habermas, Modernity and Public Theology*, 19–42.

Wall, John, *Moral Creativity. Ricoeur and the Poetics of Possibility* (Oxford: OUP, 2005)

———, "The Economy of the Gift. Paul Ricoeur's Significance for Theological Ethics", in *Journal of Religious Ethics* 29 (2001) 235–260.

Walter, Peter (ed.), *Das Gewaltpotential des Monotheismus und der dreieine Gott* (Freiburg: Herder, 2004)

Walzer, Michael, *Spheres of Justice. A Defense of Pluralism and Equality* (New York: Basic Books, 1983)

Weber, Max, *Economy and Society. An Outline of Interpretive Sociology*, ed. by G. Roth/C. Wittich (Berkeley and Los Angeles: University of California Press, 1978)

Wellmer, Albrecht, *Ethik und Dialog* (Frankfurt: Suhrkamp, 1986). ET *The Persistence of Modernity*, trans. D. Midgley (Cambridge: Polity Press, 1991), 113–231.

Wenzel, Knut, "Gott in der Moderne. Grund und Ansatz einer Theologie der Säkularität", in Schmidt/Wenzel (eds.), *Moderne Religion?*, 347–376.

Wendel, Saskia, "Die religiöse Selbst- und Weltdeutung des bewussten Daseins und ihre Bedeutung für eine 'moderne Religion'. Was der 'Postmetaphysiker' Habermas über Religion nicht zu denken wagt", in Schmidt/Wenzel (eds.), *Moderne Religion?*, 225–265.

Wiggershaus, Rolf, *The Frankfurt School* (Cambridge: Polity Press, 1994)

Wils, Jean-Pierre, "Sensus communis – ein 'Vermögen'? Quasi-anthropologische und hermeneutische Aspekte in John Rawls' Sozialethik", in Wils, *Handlungen und Bedeutungen: Reflexionen über eine hermeneutische Ethik* (Freiburg i.Ue./Freiburg i.Br.: Freiburger Universitätsverlag, 2001), 126–163.

Wimmer, Reiner, *Universalisierung in der Ethik. Analyse, Kritik und Rekonstruktion ethischer Rationalitätsansprüche* (Frankfurt: Suhrkamp, 1980)

Person Index

Abraham 251
Adam 251, 294
Adorno, Theodor W. 104–05, 117, 162
Anselm of Canterbury 180, 275–86
Ansorge, Dirk 144
Anzenbacher, Arnold 86, 121, 126–27
Apel, Karl-Otto 111, 123, 125–26, 218
Arendt, Hannah 205, 213, 224–26, 249, 286
Aristoteles 24–26, 28, 30–31, 38, 42–43, 49, 102, 185–86, 203–04, 207, 209, 290
Assheuer, Thomas 266
Assmann, Jan 274
Augustine 165, 277

Benjamin, Walter 117, 156
Böckenförde, Ernst-Wolfgang 93, 229
Boltanski, Luc 31, 233
Brieskorn S. J., Norbert 162
Brock, Daniel 46
Brunkhorst, Hauke 125, 282, 287
Buchanan, Alan 46, 190, 250
Bultmann, Rudolf 155, 157, 159

Cooke, Maeve 169–72, 174–75

Daniels, Norman 46
Daughton, Amy 275
Descartes, René 199, 201
Dilthey, Wilhelm 194–95, 232
Dosse, François 186, 224, 240
Duns Scotus, John 180

Eckholt, Margit 185, 189, 192, 270
Essen, Georg 173, 252

Fichte, Johann Gottlieb 184
Forrester, Duncan 2, 33, 295–96
Forst, Rainer 48, 72, 75–79, 81, 107–08, 113–14, 121, 138–39, 141–42, 147, 163, 216, 222
Freyne, Seán 159, 200

Gadamer, Hans-Georg 125, 190–92, 197–99, 220, 237
Gascoigne, Robert 298
Gelasius I, Pope 173
Greisch, Jean 186–89, 199, 205–06, 211, 215, 217, 250
Grondin, Jean 190–91
Grotefeld, Stefan 95–99
Gula, Richard 44
Günther, Klaus 287

Habermas, Jürgen 1, 4, 17, 22, 38, 43, 46, 54, 57–58, 60–61, 63, 67, 70, 83, 85, 87, 90, 93, 99, 101–02, 103–183, 188, 192, 197–202, 213–14, 217–22, 229, 235–36, 239, 241, 245–47, 249, 253–55, 263–66, 268, 270, 273, 281–84, 286–99
Haker, Hille 129, 189, 200, 217, 219
Harrington, Austin 293
Hegel, Georg Wilhelm Friedrich 21, 23, 109, 156, 161, 168, 180, 194–95, 208–09, 235, 239, 249, 254–59, 262–66, 284, 291–92
Henrich, Daniel C. 115
Henrich, Dieter 43, 114–15, 117–18, 119–21, 131, 178, 282
Hetzel, Andreas 245–46
Hobbes, Thomas 205, 214, 298
Höffe, Otfried 8–10, 13–14, 19–22, 30, 35, 38, 48, 141, 209
Hoffmann, Veronika 190, 192, 199, 250
Höhn, Hans-Joachim 291–92
Hollenbach, David 65–66, 96, 295
Horkheimer, Max 104–05, 117
Huber, Wolfgang 32, 98
Husserl, Edmund 186, 189, 282

Iakovou, Vicky 196–97

Jaspers, Karl 99, 150–51, 154–60, 176
Jesus Christ 33, 46, 157–59, 173, 278–79, 300
John, Ev. 200

John Paul II   173
John, Ottmar   18
Jörke, Dirk   281–82
Junker-Kenny, Maureen   189

Kant, Immanuel   1, 3–8, 11–13, 17, 23–24
    28–31, 33–35, 37, 41, 43, 46, 49, 51–
    52, 54, 62, 67–73, 80–89, 91–92, 94–
    97, 102–03, 106–07, 110–12, 115, 117,
    119–23, 127, 129–32, 136, 138–40,
    143–45, 147, 149–50, 156, 158, 161,
    172–73, 177, 182, 185–86, 201–08,
    211–12, 214, 217, 219, 221–22, 248–67,
    270, 272, 274, 278, 280–81, 283–86,
    288–290, 293, 295, 299, 301
Kenny, Peter   175, 189
Kierkegaard, Soren   46, 120, 131, 146, 178,
    249, 262
Kohlberg, Lawrence   117, 130, 220
Küng, Hans   270–72, 274, 290, 299
Kuschel, Karl-Josef   271

Lafont, Cristina   125
Langthaler, Rudolf   255
Larmore, Charles   83
Laux, Bernhard   216
Lawrence, Frederick G.   157
Leclerc, Gérard   140–42
Lefort, Claude   227
Linde, Gesche   182
Luke, Ev.   200

MacIntyre, Alasdair   25
Mack, Elke   89–98
Mandry, Christof   204, 207–09, 211, 284,
    287
McCarthy, Thomas   67, 136
Mead, George Herbert   110, 119, 156, 247
Mendieta, Eduardo   152, 161, 163
Mieth, Dietmar   87, 245
Milbank, John   173

Nagl-Docekal, Herta   3, 35–36, 63, 68–69,
    84–86, 92–94, 150, 169, 177, 180
Nietzsche, Friedrich   158, 190, 199, 201,
    218, 234, 240

O'Neill, Onora   3, 8–12, 17–21, 34, 44, 47,
    72, 78–82, 85, 87, 92, 99, 300

Paul, St.   213, 252, 277–79
Pellauer, David   14, 205, 250, 252, 270, 273,
    282
Peukert, Helmut   18, 175
Plato   22, 146, 184
Pröpper, Thomas   2, 157–59, 167, 173, 178–
    79, 251–52, 264, 266, 278, 292, 301

Ratzinger, Josef   229
Rawls, John   1, 3, 5–101, 102–04, 106, 108,
    110, 112–14, 117, 126, 130, 132–50,
    163–64, 166–70, 177, 188–89,
    200–02, 213–18, 221–22, 229–30,
    245–47, 253–54, 263–66, 268, 280–
    82, 284–85, 287–89, 295–96, 299
Reder, Michael   162
Ricken S. J., Friedo   293
Ricoeur, Paul   1, 4, 8–9, 12, 14–16, 18–20,
    22, 25, 29–30, 38, 41, 48, 63, 99,
    101–02, 104, 125, 129–30, 154, 163,
    184–279, 281–91, 295–301
Römer, Inga   246
Rousseau, Jean-Jacques   6–7, 11, 33, 214,
    226–27, 229

Schapp, Wilhelm   189–90
Schelkshorn, Hans   298
Schelling, Friedrich Wilhelm Joseph   131
Schleiermacher, Friedrich   2, 4, 159, 178,
    193
Schmidt, S. J., Josef   162
Schmidt, Thomas M.   109, 173, 176, 179
Schmitt, Carl   164–65, 298
Schnädelbach, Herbert   115, 209
Schulz, Walter   194–95
Schüssler Fiorenza, Francis   132, 163
Schweitzer, Albert   159
Siep, Ludwig   45, 100
Solum, Lawrence   97
Spinoza, Baruch de   186
Strauss, Leo   165
Striet, Magnus   18

Taylor, Charles 42, 94, 206, 219, 229, 238, 269
Thévenot, Laurent 31, 233
Thomas Aquinas 180, 275 – 76
Tracy, David 128 – 29, 163

Wall, John 202, 285
Walzer, Michael 30, 48, 217, 233
Weber, Max 110, 112, 140, 221, 225, 231 – 40, 243, 246, 268

Weithman, Paul 169, 171
Wellmer, Albrecht 123 – 24
Wendel, Saskia 176, 178
Wenzel, Knut 174 – 75
Wikler, Dan 46
Wils, Jean-Pierre 31
Wimmer, Reiner 123 – 25
Wolterstorff, Nicholas 97, 169 – 72

Subject Index

agency   9, 11, 17 – 18, 35, 51, 80 – 81, 86, 89, 101 – 103, 106, 116 – 119, 123, 129, 168, 181, 184, 191 – 91, 195, 197, 199 – 202, 204, 209 – 10, 212 – 13, 231, 237, 240, 249, 251 – 253, 256, 262 – 63, 267, 291, 294, 300
– regeneration/renewal/restoration of 85, 204, 217, 249, 253, 262 – 67, 270, 273 – 74
analogy   22, 175, 178 – 79, 195, 268 – 69, 275
anthropology   3, 18, 23, 38, 50, 86, 88, 102 – 03, 116 – 17, 130, 138, 184, 187 – 88, 191, 199 – 200, 202, 207, 215, 223, 246 – 249, 263, 268, 283, 294
antinomy of practical reason   71, 85 – 89, 94, 149, 182, 253 – 62, 266, 285, 299
apokatastasis panton   143
aporia   69, 86, 154, 228, 259, 261
argumentation
– presuppositions of   107 – 09, 121 – 27, 131, 135, 268, 270, 277, 284
Aristotelian principle   24 – 26, 28, 30, 38
attestation   189, 199, 203, 214, 246, 301
authenticity   172
authority   21, 32, 70, 82, 112, 130, 145, 164, 170, 172, 174, 181, 185 – 86, 196, 207, 222 – 233, 292
– enunciative vs. institutional 197, 223, 232, 240 – 244, 247, 295 – 96
authorship   46, 50, 137, 214, 251, 256, 266, 282, 287
autonomy   4, 12, 17 – 18, 32 – 36, 44, 46, 54, 69 – 70, 79 – 88, 94, 105, 112, 127, 133, 136, 160, 171, 173, 204 – 208, 211 – 12, 220, 240, 261, 283, 290, 300
axial age   63, 99, 150, 153 – 55, 157, 165, 220

background culture   10, 13, 51, 64 – 67, 137, 141
Bible   4, 144, 146, 167, 172, 180 – 81, 185 – 86, 189, 192, 197, 213, 221, 230, 236, 242, 249, 251 – 54, 264 – 65, 267, 273 – 74, 279
biblical monotheism   85, 101, 157, 160, 166, 197, 209, 217, 248, 264, 267, 273, 290
– translation of   4, 63, 101 – 02,143, 155 – 56, 167, 181 – 82, 185, 245, 247 – 53, 267 – 79, 256
body/embodiment   38, 41, 43, 55, 62, 128, 187 – 88, 200, 237
burdens of judgement   50, 103

capability   3, 29, 34, 63, 69, 71, 82 – 83, 88, 90, 112 – 13, 119, 136, 148, 186, 188, 202 – 03, 206, 212, 217, 221, 230, 239, 241, 245, 247, 249 – 51, 260, 263, 281, 284
Categorical Imperative   33, 35, 69 – 70, 82, 86, 93, 107, 123, 203 – 04, 208, 216, 219, 283
Christendom   230, 242 – 244
church   65 – 66, 84, 132, 163, 173 – 74, 230, 242, 244 – 45
– as community of interpretation   132, 150, 163
civil disobedience   21, 209
civil society   1, 51, 60, 64 – 65, 67, 94, 113, 148, 165 – 66
Cogito   186, 199, 282
communicative action   18, 103 – 109, 116 – 17, 121 – 22, 125 – 26, 135, 151, 161, 175, 287
– and strategic action   106, 121 – 22, 161
communicative rationality/reason   see reason, communicative
competence   31, 50, 105 – 06, 109 – 13, 117 – 18, 121, 134, 136, 190, 246
compromise   56, 84, 91, 220, 233, 283, 296
comprehensive doctrines   5, 23, 36, 41, 48 – 49, 51 – 52, 54 – 59, 61 – 63, 72 – 73, 83, 88 – 90, 92, 94 – 96, 98, 100, 112 – 13, 117, 133, 135, 137 – 38, 140 – 42, 147 – 48, 214, 230, 268, 280, 288, 290, 296, 299

conscience   1, 68–70, 73, 75, 77–78, 172, 200, 209, 222, 251–52, 262, 288

consensus   21–22, 105–06, 113, 136–142, 168–174, 218–220, 224, 230, 241, 266, 272, 283, 298–300

– overlapping   51–64, 68–70, 76–77, 80–84, 86, 90–97, 101–103, 132–33, 139–42,168–69, 229–30, 273, 279, 281, 283, 295, 299

considered convictions   7, 9, 15–16, 19–22, 32, 42, 46, 50, 97, 103, 117, 126, 216, 221–22, 283, 287, 295

constitutional essentials   53, 59, 70, 78, 83, 100

constructivism   12, 15, 21, 23, 31, 52, 67, 91, 94, 106–09, 171, 195, 233–34; *see also* empirical-reconstructive method, transcendental method

contingency   36, 38, 46, 81, 120, 131, 154, 165, 249

contract   5–10, 13–17, 19–23, 26–28, 30, 42, 46–47, 49, 62–63, 68–69, 71–74, 79, 92–95, 97, 103, 106, 169, 205, 211, 214–15, 218, 223–24, 226, 228, 246, 258, 262, 283–86

cosmopolitanism   80, 194

Covenant   237, 253, 300

creation   38, 41, 46, 59, 110, 159, 181–82, 237, 251, 265, 272, 300–01

critical theory   104–05, 111, 117, 126–27, 157, 175

defeatism   102, 168, 201, 216, 243, 299

deliberation   16, 54, 64, 103, 135–36, 139, 145, 149–50, 171–72, 215, 296

democracy   14, 36, 43, 50–53, 58, 60–61, 64–65, 72, 75, 82, 85, 89, 92–94, 102–03, 106, 108, 112, 130, 132, 137, 141, 150, 165, 167, 186, 197, 202, 216, 221, 223, 226–29, 247, 283, 298–99

demythologization   157

deontology   *see* ethics

difference principle   6, 31, 33, 35–38, 45, 70, 75, 78–79, 101, 295

discourse   28, 54, 58, 65, 67, 76, 94–95, 97, 101, 103–108, 120, 132–33, 135, 137, 140, 145, 150, 156, 162–63, 165, 203, 206, 221, 240–41, 243, 255, 264–65, 270, 282, 287–288, 298

– practical   67, 113

discourse ethics   1, 90, 103–08, 111, 113, 116–117, 121–130, 135–38, 140, 145–46, 150, 156, 163, 167, 175, 218–22, 241, 243, 268, 270, 279, 282, 284–85, 287, 296, 298, 300

discourse principle   108, 122

disenchantment   235, 238–240

distanciation   188, 218, 285, 288

dogmatic authority   172, 174, 181

domination   8, 78–79, 105, 120, 221, 223, 225, 228, 231–33, 235–36, 238, 268

duty   55–56, 66, 68–69, 77, 79, 91–92, 127, 177, 184, 203, 205, 216, 255–56

emancipation   161, 181, 197–98, 220, 281

empirical-reconstructive method   9, 11–13, 17–19, 28, 33–34, 36, 54, 58, 79, 87–88, 97, 103, 105–11, 113–14, 116–19, 120–26, 133, 146, 149, 151–53, 158, 187, 265, 281, 283, 294, 299; *see also* constructivism, transcendental method

enhancement   45, 120, 282, 285, 287

Enlightenment   93, 101, 104, 147, 175, 193, 198, 242–43

ethics

– cosmopolitan   1, 3, 51, 68, 72, 81–82, 92, 102, 143, 194, 215, 283

– deontological   8, 11, 16, 21, 54, 72, 86, 103, 116, 132–37, 143, 216, 222, 255–56, 281–82, 288

– deontological and teleological/morality and flourishing life, relationship between   23–41,47, 102, 129, 138–42, 147–50, 200, 203–11, 218–220, 248–249, 279, 283–86

– theological/Christian   2, 32–33, 35, 44, 52, 65, 75–76, 85, 87, 89–104, 126–27, 129–30, 167, 204, 207–09, 211, 280, 284–5, 287, 295–98; *see also* discourse ethics

evil   16, 89, 102, 143–44, 190–91, 202, 207, 211, 216, 237, 248, 250–54, 256, 258–59, 262–63, 267, 274, 278–79, 284–85, 291

Exodus   198, 275–76

facticity 131, 178, 248 – 49
fact of pluralism 23, 41, 46, 103
faith
– certainty of 154 – 56, 170, 175 – 77, 179 –
80, 182, 292, 301
– religious 131, 148, 154 – 60, 166, 176,
178, 182, 236, 301
– Christian 72, 89 – 90, 98 – 99, 101, 143 –
48, 155 – 160, 172 – 175, 178 – 83, 198, 230,
236, 242 – 245, 275 – 79, 297 – 98, 300 – 01
– truth of 179, 292
fallibility 118, 130, 155 – 56, 161, 177, 186 –
87, 190, 206, 247 – 52
finitude 13, 248, 250, 267, 285
forgiveness 85 – 86, 102, 181, 204, 210 – 11,
213, 217, 246 – 47, 249, 253 – 54, 263,
291, 300
founding/founding energy/founding event
7, 9, 16, 45, 47, 154, 192, 196, 225, 226 –
28, 230, 243, 285, 291, 298
fragility 13, 20, 45, 187, 231
freedom
– concrete 247, 264
– of conscience 1, 75, 77 – 78 172, 200,
209, 251f.
– of religion 1, 77 – 78, 167, 172 – 73
– transcendental 16, 18, 33 – 34, 107, 121,
178, 264, 294
friendship 26, 62, 205, 300

game theory 14, 30
Geltung (acceptance) vs. *Gültigkeit* (validity) 91, 103, 110, 128, 133 – 34, 139 –
40, 145, 173, 216, 303
genealogy 99, 142, 151, 160, 162, 224,
293 – 94
Genesis 105, 118, 236, 244, 251 – 253, 294
genetics 38, 44 – 46, 110, 120, 166, 188,
201, 217, 247, 253, 282, 285, 287, 306
German Idealism 43, 105, 118
gift 37 – 38, 159, 181, 246 – 47, 260, 267,
276, 285, 290
globalization 14, 75
God 4, 23, 46, 78, 84 – 88, 95, 100, 142 –
148, 155 – 159, 161, 165 – 66, 172, 174,
177, 181 – 82, 189, 198 – 99, 240, 249,

251, 253, 260 – 61, 264 – 65, 267, 271,
275 – 78, 286, 290 – 92, 294, 297, 301
Golden Rule 14, 16, 98, 215
good life/flourishing life 27 – 28, 30, 39,
42, 47, 65, 89 – 90, 95, 102, 128 – 29,
149, 188, 202, 204 – 15, 210 – 11, 218,
223, 227, 249, 279, 284, 296
grace 149, 164, 198, 236, 253, 263
guilt 199, 248 – 53, 278, 285, 294, 300

Hegelianism 21, 23, 194, 209, 235, 255,
257 – 59, 262 – 64, 266, 284, 292
hellenization 277
hermeneutics 95, 141, 174, 184, 186 – 87,
189 – 91, 195, 198 – 99, 214, 218 – 19,
222, 237, 246 – 48, 252 – 53, 263, 268,
270, 275, 277, 288, 301
heteronomy 34, 36, 69, 261
highest good 52, 83, 85 – 86, 88, 94, 131,
177, 253, 255 – 56, 261, 267, 285
Historicism 154, 194
history of effects 125, 275, 277
Holocaust 104
hope 2, 21, 23, 29, 39, 50, 60 – 62, 65, 84,
86 – 89, 102, 142, 149, 177, 181, 192,
195 – 96, 198 – 99, 202, 210, 213, 218,
231, 243 – 44, 247 – 48, 253 – 65, 267,
270, 286, 290 – 91, 295, 300 – 01.
hospitality 185, 221, 248, 270, 272, 297
human dignity 31, 51, 68 – 71, 92 – 93, 124,
144, 172, 227, 286
human rights 9, 13 – 14, 45, 51, 71 – 77, 80,
92, 98, 137, 172, 216

idealization vs. abstraction 8 – 10, 12 – 13,
19, 56, 111, 157, 201, 294
idem vs. *ipse* 34, 199 – 200, 202, 210, 264
identity 2, 27, 29, 36, 46, 50, 57, 89 – 90,
97, 99, 102, 106, 110, 113, 120, 127 – 28,
165, 186, 189, 196 – 97, 199 – 10,
203 – 04, 206, 210 – 11, 213, 219, 233 –
34, 251, 274
ideology critique 20, 198, 226
imagination 25, 41, 185, 192 – 93, 196 – 97,
201, 208, 216, 222, 232, 252, 259, 265,
270, 274, 279, 288 – 89, 297

imago Dei   4, 59, 86, 100, 172, 181–82, 251, 265, 301

infallibility   174, 179–80, 227, 292

instrumental reason   105, 235–36, 239, 285

intentionality   282, 285

intersubjectivity   37–38, 117–21, 145, 178, 219, 234, 282

irrationality   180, 233, 258, 262, 291

Israel   161, 165

judgement   3, 12–13, 19–20, 22, 29, 31, 38, 50, 69, 81, 103, 121, 128–29, 138, 143–44, 146–47, 159, 174, 177, 188, 193, 203–04, 211–12, 216, 277, 280, 285–88, 293, 296–97, 299

justice
– distributive   78–79, 188
– principles of   5, 7–15, 18, 22, 26, 32, 40–41, 47, 50, 76, 79, 84, 94, 97, 108, 136, 140
– sense of   14–15, 20, 23–28, 31–40, 211, 214–220, 283

language   22, 74, 103–08, 111–13, 116–21, 127, 135–36, 145, 153, 155, 161, 164, 168, 172, 178, 181,185, 194, 198, 201, 207, 218–21, 248–49, 268–70, 272–74, 277, 281–82, 284–85, 289, 299–300

law   1, 3, 14, 22, 32–33, 50, 64–65, 68–75, 78–80, 82, 85, 87–92, 94–95, 98, 105–06, 118, 137, 140, 143, 145, 147, 150, 154, 164–66, 169–70, 173, 203, 206, 209, 212, 215–16, 223–24, 227, 235–36, 242, 258, 261–62, 286–88

legitimacy   52–55, 62, 68, 77, 83, 92, 96, 138–140, 147, 149, 172–73, 196, 232–33, 236, 240–41

legitimation   1, 3, 6, 101, 140, 164, 166, 186, 195–96, 198, 222–23, 228, 231–233, 235–36, 238, 240

liberation   33, 161, 236, 239, 252–53, 263, 279, 284, 299

lifeworld   1, 19–21, 66, 102–03, 109, 111–13, 116–18, 120, 125–28, 130–32, 134, 154, 160–62, 201, 241, 265–66, 281, 285, 288, 294, 296

love   86, 95, 98–99, 128, 184, 212–13, 218, 276, 291, 297–98

Magisterium   174

memory   101, 186, 204, 210–11, 213, 219, 223, 264, 270, 287, 300

metaphor   9–10, 112, 161, 185, 192, 224, 240, 272, 293

metaphysics   3, 11–12, 18, 23, 26, 36, 41–43, 54, 71, 91, 94, 106, 111, 113–15, 119–20, 127, 133–34, 138–39, 141, 146, 149, 156, 162, 165, 176, 178, 181, 195, 198, 247, 276, 280–81

modernity   2, 4, 48, 82, 101–03, 106, 114–15, 118, 130–31, 144, 150–54, 156, 160–61, 164, 176–77, 180, 185, 198–99, 217, 226, 230, 239–40, 243, 247, 281, 291–92

modus vivendi   53, 56–57, 61

monotheism   4, 21, 59, 85, 99–101, 145, 160, 166, 197, 209, 217, 248, 264–65, 267, 273–75, 290

morality   3–4, 15–16, 19, 33, 35–38, 51, 63, 68–71, 75, 77, 82–83, 85–87, 90–95, 97–98, 102, 105, 108, 121–29, 132–37, 146–50, 154, 170–74, 184, 188, 205–12, 215, 218–20, 241, 260–61, 265, 272, 282–89, 298–301

motivation   1, 7, 10, 24, 26, 28, 31, 34, 38–39, 53, 56–58, 60–62, 66, 70, 85, 93–95, 116–17, 126–30, 143, 149, 186, 193, 201, 215–16, 219, 223, 229, 231–32, 236–37, 239–41, 266, 272–73, 283, 285, 290, 294–95

myth, *mythos*/mythical   102, 127, 153, 160, 163, 165–66, 184, 187, 192–93, 223–25, 227–29, 242, 245, 250, 253

narrative   25, 62, 102, 165, 181, 187, 189, 193, 199–200, 203, 206, 210, 214, 219, 224, 226–28, 248, 250–52, 268, 270, 274–75, 277, 290, 294, 299

naturalism, naturalization   115, 125–26, 134, 177, 266, 281, 289

natural law   44, 165, 167, 198

negation   258, 263

neutrality of the state   160, 169, 172–73

New Testament   200, 209, 244, 267, 277 –
79
normativity   1, 3, 5 – 6, 13, 16, 20 – 24, 27,
32, 34, 36, 42, 48, 55, 76, 81, 90 – 91,
94, 99, 101 – 104, 106 – 07, 110, 111, 115,
117 – 18, 121, 123, 125 – 29, 133, 142,
148 – 49, 153 – 54, 164, 167, 185 – 86,
197 – 98, 226 – 27, 238 – 39, 283, 295 –
96

obligation   28, 34, 37, 69 – 70, 82, 85, 87,
92 – 93, 124, 127, 129, 133, 137, 145, 170,
174, 185, 203 – 04, 207, 210, 212, 222,
245, 251 – 52, 256, 261, 291, 296
opacity   104, 156, 175 – 77, 180, 196, 233,
266, 280, 290 – 92
original position   6 – 10, 12 – 13, 15 – 17, 19 –
21, 23 – 24, 27, 30, 34 – 35, 38, 45, 74,
78 – 79, 97, 101, 108, 116, 133, 136, 140,
214 – 25, 218, 285
original sin   274, 277 – 78
otherness   19, 160, 179 – 80, 200, 212, 219

paradox   15, 53, 55 – 56, 71, 107, 144, 149,
185, 224 – 25, 239 – 40, 252, 255, 276
parliament   51, 113, 150, 169 – 71, 271
particularity   4, 13, 35, 54, 99, 113, 128,
149, 157, 178, 192 – 93, 196, 220, 222,
247, 267 – 269, 271, 274, 287, 289, 292 –
93, 298
pathologies   0, 66, 102 – 03, 160, 162, 169,
177, 266, 281, 285, 290
phenomenology   184, 186, 188, 202, 204,
213, 215, 249, 263
philosophy
– of consciousness/reflexivity/subjectivity
104 – 05, 116 – 20, 178, 201, 247
– postmetaphysical 17, 43, 103, 105 – 06,
108 – 16, 120, 126, 133, 135, 146, 151 – 53,
155 – 56, 162, 175 – 77, 180 – 83, 198, 254,
293
– *Interpret* (interpreter)   109 – 13, 117, 131,
222, 254, 265, 281
– *Platzanweiser* (usher)   109 – 13, 265
– *Platzhalter* (stand-in)   109 – 13, 117, 222,
254, 281
– *Richter* (judge)   109 – 13

pluralism, plurality   1, 23, 30, 41 – 42, 46,
48, 51 – 52, 54, 56, 59, 61, 74, 90 – 91,
95 – 97, 101, 103, 148, 150, 168, 229 –
30, 244
poetics   193, 285
political conception   42, 44, 51, 53 – 63, 66,
71, 74, 76, 78, 82, 95 – 96, 100, 133, 135,
137 – 39, 141 – 42, 148, 230, 290
political liberalism   52, 65, 82, 90 – 91, 94,
96, 137, 139
political theology   165, 242 – 44
postconventional morality   116 – 17, 125,
128, 130, 132, 137, 220
postsecular society   99, 150 – 52, 155, 160,
167, 172 – 73
postulate of God   23, 86, 88, 177
praxis   30, 106, 113, 126 – 27, 136, 203, 209,
286, 291
primary goods   7, 24, 26 – 30, 32, 37 – 39,
46 – 48, 79, 217, 284
promise   102, 158, 192 – 93, 196, 200 – 01,
213, 217, 223, 230 – 31, 251, 258, 264 –
65, 279, 290 – 91, 295, 300 – 01
proviso   52, 58, 89, 104, 132, 151, 164, 167,
169
public sphere   1, 3, 43, 61 – 62, 64, 67, 95 –
96, 101, 103 – 06, 132, 149 – 51, 160,
162 – 63, 165, 168 – 71, 185 – 86, 213,
218, 231, 240 – 41, 245, 247 – 48, 266,
286, 294 – 96, 298, 301

rational choice   9, 13, 17 – 20, 30, 35, 43,
49, 60, 108, 146, 169, 201, 215, 283,
285
rationality   8, 12 – 13, 18 – 20, 24 – 26, 28 –
30, 50, 80 – 81, 103 – 09, 112, 114, 117,
121, 124, 131, 141, 148, 161, 177, 180,
219 – 20, 233 – 39, 248, 256 – 258, 262 –
63, 266, 268, 284
rationalization   105, 110, 151, 160, 162, 164,
167, 181, 197, 233 – 236, 238 – 40, 243,
299
reason   2, 4 – 5, 8, 11 – 12, 16 – 18, 23, 46, 51, 53,
63, 67, 69, 72 – 73, 81 – 89, 97 – 98, 101 – 02, 104,
108 – 15, 117 – 21, 130 – 31,134 – 35, 145, 152 – 56,
160 – 61, 164, 167 – 68, 171 – 72, 174 – 76, 178 – 82,
184, 186, 191 – 92, 198, 201, 209, 211, 219 – 222,

234, 236, 239, 243, 247–51, 253–66, 268, 276, 279–82, 286, 290–94, 296–97, 299
– anamnestic   161
– as faculty of principles/unconditional 114–15, 117–19, 177–78, 253–62, 292
– communicative   103–08, 112, 114, 117, 121–30, 160–62, 200, 220–21, 266, 273, 281
– instrumental/purposive   16, 102, 105, 117, 220, 234–36, 239, 281, 285
– postmetaphysical   *see* philosophy, post-metaphysical
– practical   9–12, 19, 23, 51–52, 58, 67–71, 79–83, 85–88, 94, 100–03, 107–08, 113, 121–31, 133–41, 143–45, 147–49, 170–72, 177, 182, 206–08, 212–221, 238–39, 248–56, 258–63, 266–67, 271–72, 278, 281–86, 288–89, 291, 294, 297–301
– private use of   3, 81
– public   1, 3–5, 11, 14, 19, 23, 39, 44, 48–60, 62–68, 71, 73, 78, 80–85, 88–89, 96, 98–100, 102–04, 112, 132–43, 149–50, 163, 165–66, 168–70, 177, 221, 229–30, 248, 256, 259, 280, 285–86, 288–89, 294, 297–99
– public use of   67, 88, 104, 112, 132–33, 135, 139, 141, 166
– scientific   40, 44, 63, 112, 114–15, 131, 156, 195
reasonableness   6–7, 11, 15, 33, 35, 42, 45, 49–59, 61–63, 66, 69–71, 73–74, 76, 80, 82, 85, 88–89, 94–95, 98, 108, 113, 127–28, 133–35, 138–39, 148, 156, 214, 222, 229–30, 284, 290, 295, 298
reception   4–5, 11, 28, 33, 85, 91–92, 95–96, 104, 127, 157–58, 182, 191, 199, 209, 221, 232, 237, 248–49, 264, 267, 274–75, 278–79
receptivity   17, 199–200, 209, 223, 292
reciprocity   35, 53–54, 62, 69, 83, 86, 93, 97–98, 127, 133, 205, 283, 297, 300

recognition   19, 29, 63, 102–03, 106–07, 117, 121–25, 150, 160, 169, 184, 201, 203, 205, 228, 231, 235, 246
– unconditional/asymmetrical/one-sided 18, 34, 37, 69, 85–86, 117, 121–25, 246, 298
reconciliation   61, 82, 112, 133, 144, 257–60, 267, 270, 299
redemption   175, 199, 237
reflective equilibrium   7, 15, 19–21, 42, 46, 50, 97, 141, 222, 287
reflexivity   29, 63, 107, 115, 153–55, 163, 184, 189, 282
– and intersubjectivity   29, 117–21, 282
responsibility   3, 21, 85, 90, 95, 122, 145, 149, 154, 204, 217, 219, 253, 297, 299
resurrection   181, 198
revelation   4, 148, 155–158, 174–75, 177–80, 275–77, 291–92
ritual   166, 291–92
Romanticism   159, 193, 230

salvation   4, 59, 146–47, 149, 164–65, 167, 173, 180, 236, 263–64, 278–79, 292
secularity   166, 173
secularization   150–51, 199
– of state power vs. of civil society   57, 61, 148, 150–53; *see also* neutrality of the state
self-communication/self-revelation of God 156–57, 172, 174, 276–77, 292
self-consciousness   118–19, 131, 153, 251
self-determination   76, 79, 103, 164, 214–15, 283
self-esteem   26–28, 33, 206, 211
self-interest   9–10, 13, 16, 18–19, 31, 33, 35, 38, 86, 92–93, 106, 116, 129, 145–46, 201, 215, 261, 283–84, 296
self-realization   24, 2–28, 30, 39
self-reflection   4, 15, 34, 68, 102, 107, 115, 118–19, 121, 123, 125, 146, 178, 181, 209, 218, 253, 292, 294
self-relation   114, 119–20, 214
self-respect   7, 26–29, 37, 206, 211
semantic potential   4, 61, 135, 150, 156–57, 160, 162, 180

singularity   67, 120, 147, 203, 208, 210 –
    212, 218 – 19, 272, 285, 291, 297
slavery, abolition of   73, 77, 100, 217
socialization   119, 125, 148 – 49
solidarity   54, 93, 95 – 96, 103, 110, 161 – 62,
    169, 181, 232, 271, 290, 294 – 296, 299
species ethics   241
subjectivity   117, 120, 178, 184, 188, 198 –
    99, 282
superabundance   218, 246, 276, 279, 290
suspicion   22, 60, 125, 147, 157, 190, 199,
    214, 218, 226, 237
symbol   119, 125 – 26, 130 – 31, 154, 158,
    160, 163 – 64, 184, 186 – 87, 189 – 93,
    196, 201, 208, 212, 224, 226, 231, 237,
    240 – 43, 245, 247, 249 – 50, 252, 254,
    267 – 68, 270, 279, 281 – 82, 288, 290,
    294, 298 – 99

testimony   155, 159, 178, 245 – 46, 275
theodicy   236, 259
theology   2 – 4, 18, 33, 65, 71 – 73, 83, 94 –
    96, 99, 104, 111, 118, 126 – 29, 132, 142 –
    51, 155 – 159, 163, 165, 172 – 183, 189,
    213, 237, 242 – 45, 249 – 50, 252, 254,
    256, 266 – 68, 270, 274 – 80, 285, 289 –
    95, 299, 301
theory of action   3, 12, 18, 24, 29, 79 – 81,
    103, 130, 186 – 87, 203, 213 – 14, 223,
    227, 229
theory of science   239
totality   35 – 36, 69, 109, 117, 128 – 29, 131,
    161, 254, 257, 261
tradition   1 – 4, 6 – 7, 10, 14, 17, 21, 23, 31,
    41, 49, 56 – 57, 60 – 61, 63, 65, 81, 85,
    89, 99 – 102, 112 – 13, 118, 128 – 32, 137 –
    38, 141, 146, 150, 152, 154, 156, 158 –
    60, 162 – 63, 166 – 67, 173, 177, 180 – 82,
    185 – 86, 191 – 94, 197 – 99, 202, 213,
    218, 220 – 21, 223 – 26, 228 – 31, 233,
    235, 241, 245, 247, 267 – 68, 272, 278 –
    79, 281, 283 – 84, 286, 289 – 91, 294 –
    96, 298
transcendence   66, 95, 118, 126, 135, 154,
    157 – 58, 177, 242
transcendental method   16, 18, 33 – 34, 105,
    110 – 11, 119, 121, 123, 135, 178, 198, 215,

    264, 294, 299; *see also* constructivism,
    empirical-reconstructive method
transformation   31, 71, 93, 105 – 06, 115,
    143, 145, 165, 220, 226, 250, 295 – 96
translation   4, 41, 46, 62 – 63, 99, 101 – 02,
    104, 109 – 10, 119, 131, 135, 143, 149 –
    52, 155 – 56, 164, 167, 175 – 76, 180 – 82,
    185, 221, 245, 247 – 49, 256, 267 – 70,
    272 – 75, 277 – 78, 281, 285, 289, 293 –
    94
transnational justice   5, 75, 79, 81
truth   2 – 3, 49, 51, 53 – 57, 61 – 63, 66 – 67,
    82, 84, 88, 97 – 98, 106, 109 – 10, 113 –
    14, 121 – 24, 128, 130, 134, 138 – 39, 141,
    146 – 49, 155 – 59, 162, 168, 171 – 72,
    174 – 75, 177, 179 – 81, 184 – 85, 190, 199,
    235, 248 – 49, 257, 265, 268, 271, 274,
    276, 281, 286 – 87, 290, 292, 300
truthfulness/sincerity   77, 106, 121 – 23, 128,
    271

Unantastbarkeit (inviolability)   31, 45, 70 –
    71, 142, 296, 300
Universal Declaration of Human Rights   73,
    75, 80
universalism   1, 99, 130, 143, 154, 193, 249,
    287, 297
universalistic level/scope   72, 101, 109 – 10,
    124, 128 – 29, 134, 144, 218 – 19, 227,
    265, 281, 284, 298 – 99
universalizability   103, 107, 116, 140, 163,
    170, 174, 209, 219, 241, 243, 286 – 87
universalization   91, 108, 122 – 25, 127, 129 –
    30, 136, 149, 203, 211, 287 – 88, 296
unvertretbar (unsubstitutible)   102, 143
Utilitarianism   14, 30 – 31, 45, 70, 142 – 43,
    215, 282 – 83, 285
utopia   102, 161, 187, 192, 195 – 97, 199,
    201, 266

validity (*Gültigkeit*)   11, 14, 17 – 18, 53, 59,
    69, 73, 80, 83, 91, 99, 106 – 08, 110 – 13,
    122 – 29, 134, 138 – 39, 148 – 49, 158,
    170 – 73, 176, 179 – 80, 191, 210, 219,
    224, 232, 261, 268, 284, 297
veil of ignorance   6, 8 – 10, 44, 50, 116, 136,
    145 – 46, 283

Vernunft   *see* rationality and reason
Verstand (understanding)   117, 260
violence   206 – 07, 223, 227 – 28, 235, 271, 274, 290 – 91
virtue   12, 14, 16, 21, 23, 28, 43 – 44, 51, 54, 56, 61, 68, 74, 82, 85 – 86, 90, 94, 113, 134, 202, 207, 209, 213 – 14, 228, 236, 239, 253, 256, 271, 294, 296, 300

will   3 – 4, 7, 35, 43, 53, 55, 62, 64 – 65, 69, 86, 102, 113, 121, 127, 134, 141, 145, 155, 160, 170, 180, 184, 186 – 87, 191 – 92, 194, 199, 202, 205 – 08, 210, 217 – 18, 222, 225 – 27, 229, 231, 235, 237, 243, 246, 249, 252, 254 – 56, 261, 263, 265, 267, 269, 271, 285, 289 – 91, 295, 298, 301

wisdom, practical   203 – 04, 208 – 210, 212, 216, 219 – 20, 222 – 23, 285 – 88

worldviews   3, 11, 43, 49 – 55, 57 – 61, 63, 66, 71, 78, 82, 84 – 85, 90, 94 – 95, 97 – 99, 102, 106, 109, 113, 133 – 35, 137 – 39, 141 – 42, 147 – 49, 160, 165, 168, 170 – 71, 174, 185, 229, 268, 283, 285, 289 – 90, 298

www.ingramcontent.com/pod-product-compliance
Lightning Source LLC
Chambersburg PA
CBHW070017100426
42740CB00013B/2535